TOUCHSTONES

TOUCHSTONES

Letters Between Two Women, 1953–1964

PATRICIA FRAZER LAMB AND KATHRYN JOYCE HOHLWEIN

Edited and with
additional material by
Patricia Frazer Lamb

1817

HARPER & ROW, PUBLISHERS, New York
Cambridge, Philadelphia, San Francisco, London
Mexico City, São Paulo, Sydney

Grateful acknowledgment is made for permission to reprint:

Excerpt from *The Poems of Richard Wilbur,* by Richard Wilbur. Reprinted by permission of Harcourt Brace Jovanovich, Inc.

"Byzantium," from *Collected Poems of William Butler Yeats,* by William Butler Yeats. Copyright 1933 by Macmillan Publishing Co., renewed 1961 by Bertha Georgie Yeats. Reprinted by permission of Macmillan Publishing Co., Inc., Michael and Anne Yeats, and Macmillan London Limited.

Excerpts from *The Poems of Gerard Manley Hopkins,* Fourth Edition, edited by W. H. Gardner and N. H. Mackenzie. Copyright © 1967 by Oxford University Press. Reprinted by permission.

"Forgive, O Lord," from *The Poetry of Robert Frost,* edited by Edward Connery Lathem. Copyright © 1962 by Robert Frost. Copyright © 1969 by Holt, Rinehart and Winston. Reprinted by permission of Holt, Rinehart and Winston, Publishers.

Lines from "Reluctance," from *The Poetry of Robert Frost,* edited by Edward Connery Lathem. Copyright 1934, © 1969 by Holt, Rinehart and Winston. Copyright © 1962 by Robert Frost. Reprinted by permission of Holt, Rinehart and Winston, Publishers.

Lines from "Ite," from *Personae,* by Ezra Pound. Copyright 1926 by Ezra Pound. Reprinted by permission of New Directions Publishing Corporation and Faber and Faber, Ltd.

FIRST EDITION

Designer: C. Linda Dingler

83 84 85 86 87 10 9 8 7 6 5 4 3 2 1

Library of Congress Cataloging in Publication Data

Lamb, Patricia Frazer.
    Touchstones : letters between two women, 1953–1964.
    1. Lamb, Patricia Frazer.   2. Hohlwein, Kathryn
Joyce.   3. Married women—Correspondence.   I. Hohlwein,
Kathryn.   II. Title.
HQ1206.L37   1983   305.4'890655'0922   81-47662
ISBN 0-06-014942-6

We dedicate this book to our five children,
with love and gratitude for their
understanding

The word "touchstone" used to refer to a stone such as jasper, against which gold and silver were rubbed to test their purity. It has now come to mean a criterion by which the qualities of something are tested or measured.

CONTENTS

ACKNOWLEDGMENTS

I wish to thank all those people whose support and loving encouragement made this book possible. Dr. Ramona Lumpkin of Lexington, Kentucky, was the first person other than us to read the original letters. In fact, Ramona helped me put them in matching order—month by month, year by year—in two neat rows along my living and dining room floors. She responded to their content with an unwavering faith that they were valuable as documentary evidence of women's lives, women's love for one another, women's truths. We owe you, Ramona.

Thanks go to all the other friends who read the letters in their various stages of editing, especially Larry Sells and James A. Perkins, both of New Wilmington, Pennsylvania. Larry read the manuscript through and made very helpful suggestions, and Jim burrowed through the library, finding the poetry sources for me. Donna Sue Kilpatrick was very helpful in editing the unwieldy original manuscript down to a readable length. And to Laura A. Dean, my friend and former student, goes my gratitude for her assistance in the last stages of proofreading and collating.

Most of all, thanks to Martha Sternberg, our agent, who believed in the book, and to Ann Harris, our brilliant editor at Harper & Row, who made this final version possible. Any faults of selection and editing—omission or commission—I take on my own head.

P.F.L.

INTRODUCTION

When the two of us—Joyce and Pat—left the University of Utah in 1953, we began this correspondence with no idea in mind except to "keep in touch." But soon, as our paths took us farther apart, and in the absence of anyone else to confide in, we began to share with one another our most secret thoughts and feelings about our lives. What began as a dialogue became, over the years, a dialectic, to which each of us contributed, from which each garnered new insights and viewpoints about her own life.

We discussed marriage, children, sex, our travels, our social and political outlooks, our loves. Now we would like other women and men to share a selection of these letters. The concerns and passions we wrote about are the same ones that all friends exchange with one another and talk about endlessly. Precisely because we were "ordinary" people, not celebrities, we could speak to each other with the unselfconsciousness that gets lost in the glitter of a public life.

To be sure, we lived in outlandish places for the first few years. In the heyday of this correspondence, two decades ago, the thick packets would arrive, to our great excitement, covered with exotic stamps, filled with the long letters, newspaper clippings, cartoons, snapshots. They would come from the heart of bush Africa, from glamorous Beirut, from a tiny fishing village in Scotland, from Iowa, from the sedate English countryside. From thousands of miles and many years apart, we went on and on writing to each other.

Occasionally we couldn't resist the urge to read what seemed to us a particularly interesting section of a letter to an acquaintance. We might mention the length of time we'd been writing, the topics we covered, the depth of our friendship. The usual response, to both of us, was puzzlement. The friend would ask (with variations on this theme), "Well, it's very nice to get news of one's family and friends, of course, but isn't it an awful lot of trouble? Why *do* you write so much to each other? I know I'm no great letter writer myself." And so on. We really had no answer to these queries then, especially since we never read the most personal parts of the letters to anyone else. We agree now that at the time, we understood neither the compulsion nor the passions which drove us to forge this unwitting document of our youth.

Today, with the aid of a vocabulary enlarged and enriched by the women's movement, by our own experiences, by reading back through the letters, we can say that the key motivation was loneliness. The letters were born of a desperate need for love and understanding. We each became willing to open our hearts to one another, on paper, to ask questions out of the most private depths of our souls, and to sit down and attempt to answer one another's agonized pleas. We simply could not keep our sense of isolation and our yearnings to ourselves. We had too many questions to ask that demanded answers, or at least the loving attention of someone else, and so we turned to one another, in the absence of this sort of communication with our husbands, and, too, in the absence of close friends, family, therapists—the usual places people are likely to go for a discussion of the subjects raised in the letters.

We moved around too much in those years to make stable and close friendships. We were far away from our families. We were each geographically removed from our own culture—Pat for the whole eleven years of the correspondence, Joyce for the first four years. We were married to uncommunicative foreigners and struggling to adjust our American viewpoints to our husbands' alien demands. Adjustments are made in all marriages, and in the old-fashioned sort, as ours were, these adjustments are traditionally made by the wives. But in the strange surroundings in which we found ourselves, we persevered in the attempts to forge satisfactory relationships and a comprehensible life style that would satisfy everybody. The letters record our partial successes and our many failures.

The point is that we could not share our doubts and dilemmas with the people around us. And so what at first were merely news-from-elsewhere letters became virtually our only pressure valves. Also important, perhaps, is the fact that for some people it is easier to say personal things on paper at a remove in time and space than it would be to say them face to face or even over the telephone.

We believe that these letters offer a truly fresh illumination of the female psyche working out her destiny in the traditional marriage forms. Our day-to-day experiences over the years tested and altered our sensibilities and perceptions with a naiveté and an innocence unmediated by autobiographical hindsight, unalloyed by public considerations. The absolute privacy in which, for which, these letters were written is their affirmation of the painful honesty with ourselves and with one another that we came to see was the touchstone of this correspondence.

Since for obvious reasons these letters neither introduce nor explain the two friends to each other, and hence to the reader, some background to each of us is necessary.

Joyce's home and family were solidly middle class. She was in fact born in the house in Salt Lake City in which her parents lived until their deaths almost five decades later. Warner and Helen Jerrell were gentle, soft-spoken Midwesterners who had fled Kansas Bible Belt Methodism to a life engaged in Unitarianism and liberal causes in Salt Lake City. They abhorred violence and any overt display of emotion. Joyce cannot remember ever hearing an argument or a fight in her home.

Music filled the Jerrell household. Both Joyce and her gifted brother Bob learned to play the piano, and Joyce took singing lessons for years. Their parents had been unable to go to college and saw to it that both their children did. Typically, Bob went away to a prestigious university at a precocious sixteen, and Joyce stayed home and attended the University of Utah. She was engaged through most of her college years to a young man who became student body president in their senior year, when the engagement was broken. She was a sorority member, popular, respectable, pretty, one of the brightest students on campus.

Joyce was raised to believe devoutly in the virtues of family life, in the traditional role of woman inside a lifetime marriage; yet she also aspired to be a writer, a poet, a scholar, a teacher. She yearned to travel, to experience the presumed sophistication of Europe which all would-be intellectuals our age believed necessary for true maturity. All these conflicting beliefs and desires led her as inexorably into her Fulbright year in France, and thence into her marriage to a German artist, as they did Pat into hers with a British doctor, as, indeed, they presumably led Sylvia Plath, exactly our age, into her marriage to a non-American writer and a life in that nebulous, sought-after "abroad."

Pat's working-class background in Los Angeles, replete with family divorces and migratory moves from one rented pastel bungalow to the next, was about as different from Joyce's home circumstances as could be be imagined. There had never been a divorce in Joyce's family, on either side. People stayed firmly rooted in their homes and their neighborhoods. Respectability was the watchword.

"Survival" would probably be the best word to adorn an imaginary escutcheon of Pat's family. Her maternal relatives had a very different definition of respectability than did Joyce's. It meant being married to the man with whom a woman was living. It meant staying off "relief," that Depression-era form of welfare. It meant being able to find a job when one's neighbors could not.

The relatives who filled Pat's childhood homes constituted a sort of matriarchal extended family. Stepfathers and uncles came and went, but the aunts, great-aunts, female cousins and siblings were a permanent feature on her shifting California landscape. Her female relatives all worked; they were mostly waitresses, cooks, manicurists, saleswomen—all peripheral service jobs, easily found and just as easily abandoned when something more interesting beckoned, whether an impulsive trip or a new husband.

She remembers them as articulate, amusing, fun-loving, supportive, strongly imbued with a deep sense of family loyalty. Education, at least beyond high school, was not considered possible or even particularly desirable, since where could it lead, what difference could it make, in a world ruled by the rich and the powerful? Pat now sees her teenage self as wanting desperately to educate herself out of her background, however caring, and to move into a totally different world, unlike Joyce, whose education was perceived by her middle-class parents as a way to go further in more or less the same kind of life they had structured for themselves.

On her own at fifteen, Pat worked her way through high school, living in rented rooms, waitressing, baby-sitting, hiring out as a mother's help. She paid for singing lessons by baby-sitting her teacher's children and typing his master's thesis. She knew she was bright, talented and well-read, but had little idea how to go about getting to college. She chose Utah simply because of Los Angeles friends who moved there. She wanted to get out of southern California and to begin a new life, away from what she saw at eighteen as the tawdry chaos of her background.

After her freshman year, however, she fell into the family pattern by marrying (the "Jones" Joyce refers to early in the correspondence). The marriage lasted only a few months. In the middle of her sophomore year, Pat's then-stepfather died. She returned home for the funeral and, typically, found herself talked into staying for three months to care for her younger sister and brothers. Her mother was quite unable to cope with the demands of the family business, her three young children, and widowhood. She had been left financially independent by her deceased husband (her third), and she more or less bribed Pat to stay for those months with the promise of enough money for a summer in Europe. It would be the student ship and youth hostel Europe, but no matter how one got there or what one's circumstances, once there, Europe was Europe.

And that is how Pat got herself to France a year earlier than Joyce and met the young British medical student who was to become her husband the following year. She returned to the U.S. for two more quarters of college before her marriage. Thus, though only a few months younger than Joyce, she had completed just two years of college by the time Joyce had earned her B.A. and M.A.

The two of us met within a few days of Pat's enrollment at the University of Utah, through Joyce's then-fiancé, a fellow classmate of Pat's in a French course. We discovered immediate rapport, through music (we sang with the Mormon Tabernacle Choir, though not Mormons), books, movies, a similar sense of humor and, most of all, a nebulous desire to achieve goals we shared but could not articulate very clearly.

For a while, the Jerrells were uneasy about Pat's friendship with their daughter. She seemed too "bohemian," as the fifties had it, disreputable, divorced, with no discernible roots or solid antecedents. But that passed, and we proved to be more alike than dissimilar in our future choices. We both wanted to "write." We wanted to travel, to see the world, to expand our horizons, to share in that great feast of the intellect for which university seemed to be preparing us. But we were obedient daughters of our time, destined and eager for marriage and motherhood. Both of us resolved the conflict between these personal ambitions and the social commitment to marry by choosing husbands who would shape the travels, the glamorous careers, the horizons, the life styles for their wives.

And out of these marriages, travels, life styles, came the years and years of letters to each other.

We have been asked two frequent questions: Why did you both keep the letters? And: Did you have an eye toward publishing them all along? To the first we have a complicated answer and a simple one. We were both young students of literature; we cherished the written word; we attempted to be truthful, expansive, even elegant, when we wrote to each other; and for all these reasons we respected what each had written and saved the growing piles over the years. Our simple answer, equally true, is that we loved and cherished one another, and the letters represented a part of one another as much as do snapshots or gifts exchanged. To the second question, the answer is an unequivocal No.

Much has been omitted from the printed text that follows; the original letters add up to some three times the length of this book, far more than anyone would want to read. We did not reread the other's letters except to answer the most recent one, nor did we keep copies of our own, so there was much repetition which has been excised here. We have cut (or drastically reduced) some of the discussions of religion and politics, old college friends and their doings; lists of books read and about to be read, movies, plays, concerts, operas; philosophical ruminations, sophomoric effusivenesses and self-conscious foreign phrases. We have omitted the itineraries, dates, and addresses of shipping companies and hotels that our frequent moves required so that we would not lose touch with each other for months at a time. The excisions are all of material that is redundant or tedious; what remains is full and faithful to our lives and to who we were and became over the years.

The names of some people and places have been changed to preserve the privacy of living persons who were a part of those lives.

Some letters were lost, and in one instance (in mid-1959) were deliberately destroyed; a transitional passage has been inserted at that point in the text to sketch the events of those months. Except for this, we have chosen to add little transitional or explanatory material because we feel the letters speak for themselves. Where there are cuts—a few words or paragraphs, even a few pages—we have not indicated them in the text, in the interests of brevity and fluency—and because this is not, after all, a sacrosanct work in which every changed comma must be indicated with brackets or a *sic.* It is, rather, the distilled story of two lives as they were lived through and transmitted one to the other. We have, however, marked gaps of time which sometimes separated the writing of one part of a letter from the rest of it, on occasion stopped midsentence by babies crying, doorbells ringing, husbands coming home. In such instances, a line indicates the break in continuity.

As is true in lives, if less often acknowledged in books, we sometimes appear flatly to contradict ourselves on some subjects from one year to the next—to present a bright and lyrical face on sexual matters, for instance, that later letters describe very differently indeed; or to profess a lack of competence because skills did not measure up to impossibly high, self-imposed standards. What we wrote at such times, and wished to believe, we have left intact and without editorial comment.

The correspondence begins in the summer of 1953. Joyce, twenty-three, had been graduated from the University of Utah a year earlier, and was completing a master's degree in creative writing at Middlebury College in Bread Loaf, Vermont. In the spring she had applied for a teaching grant to France and was awaiting news of her acceptance. At Breadloaf she had fallen in love with a Welsh poet. They became engaged after a brief acquaintance, and planned to marry the following year.

Pat, twenty-two, was living in Los Angeles with her husband, an English doctor doing his internship there. They had met the previous summer in a youth hostel in France, become engaged after knowing each other for ten days, and separated three weeks later, Philip to return to Britain to complete medical school, Pat to finish her sophomore year at the University of Utah. They married a few days after Philip arrived in the United States. On their way from New York City to Los Angeles, they stopped briefly in Salt Lake City, where Pat confessed her doubts to Joyce about the wisdom of her decision.

This was a time when women were considered to be on the shelf if they had not married by the time they were twenty-two or twenty-three. Any talents or self-generated goals that would interfere with marriage were either ignored or laid quickly to rest. The woman who gave herself to art or a profession was pitied or scorned, rather than admired or envied.

It was a time of conformity: political, social, artistic. To be twenty-two in 1953 was to be a decade too late for the self-sacrificing drama and commitment of World War II and a decade too early for the political and sexual liberation of the 1960s. We were called the "silent generation" in the early 1950s. There was plenty to be noisy about, but the paranoia and hysteria of our elders in their manipulation of our world sobered us, frightened us, filed down our rough edges too soon, too thoroughly. We were perhaps too willing to accept the official version of the world we lived in. Our mostly futile rebellions were enacted one by one, as individuals, rather than as common efforts to ameliorate the conditions of our world.

In July 1953, our generation of young men was just coming home from Korea, that puzzling and, by us, unexamined earlier version of Vietnam. Joseph

McCarthy was still ruining the lives of good people. Joan Crawford was still being cast as the calculating business woman who foolishly gave up love (read: marriage, home, children) for professional success. Simultaneous orgasm as the natural culmination of romantic love was the goal of all newly married couples.

On the world scene, recently Nazi Germany, at least the western sector, was busily regenerating itself into respectability. France still seemed the desired cultural milieu for expatriate American would-be intellectuals, World War II having been only a regrettable period when its ports were closed. Britain still ruled an empire, although it was truncated with the loss of India and Burma. Germany, France, Britain and her empire—all these would play roles in our lives. We were to become involved with Germans and Britons. We were to walk the streets of German and British cities. Our American lives were to be shaped by forces from the other side of the Atlantic, but we would remain quintessentially American women in the end.

PART ONE

JULY 1953 – AUGUST 1954

The vacuum a really good friend leaves is a sad thing

Touchstones accurately portrays our lives in Africa, Europe and the United States. However, to protect the privacy of people who were part of those lives during that time, the names we have used in the book are fictitious, with the exception of our own names, those of prominent individuals and those of some members of Joyce's family. The descriptions of certain individual traits and the locations of certain events have also been changed.

P.F.L.

K.J.H.

(Postcard)

Dear domesticated Pat,

So it is in my stars to be eternally the follower. You've ruined me for forging any horizons of my own. Since it is obviously the clear fashion for young existentialists to fall in love with Englishmen, I catered to the public trends, with slight individualistic tendencies, and fell in love with a Welshman. Dear Friend, I did. His name is Lloyd James, and he is here for the first time. He is over here on the reverse Rhodes Scholarship, called the Commonwealth Scholarship, and I'm afraid I have failed you in our anti-poet league. He'll finish his Ph.D. on poetry (modern) this year. Twenty-seven years and skinny as a sparrow, and has a face like Jean-Louis Barrault. He's terribly witty and his basic seriousness is pretty private. He's quite quite wonderful and I'm horribly in love with him. However, he is engaged to a girl who teaches at Cambridge. So what can I do but

> Stand in the hard Sophoclean light
> And take [my] wounds from it gladly.

I'm very afraid. Work is excessive. I will graduate Aug. 9. If I get the chance, I'll elope at first opportunity. Sail early October.

Joyce

3

(Postcard)

Do you realize my married name will most probably be Joyce James, and I'll have to write a book called *Finnegan, Wake Up!* I guess I'll slip out in a little schooner one night and pull a Richard Halliburton on all my enemies, who will be very dismayed when Dr. Livingstone stumbles across me in Tanganyika, leading the Mau Maus, and says, "Miss Jerrell, I presume!" My new anti-Nixon slogan: I don't like Ike, but DON'T DIE, IKE!

(Postcard)

NEW YORK CITY
September 24, 1953

Dear Pat and Philip,

You sphinx-like duo, you. You'd better write me soon, or I won't give your regards to Paris. I sail on the *Queen Elizabeth* the 30th. I've always been a Royalist at heart. It's the English blood in me. Isn't it grand that we are all being so true to the Commonwealth? Am really much in love. Hate to leave him for any reason. Wish me luck. I'm scared spitless.

Love,

Joyce

(Greeting card, with letter enclosed)

LOS ANGELES
November 7, 1953

(Printed message:) "I've got a story for you! Once upon a time there were two little birds who lived in the center of an oakleaf. One day one little bird flew way past the edge of the forest where it saw and heard many, many things. When both little birds got together, they talked and talked and talked and talked and talked and talked."

Yr. obt. serv.,

Pat, a domestic drudge
(formerly Jones, Lamb, etc.)

4

(Letter)

ANOTHER STORY (but v. sad)

Lover:

Once upon a time there was a young bride who was living with her husband (a young doctor) in a horrible town where she had no friends, nor the surroundings nor the occupations she loved so well. She became "in the family way" after she had been married a couple of months, and though she was quite ill, and had to work in the library typing little nonsensical things all day long to help support herself and the doctor, she was very happy and spent her few leisure hours knitting tiny things and thinking of the small life soon to emerge. But alas! It was not to be, and (just a week ago) she lost the little one—

FIN

So, my dear, I haven't written for just ages, I know, but I haven't done anything else but be iller and iller. Now I feel great, but hope to be ill again next month. We're trying again so soon for some obscure medical reason P. dug up.

Are you happy? Is your French rapidly improving? Do you miss your Welshman greatly? How I wish I could have a long long jabber with you till 5 A.M. The honeymoon's over, and though I love P. dearly, I miss all my friends and carefree drunkenness and gay times and school and such.

I read incessantly, especially since I've been working in the library. I quit school and my part-time job when I got pregnant, and went to work in the Order Dept. in the main Los Angeles Library here, full-time. I work with myself, one very pleasant woman and 10 fools. But it pays well and certainly isn't taxing. Since we'll be leaving this smog haven in 8 months anyway, I may as well stay.

About 3 months ago we wrote to Albert Schweitzer, mainly on an impulse, asking if he had any 2 or 3 year vacancies in his hospital in Lambaréné, and last Friday received a personal handwritten letter in return! (saying non, non!) Mainly because he dislikes taking married couples because of the health problems involving children. But it was a very kind letter. We're framing it, I think.

Much much love to you. I can't tell you in my poor prose how much I miss you.

Love,

Pat

5

November 16, 1953

Dearest friend Joyce,

I have absolutely no excuses; I just love and miss you dearly, and hope you will forgive my long silence. As you will note from the enclosed, I sent you the card days ago, which, through my usual negligence, was returned for extra postage. Shall I give you a short history?

I spent the summer going to school at L.A. State College taking two abominable courses. As I planned to enter full-time at UCLA in September, I kept on at my part-time job at a hospital in Hollywood, a job most interesting which I dearly loved. I realized I was pregnant just before school was to open, so I quit the job and went to work full-time for the L.A. Public Library in the Civil Service. I've never spent such a ghastly two months in all my life. The people in C.S. are unbelievably dull and monotonous, and so was the work.

So just last week I quit there and have been looking again. I've found something with Studebaker, extremely well paid, and, what the hell, only till next June. I start day after tomorrow.

I've been reading voraciously all summer long, all kinds of things, for instance Maurois's wonderful biography of Sand, *Lélia*. You must read it if you haven't. You'll soon be able to read the original French, you dog! It strikes home so very much with me, because Sand was a woman who always felt the urgency of the moment, the impelling drive to *be* whatever the situation called for, and to live each segment of her life to the utmost. Maurois captures this beautifully.

I'd like to sing in a chorus around here, but I really don't have time, and besides, now that I've started all this, I'm hoping to get pregnant again right away. Keep your fingers crossed. Maybe four tries is the charm for a successful pregnancy, since three wasn't. It was all very sad and gory. God, I had ten hours of labor for a little thing you could hardly see. Such a waste, tch, tch.

Marriage is pleasant, but takes away from one's sense of privacy in an annoying fashion. I don't mean through the other partner's blundering, but just the fact that you *are* sharing your life with another person. Certainly no one could be less intrusive than Philip, but one's impulses, such as spending the last dollar, going for a long lonely walk, and the like, have to be curbed, because there are things to be done that just can't wait for your pleasure. Cooking, ironing, and other bores. But it has its compensations too; I guess, in the last analysis, I wouldn't trade it for the misery of being single again.

I'm very glad about you and Lloyd, and do hope all comes out in your favor. I was thinking of sending you a few leeks for Christmas, but guess they wouldn't go through customs.

P. and I hardly ever drink, perhaps a glass of wine or two when we have dinner at my mother's once or twice a week, but never at home, and never, never in bars. Mostly because we can't afford it, and have better things to do with what

6

little money we do have. And while I was pregnant, I quit drinking *all* alcohol, coffee, and tea, and nearly quit smoking, and ate enough to keep a very small bird alive, all through desire! Or I should say, no desire. I certainly want a baby, though. It's almost becoming an obsession. I already had two sweaters knitted, and a layette started. I guess it's the challenge of the whole thing. There seem to be so few challenges in my life these days, except getting up in the morning. Why don't you get married, and we'll share our woes?

I guess I'd complain even if I were married to our god, Adlai. I meant to write you a very very long letter and philosophize beautifully and at length about souls, the universe, modern society, and such, but I'm not much good this month.

I suppose the nicest dreams are always those that aren't fulfilled. Yeats: "All my life seems to me a preparation for something that never happened." Dear soul, when may we two walk again through the autumn leaves, innocent, young, bright and eager, waiting for winter, our next date, skiing—

Much of my heart is with you,

Pat

LAVAL, MAYENNE, FRANCE
November 24, 1953

Dear old bean,

Why don't you just skip town for a while? I'll forge you a seaman's passport, and we'll "do" the chateaux together. Damned if I don't miss you enough to make me angry. Besides, I could use you as an interpreter. I'll be lucky if I can read the Cinzano ads by June. Honestly, I'm going to have to learn this language. It seems to be quite the vogue here, at least in Laval. About my only chance to speak English is to indulge in my inherent weakness for dramatic monologues. And as for my French, when some wobbly fisherman greets me with Bonjour! I'm pretty much stuck for an answer.

Enough of that. I'm so glad you finally broke down and wrote, but I wish you could have had a happier excuse. It made me sick that you keep having all that trouble. I do hope it works out this time. Your maternal instincts seem about as ripe as mine. Funny how I, too, and quite seriously, am more attracted by the idea of being a mother than all the other diversions. I wonder if I would feel so married, or if the Damoclean sword would sway over my liberty too much.

Hang on—I have to go wrack myself in the interpreter's role, for my class, who only understand "cat" if I draw them a "chat." I'll be back.

And after that last comment, here I am practically in tears because of the sweetness of these élèves—here I am about to dissolve in the sentimental

7

muck of one of the lesser emotions. But who cares? When I went to all my classes today, they were all decorated for me, and the desk was either bursting with gifts, or the blackboards were playing at hiding them. Honestly! And all because it is St. Catherine's Day in France, and my first name is the same. I really think they went too far. The candy and nuts and roasted chestnuts were a suggestion, but when these lovely, dirty little bilinguists raked up their "egg money" to buy me two bottles of perfume wrapped in hand-stitched handkerchiefs, and a lovely leather photo album, I felt conspicuously appreciative. I mean, really. It's like 2 weeks ago—my presumption in going on strike ("faire le grève") when I'd only been here 3 weeks and only taught 12 hours a week. Sirrah! And to think I went to Paris the same time I was contesting for higher wages—which would help. Ye gods, France is expensive! I can't even afford the necessities of life. I guess I'll just have to make do with the luxuries.

But I really do have an ample supply of all the conveniences current in contemporary France—fresh *cold* running water, camping stove, foot warming brick, and choice of pot or path. It's lovely. Don't misunderstand me; we do have hot water—every Wed. from 8 to 8:10—and it's great fun waiting in line for the cleansing dash, trying to cache enough away in your pants pocket to do the weekly wash in.

Of course you and the clichés have it true that Paris is beautiful. It is. It's so spectacular at night that I have the sensation of being in some grand theatre, and that when I leave the Tuileries, I'll find myself outside some dingy stage door, as if it were the Ice Follies or something. And even if it's true, that stage door is, if possible, more charming.

But Laval is lovely too, in a thoroughly un-Parisian way. Everyone claims it is dead, and I would have to agree with them, if I weren't somehow lucky enough to get a tremendous joy out of simply observing medieval chateaux and prejudices, old streets and smells and crooked chimneys and fruit vendors. If it didn't somehow excite me to watch the lovely silhouette that the clerical robes fan into when the nuns and priests go bumping over the cobblestones on their bicycles (by the way, I bought a bicycle, 3 days before I broke my foot). But for all of it, I'm quietly rotting away living a noble existence. So I make a supreme effort to get to Paris each time saints' days and checks coincide. Tomorrow, for instance.

Details: I got my M.A. I'm going to the University of Rennes each Thursday in hopes of passing my "certificat d'Études Françaises" by June.

I am still in love with the thinnest of them all, my scraggly and magnificent Lloyd. He really is a joy, and as amazing a "catch" (what a hideous term) for me as Philip for you. I'd like to have you meet him, and I know you would too. I really am poor. Ye gods, I went through Paris for two days on 100 francs. I'm getting more and more skillful.

Well, I miss you. I'd drop half the population of Laval in the Mayenne if you could take their place. Now write, Pat. You've no idea what it means. The vacuum a really good friend leaves is a sad thing.

My love,

Joyce

Dearest friend J.—

I am so glad we were both born of the same sex. I can feel lifelong gratitude for a lasting understanding and the deepest sort of friendship between two women. My singing teacher once told me that a close friendship between two women was impossible, because sexual jealousy always spoiled it eventually. I think we have each experienced this with the other on a few occasions, but I hope our own self-understanding was able to penetrate the motives and feelings of the other to a realization that it basically didn't matter. I love you very dearly, in short, and treasure your respect and love as I do hardly anybody's. I wish I could see our mutual states, in, say, fifty years?

A different part of the same subject—I really feel that a man and a woman can reach an empathy that is impossible between two of the same sex (save homosexuals); that is, lovers find something that friends don't.

I am once more slinging the old hash, but this time à la Français. I'm working in a little French restaurant in downtown L.A. It's rather fun; I work banker's hours, make fairly good money, and intend to quit in Feb. and go back to school, because I get bored working all the time.

Oh! Now I remember what I was going to say at the beginning of the letter —continuing—*but,* friends reach a state of mutual behavior on the same levels with the same motivations and deep sympathies of such intensity that is impossible between lovers. Thus the advantages of a great love plus a great friendship (or two or three, but I doubt very much if that is possible).

We're so terribly, terribly alone, Joyce. You, me, everyone. I imagine it's the most obvious and basic fact in the world, but I'm just beginning to realize it. I think one sees this fact more when one looks deliberately for the perfect understanding one is supposed to find in marriage. Perhaps that is why my aloneness (and consequently, everybody's) is becoming so vivid to me lately. Because I really think I have a very wonderful marriage and that it will last as long as Philip and I do, but it certainly is not everything in life to me, because it (meaning Philip, our social pattern together, I guess) cannot cover every bit of every complexity of my ego, my life, my personality. There are too many parts of me concerned

9

with other places, other people (other voices, other rooms?). I'll end this train of thought, and go on to something else.

Philip and I, since we're not pregnant any more, are thinking seriously of going off into the boondocks next year, Africa or South America, or someplace, and putting another notch on our "finding ourselves" guns. We'd like to find a little mission or government settlement in the jungle (or on the plateau!), and save everybody's souls and bodies, and find ourselves a diamond mine so we wouldn't have to work any more, but could travel about and write books and poetry, and read philosophy, on our income. Wouldn't that be pleasant? But it isn't likely. So, I suppose if we really *are* in a suitable place next year (Canada, most likely), I shall return seriously to school, equip myself with a B.A., and begin teaching Freshman English to all the dolts from the hinterlands. If I only had anything pertinent to say, and some time to do it in, I'd write the Great American Novel.

I think so much about my past years, and wonder if anything in the future can hold the excitement and thrills of the unknown tomorrow, as my past few years have. Somehow, an evening out with the beloved date of the moment can never quite be surpassed by the hubby taking you out for a movie or a party. I don't mean that I'm really dissatisfied, though, don't mistake me. I only feel that this is a stage of my life, irrevocable as it is, that can never be recalled, and I feel a bit sad about its passing. However, some new experience must be just around the bend, to intoxicate me with its newness and vigor and life-giving originality.

I felt much the same for about the same period of time as when I broke up with my first great love at 18. I guess something new always has to be around the bend, or life would be unbearable. When I think about it, it makes me feel rather like a heroine out of a bad 19th century novel. If I don't become satiated with life's adventures first, perhaps life will become satiated with me, and I'll be left with a cat and a parrot to exist away the rest of my life in effigies of what has been. But I don't think so. So many little things *are* terribly exciting most of the time, the downtown skyline from our window on a bright sunset evening, the funny different customers in for their coffee in the morning, Bennett Cerf's column in the *SRL*, memories of skiing, good old Gallo Zinfandel, the look of a foreign postage stamp on an unopened letter. (*Trite!* Oh, so many things!!)

But I guess, in the last analysis, I enjoy my life very much and wouldn't exchange it for practically anybody's. Mostly because I don't know what's going to happen next, and that's about the greatest thing in my life. Isn't it funny? Because most people are quite happy because they know, *precisely,* what's coming next.

Well, I'm running dry, so—

My greatest affection and love,

Pat

10

December 21, 1953

Dear friend of sorrows and of joys,

Well, I'll fit in Merry Christmas and all those perennial optimisms that get around. I'm sure that this will arrive too late, but I'm also sure that your Christmas wouldn't be much the merrier if it arrived first. But the point is, I *do* hope it will be all the things it should be, but never is, for you, this year. I also hope that on some remote Algerian coast or another, we may be able to see each other again.

I'm setting off on the early train tomorrow morning for Spain and the Baleares via Paris. I'm feeling a bit like George Sand, escaping to the island. Too bad I don't have like company.

From all latest reports and intentions, I'll spend next year in Paris if it's humanly possible. After two years in France, I ought to be able to make myself understood in a café. God! I'm hardly what you'd call precocious. I still can't talk about the weather and make them understand the subject.

There are so many things I would love to talk to you about, but sitting on the floor smoking or eating your Mexican specialties, and at 4:19 in the evening watching each other for the darkest eyebags. I do miss it all, like you do.

I don't feel at all Christmasy, and the French don't care a hoot about their elections. I know more about them than they do and *I'm* not sure how many candidates there are.

I'll write more soon. You too. Merry, merry Christmas.

> I love you,
>
> *Joyce*

December 22, 1953

Dearest Joyce,

Things are very quiet here. Just work and housekeeping and cooking and movies and the Metropolitan Opera broadcasts on Saturday mornings, sending and receiving Christmas cards.

I don't remember if I told you that P. gets two weeks' vacation with pay during the year whenever he wants it, and that I am returning for spring semester at State College. So I'm quitting work two weeks before school starts and we're going skiing up near Reno or Yosemite.

11

December 28: Time does slip by. But now I can tell you all about Christmas. Philip gave me—(dramatic pause)—a recorder! Alto, German, etc. Just gorgeous. And already I can play Three Blind Mice and Merrily We Roll Along. I'm beginning lessons at USC next week. We had a lovely family Christmas. Spent the weekend with Mother, played Scrabble (a wild new word game), drank wine, and lazed around generally.

I've now decided to go to USC instead of State College next semester. What the hell, we can't afford for me to go to school at all, so I may as well go to the most expensive of all. At least half this poverty-stricken year is over. P. and I were married 7 months yesterday, and getting to know and love each other better all the time.

Love,

Pat

January 12, 1954

Dear friend,

I cannot perceive what form this letter will take. I want you to know that I got your letter at a time when I was peculiarly in need of it. A time when I needed most of all to feel that certainly one was not out of touch with Hawthorne's "magnetic chain." To be assured that somehow one's individual needs and reasons for needing idiosyncratic things (such as a lust for life) are understood and echoed somewhere, even the other side of ocean and environment.

I have had insomnia of the worst sort the past 3 weeks and dreams of an almost serial nature. Last night I dreamt I died and not only that, but the whole dream was what happened to me when I was dead. I blew my breath on a window filled with music to see if it made an evidence of steam. It did, but I was told that that was not a sign I was alive. I tell you this for no reason. It was on my mind.

School finishes July 1st. I'm going to bicycle the Loire Valley in July, and England in August. All beyond that depends on if my fellowship to Paris is granted (things look hopeful, surprisingly so), and when I am going to marry Lloyd. It will be soon. (Think of being around. I want you to be.) There are so many things to talk to you of, but everything conspires against it. It is almost false to our friendship to talk in the résumé style of false summaries that letters entail. I need to talk to you of my coming marriage, of all the doubts and certainties and problems. There is a nice Irish girl here, but I would trade a month of talking to her for one bleary-eyed session with you. I will marry Lloyd; I want to. And he will teach most probably in Britain. Right now, an international marriage pressures me with the separation from the family. You know me too well to think I can't be severed reasonably from the womb. It's just that last spring our home was filled with the ache of possible last times, and now with Daddy ill, the point is italicized.

I am too mercurial. When it rises, I'll write you of events and less of moods (though, thank God, you are a friend for the latter). I'll write you how you can live in Spain on the old proverbial, with a little energy. I want to tell you more of Lloyd and the problems thereby, of school, and of my writing. Because at last I am. And reading. Just finished all Faulkner. Will read your *Lélia* soon. Many things. I need you here. Come quickly.

My best love,

Joyce

(Birthday card with printed message)

LAVAL

January 15, 1954

Were I a disciple of Sartre
Reflecting on life in Montmartre
I would simply exist
Not attempting a new twist
To WISHING YOU A HAPPY BIRTHDAY.

I bought this 6 months ago in New York just for you, and here I am getting it off too late. But you have all my *meilleurs voeux* for a terrific year, dear friend. You seem to have every chance. And I hope somehow we may meet working for the Mau Mau underground before we are both driven to that unhappy state of senility where our only means of reminiscing is to rock our rocking chairs at a breathtaking pace. And I fear that may be here so soon that I could swear we parted in Salt Lake only a few years back, since life has a nasty talent for "slipping by like a field-mouse scarcely rustling the grass."

Love,

Joyce

Beloved friend,

I am getting older and older, and sadder, but, I think, less wise than ever. I intend to return for "just one more" semester at college, and went there the other day to see about a job in the English Department to scrape in a few extra drachmas a week, and was weary and depressed for hours afterwards by the youth, the cruel heartlessness of the fact that I can never be seventeen again, not know a first (or second, or third) triumphant, secure, cocksure love for a boy, that I can never discover again modern poetry all by myself and think, "What a genius am I!"

The weather is like spring here just now, and spring, with all its blatancies, its too bright sun and colors (in Los Angeles, I mean), has always greatly depressed me. I feel my life flowing effortlessly, ceaselessly, painlessly away—not onwards, notice, but away, away. I sat in a little coffee shop by school and deliberately conjured up visions of my youth (for I have faced it, and believe it truthfully now —I am a woman).

I felt a twinge of my old self just yesterday, though, and tears came to my eyes, tears of gratitude for being able to be moved—at what? The words "Thermopylae, Salamis, Marathon." I was reading Edith Hamilton's *The Greek Way*, and nothing, but nothing, in the entire beautiful book stirred me so much as just her simple description of those glorious battles. Oh, God, Joyce, I feel in *such* a godawful vacuum. None but minor feelings—slight irritations, pleasurable seconds—never rage, tragic pain, elation, the belly laugh, the crying jag. I feel I'm *dying* inside, and that if something doesn't stop it, soon all of *me*, the me I know and want to keep on being, will be utterly dead and gone, leaving only a husk that can respond mechanically and live, exist, only in a behavioristic universe. My God, is this a terribly long-winded way of saying, "I'm bored stiff"? I don't think so; it really does seem to go deeper than that.

Doesn't being gone from everything and everyone familiar and beloved do terrible things to you? This is the first time I can ever remember being lonely, bitterly lonely, for so long. I think it just gets less easy to open oneself to new people as the years go by. It's so terribly funny that a year or two or three could make such a difference, but perhaps it's only because I've learned to introspect deeply in the last 3 or 4 years.

Poor us, Joyce, you and I. We're so gregarious in the things of the soul, so quick to love and anger, to giving. And I'll wager Lloyd is every bit as reserved and difficult as Philip is when you've been married 6 or 8 months (or years, even, though I won't have the proof for a time yet). I love P. deeply, and another man would revolt me, but I still get lonely for the electric response, the quickness, empathy, simpatico, that I've had with others, though damned few others. If only

14

I could open up and write, I think I would feel better; therapy, I guess—sewing, cooking, knitting, reading, keeping house, just don't fill my awful vacuum.

I think I'm pregnant again, but I won't be turning mental handstands till another month is past. I hopetogod, hopetogod, I am. P. and I went skiing in Yosemite for a week, got back last Sunday, both tanned, me bruised, and very blue at having to return to this horrible city. I sure seem to feel awfully sorry for myself lately. Well, well.

If we really do go to Africa, why don't you come and shoot tygers and marry Ernest Hemingway?

I'll try a brighter letter in a day or two.

Love,

Pat

LOS ANGELES
February 2, 1954

Dearest Joyce,

I have not mailed the morbid depressed letter I wrote the other night yet, but I'll send it air mail, and this one surface. I'm feeling much better now, thank you. I had a long monologue with Philip the other night, and he sympathized and agreed and was very logical, and, oh, I don't know, I'm just better. Guess what? I'm writing a novel! It'll probably be lousy, but it's a lot of fun. I've been working on it (in my mind) for the last couple of months actually, and I finally got the first words on paper today. Guess what it's about? US!! Well, all the creative writing teachers say write about what you know and love, and what do I know better than university life? If you like, I'll make you my critic. Do you want to read the first couple of chapters when I'm finished? I haven't told anyone else, even Philip or my mother. Until it's well along the way, I don't think I shall. I hope I don't get sued for slander by all my old friends. Of course, I'll probably never finish it, and even if I should, it'll lie in a drawer somewhere till I die! I'm thinking of calling it *The Island That No Man Is*, from Donne. Profound title, no? I now have a title and half a chapter. I don't know exactly how it's going to run, just our life, and our loves, and our fight for knowledge and recognition, and our good times and drunken parties, and all the little intrigues, love affairs and political battles, our seminars and the exhilaration of a really good lecture, and all the coffee times and good friends we've left behind us and won't ever see again. Maybe if I do finish it, I can get my adolescence out of my heart and head once and for all. Why *do* people want to write?

Are you knitting any more? I just finished a pair of ski socks for P. and myself

15

each, and am on my third baby sweater. I always get carried away, you know. I feel so very much better this time, it seems like a good omen. I wish I had that old book of Anglo-Saxon charms and spells I showed once to you from the U. Library. I'm sure they'd be quite efficacious.

I'm coming along famously on my recorder. I'm learning both parts to a fantasy in F for 2 recorders, a charming little thing. My teacher from USC is a panic. I was looking for blank paper today when I ran across the notes from our old Philosophy 102 class, and I couldn't resist sending them to you. Will write again soon. Be good, dear. We'll see you soon.

Love,

Pat

(Enclosure)
The Importance of Being a Philosophy Professor
Act I, Scene 1

> Go Spinoza your top.
> I Kant.
> Oh, go to Hegel.
> I'll have a Plato spaghetti.
> Let's ride Descartes Hume.
> I won't go Hume again.
> My dog said, woof, woof, Berkeley, Berkeley.

LOS ANGELES
February 15, 1954

Dear Joyce,

I feel as if this is going to be one of my crying letters, but I will do my best not to make it so. I think my main trouble is that I am nauseated constantly and throw up at the drop of a hat. Pregnant again, of course, and we're both keeping all toes and fingers crossed. I've safely passed one period and the date for the next begins next Friday. After that, only one more, then I'll feel fairly safe. When registration day arrived, I felt so wretched, I could just crawl out of bed at noon and get to work at the hospital on time at 3:30, so I guess my school days are over. I can't handle working an 8 hour shift 3 days a week *and* school both, and we need my salary desperately, since P. only gets the usual intern's pittance.

I popped around to the County Museum the other noon, for the dullest lecture I've ever heard, and beginning tomorrow, a series of 6 philosophy lectures at USC in the afternoon once a week; I guess I'll attend for want of anything better. I've never had so much leisure time. We're so broke we hardly ever go out, and I only work 3 days a week from 3:30 till 11:00 at the hospital. The other 4 days I get up at 10 or 10:30 usually, mope around for an hour or so, have a cup of coffee and some cereal, throw it up, read and smoke for a couple of hours, have a baked potato or some soup and a glass of milk, throw it up, make a few minutes' sporadic attempt at cleaning, take my pills, brush my teeth, work crossword puzzles, sit and look out the window, and, as it's then late afternoon, go to the store and get something for P.'s dinner, fix it, he comes home, we eat, I throw up, we read for a couple of hours and go to bed. Isn't it an inspiring life?

I usually don't even go downstairs to get the mail till I go to the store. I have so little energy. About the only thing I do with any gusto at all is thoroughly loathe myself. But nothing ever seems to happen, and I can see this life stretching on into infinity, when, one day, I'll just die quietly.

We aren't even going up to the mountains on Sundays to ski, because it's too dangerous for me now, and I won't go if I can't ski, and P. won't go alone. We're charming company for each other. I think I'm just fatal to men who love me or something, but he seems to have less initiative than a garden worm. He never suggests doing anything, never initiates a conversation, never makes friends. He seems to exist quietly, apprehensively, in a little world all his own. He's terribly nervous, is always twitching and squirming, or drumming his fingers, or tapping his feet or swallowing in a (to me) peculiarly offensive manner. I wish I knew what manner of beast I am to bring out all the worst in people. Perhaps it's because I'm so discontented myself. But if I weren't so lazy, I'd be less discontented, I'm sure.

Here I am, in another damned vicious circle. I feel like breaking a leg or something for a little change and excitement. My God, but we're humdrum. I hate brushing my teeth in the same stance over the wash basin every morning, and making the bed in precisely the same efficient manner, and oh, I give up— but you get the picture, I'm sure. How *do* people do it, Joyce, year after year after soul-absorbing year? I wish I had someone to talk to. You, mainly. I will end with my two liner:

> So about Los Angeles I will jog,
> To see the palm tree draped in smog.

If you'll stick around till Aug. or Sept., we just might make it by then. We're very vague on plans for next summer though. Hope this letter cheers you up considerably. God, how I miss you.

Love,

Pat

February 16, 1954

My dear old standby of a wonderful but too far away Pat,

Zut! as they say here. or MERDE! in my really down at the heel moods. I've been carrying your addressed envelope around with me for the last "quinzaine" and I haven't set a word down or all the thoughts of you and feelings toward you I've been having. Your letter made me feel so much with you again. Strange how the words can come so far and yet seem closer than my own thoughts sometimes, which these days seem too often to be wandering aimlessly among the trivia. Your letter brought it back to me all too poignantly. It really was too much. Laval is a dangerous place for someone walking the cliff of self-pity or nostalgia. I sometimes think of it as little more than an incubator for lost emotions (which unfortunately are not successfully displaced). Bill Wanless haunts my dreams as if it were only last night I slept with him. And it shocks me even more to realize it was just exactly, and only, 2 years ago, that we broke so cleanly, so completely, and yet so slowly has it settled, the dust into its place, but some still breeze can yet lift the particles into a painful presence of the life we had.

> We fray into the future, rarely wrought
> Save in the tapestries of afterthought.

I know so much the mood of your last letter. We're both at that age when that mood begins to have relevance. I thought how I'd just like to go on a midnight walk with you, in silence that perhaps you and two or three others could articulate by. Unfortunately it's damned difficult trying to communicate silence by letter. Well, hell, we always claimed to have a certain respect for the written word. (And by the way, I have been writing. It's the least—and the most—I can do. If you're interested, I'll plague you with them.)

The point is, you see—I've lost Lloyd—or he's lost me (as his reward for making me love him)—and consequently I don't give two consecutive goddamns about much of anything at the moment. I suppose I'd feel cheated if I could feel anything, but I just feel a bit dead (I suppose even that is elaboration. Can a person "feel" dead? [especially if he grew up outside fundamentalist beliefs in later consciousness?]). I do feel as if some cosmic Iago were just taking over and getting away with it. That's the trouble with grief, isn't it? And death? That they always get away with it! Someday I'll explain to you what happened, if I ever find out myself. It's as if some part of me insists on overbalancing the teeter-totter.

The trouble was, he was already engaged when I met him, and all the passion and poetry and childlike pledges (with adult repercussions) were not sufficient to counter the deficit we began with. And I say "we" because if he returns to her, it's out of reasoning and not impulse. That much I know. He has told me. But Frost's words are perfect—

Oh when to the heart of man
Was it ever less than a treason
To go with the drift of things
And yield with a grace to reason,
To bow and accept the end
Of a love—or a season?

The fact that I can quote comments on my own unhappiness is evidence to the rising graph and fleeing time since I heard from Lloyd 3½ weeks ago. I was really physically ill, but I'm up on two feet and half a spirit again. Oh hell, I don't know if it's really definitely over or not. I have at least a little waiting more before I know. But God, Pat, the worlds that burst apart! I don't expect anything. I don't even want anything, and I feel it will be a long time before I can give anything.

I wish you were here. It's agony trying to write it out, and I haven't succeeded. I feel bereft, but I suppose that's one of the less mundane agonies.

My best love,

Joyce

March 23, 1954

Dear Joyce,

This will no doubt be a most boring letter, because I have been doing absolutely nothing. I am pregnant again, you know, nearing my 14th week, which will be the longest I've gone so far. Except for morning sickness, I'd been fine this time till three weeks ago, when Philip and I borrowed a car and drove down to Mexico for the weekend. P. doesn't have a license, so I had to do all the driving, and when we got back I started hemorrhaging a bit, went to the doctor, and was peremptorily ordered to bed.

I spent nearly a week at my mother's, poor P. commuting interminable L.A. miles to the hospital and me flat on my back with all and sundry waiting on me hand and foot. I felt fine, but got bored as hell after a couple of days of it. I lost my job, of course, it being the kind where you show up or else, and haven't received permission yet to get another. I can't even sweep a floor or do any ironing or anything. I am allowed one outing a day, a ten minute trip to the grocery store and back, and my only work each day is cooking P.'s dinner. I can't even knit or sew, because these require sitting up, and I'm supposed to be prone practically all the time. So I read, read, read, and get splitting headaches and violent nausea as a consequence. What a project having a baby is. But I'm being a very good girl because I want this baby so badly.

19

It looks as if there is a good chance that Philip can join the British Colonial Service and be interviewed here in the States without having to go to England first, as we had previously thought. If the Colonial Service will send us from here direct to Africa and pay our fares, it'll save P. having to get another ill-paid temporary hospital job here in this country to save the money to get to England. Of course, I don't know if I'll be able to travel at all—so? I may have to stay right here in L.A. till the baby's born (if??), no matter where Philip goes. All very vague and unsatisfactory. Except for our sex life, which has of necessity been totally nil for three months, we get along surprisingly well for having been married nearly a year.

He really has been so very steadily sweet and understanding to me the past few months, it's unbelievable. I feel so perfectly lousy both physically and mentally because of my enforced inactivity mainly, that I know I get unbearable at times, but P. and Mother are my mainstays. I go on crying jags and he brings me a Kleenex, an aspirin, a glass of water, and a kiss, and retires to read his newspaper, which is the best possible thing he could do. I feel terribly unattractive; none of my clothes fit, since, though I've gained no weight, my waistline has already expanded an inch; my complexion is ghastly and my hair a horror, it just sticks out in tufts all over my head.

We have our moments when we snap at each other (practically always instigated by me), but usually we just exist quietly and warmly with each other in our little hovel. My whole life at this moment is entirely centered around keeping this baby. Another month should tell the story, though I'll have to be awfully careful the whole time. I'm due around Sept. 15th, if all goes well. If it's female, it's Deirdre, and if male, Trevor. Dear Joyce—why don't you come and live with us next year and write a novel or something? Would you like Afrique? Sorry such a dull letter. Will try to do better next time.

My deepest love,

Pat

LOS ANGELES
May 6, 1954

Dear Joyce,

I hope to God this reaches you somewhere in Europe in case you've left your school. This is the first letter I've written to anyone in months, literally! I'm very pregnant, you know, successfully at last, and even started wearing my maternity clothes last week. I look like the latest model tent.

I've been working in a place downtown punching a typewriter for 6 or 7 weeks, and am quitting around June 15th or so. I've been feeling very lousy, about half-alive, till just recently, and now am on top of, yes, I guess the world, physically and mentally. It's so funny, but I've struck the most peculiar vein of lassitude in myself since my second month or so. When I'm not actually at work, I merely lie around from A till PM, doing and thinking absolutely zero. I don't even read very much. I'm getting so damned domestic and maternal you'd hardly know me. I'm even making, of all things, a quilt! For the baby. The greatest symbol of all, I've neatly packed away all my mildewing stories and turned the little notebook I kept them in into a recipe book. Ah, me.

It looks very much as if we are going to Saskatchewan for the summer and returning here for the great event in Sept. P. has an offer of a well-paid locum for an M.D. going on vacation in July and August. After that, who knows? Another job somewhere till we have enough to get to either England or Africa. The Colonial Medical Service, with which P. applied, moves very ponderously and hasn't come through with any fabulous offers for an all-expense 2 years' trip to Africa.

The Army-McCarthy hearings here have been the big thing lately. P. and I hunch over our battered little radio every night listening to the unbelievable name-calling, and I at last feel that all the paranoia our *Forum* bunch carried around on our radical little backs was justified. What are your plans? You haven't made one concrete statement in a letter yet! And if you do come back here in the fall, you must come down to L.A. and play Aunt Joyce for a bit. Or, if in late summer, up to Saskatchewan and fish with us. We're very back-to-nature these days; must be parenthood descending rapidly upon us. You're my one friend, whom I really miss. Do give us a line.

All my love,

Pat

LAVAL
May 18, 1954

Dearest Pat,

It's my birthday and I don't like it and getting old reminds me of how you don't want to either, which reminded me of how I miss you and having you to discuss it with, which reminded me that it was time one of us broke this silence. When you don't write, I cannot help but envision you in the sorrow of another miscarriage and it worries me to the point of writing it.

My telepathy isn't working lately. Due to the H-Blast, no doubt. Dusty atmosphere. Don't forsake me, friend. I need your insults to keep me kicking.

21

And I haven't seen so much as the tracks of a missed friendship this year. No relationship worth even the name that Henry James would give it. Disgusting to have spent one whole year recuperating from the blow of the realization of perfidy. Convalescence—that's really what this year has been for me. And all because I once read Shakespeare, and learned of Merrie England, and thought, "You, too, can love an Englishman." Have you read Joyce Cary's *The Horse's Mouth*—which means to say, have you learned to "Go and love without the help of anything on earth?"

Does it really come down to that, Pat? You're the best friend in the world to turn to when I'm blue, if only because you help me find reasons for making it bluer. You're good when the sun's up, too, I think. It's been so long I may be mistaken.

No, I'm not really feeling so Philip Wylie-ish as I may sound. My bitterness against Lloyd is just a canker, not a cancer. But it made a sort of marmot out of me when I should have been marveling over medieval moods and moats. But, God damn, it's hard to think that even the Bayeux Tapestry matters, that it really has much to do with our experiencings and feelings and disillusionments, when one's worlds are blown apart. Even if they do matter, it's hard to care, selfish little beasties that we are. There's a lot of disgust behind it all. The way we go along in our rut, kicking the future into a ball that rolls in our idealistic gutter, watching our feet, or the place we think our feet will be. Then when we realize that the ball rolled into a funny side street of its own that we never expected, we want to go back to the alley and see the sights we could have seen along the way, after it's too late to see even where the alley changed. So I find myself thinking I have to compensate for nine months of missing with six weeks of seeing.

It's like living on credit. Always overdue, paying for something you didn't have or enjoy with the only minutes you'll ever know. Hell—I want long clean wind and a clear emotion. Perhaps our kind of hypocrisy is the worst of all, not living, just believing in living; not seeing, just defending one "vision" after another that doesn't belong to us; not feeling, just arguing that to live is to feel; not even loving, just being persuaded that loving is the most valid way; not caring, just wanting to.

Oh God and time to wrap this letter up with those delicious, all-saving miraculous "details." I made a 50 mile pilgrimage to Chartres, à pied, last weekend, with 10,000 students from Paris, with beautiful balloony blisters. One American girl was so conscientious that she told me I should be ashamed of myself when I fell to the ground from fatigue, on the grounds that "You should remember you are an ambassador of America!" Lovely, isn't it? Laugh, I thought I'd die.

I won a scholarship to study in Santander, near San Sebastian, Spain, during the summer. I'm staying in Europe next year, foreseeing quite easily the difficulty in rowing back.

Well, I'll let you off. I've demanded too much already. But it's disgusting, being 24, especially since I was never so old before. I love you, because of all your faults. But I wish you were a little more vocative.

Joyce (or the facsimile thereof)

P.S.   Got your letter—now that's intuition! Same day! Awfully glad you're pregnant, domestic, and happy. Canada sounds good. I *have* sent concrete statements. Besides, the only important one is that Lloyd and I are through, and he is about to marry, not me. Next year's plans are vague, but vague! Another tacit word—am doing lots of writing. How—or is—your novel? I speak French now, like an illiterate native. And your recorder?

LAVAL

May 31, 1954

Dearest Pat,

Good news! I really am pleased you're progressively pregnant, and I'm as jealous as my thwarted maternal instinct will allow me to be. It has been ages since I've heard from anyone, even YOU in length. I love you anyway.

Who would I write this letter to, but you? And it's your fault that I can write it at all. You're the one who talked me into buying a douche bag. Anyway, you can't buy contraceptive douche powder over here, for heaven's sake, and so I'm writing to ask you to send me some. Air mail. Unfortunately, not because I need it in Laval, but because I'll be pulling up my unromantic roots before long, and I won't have an address. And, in the immortal words of Fats Waller, "One never knows, do one?" So I know you'll do that for an old buddy. And don't forward this letter to my home.

You see, in September I am going to rent a chalet in Austria or Switzerland with a boy I met on the boat. It's all been arranged by letter, and incredible as it is, our whole relationship is becoming quite sensual through letters alone. We write 2 or 3 times a week and I even have a teaching position in Beirut offered to me. I might take it because that's where he lives. I'm not really as resilient, after Lloyd, as this sounds. I'm feeling in a particularly good mood, but actually I'm skeptical as anything about any relationship that might be mis-termed love.

But I have had a too-celibate year here and—you understand. I can't write about Lloyd—impossible. I have to go teach now. I hope you can fathom the profundities of this letter. Nothing but ideas, ideas! I sometimes exhaust myself, always being so deep. Will write something more than a scattered, battered, shattered letter later.

My love,

Joyce

23

July 28, 1954

Dear (I assume) Pat,

I'm one hell of a better correspondent than you are, and I'm no Madame de Sévigné. Damn it, Pat, motherhood's all to the good, but a friendship is a friendship, and kindred spirits aren't to be found in the Annex Coffee Shop every day!

Still, I'd rather have your silence due to indifference than a relapse on your pregnancy, and I do hope you're just being a dullard, a slackard, and a damn lousy friend.

I suppose I should thank you for the package you sent me [contraceptive jelly.], even though it has proved most inutile, not having met anyone I could shake souls, or ideas, or anything but hands, with, since I left Breadloaf. Except for the philosophy professor at Rennes who has turned into one marvelous friend. But, NO, Catholic, and decidedly a "célibataire."

We ought to start talking about meeting in the Belgian Congo under a 40 foot fern pretty soon. Is it true—yes or no—that you and Philip will be in Africa next year? Mother says that you called her on your way, hitchhiking (bless you!) to Canada, and that your plans were oriented towards Kenya or some outpost (as Americans think of them).

I'm going to be in Lebanon next year, teaching lit. in the Beirut College for Women, to Greeks, Arabs, English, French, Italian, Lebanese, Americans, and Iranians. It's a real scandal, this jumping around from hemisphere to hemisphere like a lesser Barbara Hutton—and all of it at somebody else's expense—but I'm not about to make a moral issue of it. Write me right away in Santander, as I'll only be here one month before I'm off grasshoppering around again, so please take me seriously.

After school was out, I hitchhiked down to Biarritz and then went on to Pamplona to see the bulls chase the boys down the barricaded streets at 7 in the morning. Lady Brett was still walking the streets, although the sun wasn't rising also. And still isn't. What schmutzy weather. All foreigners blame it on the atomic bomb, you know. I turned into a really bloodthirsty fan of the bullfights —sadistic Spanish and I shouting Holá!—can't stand the sight of Band-Aids usually. I really did love it; might as well be honest.

From there down to Madrid for 2 weeks in the hellish heat of July. All alone, wandering through the Prado, and the museums of Sorolla, up and down the tiny turning streets of Toledo, and then back to El Greco.

My Santander scholarship is going to be terrific. Brahms cycle, Lope de Vega, Shakespeare, Helsinki Ballet, Beethoven cycle and Greek tragedies. And what a beautiful city. Water, water—what a difference it makes to a city. Will swim every day on these beaches. I'm already speaking Spanish so well I astound myself. How easy it is after French. It's pronounceable!

Malgré tout—I love you
and hope you'll write,

Joyce

WALTON, SASKATCHEWAN
August 5, 1954

Dearest Joyce,

Well, I know I've been a rotten correspondent, but this is the goddamnedest hole I've ever lived in, seen, imagined, in my whole life (such as it is). I'll bring you up to date. We obviously got to Canada, by hitchhiking, with me almost in my 7th month, if you can imagine. I wore one of Philip's shirts over my jeans, held together by a row of safety pins in a daisy chain across my stomach. And we have 3 more weeks to go here. We had intended to go back to L.A. at the end of P.'s job here, but he lost his U.S. visa crossing the Canadian border, and the wheels of bureaucracy grind so slowly that it doesn't look as if he'll get it back in time for the baby. Then I wanted to go back to L.A. to be with my family (especially my mother—God, how I need her right now! You'll see, when you have your first) and have my family doctor deliver me, but Philip wanted me with him, wherever he might be, and I realize it's my duty to break the old ties and consider *us,* P. and I, the family unit, and not to snivel like a baby. After all, good medical care is what counts, and I'll get it where we are going, which is ENGLAND.

Philip thought he'd get another job in Canada while we were waiting for the Colonial Service to hire us and send us to Africa, but all the contracts here are too long. The thought of a Canadian winter petrified both of us, so we've taken the plunge and bought tickets on a Cunarder sailing from Quebec on Sept. 1, arriving in Southampton Sept. 10. Now, of course, I'm scared stiff I'll have the baby either on board the train from here (a 3 day trip) or on board the ship. I'm due only 3 weeks after we arrive in Southampton, after all. But P. reassures me and makes fun of all my fears.

Anyway, we're going. We'll be met by Philip's Aunt Sallie, who is also a doctor, and staying with her until after Baby is born. Then a job somewhere or other, preferably in or near London, till we finally prod the Colonial Service into action and get out to Africa (East, we hope).

That's my news. I'm still very pregnant, as you see; Baby plays wild games inside me. I'm beginning to agree with an old high school pal who's beaten me

25

to it—she has 3—and who says the whole thing is a pain in the neck, except for Baby itself. If only I weren't so damned hot and covered with Canadian mosquito bites. And so bloody bored. There isn't a *thing* to do in this place except read, and there aren't any books, and because we were hitchhiking, we only brought a rucksack and a suitcase, and I brought *one* book, Cellini's autobiography, which I now know by heart. I've also read the complete works of Zane Grey, knitted enough for triplets, and learned to play two-handed bridge, and, best of all, I've been helping Philip in the doctor's office, doing urinalyses, X-rays, accounts, all sorts of things. The office nurse has, thank God, been away all summer. I also cook a terrible meal every night in one pan on a one-burner hot plate. What a dump this place is.

How I look forward to what he tells me about life in East Africa. Sunshine, servants! Funny to think that girls my age might be going to England to do their Junior Year Abroad on the same boat I'm sailing on, a pregnant housewife.

Write and tell me where you are and what you're doing. Are you really going to Lebanon? Maybe we can get together in Timbuktu. How I envy you your summer. I'd trade anywhere and anything for Saskatchewan. I'm sorry this is such a stupid moany groany letter, but that's how I am these days, stupid and moany groany. I miss you. I need to talk to someone, preferably you.

Lots of love,

Pat

PART TWO

AUGUST 1954–
DECEMBER 1955

He is so much more
sincere than I am

(Postcard)

SANTANDER, SPAIN
August 15, 1954

Hoop-la! What delight to hear from you, being still pregnant. How I envy you, you lucky son of a gun. It sounds frighteningly as if we just might *miss* each other—my sailing on the 9th from Cherbourg and your probable arrival the 10th at Southampton. Hell! Still, next year I may be in Paris instead of Beirut. New job, more money—PARIS! And if so, London is just a hop. So we won't despair, yet. Write immediately *when* you'll be in Southampton. Do take *good* care of yourself. On my return it will be perhaps easier to see you. And I do persist in feeling *aware* of yourself and your friendship. Do you need a spare godmother? Love, Joyce

Just before this postcard (August 15), Joyce met Hans Hohlwein in Spain. They fell in love and decided to marry within a very short time. Joyce's teaching grant included her return fare to the U.S., and the job awaiting her in Beirut was paying her fare from her "point of origin" as an expatriate American teacher. She took advantage of the two paid-up fares to make a quick trip home to Salt Lake City, where she informed her parents of her impending wedding. They accepted the astounding news in good grace, informed the Salt Lake City newspapers, and had engraved the following wedding announcement. The date and place of the marriage turned out to be otherwise, as the letters tell. Joyce packed up her hope chest, that emblem of solid respectability which Pat had always envied her so, and set

29

sail again to Europe and Hans. In Paris, he too had been able to arrange a teaching position for himself in Beirut.

September 18, 1954

(Printed announcement)

Mr. and Mrs. Warner Phillips Jerrell
have the honour of announcing
the marriage of their daughter
Kathryn Joyce
to
Mr. Hans-Jurgen Hohlwein
on Thursday, the seventh of October
Nineteen hundred and fifty-four
Paris, France

At Home
Faculty Residence
Beirut College for Women
Beirut, Lebanon

Added by hand: And PLEASE use it!

SALT LAKE CITY
September 25, 1954

Dearly loved Pat,

I literally have only one minute. Sorry not to have written sooner.

But know my thoughts were with you during your time of motherhood. I am getting married October 7th in Paris, Pat, to Hans-Jurgen Hohlwein, a German painter I met in Spain. We will be there only 3 days before we fly for Beirut, where he'll teach art and I lit. and Freshman English. It's all incredible luck, as good as yours, and I'm still staggering from the blow.

The Beirut College for Women is flying me to New York the 4th, to Paris the 5th, where I will meet and marry Hans, and then we both fly to Beirut to begin teaching the 11th of October. They furnish us our apartment, 3 rooms, bath, and a studio for Hans, laundry-maid, meals, and medical service. And they pay us each $1,100 on top; not much, but it will be all ours, enough to see Damascus, Jerusalem, Cairo, Istanbul, and so on.

30

Anyway, if you can't come to Paris, and I know you can't, write to me in Beirut. And remember that I'm loving you, in all those foreign parts. I am very happy. He has it!!

Joyce

September 26, 1954

Dearest Joyce,

I'm sending this to Salt Lake, hoping it will be forwarded to Paris, if you're still there, before setting off for Beirut. You lucky girl! How wonderful for you —if it weren't for the fact that on October 7th I'll be proudly and gratefully dandling my wee babe on my knee in the hospital, I would swim the Channel and be there as matron-of-honor for your wedding. I'm dying to hear about how you met, fell in love, what he's like, what you're like, etc. And BEIRUT! As romantic as Africa. Aren't we marvelously fortunate in having found great husbands so out of the ordinary and going to such great places instead of settling in some dull suburb?

As you see, I survived Saskatchewan and both train and boat trips, and have been twiddling my thumbs here in the Midlands ever since, in this dreary carpet-manufacturing town. I wouldn't dream of letting on to Philip, but his Aunt Sallie scares the daylights out of me, and baby that I am and much as I'm charmed with just the fact of being in England, I'm awfully homesick, miss my mother, and am rather scared at the approach of the great event. I'm in good health, have religiously done all my breathing exercises and taken all my vitamins (vihtamins, as the English say) and so on—but . . . For instance, the baby's trunk (layette) got left behind in Montreal in the bowels of Railway Express, and I was practically hysterical. Philip was very cross with me, but I just couldn't help it. I felt like an Armenian refugee, and *that* was the last straw. Cunard, of all people, traced and found it for us, and shipped it free. It arrived a couple of days ago—thank God for efficient British firms.

Philip was awfully sweet on board ship, very thoughtful and considerate. I remember having a lot of objections to his laying down the law and ordering me around in Los Angeles, but either I'm getting used to it or else it's particularly nice to have someone take over your life when you're pregnant.

How shall I begin to describe Aunt Sallie? She's enormously fat, has tiny little pig eyes, is a dreadful slob, wears no makeup (even lipstick), wears her hair parted in the middle and hanging down straight as straw either side of her fat

31

purple face. Her first half-dozen sentences to us when we disembarked on the 10th were that we must face our responsibilities now and not go gadding about the country sightseeing and being selfish about it, when we have a baby on the way. So, in short, we didn't go the twenty miles out of our way to or through London. Philip argued a bit, but it didn't do any good. I just kept my mouth shut. She's a holy terror. I feel very ungrateful when I'm sleeping under her roof and eating her food, but I simply can't feel otherwise. I hope Baby comes on time. Even three weeks will seem an eternity.

I feel so helpless at this point, but I guess that's natural. I get weepy a lot, which then upsets Philip, so I try to hide it, or go to the bathroom (my God, English bathrooms are cold) and have a good cry on my own. My face is so red from the cold and puffy from the last stages of pregnancy, that a few tears never make any difference.

Philip is spending a lot of time looking for a hospital job to give us something to live on while we wait for Imperialism to do its duty by us and get us off to East Africa. Philip simply hates it here at Sallie's too. I told him I think he married me just because she told him not to. I suppose the situation is really quite comical, if I can just get myself to look at it that way.

———————=◄ ►=———————

Later: And it's all very well living in this exquisite country, but I'm so damned lonely and depressed and homesick at times I could die, and I haven't had so much as a postcard from my twenty correspondents. If you don't write to me I won't even send you an announcement! I mean a real letter, not just an address for me to write yet more unanswered letters to. Come on, take time out from honeymooning and being in love, and be a brick.

This is possibly the dullest spot in all Europe, all the world! And Sallie the dullest person, most of the time.

I feel so alien here. The biggest, most intimate event of my life is about to occur, a period in which I'm practically helpless, dependent upon others, and I'm among strangers who aren't the least bit interested in any part of it. Well, I suppose after Baby finally does come and we can get away from here, I'll be too busy to be lonely or homesick or dying for letters. I dread going into that damned hospital; not from the delivery standpoint, which doesn't bother me at all, but from the alienness and strangeness of it all. They're quite old-fashioned and dictatorial in English hospitals, from what I gather, and fuss and poke about one a lot, which I hate. When I do go into labor, I've made Philip promise he won't say or do anything till I'm nearly ready, and *then* we'll go to the hospital. I know I sound depressed, forgive me for pouring it out to you but I can't to Philip; he's British, after all, and it's not strange in the least to him, and he doesn't like it here at Sallie's any more than I do. He's done his best for me, which is all I can ask. He loves me, takes good care of me, is very sympathetic, and is as thrilled and excited over Baby as I am. But I *still* miss and want my Mother and a friend like you. So damn it, WRITE to me! It helps.

> Very much love—
> and all our felicitations
> and best wishes on your forthcoming
> nuptials. I wish we could meet.
>
> *Pat*

Dearest Joyce,

A sad, sad letter. Our poor little baby died about a week ago, and I delivered him four days ago. The doctor and Philip hadn't told me, as they thought it would only make my labor so much worse. I thought I hadn't felt any life for the last couple of days or so, but Philip kept reassuring me everything was okay and that he simply didn't have room to move about. I won't go into the details about the delivery. When I came out of the anesthetic, the doctor took my hand and told me that I was fine and would have lots more babies, but that this one was dead. It was a little boy, seven and a half pounds. I think of him as so real that my tears keep coming and coming for little Trevor who lived inside me all those long months in California and Saskatchewan and across the Atlantic and in England, and never even had the chance to breathe. Philip came in after the doctor told me, and we cried and cried in each other's arms, and all the time I just didn't believe it.

Everyone is very kind and considerate, and Philip and I have comforted each other enormously, and if this has done nothing else, a tragedy like this (even though I know it's a minor one) has cemented us together and given us more love and understanding and compassion for each other than I thought possible.

I'm going to get pregnant again after my first normal period, and just try and forget all the difficulty and disappointment. I had a wonderful pregnancy the last three to four months. And my labor and delivery were unbelievably easy and good and fast. I'm just like you, apparently, made for childbearing. So there's still a family ahead for us. There just wasn't anything that anyone could have done. Baby just died quietly without any of us realizing it, and that's that. I'm forcing myself to stop thinking about it and to stop crying.

The very hardest thing, almost, was Philip and I having to sign jointly a burial order for the poor little lifeless thing. We just couldn't afford to have him cremated after the postmortem, and British law demands burial in a cemetery otherwise. It's all fearfully gruesome and was done yesterday; I had awful nightmares last night listening to the rain pouring down and thinking of him so recently safe inside me and now under the cold cold ground in Meadowfields cemetery. I shall never want to come back here as long as I live. But enough of this.

The doctor suggested to Sallie and Philip that I be taken somewhere nice for a few days, and good old much maligned (by me!) Sallie is giving us a few days in Paris, which is really why I'm writing you so soon. Otherwise I would have waited till you were settled in Beirut and we in London. I know you'll be married by the time we get to Paris (Oct. 12) but I pray you'll get this letter and that you'll still be there and that we can meet Hans-Jurgen and see one another for one more time for God knows how long.

You see, I was right all along. Growing up is plain hell. But I won't be a weepy bore in Paris, I promise. I *so* want to see you!

Very much love,

Pat

(Note left by Joyce on hotel door for Pat)

PARIS

Mid-October 1954

Dear friends:

Sorry, but one hell of a day. We CANNOT be married here in Paris. We'll have to wait till Beirut. Tonight we go to Bach's B Minor Mass over in the cathedral near Les Halles. May look for you afterwards. Won't be surprised if you can't be there. At any rate, I still love you and hope to see you tomorrow. I promise to call before 10. OK? If not, call us. Joyce

Despite their frantic efforts, rushing from one government office to the next, Joyce and Hans could not be married in Paris, because Hans, born in what was to become East Germany, lacked the requisite documents. In the midst of the rush, the two couples managed a few meals together, a concert, a movie. Pat and Philip expected what was then called a bohemian artist—unkempt clothes, long straggly hair,

34

slovenly habits—but to their surprise they met a very proper German in suit and tie, every bit Philip's equal as an urbane young European gentleman. Each woman, they confessed later, felt the other's husband to be stiff and a little cool. Joyce of course had met Philip briefly in Salt Lake City the year before. Perhaps each husband felt somewhat ill at ease in the presence of his wife's closest friend. All of them loved Paris and knew it well; they were undergoing some pre-nostalgia at the thought of a couple of years "exile, even with the excitement over the new lives they were all about to embark on. It would be seven years before Pat and Joyce met again, and ten years before Philip saw the other couple.

LONDON
November 12, 1954

Dear Mrs. Hohlwein,

Oh, it was so fine seeing you and your Hans-Jurgen, so happy, so in love. We like him very much. How good it would be to get to know each other's husbands, wouldn't it? And how good that life has worked out so well for both of us. All I need now to make my happiness complete is a baby or two. And we'll be working on that soon. I'm feeling very well, am thin again, working part-time at a dull job in a funny little Dickensian office in Soho; we live in the great flat I told you about in Paris, very near the British Museum which I pop in and out of on my way home from work. I'm taking a course in pottery which I love.

We have got our acceptance into the Colonial Service—now very grandly (and with a splendid anti-imperialistic euphemism) called Her Majesty's Overseas Civil Service. But it's still uncertain when we'll go, though we got our first choice of where, Tanganyika. We'd like to go in the spring.

I'm falling madly in love with London, though it's so different from our beloved Paris. I just wander around here and there by myself, for hours on end. I'm writing this in bed because it's too cold to be anywhere else, and I haven't got any shillings to put into the gas meter. When I'm home alone, I spend most of my time in bed reading or writing, with three sweaters and a pair of ski socks on. Just like La Bohème. What an abominable climate. I now see why the British were such great explorers—they were trying to find a decent sunny climate to live in. But no doubt I'll be writing you in a year's time complaining about the heat of Africa.

I can't say I'm doing much in the way of profound thinking these days. I'm just drinking in London and the English and all there is to do here, perhaps in preparation for three years of life in the bush? We seem to have met a lot of people and go out to lots of parties with cheap Algerian wine and cheese and good companionship. I begin to see that what I've always thought of as vaguely and

35

generally British has many ramifications, and, I suspect, snobbish ones which I can't see as yet. I am barely able to begin to distinguish among the various accents, for instance. I can sort of tell a South African one from "pukka" English, and Scots (not Scotch, as we always said in the States) and Irish, but *class* differences make it harder than regional ones. More of this and the behavior that goes with it later.

Our finances are terrible, as no doubt yours are too. Do you think either of us will ever be rich someday? I'd like to get you a scrumptious wedding present. Will you accept the thought for the deed, at least for a while more? I have to go out and shop for dinner; I must do it every day as we've no refrigerator and everything gets high as a kite in no time, despite the indoor temperature. Mostly we live on spaghetti, Spanish rice, and albóndigas. But I have an awful time finding the vegetables I'm used to.

Write and tell me all about Lebanon and your life,

Lots of love,

Pat

BEIRUT
November 30, 1954

Dearest old Pat,

Well, even though we only managed it between two crises, I was glad that our Parisian meeting happened. It did me good to touch again the old contact, and to see, especially, that you are happy with Philip. And since the subject is on its way, I'll only say that I, too, am even happier than my thoughts had aimed towards. Unfortunately, you only met the rather more or less unsocial profile of my husband, as does everyone who sees him only passingly over at least a one-month trial period. All I can say is that he needs no apologies and that I could not have dreamt he would be so exciting to live with. There's a good deal more movement going on there than I was prepared to believe. No, in every way that I have even begun to discover, there exists the "Everlasting Yea!" of the rightness of this action. Which, by the way, *did* take place, if not until October 30th and here in Beirut.

Actually, I suspect that Beirut is beautiful, but we've not had time nor opportunity to verify either assumptions or local exclamation marks. We seem to be spending these vacation hours listening to Bach in our funny little linear and freezing and unfurnished apartment. About all we have in the way of furnishings are books, orange crates, itchy khaki blankets, 15 drawings and all the utensils thereto, poinsettias, a spouting toilet, a plugged bidet, cans of Nescafé,

Kleenex, and each other. Luckily the place is so small that if we had much more it would seem tastelessly crowded.

I'm teaching five classes. Hans-Jurgen has two unhappy courses in "Art of the Home" but he can compensate for that by his three hours of studio art. Also I have begun German lessons. Ich gehe in die Schule und lerne Deutsch. En principe. Oh well, luckily I can communicate with my husband in other ways.

How are you feeling, friend? I've thought often about your summer months and September days and of your ever amazing courage. It helps me always just to be able to watch it. But much more importantly and sincerely, I hope that you're not having to read Norman Vincent Peale's *Power of Positive Thinking* and its ilk. Knowing your resources, I should doubt it. Write me, please, of your psychological graph, if just briefly.

Do, please, count on me, Pat. So much so that you insist on continuing participation in our two lives. Geography is everywhere, so let's not concern ourselves with it too much. Please write soon.

Love and gladness
at having been with you,

Joyce

LONDON
December 7, 1954

Dearest Joyce,

Your ecstatic life with your husband is so good to hear about. I too am very happy, except for the ever-present ache of wanting a baby. You say that you admire my "courage" in wanting another baby right away, but far from being courage or anything of the sort, it's more like an obsession. I am absolutely *determined* to beat it this time, and if not this time, then next or next. . . .

I went to a specialist in miscarriages and stillbirths the other day and he suggested I get pregnant as soon as I wish and then spend the first 16 weeks in the hospital, flat on my back. I know I'd go crazy, and Philip and I talked it over and decided to take our chances with Nature—no more drugs, no flat on the back stuff—though I'll play it cool and stay very quiet, but still lead a reasonably normal life. Keep your fingers crossed for me. I'm lucky to be as fertile as a rabbit and not have to wait months or years for each pregnancy to come along.

Oh Joyce, Philip and I are finally so happy together. Since the baby died, he's opened up to me like a lovely rosebud come into full mature bloom. You know how hard I found his silences and reluctance to talk about anything, even the weather, let alone how he felt about things. I guess he really doesn't talk much

37

more now, but it seems to mean a great deal more; I seem to understand his silences. And our personal life, which I told you a little of on our way through Salt Lake on our honeymoon, and which was so awful that terrible first year in Los Angeles, full of difficulties about which I couldn't seem to do anything and about which he wouldn't talk, nor even let *me* talk about, well, now it just happens, without my having to do anything at all, all by itself, if I'm not being too vague. We don't talk about it even now, but it's finally okay.

I hope life can go on being this good forever. I feel as if I ought to be doing something more than waiting to get pregnant, waiting to go to Africa, loving Philip, and making pots, but I don't really want to. What a waste of three years of college! And I didn't even marry a man who wants to talk about books or listen to music. I think I should have majored in Home Economics, as I'm not a very good housewife, and except for decorating, I don't really take much interest in it. Carol Selby's mother wrote to tell me that she's subscribed (for five years!) to the *Ladies' Home Journal* for me. What a joke, me playing at being Mrs. America —or I guess now it's Madam Colonial England—from the suburbs, à la *LHJ*.

I have the feeling I'm writing too much about housework (well, and why not? I'm now a full-fledged housewife, except for my piddling little job), but oh, I'll be so glad when we get to Tanganyika! Warmth all the time, someone else doing the laundry. It's no easy job being a housewife here. I'm now addressing envelopes in the afternoons at home to make a little sorely needed extra money. The pay is terrible—I got more (double, in fact) at home for baby-sitting or slinging hash. But I have to think again where "home" is now. I surely could do with a phonograph and/or radio to help the tedium of the typing.

We read much about Mau Mau in Kenya, and I do hope it doesn't spread southward; I don't think I'm very brave. Anyway, somehow it doesn't quite seem like my war, though I'm sort of involved in it by marriage, with a brother-in-law and mother-in-law both in Nairobi.

I'm too cold to write any more. I too want a "continuing participation in our two lives." There really isn't anyone else I care about, except for Philip and my family.

Much love,

Pat

BEIRUT
December 18, 1954

Dearest Pat,

I've had a lot of nonsense to take care of and swim out of, besides such a rushing reversing tide to swim into, and the two directions have finally managed

38

to pass, somehow without a resounding, head-on collision. Until at last, I find myself sitting on top of these whirling worlds, and sailing, even happily, straight into bright countries.

Paris, although as seductive as ever, was just nonsense so far as the possibility of our actually getting married. In France? In the Mairie of Saint Sulpice? An American marrying a German in Paris and on their way to Lebanon? Mon dieu, impossible. So we flew away from all that always bursting French scene, across Italy and Greece and into the still bright Syrian sky. The only thing that belongs to Christmas weather here is the immense quantity of gigantic poinsettias—and even they have never belonged to Christmas except in a very theoretical or expensive way.

We were plunged immediately into three big worlds—the Orient, teaching on a university and not undemanding level, and marriage. We were also plunged into some wearisomely small worlds, the most exasperating one being the Presbyterian climate we're always shoveling our way through. The Lebanese were much more generous about acknowledging German existences than the French are ever likely to be, and on a sunny October 30th we were married in a very still but moving ceremony on a hill overlooking this aged and ageless sea. It was what I have long wanted—very unified, and having its proper substance.

It is funny to say that I am happy. It almost makes me feel that I'm losing a very old and cherished friend, my disillusion. One can get enchanted by his disenchantment to an almost treacherous point. I think it's even possible for a person to get attached to the image of himself as lonely. Not that I feel I've sacrificed an essential part of me. No, I really feel as if I were just being born. It is really the kind of marriage I have long directed myself towards and it is to be hourly rewarded with the proper pains and difficulties of its kind. It is curious how I have so long inclined toward marrying a "creative" person, whatever absurd definition I meant by that unattractive label. Not that the quality doesn't exist. It is just that now I am caught, exactly where I have dreamed of being, and I realize that the word had rather limited implications as I thought of it. For now I find myself daily tortured by the sense that I am very possibly just not creative enough in spirit to belong here. It's not so easy as I imagined it, but assuredly twice as fruitful.

My evolution to the person I am must have been quite slow and collectively constructed. I did not grow from the inside out, I suspect, but from the outside in. I was one of these poorer ones, who was "cursed with a little gift" and who needed the right influences, and was, I think, lucky enough to find them. At best, I can feel that some little core which I had found and forged myself was just enough to pull me to the kind of person who would at least get involved in this sort of marriage and the premises it involved, and who, with energy, might be able to live it.

Every day I am caught in realizing that this is a marriage of private people, with, as you would suspect, the privacy beginning on his side. But in a sense it is this difficulty I have always wanted. For I am so much more academic and full of things inexpensively learned, although the things I most know I have paid for. Perhaps I am more even on top, but he is much more whole underneath. I am no less modest than he, but I'm so much less *involved*. And this is what weakens my blood somewhat and disarms me. Because he is so integrally creative, or spiritual, or both together, I think, in one quantity.

It was so different with Lloyd, for example, whose silences frightened me with their aggressiveness. It was as if each unspoken sharing was a cautious attack, for we were observing each other so soundlessly. But my husband seems so much less self-conscious about the processes of being an observer. Consequently, he is less aware of me, or of my mind's operations, and of the wars and peaces therein. For he is more integrally a part of the world that absorbs him. His is not primarily the critical spirit. Lloyd's was. Mine is. And in the world of criticism there is room for competition, while in the realm of spirit, there is not. And Hans-Jurgen's is the purest way; it is not directed towards being humanly perceived from the outside, nor even from the inside by those intent on dissection. He is hiding nothing; he is just operating on other terms. At its best, and without exaggerating, this kind of absence must lead to mysticism. My critical involvement never could. At its best it is a kind of Henry Jamesian receptivity to human relationships; at its worst, it degenerates into a cat-and-mouse game of the intellectualized soul, where one human mystery assaults another human mystery with a formula for testing sensitivity; Plan A or Plan B. I can't help it; there's something damnable in the spectator.

This is a good thing, I'm sure, our marriage. He is so much the synthesis of the best things I have felt. He is so rich in emotions without ever trespassing on sentimentality, so respectful without being a traditionalist, and so conscious without being tiresomely conscious of *being so*. And he is an artist without beginning to be bohemian. So much so that when you met him in Paris, I think you felt shocked or disappointed about the shedding of a certain artistic flavor to my life. And he is intelligent without being an intellectual. Even conservative without being frightened. I could go on and on, and probably will from one letter to another. He is so single without being either a cynic or a snob, and so private without being selfish. And he isn't soft, although he's very gentle. And perhaps most important of all is that he is religious without being "caught." He's moving so rapidly inside it.

We're really ridiculously busy. Now Christmas vacation is upon us, and we have not had time to get the desired visas to enable us to go to Egypt, and there are only two or three days left. I hope we don't have to stay here in our thin little viewless apartment, whose only valid claim as a home is that we move around in it happily together, and that we have some loved books, records and many paintings in many different stages. Well, that's already enough. What am I complaining about? The lack of furnishings, I suspect. Can you imagine this: those malicious authorities furnished our house with little else than twin beds!

I am teaching wonderful things, however, and just outside the college walls is quite another world, and language, and religion. The latter of which we are obliged to acknowledge at least 5 times each day, and innumerable times on Fridays, because of the "muezzin" who shouts from the local mosque, which is only about 20 yards away, to join in the praise of Allah and the turning toward Mecca.

But it is funny, you know, to scan the outline of a large city and fail to find even one Christian comment etching itself upon the sky. Gives one a sense of dislocation, in spite of himself. The contrast is, of course, exaggerated after a year of the French and Spanish spired horizons. But, as it stands, we haven't really had the chance to say what it feels like to live in a Moslem community. One is only slightly aware of the discrepancy in religious reactions among the girls. But they are quite willing to absent their faith long enough to do such things as participate in an orthodox Christian Christmas pageant. Beneath it all, however, I suspect that feeling on the subject is not weak. It is still very strong against the French, although the influence in the culture is remarked quickly. But English is rapidly taking everything over and the whole life is becoming sadly American-ized.

You really DO know that I'm concerned about how you are. About whens and whys and all that. And though I haven't mentioned it, you know that Christmas wishes are strung throughout.

Last night I had the most realistic dream imaginable about having a baby, or about having had a baby, and people were using clinical jargon all over the pillow about "lactation" and other such shocking words. I think it must be your maternal influences working upon me.

Or more likely, and even certainly, it is the result of loving him. God, Pat, you can't imagine (although you certainly can, and that's why I'm addressing this to you) how terrifyingly fast the ties are being formed, deeply soldered way in the underground. I can't imagine how I must have lived before him; I only know that life must have been terrible (although of course it wasn't). And perhaps I am equally terrified about the oh-so-many chances to have missed going to Spain and to him, and about the terrified reality of having him, of being caught *exactly* where I have most dreamed and directed myself toward being.

All the most vile and virtuous womanly characteristics are being boilingly born inside me because of him. I always wanted to and talked about it, but I never have been so INVOLVED in minute-by-minute loving. Friday he is having a French ballet dancer come to our house to pose for him in the nude, and I'm shakingly, terrifiedly, almost weepingly upset inside, and yet without a word to him. That would not go. And so I write you.

I really wish I had known before the agony a married woman in love must go through in seeing her husband wander from her. Oh, Pat! I can't be liberal any more. Isn't that typical? One can be so free with everyone else until it is himself and then he is uncontrollably, irrevocably, subjectively, unreasonably selfish! Do you feel the same? Because I was never so truly formed before, as you know, never so that all the sunlit evidences of my features and angles and thoughts said very explicitly without the least italics forced beneath him, "I belong to this man, and I am oh so very married."

He is so demanding. I have never lived with or near anyone so constantly insisting on the living pure directions in the daily life. It means and includes everything. It means the time and place and way of playing records; it means the absolute openness of spirit that is almost too continuously hard and yet the healthiest and finest way I've ever had. And most of all, it demands the most integrally molded language, the search for the real verb. I cannot settle for less or he will say, "Oh, watch your language! You can't call Braque's face 'nice'! The least you can do is say it is 'fine.'" And he is so right. He keeps me seeing sò, so continuously. Oh, Pat, I might have married so much less. It all means that I am terribly happy, terribly sure that I have done the right thing, and terribly afraid of all the stupidities I am bound to occasion which might mar, even slightly. Now I have everything given; if I cannot live it, it is not the fault of the thing itself, but the fault of a limited and too sophisticated spirit that could not hold to its proper substance and heart.

I have the sinking feeling that it will be many moons before we bump into each other again, whether in one of the universal College Inns or another of the Parisian Mabillons. With your going to Tanganyika, how can we ever manage? And are you pregnant as you hopefully hinted in your last letter? You know that I do hope so, and that your courage is answered by your desire. This is probably not successful as a Birthday letter, but I am sure that by now you do know that I love you and that I do think about you, so I'll close.

Joyce

BEIRUT
February 17, 1955

Dearest Pat friend,

Or are you and Philip in the deepest depths of what we think of as darkest Africa? I haven't heard from you for sooooooo long that I think your ship must have sailed by way of British Columbia.

Shall I be awfully transparent and tell you that this is going to be a rotten letter, or shall I allow you the joy of discovery and let you find it out for yourself? I suppose that I can save my and everybody else's precious time by not bothering with the meddlesome details of how little time I have and how therefore I cannot write a good letter but only a bad one making excuses for its insipidity.

But to make a long apology short, I'll be terse and snappy and tell you that I just simply want to know where you are and when you're not likely to be any more. Before you sail away from the enchanted isles, please let me know what your itinerary is supposed to be, and I will see that my apologetic letters plague you with good will as you go.

I suppose the most important thing to tell you is that I married the right man, that I am more and more and more sure of it every day. He is so much, and I can hardly believe, each day, that I DID actually make the right choice, when choosing was, for once, in time. We are wonderful together, in every way, and I love our life—our privacy, our arts (or more especially, HIS, although I am doing more work on my own than I have done in a very long time), our attitudes, our gifts to each other. I'm really trying to learn this German language, and I even study it regularly. We read in bed to each other, and if I can't read Rilke in the original, I'm certainly becoming familiar with the sound of it. And when the failure of that language to register begins to exhaust, he switches to Camus, or Gide, or Pascal. All I'm saying is that I am happy happy happy happy with Hans-Jurgen, and I'm going to devote any energy I have to generating the lifeblood of this marriage! It is so good a thing. I can't help it, it is.

From the looks of things we most probably will be in Beirut another year. Enough nonsense for now. It just comes to say that I wish you would hurry up and write me some quick little epistle about the state of affairs in London. Please do!

It does matter, after all.

Love,

Joyce

(Postcard)

BEIRUT
March 1, 1955

Dearest Pat:

I begin to worry. The silence has spread almost across a winter. Are you all right? and there, or in Tanganyika? This is part of the Via Dolorosa, where we were in early February, quite alone in these wandering streets of the Bible and the Old Jerusalem. It is really a noble and handsome city, that high-built Jerusalem, though pathetically split through the heart, with a "No-Man's-Land" bracing one hate against the other, only a stone's throw from Calvary. Please write!

Joyce

43

March 10, 1955

My dear Joyce,

I'm a pigdog, and don't deserve your love and friendship. If you knew the kind of life we've been leading here, I'm sure you'd understand why I haven't written for so long. It's just been busy, busy, busy all the time, and getting worse every day, as we sail in exactly four weeks! I am getting so excited about it I can hardly think of anything else. I would love to hear from you along the way; or better yet, meet you somewhere? We are going through the Suez Canal and down the East Coast to Dar es Salaam, via Zanzibar. Who ever would have thought I'd get to Zanzibar? (I did, that's who.) Could you meet us at Port Said? Wouldn't that be fantastic?

I've been sewing what amounts to a trousseau for the trip (since I never had a "proper" wedding or honeymoon or trousseau), on a borrowed machine. I had to make three long evening dresses and a couple of long skirts and fancy blouses for them too, because we go first class and Philip says we'll "dress" for dinner every night—just like a Victorian novel. Also I've had to spend huge amounts of time filling in the million and one forms and documents bureaucracy demands of me (an American going to subvert the natives, I guess); I've been shopping carefully for all the things we'll need for housekeeping out there, where you can't get anything—needles and thread, for instance. And lots of stuff for entertaining.

I can't tell you how excited I am about going out to East Africa, although I will miss England—London, I mean. I've come to love it here so much. There's so much to do. I've scarcely read a book since our arrival here last September. I'd be illiterate if we lived here and rushed around all the time the way we do now. But I'll no doubt have plenty of time to catch up during the next three years. What I love about England, I guess, is how very civilized so many of the important aspects of life are. Putting my messy thoughts together on this subject, I'd say that the very civilized standard of living which Philip is used to and has every right to ask of me is precisely what makes life just a drudgery without money. Well, we'll just have to enjoy it in small doses.

I loved your description of Beirut and your new life with Hans. I too would love to visit Jerusalem someday. I'll be good and write again soon. Don't cross busy old me off your list (busy old unpregnant me).

Very much love,

Pat

March 20, 1955

Dearest Joyce,

Very briefly: to say hello and goodbye, as an excuse for not writing a real letter. I'm more in a whirl of last minute things than ever. Forms to fill out, the flat to transfer the lease of, stuff to sell, and PACKING. What a chore. Do write me along the way! We're in a fever of quitting jobs, seeing last minute plays, one or two last pub crawls, a farewell party or two. Goodbye Europe! Hello Africa! Write!

Lots and lots of love,

Pat

BEIRUT
March 26, 1955

Dearest ol' Pat!

I received your last (short!) letter yesterday happily, gratefully, almost tearfully, and it saved me from taking my ritual double aspirin during these last sick days. Will you forgive me for now if I write what could barely be termed a civil reply?? I'm just not up to the old de Sévigné standards. But I want to get some word from us into your hands before you sail off exotically into the bleak, or glorious, unknown (take your choice, depending upon the mood of the day). I did receive your letter à la itinerary, and I can't even remember whether or not I acknowledged it and told you that, at the present state of our finances, Port Said sounds just about as far away as the Thrifty Drug Store. I don't know if you'd be glad to see me, as I would make everyone miserable and nauseated by my repeated attacks of morning (AND evening AND night) sickness.

Yes, I think it's true, Pat. Ironic to think that the first and only person I have written about it to is *you!* Perhaps during the next nine months I can write to you and your doctor husband for all the little important medical advices that we cannot afford to pay these capitalistic, imperialistic missionary-spirited Americans who make a living off pregnant women in the Near East. Anyway, I feel like hell, and I must teach every hour like someone up on a one-hour pass from same.

It makes our plans for next year shift a bit, but neither of us can yet tell in which direction. We talk of going back to Germany, where he could teach in Hamburg or Köln and I could generate a generation of my own, or sometimes we talk of taking off like two big birds and heading for America, where we would be greeted with open arms and hearts by the family. I'm pretty sure that we will simply end up for another year in Beirut, with both of us trying to teach and make enough money to have one of the many lovely apartments that one can find here. With dog. We have not only decided upon baby, but on dog. Extravagance.

Well, I have to go throw up again, so excuse me. I hope you have a great trip going south. Please write me again before too long.

My best love,

Joyce

June 20, 1955

Dearest Pat,

If a combination of pregnancy, finals, term papers, yearbook, and a month of hospitalization for some vague subspecies of meningitis doesn't form a pact strong enough to keep our friendship intact, then NOTHING will.

Anyhow, it's great getting letters, even undeserved ones, especially when there is a noticeable aura of feminine data in the air mail. Well, I'm still in the hospital, still feeling like sin boiled stale, and still happily pregnant. I don't know where this godawful onslaught came from, but certainly somewhere from behind —rearest flank. It's a combination of encephalitis-meningitis (God!) and it's no toy. Only my back is still partially paralyzed, but I can walk by now. At first even the humbler gestures, like turning over in bed and drinking from a cup, downed me. But after "lombard punctures" and other better-to-be-avoided subjects of conversation, I'm getting a bit of wind back. Enough, that is, to correct 6 or 7 finals during the long and oh so lonesome and hot day. But next Thursday the chips either fly up or fall down. We're due to sail and we're *determined* to sail on the 24th. If we don't make that, we don't go to Europe, and we must and shall go to Europe. Anyway, I hope I can still button a skirt by then.

I have an excellent gynecologist from New York who assures me that the disease could not affect the child in any degree, as the whole thing was centralized in my head and the vertebrae between the shoulder blades, so I'll not worry. Actually we are not due so very far apart. I'm about 16 weeks now, and the baby's due November 10th or so. My figure has only taken a change toward the lesser through all this, but I'm beginning to suspect a growing firmness in my lower abdomen. Anyway, no movement yet. I can scarcely wait. It is thrilling, Pat, and I'm beginning to understand the indomitable insistence with which you confront the mystery. But I read lately that the maternal mind is born with the first stirrings of the embryo, and if that's true, I should only have a bit more waiting. Until then, a woman does sort of feel that things are going on of which she has no part.

It's good to have you as companion these days, Pat. Wouldn't it be just like Hollywood if the two grew up and married? Ho, ho. Anyway, let's do keep up a spastically regular correspondence through the summer, shall we? I want to avoid that with everyone else, because we'll be a bit on the move, but still. You have *all* my good luck wishes—truly.

Just where are you living anyway? Did you take over the tent that Gregory Peck deserted, or what? Are there no whip-swinging, mustache-stroking Englishmen? Is it a town or a city, or just a medical center—or—?? By the way, is Philip your obstetrician?

Beirut begins to get smuttily hot and humid. I can't sleep even with the sleeping pills. What's more, I can't write a decent letter, and my tailbone is shrieking to be let off easy. But I will have time and the will to write from Germany, and, I hope, the energy. Your life sounds good and ripe and promising of the best things. So does ours. I love Hans-Jurgen terribly; he's so much more, and more, and more. His exhibit was very successful with the people we cared about. We'll all wish us all the best.

My love,

Joyce

MAHALI, TANGANYIKA
June 23, 1955

Dearest Joyce,

Here I am, in the heart of darkness, sweating away, but happy to *be* in Africa, in our very own home, Philip at a job he loves, and me, as I told you briefly in the airletter, pregnant. Did you also get my postcards en route from various places including that sinister locale straight out of Somerset Maugham, Port Sudan? I haven't said much to anyone here about my pregnancy out of sheer superstition. But what a glorious way to begin our African life! I'm due around the end of December, as I think I told you.

We have a large rambling old German (pre–World War I) house, a wilderness waiting to be turned into a garden (after Philip turns me into a gardener), four servants, a cook, a houseboy, a dhobi (laundry boy) and a garden boy, all for about $35 a month. It's positively sybaritic when I feel like lazing about all day doing nothing. But there's plenty to do, all the same. We have a refrigerator even, a late wedding present from P.'s mother, a 5 cubic foot Electrolux which runs mysteriously on kerosene, but won't quite make Jell-o set. No electricity, but hallelujah, running water and indoor toilet and a bathtub, far more than I expected.

The heat lives up to my literary expectations, and is simply appalling from about 10 to 4, but the rest of the time it's quite nice, especially in the evening. Of course, as everyone is quick to tell me, this is the cool season. We sleep nude under just a sheet, and of course a mosquito net, though the mosquitoes aren't bad inside the house, with lots of assiduous flitting.

There is a "gymkhana club" (wonderful expression) which all of the Europeans belong to (i.e., whites) and it has hordes of fruit bats which come flying out on the veranda at night disrupting the perennial drinking sessions there. The club has a bumpy tennis court and a sort of golf course only usable four months out of the year.

We have three seasons a year: the rains, the hot dry season before the rains, and the not-quite-so-hot dry season after, *called* the cool season. We are at the end of the rains now and at the best time, when everything is green and lush, other people's gardens blooming, and the occasional sprinkle of rain. The club has a dance now and then, and people play cards and tennis and so forth. I'm still determined to remain ignorant of bridge. I shall read, garden, cook, sew, do embroidery, and maybe even have a stab at learning Swahili. I'd like to do pottery too, if I can get the equipment. I shall live my own life.

The Africans are not really what I expected. I guess I've seen too many National Geographic pictures. But they are so very raggedy in old European clothes, and so very black and *small*. Not at all like American Negroes. I'll bet it's because most American Negroes have a good dose of white blood in them. We haven't been on a long safari yet, just 10 to 30 mile forays around Mahali (everything over a mile is apparently called a safari). It's a great country here, with a tremendous future, and I feel lucky to be able to see the last days of one of the few primitive places left. My children will never be able to live this sort of life, nor, I think, will we, in another 20 years or so.

I'm also planting a garden, prodded on by Philip. We're surrounded on all sides by encroaching bush, between our house and the next, and every day the garden boy whacks away at it with what looks like a flat metal hockey stick, sharpened at the bottom. The result isn't much like a lawn, but it's better than ten foot high bush up to the windows. All the house except the bedroom is cleaned every morning before breakfast. The cook comes in after breakfast and I tell him (in a garble of English and Swahili and sign language) what we want for lunch, tea and dinner. Philip goes, then I write letters, garden, sew, have morning coffee, read, knit, have lunch with Philip when he gets home at 12:30, afternoon much the same while he's at the hospital. He's home at 4:30, tea, walk or garden a bit; then comes what people here call the sundowner hour; they appear to drink steadily till dinnertime—there are exactly 12 hours of daylight and of darkness, no dusk or twilight— but we play Scrabble or read till dinner at 8, and go to bed around 11, as we get up with the sun at 6.

People tend to be very sociable here, in and out of each other's houses all the time, or in the club, and I'm afraid they're going to find us antisocial. We're happy just with each other and our house and garden. We are so very happy. We never argue, and our silences these days are happy ones. We are very self-contained. Company's nice, but in small amounts.

Well, now you have some idea of my quiet and happy life. All we ask of the future is a baby, delivered whole and safe and sound. I feel very certain that everything *will* be all right this time. And if I don't hear from you, my girl, this will be The Last Letter I shall ever write, and the end of A Beautiful Friendship. Come on now, I've atoned for my sins of the winter with letters and p.c.'s and now this. Your turn!

Very much love and affection,

Pat

MAHALI
July 4, 1955

My poor dear friend in need (and in bed),

I wrote you a long letter about a week ago, and just received yours from hospital. I presume you are now "in Europe." My God, you should *not* be traveling in your condition! I mean the dreadful meningitis and its complications, not the pregnancy (*I* should never have the nerve to scold anyone traveling throughout pregnancy!). I wish you were here so that Philip and my servants and I could all lavish loving care on you. Be good! Be prudent! But as long as you're there, have a good time, wherever it is. Congratulations on the pregnancy! Imagine us having our first (sort of my first) so close together; I'm only due a few weeks after you. I'm knitting now for your baby too; I presume he/she will need "woolies," as the English call them, a lot more than mine will here. Would you like me to make you some maternity smocks? I am certainly going right ahead (without even asking you) and ordering a marvelous vitamin-iron-mineral compound especially for pregnancy. I found out the nearest suppliers for myself, and it's Baghdad, so I've written off to them and ordered some for you, and it should be with you soon.

I wrote you pages about our life here in the last letter. I love it more every day. Philip is "Bwana Mganga" (Mr. Doctor) and I am "Memsahib Mganga" (Mrs. Doctor). Fancy being called Bwana and Memsahib. Three of our boys are Mohammedans and one is just plain pagan. Some people call their boys just "Boy!" or "Cook!" but I hate that. People have names and I think it's polite to use them, no matter if they're black or green or have two heads. Our house has been freshly white-washed and I shocked our conservative little community by painting the front door fire-engine red, for a change from the everlasting white. Clearly, it doesn't take much to shock people here. Frankly, most of them are

49

duds. But then any town of this size is bound to be that way. I don't mind in the least, as I have so much to keep me busy, but it would be nice nevertheless to find a kindred soul or two amongst the gin-drinking and bridge-playing types.

No more room on this stupid airletter, no matter how tiny I write. So I'll sign off. Look after yourself. Let me know how you are.

Much love,

Pat

SOLINGEN, GERMANY

July 23, 1955

WARNING: A <u>DUMB</u> LETTER!

Dearest Old Pat,

I know I've been a heel of the first water (and the sixth month), but God! I'm not *that* unappreciative! I just today received a letter you wrote June 23rd, sent to Beirut, and forwarded here, swearing (almost) the end of a beautiful friendship. In my present enfeebled state, I take such threats (though I realize they weren't) tragically. Can you imagine the thing that is (or was) me having fallen into that unhappy category of "delicate health"—a "fragile wife"? ME!! But I have; it's hell and I hate it! My God, my mechanism is really kaput. I wish that we all could attribute my silences to maternal lethargy, but unhappily, it's not such a joyous infirmity. Twice since we finally made it to Germany and to the in-laws, I've had relapses from the meningitis, with fevers going indecently high. We always try to be interesting; this time we call it nephritis: another two weeks in bed.

Ugh, what a bore. I've been a spiritual, intellectual, sexual, physical nil for five months now, and I felt so sorry for my burdened husband today that I told him to go out and have a hair-raising affair with someone. He's been so thwarted, I'd not be surprised or annoyed if he did.

Your calculations were brilliantly deductive. November 10–12 is just when he (Stefan, we think) is due. He is extremely active lately, to the point of my steady insomnia, but this I love; it counteracts the disgust that comes from my inability to walk, climb—think! I lost 20 pounds because of all this tomfoolery, dropped from a big 145 to 124 now, and for that, am essentially glad. So is my obstetrician.

I'm so glad your pregnancy goes smoothly. I hope it will for the whole run. I've given up hope of feeling good for some time yet. Good Lord, I'm a BORE! But I'm doing my ineffectual best. Thanks for the suggestion about the maternity clothes. Actually, Mother sent me all I need. And the pregnancy compound sounds very good. Mine is almost over, and I doubt it was so good.

50

Please believe that this slump has not been a forgetting or an indifference. Your concern in the baby brightens up my loneliness and depression a good bit, and I've never had the intention of letting our friendship fade, meningitis or not!

My real love,

Joyce

August 15, 1955

Dearest Joyce,

I'm so very sorry that you're still so ill and in pain, but glad you're still pregnant. Me too, very much so, just entering my sixth month now, and feeling marvelous. *Finally* no morning sickness. I seem to have spent most of my adult life leaning over a toilet heaving up my toenails. I hope you too are relieved of it. I too feel much life from Baby, enthralling and awe-inspiring, as it was last time.

Life goes on here, outer as well as inner. Something is going on in our social life that I'm uncomfortable about, and can't quite come to terms with. You know how political and in the thick of things I've always been (and loved to be), and how I love talk about politics and the world situation till the wee hours. And I'm not exactly illiterate. I find it hard to remember that I campaigned for Henry Wallace when I was in high school, and for Adlai with you. Remember all those doorbells we rang? I signed the Stockholm Peace Petition in '47. I worked for three different labor unions—I even got fired from Prudential for trying to organize the office staff right after I graduated from high school. And here I am, finding that I'm expected to keep my mouth shut and listen sweetly to the men, along with all the other stupid uneducated wives. Philip gets quite cross with me when I forget myself and break in with my two cents' worth, so I'm learning painfully to keep quiet. What a comedown from the radical old *Forum* days and me writing articles about the international oil situation. I imagine it must be different with you and your life, since you're teaching and palling around with a university crowd. Sometimes I miss all that.

But there's a lot to make up for it here. We had our very first long safari recently, when Philip visited several outpatient dispensaries scattered over the northern mountains of the district. Once we got out of our steamy hot valley, the country became much rockier and drier, and to my Western mind, much prettier. We went through a place which was an old slave-trading center, and on Stanley and Livingstone's route. We drove into a little valley reminding me so much of home, with its huge boulders, scrub bushes, cactus, wildflowers, and funny-shaped hills all round. We kept an eye out for game for the pot, but didn't

51

see any the whole trip. God, are the roads terrible; you simply rock and crash over ruts and sand and rocks and gullies worn across them by the fierce rains. And narrow. Very hair-raising, and exhausting. We averaged about 10 miles an hour! We visited a mission hospital (U.S. Protestant) and were fêted on tea and oatmeal cookies (first I've tasted in a coon's age) by the three dowdy bobby-socked and lipstickless mission ladies.

We snaked up into the mountains, about 8000 feet up, on another awful road, into a high-up little valley where the Englishman lives who built the road we were to go on next. He built it on contract from the government. He's lived a hermit's life up there for nearly 30 years. It was just like something out of Maugham or Conrad. He was in bed when we arrived, so while we waited, we looked around. He lives in a two-roomed mud-walled thatched hut, his boys' houses were a few feet away, all in a row, the chickens were scratching in the dust by the front door, and a couple of mangy mongrels sniffed and yapped at our heels. Finally, he opened the door and greeted us in an old dirty bathrobe, unshaven and shivering and shaking from head to toe with "a dose of malaria." We went inside his tiny "sitting room," furnished with a couple of rickety armchairs, some sort of table to match, assorted boxes and crates, and a bookcase filled to overflowing with good books, and topped by a dusty empty whiskey bottle. He told me that I was the sixth white woman ever to visit him, and that he'd only been in Mahali twice for a day in the past three years! But he was very sociable, if a little mad, and talked a blue streak. He told us of the condition of the road ahead ("good"—ha!), gave us a lot of oranges off his trees, and blessed us away on our safari. What a character.

Dear God, that road! We were the first vehicle over it ever; it had been built with just little hoes and shovels by some Africans he'd hired from round about. It was absolutely the worst road I've ever been over. It took us ten hours to go thirty miles. You could walk as fast as that. We got stuck twice, once for four hours. It was terribly steep, and the sides of it got progressively jungly (as opposed to bushy) the higher up we went, enormous trees festooned with creepers and lianas and brilliant flowers. The undergrowth must have been six to eight feet high and was completely impenetrable. Up, down, up, down, creaking with inches to spare around corners and hairpin turns, and over rickety never-before-used wooden bridges. We slipped a wheel once over the edge of a rather alarming cliff, but pulled out okay. But mud did us in finally. We had to unload every last box and tent and bed from the hospital truck, and with the help of about thirty Africans who magically appeared out of nowhere, simply push it by main force up a long muddy road. And then of course carry all the stuff up the hill too and reload the truck. Anyhow, we finally made it (two days on the road from the last rest house—we slept on the side of the road overnight). And at our campsite, we slept in the truck in the end too, as the rest house was appallingly dirty and muddy and buggy. We camped by a rushing stream, cascading down over rocks and rushing into the valley on the western slopes (the mountain chain runs north to south), where Philip's dispensary is located six miles from the road. He walked to and from it each day.

While P. was at the dispensary each day, I got visited by the local ladies and their tots, who casually looked through all our belongings, chattered away to each other and to me, but not even in Swahili, which I'm beginning to recognize a word or two of, but in some local language. Annoying not to be able to communicate, but just to have to sit grinning like an idiot. They're terribly friendly and generous with their meager little piles of food and tatty belongings. The shirt off their backs sort of thing. I'm getting to love the African, the more and better I come to know him (and her).

Anyway, it was a glorious time and I want lots more safaris all over the district. It'll be fun taking Baby up there and showing him off to my lady friends of the mountains. Notice it's a him.

Philip plays lots of tennis now at the club, and is very good indeed. We've been married over two years, and I never even knew this! I'm of course like a Hungarian who doesn't play the violin, a Californian who doesn't play tennis, but I've taken it up out of desperation. The tennis players tend to drift into the club for a drink or two, and it meant that besides being alone all day long, I was now bereft from immediately after tea until just before dinner at 8. So I go along now, and have visions of myself becoming a colonial barfly.

Would you believe I'm playing my recorder in a little concert which our next-door neighbor has gotten together? The District Commissioner is playing a soprano recorder, I my alto, and the District Officer his guitar as continuo. It sounds a little weird, but it's as much our bad playing as anything.

We've had a lot of parties recently, to begin "paying back" (awful capitalist expression) hospitality. It's *so* pleasant giving parties and having guests when you don't have to wash dishes or cook or sweep or wash and iron. Even our house-guests' shoes and brass buttons get cleaned and polished daily without my having to lift a finger. It's a good life out here. Africa already seems like home to me. It's so quiet and brooding, yet teeming with life if you look under the surface. There's so *much* of everything—plants grow so quickly under the torrid sun, the torrential tropical rains give it all so much water and nourishment. Glorious, glorious. Of course it's the cool season, such as it is, more like a southern California summer, but not unbearably hot, hardly any rain, and even chilly nights. I wish you and Hans-Jurgen and Baby could visit us here. I've written reams and must close. Write and tell me how you are. I *miss* you!! I worry so about your health and you and the baby. Let me know.

Much love, dear friend,

Pat

(in class)
October 15, 1955

Dear friend Pat,

Time at least for brevity, the art of being succinct. It's damned hot, and I want a letter from you.

I'm fine, skinny (!), and very pregnant, though far from massive. Nevertheless, I feel very "great with child" even though everybody thinks I'm beginning the 7th month. My illnesses left me weak, but not damaged, I think. When we were in Rome in late September, I had the "slipping" pains, I guess. And his head is very low now. She predicts he'll be early more likely than late, which makes it an affair of 3+ weeks, or so. I'm getting just vaguely jittery.

Back home

We've very little as layette so far, but everybody says to postpone buying much, as Arab hospitality extends over to baby-gift-giving with a fury. So much so that several other Westerners have already offered to give us their unused gifts from former years, and in one case, that even includes a baby bed! Well, that's fine; we've not money to spare, that's for certain.

We're living in a sad arrangement just now, one of the very provisory "salles d'attente" that seem to be awaiting us the wide world over, furnished more with orange crates and Gordon's Gin boxes and husband's decorative ingenuity than anything else.

To continue with our house. We were promised a four-room brand-new faculty apartment on our return, but as with all time schedules in the Orient, they're only half finished, and until then we're living in a scarcely furnished apartment next to the one we had last year. We didn't mind it before the baby, but it really won't go afterwards. A tiny little sink to wash all those diapers in??? My doctor insists that we have a maid, and I think we've found one (for $13 a month) and that should help some, but this barrack which we imagine into a residence is far from satisfying. We should be moved into the new one by Christmas, but until then?

Hans-Jurgen is so busy on his two jobs that he has to commute between them on a bicycle without brakes; then we both want him to find time to paint for himself. I'm teaching only one hour each day, Junior-Senior courses in Modern Lit., and in Writing. Nice schedule, I enjoy it.

Well, I didn't really have time to begin this letter today, so I'll close before it loses any form whatsoever. You're right about this uncreative psychology that accompanies pregnancy. Let me know how (and where) you are. I'm really concerned.

My best love,

Joyce

October 27, 1955

Dearest Joyce,

I've been very naughty, I know. A good deal of our correspondence seems to be spent in gentle friendly reproofs for not writing, doesn't it? But there you are; we'll probably still be corresponding in fifty years' time. I'm so glad everything's going well with you and Baby. Be a good girl now, and take your pills three times daily. You *have* gotten them, haven't you? I shall write a terribly fierce letter to the place in Baghdad if you haven't. I also sent off a little box with something for Baby and something for you and Hans in it. Happy wedding anniversary, Merry Christmas, and a belated wedding congratulations, though the thing isn't nearly big enough to merit covering all three.

We just bought a Peugeot station wagon. The horn makes me nostalgic for Paris, it's so screechy and funny. The seats pull down, and we sleep in the back on safari. Safari is the best part of life out here, and what I shall remember when I'm old and gray and telling my grandchildren about Life in Africa.

I've just been rereading the letters Philip and I wrote to each other the year we were engaged, and I've only now realized that so many of the promises we made each other, so many of the fulfillments of a good marriage we foresaw, have really come gradually into existence, quietly and slowly crept into our lives to become lovely habits, unconsciously have we stepped, emerged, I should say, into the world of us, which we only saw through books and other (very few) happy marriages before we married, and looked for so eagerly at first. We felt a terrific sense of anticlimax the first year, I know, or at least the first few months, because these sweet unspeakable intangibles of the Good Marriage come so slowly and stealthily, one can't look for them, but only feel a sense of them being all around you once they're there. Vague, I realize I must seem, but you catch the meaning, I'm sure. I only wish he would talk more to me, open up and share the things of the heart.

We have a dog now; he's Alsatian, 4 months old, named Brando, because he's going to be very fierce and cool at the same time.

How lucky you and I are with our full, rich and varied lives, so happy in our marriages and adventures and children coming, our lives so full of promise and excitement and coziness too. Oh well, it's there for those who will seek it out and be brave enough to do the unorthodox, the unexpected, to go into an unknown situation and fight it out, even if one's wrong once in a while.

55

I find it hard to believe I was legally married before, because nothing P. and I have ever said or done, nothing we have between us, have I ever remotely experienced before. I hardly ever think about it, but I suppose reading the details of those letters made me remember trifles like getting a divorce and such. To think I'll be 25 in January, nearer 30 than 20, as P. gleefully reminds me. But for the first time in my life, I'm glad and not sorry to lose the fresh bloom of youth, for with the few sensible years I've had has come a curious sense of well-being and particularly the sense of strength, of being loved and loving, of needing and being needed, of seeing my world through increasingly understanding eyes. These must be the things age brings, not as compensation, but as a goal. You'd think I was nearer 80 than 30!! All my thoughts and love are with you in the coming weeks as you go to do alone what every real woman must do alone. It's a grand glorious time of creation, nearly all too short. Godspeed. All, all my love to you.

Pat

MAHALI
November 15, 1955

Dearest Joyce,

I haven't heard from you since my last letter, but I know you must be incredibly busy and in that last stuporous waddly month anyhow, so I forgive you. I am filled with nervous anticipation and try to push away bad thoughts and forebodings when they creep into my head.

I now definitely have to have the baby in a proper hospital with "European beds" and another doctor, as the whole damned Medical Department from the Director down seems frightfully concerned about my having it here, in case the impossible should happen and I had a blue baby or started hemorrhaging or something, and Philip has been commanded to see me into a hospital.

So we'll take me down to our provincial headquarters. It's about 64 miles from here as the crow flies, but during the rains (which it is now) 100 miles or more the long way, still over terrible roads. And of course, with the rains here, and as it's very likely I'll be quite quick this time, Philip probably will be here in Mahali when the baby comes. Damn them all for a bunch of interfering idiots. Bureaucracy, hell. We will bring me home in the train a few days afterwards. Of course I might fox them all and come early and jolly well have to have it here, but (being my usual pessimistic self), it's more likely I'll have it alone in a horrid old hospital with peppery impersonal nurses and some clod of a doctor I've never seen before, not to speak of spending Christmas in hospital. I thought that this time at least I could have peace and familiar faces around me and someone I knew and trusted instead of being surrounded by strangers who couldn't care less, like last time.

I haven't thought about it now for months and months, but it's so hard to believe that Trevor would have been a year old six weeks ago. I'll admit to a few tears in private every now and then, though I haven't said anything to Philip. He hates me being "morbid." Probably just the supersensitivity of pregnancy. I'm terribly asthmatic too—as a matter of fact I have been ever since leaving California, for the first time since I was 14 or 15. I thought I'd outgrown it! I'll bet you didn't even know I was asthmatic. Actually I had one terrible attack the summer I was in France, in fact on the Ile Ste. Marguerite, where Philip proposed to me. Poor thing, I seem to burden him with all my wheezes and gasps. At least it isn't catching. Sorry about all the whining; I really am very happy with life, and feeling very well. I've only gained 6 pounds, and am very sleek for being this far along. I weighed 112 in April, and now am 118. I'll give birth to a midget. It's just too appallingly hot and humid to eat now; morning sickness is gone, but most food makes me throw up, especially liver, which I've always hated (and it's so horrid here, ghastly stuff), but which Philip says I must eat, for the baby's sake. I keep trying, but I promptly lose it. P. says it's psychosomatic and that I could keep it down if I tried, so I'm not only nauseated, but guilty as hell!

We are very busy with all the things I've told you of—tennis (I've quit playing because it scared the daylights out of everyone else), parties, guests, garden, dog, sewing, knitting, our little concert, which was a great success. It was pretty awful, but the deprived audience loves anything, they are so starved for anything out of the ordinary. My madrigal singing was distinctly better than my recorder playing. Do you ever sing any more? I miss it. Remember our crazy duets and "Il Bacio"? *What* a long time ago and long way away. How nice to live on hamburgers and milkshakes and French fries instead of fried liver, boiled milk, and glucy bread that tastes like stale beer. Maybe I'm just a touch grouchy and homesick.

We do a lot of shooting these days. The game herds are in migration and there's lots of wildebeest, kongoni, hartebeest, as well as the usual little buck like Thomson's and Grant's gazelles, and oodles of different kinds of birds. All make scrumptious eating. We talked about shooting some zebras for rugs, but I *hate* trophies—we never had horns or heads or skins at the ranch—they give me the pip, and P. isn't really all that keen, so we'll soldier on with our grass mats.

It seems impossible we've only been here six months. I feel as if East Africa were part of me. My Swahili is slowly progressing, with much encouragement and help from P. and the servants, although actually the latter are useless when it comes down to it, because they're far too polite ever to correct me, even when I ask them to. Are you learning any Arabic? Or is it all in French?

We went down to Dar es Salaam for four days last month. I went mad just turning the light and ceiling fan switches in the hotel room on and off. What bliss to have an electric fan, but my word, it's hot at the coast, like a Turkish bath. I wanted to get some terry cloth to make your babe and mine some wrappers. No soap. Then I tried flannelette; there's only one kind in the whole of Tanganyika, a hideous pink with Donald Duck and his beastly nephews printed all over it, so I had to settle for that. Sorry! I tried to get a Bathinette and a playpen, but they don't carry them. What a frustrating place to shop, and *it's* the capital. I guess we'll do without. I hope to God I can nurse, because I've never seen such crazy baby bottles as the English use. I think I'll have to get my mother to send American ones and a sterilizer. Mostly I get along fine with English or South African things here and never give it a second thought, but something primeval rises up in me when it comes to baby things, and I go all over American and stubborn. P. thinks I'm silly and no doubt I am. How do you feel about these things?

I thought I'd go balmy the last few weeks with the heat, sweat always trickling down my neck and chin and legs and arms. My scalp even always seemed to me to smell of sweat. I'd been taking two baths a day in tepid water (there isn't any cold) just to get through the days, and was beginning to look like a prune. But the blessed rains finally broke; what a joyous noise, crashing down on the corrugated iron roof.

This seems to have been a very crabby letter, but I'm sure you'll understand. I think of you about 10 times a day, also about to (or already?) deliver your first in a strange country, thousands of miles away from home and family. Write when you can. I'm dying to hear from you.

> So very much love—
> and happy first anniversary!
>
> *Pat*

BEIRUT
(in hospital)
December 1, 1955

Dearest friend,

I'm still somewhat too ecstatic to be very voluble about it all. On Tuesday afternoon at 12:45, our son was born, beautifully, and I'm happy, Pat, oh God! I am so happy!

I'm thinking about you too, very much in these days, as I know your time is soon, and I can guess with what anticipations you are waiting. May God bless you and bring you a happiness as certain as ours!

I was too nervous and full of false pains the last weeks to answer your letters or thank you for the Christmas card. And so, on the 28th, we went down to the hospital and the whole amazing thing began. It was a fairly long labor, but Hans-Jurgen was by me all the time, rubbing my back, helping me count for the deep breathing exercises, reading to me little novels of Giovanni Verga when I was in peace. It was a great good having him there, so calm, unhysterical, and loving. I wonder how I ever thought of marrying anyone else.

I was in the delivery room 20 minutes and was fully conscious when Reinhard (nicely German) was born. I saw the placenta and cord and felt a glorious sense of participation. It's the only way, I'm convinced. He weighed 6 lbs. 2 ozs. and had all the proper qualifications, such as toes and things, and great quantities of straight brown hair. His eyes are immense, and synchronized, his nails are lovely, and he looks like the Hohlwein line, I think. And so sweet and *klein*. I'm already nursing him on newly swollen breasts. And I already feel possessive as anything. I can't stand to see him taken away. We'll send pictures soon as possible.

I only sense that life can never be this good again. If so, I'll clasp it now, right to the breast! My very closest thoughts are with you,

Joyce

ZALIWA, TANGANYIKA
(in hospital)
December 31, 1955

Dearest Joyce-Mother!

I am so *so* happy for you! How marvelous all is over and all is well with you and your wee baby. I wish I could say the same. But I wait and wait, overdue ten days now, and in hospital since the 17th. They wouldn't let me stay in the hotel as I'd planned, where at least I would have been free to come and go as I pleased. The fretting and stewing is as much on the medical establishment's side as it is on mine, and with my rotten obstetrical record, I can't really blame them. Very aggravating to sit and wait for God's (or fate's) will to be done like someone out of the Old Testament, and not be able to do a blessed thing about it, considering the modern civilization we think we live in, full of progress; I mean, we can split the atom, but we can't ensure the safe arrival of one little tiny baby.

I'm still feeling fine, though I've started throwing up again, and getting "the vapors," i.e., fainting at the drop of a hat, which I ordinarily do only in the first 3 to 4 months. It's very embarrassing, especially in front of Philip and his mother, who I think consider me the original 97 pound weakling. Sometimes I get the feeling I can't do anything right, even be pregnant the right way, let alone produce a baby.

Baby's still kicking, though not so much, but then he hasn't got much room, either. I'm frightened, of course; that's perfectly natural after our experience, and I'll be terribly glad when this whole jittery period of waiting is over. Every little possible ache or pain (mostly gas!) I get, I glance at my watch, then sit hopefully waiting for the next, which never comes. We haven't really let this baby take on a personality for us like the last, but I suppose that's a defense mechanism. Poor old Philip's nerves are wearing thin too, the heat, the waiting and suspense, the awful drive back and forth between Mahali and here every couple of days, and the almost pessimistic feeling we have. Every day seems a month long. I've made a darling frilled mosquito net for the crib, yellow and white curtains for the nursery, and taken an old falling-to-bits table, painted it white, put a ruffled curtain of white and yellow muslin all the way round it and covered the top with white oilcloth. Philip is building shelves under it for Baby's clothes, and with a plastic dishpan for his bath, that's the nursery. We decided we couldn't afford any (necessarily) imported furniture. I also made a few little cotton jackets and one funny little jacket and bloomer set, lined with plastic I cut from an old shower curtain I've been carrying around for years (there are no showers in the houses here). It looks a little strange inside out—swans and boats on a blue watery background, but it serves the purpose. Baby won't be wearing much of anything except diapers anyway, it's so damnably hot. God, what a climate. I sure have to admire the English for taking all these tropical countries, and then sticking it sweatily out.

What was your social life toward the end of pregnancy? People here were very shocked at my continuing to go to the club and to dinner parties right up till I came to the hospital. I really *was* expected to go into "confinement" and not put my nose outside the house during the last couple of months. I didn't mind leaving my garden as much as I thought I would, since practically everything in it is dead anyway, from the heat. Not only does the sun wither everything, but the ground is baked to the consistency of marble. What looked like the rains breaking was only the short "mango" rains, not the long rains. Ah well, everything must come to an end sometime.

I'm sorry not to have better news to send you, to match your wonderful news. But next letter I will, I'm sure. I'm so very happy everything's fine with you both. Would you find it hard to believe of messy, undomesticated old me that I've at last finished a huge quilt, all appliqué pictures and border, that I've been working on two years now? And reading, reading, reading, also for the first time in two years. I mean, quilt and reading since I came to hospital. So it's good for something. Stay as well as you are.

Much, much (maternal) love,

Pat

PART THREE

FEBRUARY 1956– JANUARY 1957

*I have an appalling sense
of the nearness
of old age and death
before one has ever lived*

February 10, 1956

Dearest Joyce,

Nothing from you since Reinhard's birth, but I can imagine how busy you are. Are you trying to teach too? I find a multitude of things to keep me busy all day, and I don't work and I have servants to do all the necessary for me, leaving me totally free for Christopher, which is gorgeous. This is a wonderful and marvelous time, the happiest I've ever known in my life. I want to catch the moments as they go by and say, Stop, I never want things to change, they can't get better, only worse. What an incurable pessimist I am!

I meant to write immediately after my cable to you, but never got round to it somehow. Christopher's birth itself was quick and easy, and without anesthetic of any kind. There was a hell of a scare at the last moment when the doctor thought his heartbeat was not recovering quickly enough after each contraction, so I didn't even get the gas and air mask (self-administered), but it was all so fast, three hours from beginning to end, that I didn't mind. In fact I barely made it to the delivery room on a stretcher, bellowing my head off; I was delivering the head as they carried me out of my room down the open veranda of the hospital! What a to-do, after all those endless weeks of waiting. In fact I want to have another baby immediately, for several reasons, first because it's just so bloody marvelous, second, to have a companion as near Christopher's own age as possible, and third, so that the new baby will be at least a year old when we go on leave to England in Feb.–March '58. Philip isn't very keen, but maybe I can talk him round.

The ride home from Zaliwa to Mahali was really something. We came home after five days because I was beginning to climb the walls in the hospital. It was pouring with rain, and thirty miles out of Mahali we came to a great torrent of water rushing across the road, instead of what was supposed to be a tiny trickle (over the road, which is dirt, but which has streams a few inches deep crossing over cemented places). Anyhow, Philip poked a stick in it, and it seemed to be a couple of feet deep in the middle, so he drove the car across in a great rush, hoping he wouldn't drown the engine (he did), and I very gingerly made my way through muddy water halfway up my thighs, shoes and all, clutching Christopher to my bosom, hoping I wouldn't stumble. I didn't and all's well that ends well, but my God, Africa!

He seems to be feeding beautifully, and I have lots of milk, and have had no trouble. I've never in my life experienced anything so utterly satisfying and lovely as feeding our darling. I just cannot imagine how any woman out of preference would shove a bottle into her poor little baby's mouth and rob herself and him of one of the greatest pleasures in the world. I tell myself, *this* might even replace night baseball!! I have to tiptoe in several times between each feeding to assure myself that the fairies or Peter Pan haven't stolen him away from me.

I only a couple of weeks ago began to feel like a human being again. I felt fine in the hospital, but for the first two to three weeks I was home, I felt more exhausted than anything I'd ever known. And I have four servants, thank God. How anyone could drag around and cook and wash and keep house feeling like that is beyond me.

Philip is so funny. He loves holding him and playing with him, and pops right up to change him when he cries and makes up funny little songs to sing him. He isn't the least bit awkward or shy about it. He's going to be (and is) the most wonderful father. I'm always telling him he ought to be a pediatrician. One very odd thing bothers me. I'm rather jumping the gun by being afraid of a problem remote in the future, but I'm terribly afraid I'll never feel about any other children as I do about Christopher. I'm so frightened I'll be a possessive and clinging mother. He's just so very precious to me, so much an extension of me, of Philip, an outward sign of this good marriage, so much more so than following children can be, I fear, although I'm probably being silly. Each moment I'm alive is filled with a boundless love for him, and a gladness at his creation and being.

Enough ravings about the joys of motherhood. You too, I know, are filled with it all, and I long to hear from you, to share this with you. How I should love to in more than letters.

Much love,

Pat

February 21, 1956

Dearest Pat,

I was so glad, really so very glad to get your letter just now, and to know all goes well with you and Christopher. I've been waiting for what seems a good long time for a letter from someone I cared about besides Mother and Daddy, and I especially wanted to hear from you. Still that was no excuse for not at least sending you birthday greetings. Are you 24 or 25? I've lost all sense of the difference in age between us, if there is much. I'm certain that your boy was what you considered your best gift, whatever the rest may have been. Are you as happy with him as we are? Really, Reinhard *is* a lovely child. I cannot deny it. And he's so beautifully temperamented. He literally NEVER screams. And I know he is hungrily unhappy when he makes little half-choking, half-whimpering cries for help. But he's never insolent or demanding. I don't know how we deserved him.

He's beginning to get a little too fat, and is not quite the aesthetic and elegant little boy he used to be. He has a double chin so fat that I have real trouble finding where the crease ends underneath. Do you have everything you need, or is there anything I can send you, as things are quite accessible in Beirut. Have you these wonderful plastic nylon panties, or the indispensable Carter's nightgowns?

I'm glad to hear the nursing goes well. I really had an uncomfortable time with it for about a month, but now it is running (literally) beautifully, without any pain, and I never have to supplement. I don't know how long I'll continue. Maybe until he gets teeth! And, unless I want to do some extensive traveling over the Easter vacation in April, almost certainly the rest of the school year. I think it would be easier nursing him at least until we got to Germany if I could. But one cannot project these plans too far ahead. At any rate, I don't have the ambition to stop for the reason you do. You ever were more courageous than I. We really will try not to have another baby soon, although I admit your attitude and reasons are the right ones. Still, you do make more money than we do, and as things stand now, Hans couldn't even support the two of us, unless I were working. I'll surely have to work again next year, and I don't know for how long after that (but I hope not endlessly). It will probably be a good four years before Hans is making enough money to enable us to dare a second child. This may sound selfish, but I suspect it is true. You really are dauntless, aren't you? God, I can't help admiring you, even from a distance.

How is your figure? Did you flatten down nicely? By the way, are you cooking? And if so, American, English, or African cuisine? I'm doing all the cooking, finding it quite expensive, and that I can't really satisfy my husband unless I cook German food. He'll not admit to this, but the truth is, he eats twice as much when I have "coll-rolladen" (rolled cabbage) than when I've beef-

65

steak, for example. I really do ache for a good American meal, but oh well.

The second semester has begun now, and both of us are attempting to teach additional courses. Hans teaches half at the university and half up here. I never see him, and I'll see less of him.

Damn it, Pat, I need someone to talk to, and you always were the best one, whether near or far. I know that all the good books say that one goes through a depression after a new baby, and it's understandable, being tired and sort of overcome by it all. And I surely have been. But I swear it cannot be because of Reinhard. He's not nerve-wracking at all, and I'm not honestly overworked or tired. But I've never been so manic-depressive in all my life—one day full of the joy of living, and the next day, tears (which I dutifully try to hide). Indeed, at times I'm almost maudlin. But only with myself.

I can't really figure it out, but I feel a sort of *prémonition du mal* that I cannot explain. But if you want the truth, and I guess I do, it's our marriage— me in our marriage, Hans in our marriage. I write now the most personal of things, so take it as such, as I know you can. There's no one else I talk to like this. Don't become excited, there's nothing dangerously wrong. Perhaps that's the fright, the danger is latent, suggestive, subtle . . . but undermining, and *there*.

We are not unhappy with each other, not that. We did marry the right persons, I know. And maybe I'm just a big blasted sissy. But I weep. I lost something in Lloyd that I NEED—tenderness, overt affection. I'm quite simply not complete without it. And Hans is not active there. I mean, he hasn't kissed me good morning (or good night) for months. It isn't—oh! it is not—his Germanity. Don't think so! He makes no hausfrau out of me. But he just doesn't watch and know my needs, and it doesn't seem to matter. He's intense; he's concerned; he IS an artist (I learn now almost to my horror); not just someone loving the arts and spasmodically participating, but someone whose every waking moment is consumed. He is therefore dynamic and intense in a way very different from those half-blooded bohemians we knew at Utah (or anywhere else). He's not bohemian. Never was. Just quite capable of going for two days without talking. That doesn't matter. I married him partly in that realization.

But I just quite simply don't feel really loved. It hurts to write that, but it's what it boils down to. He's utterly adorable with Reinhard, and will be a wonderful father. He loves him dearly, and plays ingeniously with him by the hour. But I just ache to go walking with him, or dance with him, or sit in a café and talk about relationships (stupid admission, but true). But he never will. He hates analyzing, never does it. He's infinitely more creative than I ever can be, and I fear he knows it. But in a different way. I'm beginning to feel totally DAMNED by my years of talking too much—too much stunted psychology. He doesn't work that way, and it throws me off.

I love his painting and his painting presence. He works hard, is really continuously absorbed, and that never hurts. I don't feel neglected from that in the least. And I certainly am learning what art is. But as man-woman, husband-

66

wife, friend-friend, something is anemic. And it is so with him that I end up feeling it is *my* broad deep anemia of spirit which is damning the whole thing. And I'm scared. He thinks I'm doing a very good job with the baby, but he never tells me I'm a good wife, or that he is happy. And God damn it, Pat, I've never tried so hard at anything in all my life (one always says an honest effort interferes). I'm really trying to make the house pleasant, to keep myself attractive, to dress well, to read and think and activate, and write. I am writing. I stay up late hours and work after nursing the baby in the mornings. But I never see in his eyes any gladness at having me. Hell, I'm on the verge of tears again. Which naturally leads me to feel I just don't have it.

You see, it's funny to find myself loving. I am in love with him. Lawrence said there always was the lover and the beloved in any relationship, but I do NOT want to be as active as Hans's intense living makes me. And another funny, unknown part of me was born. I never was really jealous in my life, except of the *shock* of another woman taking a man from me in the past. But I live in the danger of becoming a jealous wife. Let me tell you a strange story.

It was in Rome last September at the end of our European summer. I was seven months pregnant, and it was good being in Rome together. We spent afternoons sitting in the big sidewalk café just because. And three times we went to the slickest, chicest nightclub there, small, intimate, cleverly thought out. The last night we were sitting there, and I noticed a beautiful Grace Kelly-ish sort of woman staring at Hans. He noticed it too, and could not help (literally could not help) staring back. She did not flirt. She simply looked, almost with a full innocence, into his eyes for well over an hour. And he looked back. Not even the hint of a smile traced her lips, and it was so obvious that both of them were simply transfixed in an unpremeditated and uncontrollable attraction.

Finally he said, "I must understand this," and went out. He came back in fifteen minutes, nervous, but less so than I, and I begged him to leave. We returned to the hotel, and I could tell he couldn't talk about it, so we slept. The next day he mentioned it. I had hoped he would. He had talked to her briefly in the corridor. She had said, "Are you an American?" and he, "No, but WHO are you?" They talked a bit, exchanged names, and discovered that they both were German. She asked if he was married, and he said, "Yes," and she said, "Are you happy?" and he said, "Yes." "Then there's nothing to do," she answered. "Only, here are two German kids half in love with each other, meeting in Rome, one on his way to Beirut, and the other to America." That's all. He kissed her goodbye. He told me that. I understood, though it just about shredded me inside.

My God, I'd shatter, Pat, if one of us couldn't hold out against those things, and left, however briefly. I never thought I would, but I would. The thought of infidelity panics me. I'm not obsessed by it, but another few experiences like that and I could be. Because the point was, they couldn't help it. There was nothing cheap in her. She was lovely, a lady. And she didn't try to catch his desire. It just existed, a priori, so to speak. It was Meredith's

In Tragic Life, God wot,
No villain need be.
Passions spin the plot.
We are betrayed by what is false within.

And I didn't blame him in the least. But I can't get over it. It frightened me so. I never did think I'd become this way. Hans is no flirt or ladies' man. And yet a part of him is quite willing to go along with that sort of thing, how far I don't know. We've never discussed fidelity. I don't want to.

How do you feel about it? Or how would you feel about it? Before marriage, I was quite capable of cheating on a boyfriend. But all that is so far beyond my ken now, so so far. I'm sure one day I'll meet someone who calls to me as this w man did to him, but I really don't want to. I only want us to be complete. Tl t's all I want. That is everything. I'm really writing to you from my heart now. You can tell that. Please answer me soon. I cannot help but feel that there will be a tragedy somewhere along our marriage. It's a dreadful way to think, I know, but I cannot avoid it. I could perhaps, if he would ever tell me he loved me, or sleep with me a bit more often. Oh, Pat, maybe I'll not even mail this. And if I do, please hold it closely to you alone. Will you do that?

We sail on the *Ile de France* for America on August 3rd from Le Havre. We love the little yellow sweater. It's the prettiest of all on him.

My love to you and yours,

Joyce

MAHALI, TANGANYIKA
March 5, 1956

My dear, *dear* Joyce,

Where shall I begin? How to tell you, now that my rusty unpracticed pen no longer facilely spins out the phrases with ease, how to tell you how my heart aches for you in the loneliest, awfulest, of worlds? Perhaps, because everyone analyzes everyone else from one's own inner being, you, being an impingement upon *my* consciousness, can only be seen by me through the light of my own experience. Perhaps, then, I'll tell you a little of myself.

God knows, the first year and a half of our marriage was hell from some aspects (mainly sexual—all this is for your eyes and heart alone, it goes without saying). I was used to virile impatient boys who literally hopped on and off and included sex in that hideous American pastime of "going together"—but with Philip, it meant a giving, an extension of himself that he just wasn't prepared for, nor I to draw it out of him, apparently. Months and months of nightly attempts,

68

Joyce, with perhaps half a dozen successes (out of which came my first two pregnancies, unbelievably!). I cried in the bathroom as I used to when I was an unhappy child, holding my breath till I nearly fainted, hoping I'd die, from the rage and frustration and shame and impossibility of it all. And then after we lost our baby, something snapped, and Philip has had no trouble since. It's still difficult, and a trifle forced, five times out of six, but in a personal way, as though we have a silent understanding about it.

And Joyce, knowing me and my great big flopping jaw, can you believe that never once in our nearly three years of marriage have we discussed this problem (though I've tried, timidly, to introduce it—he hates personal subjects)? *Everything* else, yes, hundreds of subjects, but never Philip's and Pat's difficulty in copulation. God knows *why* it resolved itself after Baby, but thank God, it did, to all intents and purposes. It's a dreadful shameful burden off my soul—that I couldn't *do* this for him.

We (since baby no. 1) have discussed fidelity, usually appropriate to private gossip about a neighbor's indiscretion, and seem more or less to have the same mid-Victorian views about it. I think that the first infidelity is the only really important one, because it's the rip in the fabric of the unity of marriage that perhaps can be repaired, but never invisibly. Perhaps one can come in time to ignore the scar (switching metaphors in midstream), but on rainy days, it'll hurt, if you see what I mean. And if it's happened once, well, who knows, similar circumstances, temptations, and people, will almost certainly lead to similar results.

It definitely wouldn't kill my affection for Philip for him to be unfaithful, he's too much my life, but it would maim it in such a way as to make it unrecognizable, a parody of its former lovely pure self. I have not honestly been once tempted since our marriage, have not met one person I'd be remotely interested in going to bed with but conceivably I might have been vaguely interested in in pre-P. days. Especially now, with Christopher, the three of us make such a unity that the intrusion of another person into our privacy would be obscene. I can't bear to have anyone else even change Christopher's diapers, let alone have his care for any time at all. It's all part and parcel of the above notion.

To move on to another subject, Philip talks very little more now than he did when we were first married, but I've learned to interpret his silences a little, and to value his every one word to my hundred (or thousand!). Our conversations have reached that (to others) incomprehensible marital stage of grunts and ums and private frames of reference that only time brings. I'm just telling you about us. I'm not saying cheer up, dearie, it all comes out in the wash, because I believe Hans and Philip to be two totally different kinds of men. Philip's silences and quietness of nature I attribute to his background, his Britishness, his innate shyness, having a very flashy elder brother, never feeling quite satisfied (in his childhood) with his relationship to his mother, and a host of causes which *in their totality* make up a naturally quiet Philip but which, if they had been different, might have produced a talkative, demonstrative P. For he *is* the latter two, but in such a tiny tiny way you must be forever on the watch to pick up any stray bits that quietly creep out. He too does not kiss me good night or good morning, nor does he demonstrate love verbally, but I'm sure he would if he were different. But Hans, I think (now I'm just speculating, mind you, quite unjustifiably), is by the deepest core of his being one of those who burn with a hard gemlike flame, and one can't in imagination warm one's hands and bottom before a flame like that, can one? One can read by it, be inspired by it, build an altar to it and place ikons before it, but it's inconceivable to think of cooking by it or making a wine cup over it. Am I being too easily metaphorical? Forgive me, dear friend, I only ponder over our fates and wonder. . . .

Philip and I live such easy easy lives. We're so intellectually lazy. We read the reviews faithfully, and order books and read and discuss them in a desultory fashion (I should say, I do, and he nods wisely). We garden and I look after Christopher and plan rather dull meals (I don't cook, since we have a cook to whom I demonstrate, uselessly, the ways of cuisine).

We go to the club every week and get dutifully tight; I fend off passes from the local Greek sisal barons and Philip stands on his head and is the life of all parties, in an odd reversal of his sober self; we give occasional proper dinner parties in return for other very proper dinner parties we've been to; we play a little tennis; I write letters and fuss with our photo album and the baby book. I sew a little but only fancy stuff, as it's too cheap to have plain things made by the Indian tailors—shirts, shorts, etc.—to bother to do it oneself. I keep threatening to have a potter's wheel made and take up potting again, but I shan't, because it's too much trouble and too expensive. I keep saying to myself I really *must* write but I most probably never shall again.

My youth, my glorious, aware, crystal clear, exciting and promising youth, has vanished, and I'm now nearer thirty than twenty, contented most of the time with my husband, baby, dog and home, conservative in politics, agnostic in a bored disinterested way, in a word, thoroughly and respectably bourgeois, although consciously so, and being so, tempered with irony, perhaps is what saves P. and me—though from what, I don't know.

You, I think, in your marriage with Hans, perhaps will never know this neat, orderly pigeonholed housewifeliness, and perhaps it's just as well. God, my mind turns on such small things! Surprisingly enough I'm not bored, ever. Only the feelings of guilt which rise now and again, as I sit reading, reading, reading, all the time, stir my mundane life. But why should I bother when I can pay someone else such a tiny sum to do it for me?

P. and I occasionally once every couple of months start talking about this whole business of vegetation and a few nights ago got really good and drunk and maudlin for the first time in years. It proved to be an unfortunate thing to have done, for I am still expecting him to respond intellectually and emotionally to me in a way that I feel I need, but simply will never get. But other things in the daily rounds of life must (and do) suffice. There *literally* is not one person out of the hundred or so Europeans here (and that very charitably includes the Greeks, all Cypriots) who has heard of Joyce or Brecht or Epstein or Proust or the great 15th century vowel shift. So P. and I are thrown entirely on each other for intellectual stimulation, and after a time, living as close as we do, it's like playing Chinese checkers with yourself. We shall *definitely* do only one more tour out here, and that only because P. can get a year's study leave for a degree in tropical medicine at London U. And a year paid for in London would be rather nice.

But I don't know if I can stick it for another two and a half years. We don't think about it much, but when we do it's more and more with a feeling of desperation. Vegetating, I mean. But what else we'd do, I sure as hell don't know. Both of us have the terrific urge to be creative, but are afflicted with the awful lassitude that comes with the certainty of your own mediocre talents. But I'll tell you this much—if Philip decides he wants to go to Paris and write a novel, I shall sell all the clothes on my (and Christopher's) backs, live in a nasty unheated room, carry water up three floors, beg and borrow from my family till they disown me. I shall *never* become a *frightened* bourgeois. If the revolution does come, I'll jolly well join in, even though I'm too lazy to work for it, if I'm not being too vague.

March 6

I got interrupted by our Labor Officer, who came to pick me up for choral practice. Yes, way out here in the toolies, we have actually got eight madrigal singers and someone knowledgeable and strong enough to conduct us. He also has an African male choir of twelve voices and we've been working on a concert which is to be this evening. Our rehearsals are the only (two, rather) bright spot in my week.

I miss music more than ANYTHING ELSE out here. No radio—it's not worth it, even with the best, reception is so bad, and no phonograph, as we have no electricity. No films either. But I don't think about it too often, and just sing to myself in the bathtub and to Baby. Have you found yourself singing a lot of nonsense songs, lullabies and nursery songs that have come back to you, so many forgotten songs that just creep into your consciousness with the baby? P. asks me where in the world I learned them all, and I honestly don't know. They're just there.

He's so sweet, Joyce. He has such deep intelligent eyes. We seem to share the loveliest secret sometimes when we're just smiling at each other, but I guess it's just being mother and son. I'm still nursing, but my milk seems to be diminishing. I rely on Dr. Spock for most of my information. Mother sent me the Pocket Book edition, and I've found it absolutely invaluable. The first three or four weeks I came home I was in a horrible postnatal depression. I cried and moped and shouted at Philip and hid myself in closets. But it did pass off.

Yours however doesn't sound in the least to me like the above. You know, Joyce (more unfounded speculation follows), Hans would probably be amazed to realize how much you (and all intelligent non-Continental European women) need reassurances and pats and kisses to keep a glow going. I think he probably feels—here I am happily married, with a lovely baby, working hard, my wife attends to her affairs and I to mine, and we meet quite satisfactorily on the appropriate occasions in the business of marriage. And ceases to think about it. I *know* it isn't satisfactory (believe me, I do), but, Joyce, though you say it isn't his Germany, I have never seen or heard of an un-American husband any different. Have you read Lawrence's "The Lost Girl"? Italian, yes, with the expected temperamental differences, but the essence of the idea *or* ideal of marriage was the same. Perhaps I'm just flying my kite, but I do think that kind of marriage is in fact different from what we've grown up with, but I think it can be a very happy and successful one if, I grant, most of the changes in attitude are made on your side.

I know, Joyce, God, how I know, how terribly frustrating and senseless it seems, when only a word or a gesture could resolve days of private tears and rages. But if it won't come, it won't. Am I not being helpful or soothing? In the matter of trust, well really, *getting* married itself is a sign of distrust in a way, isn't it? I mean, neither party can just pack up and hop the first train out of town once a contract is signed and sealed. But that's as far as I think one can go in forcing the issue with a terribly independent self-willed husband.

I seem to have maundered on and on and said very little of much sense. How much better it would be over cups of coffee! I am enclosing a couple of snaps of Christopher, both very bad, as we have only a little Kodak, useless except in bright sunlight, where Christopher of course closes his eyes.

I loved your pictures. Actually they are quite alike (C. and R.) in their facial bone structures and funny little serious expression and alert eyes. R. has far more hair, as you can see. How I wish sometimes we were in a city of sorts where we could get amenities like a photographer. And I do so miss good food.

It's pretty discouraging trying to cook anything decent, especially as we have ancient, tiny wood stoves and the kitchen is fifty feet from the back of the house. Custom. So I've given up the struggle except for baking and a few fancy dishes now and then.

I've run out of space. My love and hope and heart to you.

Pat

April 5, 1956

Dearest friend in all the world,

I hope my last letter in answer to your worried and sad one got to you okay and maybe helped some, though I can't remember much of what I said in it. I haven't heard from you since then.

Alas, one of my great pleasures in life has come to a premature end; I've dried up, very suddenly, and had to put Christopher on formula. Isn't that ghastly —bottles, sterilizing, all the fuss and mess, not to speak of losing our wonderful feed times together. Makes me sick, but there's nothing I can do about it.

The long rains finally came and my asthma worsens daily. We're invaded by hordes of nasty bugs of every description and everything is always damp and moldy. But it has its bright side—it's cooling off and the garden and countryside are looking lovely for the first time since just after our arrival (almost a year now, unbelievably; seems like forever in some ways). And I love the sound and smell of the rain here, different from anything I've ever known. I've been reading a lot more lately and going out less. Some friends in Los Angeles wrote a few months ago and asked if we needed or wanted anything, and my plea was books, books, books. A big carton of paperbacks came, and I've been having an orgy— *everything:* science, philosophy, political science, poetry, novels—wonderful.

I've gone into journalism again. The lady who writes up Mahali for the English-language daily published in Dar goes home on leave next week for six months, and has delegated her duties to me. I get paid! Not very much (28¢ per column inch), but still, paid. My very first story was about a Danish farmer thirty miles south of here who raises nutrias (horrid little animals that deservedly end up as fur coats). He shot a leopard a couple of nights ago near the animal pens and only wounded it, and when he went back the next morning, it leaped out at him and mauled him very badly. He was jolly lucky to have escaped with his life, as they usually play around with you till you're hamburger.

Anyhow, even with the little amount of news to write up from here, it'll be good to use my mind again at something, however trivial. I would so like to see you and your baby, to talk with you about how motherhood suits us both, all the things I don't seem to even want, let alone be able to, share with anyone else about life at this stage. Do write. I cherish your letters.

Love and affection,

Pat

Dearest Joyce,

It's nearly midnight and I cannot go to sleep, my head is all in such a whirl. Why, I don't know. Today was a perfectly ordinary day, the baby good, a row with the cook, planning a dinner party, P. and I quietly reading after dinner till bedtime. Perhaps it's because I'm reading Walpole, one of the *Herries Chronicles.* Somehow, these long rambling family histories, like the *Forsyte Saga* too, always move me deeply, perhaps because I've never had a real home or any continuity or security in my family life or background. Anyhow, I feel like talking to you. I've worried ever since I sent off my stupid letter to you.

Did I preach? Did I sermonize? Was I deadly dull and prosaic in my pronouncements? I fear so, but God! Joyce, you know how poorly I express myself compared with you. So forgive me, dear friend, if anything I said offended you, and know that I lay in bed tonight thinking and thinking on you and finally had to get up for a talk.

Life is good, but oh, so dull sometimes. I whisper to myself, *"Most* of the time." Strange that I of all the people I know should end up such a middle-class housewife, even in the midst of Africa. But what's *our* Africa, after all, but Middletown, with cheap black servants and a foreign language thrown in to confuse and irritate one the more? I admit, I quite freely admit, I now see myself as a weak person needing the stimulation of sharper personalities than my own to feel alive and aware.

It's hard to say, but I realize now that I was never more than on the fringes of the "crowd," no matter where. But better to be Lamb, girl-hanger-on, than Lamb, girl-nothing. Unhappily though, I still feel on the fringes of my present social group, though now, of course, I'm snobbishly proud of it because they're too crass for words, I tell myself. Ah, I'm suffering the later-in-life penalties of the dissipations of the pseudo-intellectual.

But I must stop. It's so silly to feel as if all the exciting parts are over and done with when I'm only twenty-five. Maybe I'm jaded, sated. Perhaps too much has already happened to me—poor, then well off, loved, then jilted, then married, childbirth with tragedy, finally a beloved son, Paris at twenty-one, Africa at twenty-four. But then only stupid people get jaded or sated. And I keep telling myself, perhaps this is one of those transitional phases in my life. I wonder to what? For after leaving Africa, I see ahead only a practice in some small town, security, the children growing up, and me suddenly fifty and all over and done with. I have an appalling sense of the nearness of old age and death before one has ever lived. I always have had, I think. Sometimes before I can stop myself I'm weeping at the thought of the swiftness of it all. Doesn't sound very healthy, I suppose. Enough puzzlement and moans.

Why on earth do you suppose we two in our latter days have become so ghostly and wraithlike? For the first time since I had Christopher I weighed myself last week and I'm 107! A dress which my mother made for me when I was seventeen actually hangs on me. 120 is my norm. I have less bosom since I quit breast-feeding than ever in my life! I feel healthy as sin though, even though I never eat anything.

What a selfish letter! Not a word about my darling son who is thriving and loves his Heinz vegs. and fruits, his cereal, orange juice and milk, his teddy bear, his rattle, his blanket, his mother and father, the poinsettias blowing in the breeze outside the window, playing two or three games I've invented. His world enlarges daily as does his huge appreciation of it. It's really too early to speculate, but I think he's going to be very delicate and sensitive (probably a boxer!), and I feel terribly fierce and protective when something startles him and he puckers his lower lip, quietly gulps and sobs and turns his head into my shoulder or the pillow. I love him so very much, but am I horrible and unmaternal when I whisper quietly to you alone that he is not my whole life? I know I'll be a good mother, perhaps the better for wanting him to develop and stand on his own feet, and not wanting to clutch him to my breast always. Have you felt anything conscious of this sort? Do all mothers feel it and are just ashamed to admit it, or am I unnatural and different? I have talked myself and no doubt you too to sleep, and will close.

All my special love,

Pat

BEIRUT
May 4, 1956

Dear abiding friend,

Your letters, your confidence and concern don't merely fade into the upper air. They're received with gratitude, read and reread, and once even wept over.

It's been such a strange year, so full of misgivings about myself (in spite of the certainty that I *can* produce a handsome son), and some despair. I've done little that is truly creative. After all, giving birth is physiological; they (Reinhard and Christopher) will test our scope, our range, but not yet. I've read relatively little, written some slight things, learned how to be a fair cook, taught well, made poor conversation, made muddled attempts to understand this Arab world and given Hans very little.

And of all, it's only this last that really matters. I am haunted by his spiritual energy. Things really do go on inside him. Watching him, I begin to think my world is all shadow play, or a jigsaw puzzle of abstractions that were stillborn.

When he got excited about Islamic pottery, there was an intense and exclusive romance going on between him and them. The same now—the entire year—with the Romanesque. He pursues it all the way through. And when I become upset, I must acknowledge that it is because he throws me on my uncertainties, on those areas I used to pride myself upon, that probably never existed. Or only in my weak-kneed self-assertions. Hans doesn't allow analyses. *Never* do we discuss human relationships in the analytical way I used so to love. I still do, in fact. No —and he much prefers me simply, vividly, honestly responding.

And he's right. But I punish myself that it doesn't come more naturally, and I detest myself when I try to force it. So, I've been caught between resolutions and disgust. And all I've needed to help me was the certitude of being loved. Lacking this, my world often fell apart, and I wept, or wrote you, or went out for walks. Then with a physical despair on top, I was crushed. Mind you, Hans is not the aesthetic young man uninterested in sex. In fact, I remember D. H. Lawrence's "The higher the brow, the lower the loins" in this connection. But it had been many months carrying Reinhard, and he didn't care enough about our togetherness to make it good. We have far to go. *If* I can satisfy him in the living, then he can me in our love. It leads to a vicious circle that scares me. I can only trust that I'm not unloved, and keep trying.

No, Pat, I am not so maternal. Reinhard is lovely, beautiful really. I adore him, but never can he make up for the vacancies and gaps between Hans and me. I simply CANNOT find compensation there. His happy baby love does not answer the problem. He *most certainly* is not my whole world. And actually, this is probably good for both of us. He's five months now, and weighs 8 kilos, 300 grams. He is incredibly alert and full of character and almost crawling. His motor development is marvelous and he's so good. It's a dear age. Please send more pictures of Christopher.

What are your summer plans? We leave June 19th, jobless, to go half around the world. Hope to stop for a week of love-making in the hay of Austria. I've *no* interest in going to America. Here are some photos. Write soon.

> My love, my thanks,
>
> *Joyce*

MAHALI
May 30, 1956

Ever dearest friend Joyce,

The tone of your last letters is so sad, I want to be able to reach out to you and say something encouraging, but frankly, I don't know *what.* Our lives, yours and mine, have taken such very different turnings, although we have married rather similar men in some ways, I think, except for their work. I of course cannot really share in Philip's, as I'd always hoped to in my husband's, but he brings home funny and sad tales from the hospital, I do rounds at night and on Sundays with him, we go on safari together, and I help a bit there, and mainly I know what he's doing, and why and how, as much as any layman can. And then we are together all the rest of the time, gloriously so, though maybe a little too much. I begin a little, for the first time since the early months of our marriage, to crave privacy again. It's silly, I know, but I remember in hospital, waiting for Christopher, the treacherous notion just popping into my head of how nice it was to go to bed and sleep and wake up by myself. I could read or eat crackers or be asthmatic or cross, and do it all alone. But I'm fighting this feeling, and want to do everything with him that he wants. In fact I'm frightened that a day might come when he might *not* want me to do things with him. After all, I have privacy (except for servants and baby and people dropping in, and those don't really count) the hours each day he's at the hospital, so that should be enough.

I've more or less given up trying to converse with him as you and I and the old U. crowd all seemed to talk together, so easily. I think perhaps it's very adolescent of me to go on wanting it. It's not only not easy with him, it's impossible, and he's the adult in this case, it seems to me. He too hates analyzing and the whys and wherefores of behavior and motivation. He just will not talk about useless things like the past (even history, in its broader cyclical sweeps) or God or souls or what we're doing here. And I think he's right; perhaps it is unhealthy and pointless and time-wasting ("non-productive"). At any rate, we don't do it any more. And I have not a single friend, here, nor have I made one since leaving college.

I get the awful presentiment that at this level of existing, I never will again. Maybe that's part of growing up, learning to be self-sufficient inside yourself, the way Philip is, not needing close relationships. He makes me feel desperately adolescent in my enthusiasms and unprofessional fads. So I try when I think about it to put a lid on the old pressure cooker that I seem to be. But values there must be, and I think I've found one. I'd like to finish my B.A. and perhaps teach when my babes are in school, wherever we're living then, so I've written off to three American universities for correspondence courses and am keeping my fingers crossed that first, it's allowed and second, that we can afford whatever it costs on our paltry Colonial Service salary. I must assure you that I don't think about all the above very much. I'm far too busy with the necessary (and enjoyable) things of my everyday life most of the time.

We seem to have gotten in the way of doing a lot of entertaining these days, and being entertained. It's all very formal, dinner jackets for the men and long dresses for the women. Philip even has his father's tails packed away in case we go somewhere ultra-formal. I guess it livens up people's existence, and makes them feel civilization isn't so far away after all. There's more to that old joke about the Englishman in the jungle having dinner in his D.J. than a foreigner realizes. I mean more sense.

About entertaining—golly, I ought to go to Washington, D.C., or its like, after what I've learned out here. One does it all so very properly. It's so hard to think up new ideas for hors d'oeuvres and fish courses and new soups and especially desserts, all the time, considering the scarcity of decent food available or anything interesting in the so-called store. As for cocktail parties ("sundowners"), I've just given up and copy what everyone else makes. But one can't call them cocktail parties anyway, because no one ever drinks anything except whiskey and soda or whiskey and water, with maybe one person out of twenty drinking gin and lemon or a pink gin. You can't even buy rum or vodka, etc. But I'm just as happy to stick with whiskey anyway, as I don't particularly like drinking; I just like getting drunk every now and again, as you may well remember! Philip hates me doing it, and I try not to. Ladies don't get drunk, maybe a little tiddly, but definitely not drunk. I just feel like letting go every once in a while, dancing the night through, telling rowdy jokes, but quite seriously, women really *aren't* supposed to do that, no different, I guess, from suburban America, where I'd probably have ended up otherwise, but aggravating, when all the men can have such a good time. I wish Philip liked dancing better, but he can't keep time and doesn't know any of the basic steps, let alone anything fancy like the tango. You remember how I adore dancing all night, but I do it anyway, with lots of other partners. He doesn't seem to mind. You should see him reliving his wild Irish medical school days on club dance nights. He's the life of the party. I will go home early, because of Christopher, as I did when I was pregnant, and also because, unless I'm dead drunk, I get bored. But I'm glad he enjoys it so much.

We are making exciting and grandiose plans to go to the Belgian Congo for our local leave, which we'll take in August. Everyone thinks we're mad to drive so far in such a short time (four weeks) via Nairobi and Kampala, but I think it'll be great fun, baby and all. We'll take a boy and manage nicely, I'm sure. And you going to Palmyra! And you thought of my childhood heroine, Zenobia. Now *there* was a life to have lived! What fun to be a queen and lead your troops into battle. Even if you lost, by God you'd fought!

Must close. I hope all is well. You say you leave June 19th. Where to and what to do? What a prospect with a tiny baby. Write me every step of your way.

All my very best love,

Pat

And a late happy birthday!

July 4, 1956
(a moment of patriotic indulgence)

Dear sorely neglected Pat,

Did you ever get the last letter I started and don't remember finishing? The tempo of our last week had been such that I've not written to anyone, that I've lost our suitcase, a diary, one glove, two scarves, four pounds, disrupted our son's life, and finally arrived, wilted, at my in-laws'. The boat trip was calm enough and lovely, the departure from Beirut sad, hasty, hot and incompetent, and the trip since Venice misery for all. Poor little boy—sleeping in a suitcase across Europe! Thanks to God I could still nurse him.

Immediately that we hit Europe, the sky shrank and muted, the people became gayer, but quieter, the relationship with our cultured selves was reborn, revitalized. Reinhard does beautifully and is indeed beautiful. He's a terribly sweet little package and good, good, good. With a great wincing of my maternal instinct, I am now in process of weaning, and it seems to be more painful for me than for him. The pain is that emotional one rooted in bodily sensations, in the same way that happy or unhappy sexual emotions are. I wean him only because I want to go with Hans to Berlin a week from Sunday.

I'm thrilled at the prospect of learning his student days' city, as I know how a city takes on the contours of meaning provided by university loves, discoveries, work and unhappiness. So Berlin becomes even more pertinent to me in relation to my husband's than to the world's history. I want to see his academy, meet the professors, meet the girl who broke his heart.

You'll be surprised at our news, but knowing me, not too surprised. We have canceled our reservations on the *Ile de France.* We're not going to America. Nor staying in the Lebanon. By accident (as these turns in life are most always accounted for), we learned that the western coast of Scotland is depopulating, and that cottages are abandoned and dirt cheap in rent. We're taking luck in our armpits, and the little money we got from canceling our transatlantic voyage, and setting off for 7–9 months in one of these cottages, for the express purpose of trying to come to terms with ourselves artistically, and in our family.

We're not going off to play Thoreau (or E. B. White), nor to wear tartans and go barefoot. Hans is bursting to the seams and to the edge of his unpredictable sociability with the need and the ideas to realize the need. I'm just at the point where, if I don't write out the diffuse directions in me, I'll just disperse and blow away. You see, Pat, 26 is no longer really young. We can't go on thinking in terms of ourselves producing, without getting to work. Between 26–30 is a kind of second awkward age, with ideas, influences, experiences knocking clumsily around day after day, formless. A bit of crystallization is due—the virtues of limitation.

Hans will leave here in mid-August and sail to Edinburgh. Our modicum of luggage is already in Glasgow. From there northward, he will search for a proper place, costing not more than 4 Eng. pounds a month, probably without running water or bathroom and almost certainly without electricity. We shall be near enough a village for grocery and medicinal purposes, and otherwise live as simply as possible. We shall have at best $60 a month for 8 months, but will live as the poor Scottish do if need be. We're fairly optimistic and cheerful about it all. I am sure we'll manage. Doesn't one always? We shall count on going home off season, around May, and hope that somewhere in the Anglo-Saxon world, Hans can have a decent-sized exhibit.

Do wish us luck and please interrupt our isolation with frequent word of you. I shall be here probably until Aug. 25th or so.

Tell me, dear Pat, would you like to be Reinhard's godmother? He would like it, I'm sure. He is to be baptized on Sunday, July 15th, by his paternal grandfather. Custom has it in Germany that a member of the family shall also be a godmother, so Hans's oldest sister, Marie, is that. But we would like it if you, too, would watch him throughout his life. Write soon.

All my love,

Joyce

MAHALI
July 15, 1956

Dearest friend,

First, I presume you got my crazy cable telling you I'd adore to be Reinhard's godmother. I am very honored indeed, though as a kind of lapsed Catholic deistic agnostic, I have qualms about really qualifying for the relationship. But I'll do my best. Christopher of course doesn't have one, because he can be christened in his own good time if he chooses to. People here think we're shocking, even though nine out of ten of them feel just as we do about organized religion, and I keep trying to point out how hypocritical of me it would be to enter him into a system I didn't really believe in, either just to be on the safe side, or to go along with everyone else and be respectable. Perhaps I have some sneaking feeling left over about the magic of the sacraments. Who knows? But I am delighted at least to do the right thing by Reinhard.

And as to your great news about the move to Scotland and the life there that you will try to live, I am thrilled beyond words at the prospect of it, and even envy you! (There, I've said it.) I think sometimes that we (P. and I) would both benefit from an attempt like that. He too thinks you are both courageous and wonderful in doing this. I agree with you that 26 is no longer young, but I don't really want to do anything else with my life than what I'm doing right now. I only wish I did it better, so I'd be more satisfied. I only yearn for company and conversation sometimes. I should get out my old efforts at writing and try to organize some of them and send them away. P. is always very encouraging about it whenever I say I should do it. My baby is so very much in my life, I can lavish all the affection and love and care on him that I have in me. But I have to admit there are still some chinks and holes through which a cold wind comes blowing unbidden, sometimes.

As well as with Christopher, I fill in my days with lots of tennis. It's a wonderful game. But I'll never be any good. I took it up too late and am too ill-coordinated.

So, as you go off to test yourself, I sew and garden and play tennis and entertain, and get ready for our Congo safari. Haven't our lives turned out oddly? I'll be longing to hear about your cottage life and how the work progresses. *Do write!*

> Very much love, all my congratulations
> on this wonderful decision—I'm sure
> none but good can come from it,
>
> *Pat*

KENSINGTON, LONDON
August 28, 1956

Very dear Pat,

Excuses: this ragged attempt at stationery; a so long delay. Your telegram arrived in time for the baptism, in time for you to be properly represented as godmother, which pleased me. Thank you for it. My thoughts are full of you and Philip, being here in London, and I must write. It has been lack of stamp money as much as anything, which has so retarded my answer. But we've almost made it now, and the year is about to begin. Hans went to Scotland before me, and after walking over fifty miles, found an almost ideal place.

I hope you may use the enclosed address often, as mail will really be our only social life, I fear. The worst of it was that it was not free until Sept. 3rd, so we had to breach over the time here in London. Mind you, I enjoyed that, but we could scarcely afford it, even cooking package soups as we were in the hotel room. But I feel so at home and at ease here; I like London. After the Orient, I appreciate so much the lack of shouting, the unsuspicious glance, the fair trade. Even the climate. I walked for hours yesterday, drippingly along the river. I feel I could even live here happily. Perhaps we will. We've great hopes for the possibilities of exhibiting in Britain, having already some substantial leads.

But oh, Pat, how I ache at the moment for some honest female companionship. If just to talk with you for a whole afternoon. There's not been anyone really good for a very long time. In Beirut, too late came the acquaintance with a good English wife of one of the professors, just the right sort, but too late. Otherwise Beirut friendships were constituted by an English couple who admired us far too much to make it interesting, a good New York couple who always bought paintings but who were too neurotic, and a wonderful philosophy professor whose wife just barely missed being close to me. In France was no one. In fact since Salt Lake, the going has been rather solitary, so far as women friends are concerned. Why should it be so difficult to find the right sort? Are we demanding so very much? Anyway, I miss you.

I think that we have a tiny unmentioned fear about the quantity of free time with which we are faced. One may come to realize how fully he depends on schedules and duties to keep sane. Not that we've not plenty of work both to do, but such freedom to do it in is after all a bit frightening. Frightening because one can no longer fool himself or make images around what he is. I must now meet myself as writer (of any sort) or stop kidding. As for Hans, he's simply exploding with ideas and eagerness to get to the paints. We're about poverty-stricken now, but from what we see here, prices on paintings are splendid and public willing. It looks hopeful.

Our house is, after all, not primitive. We have electricity for cooking, and running water (thank God!), and four rooms. We're in a fishing village on Loch Fyne called Tarbert, with about 2000 people—doctor, supplies, all necessaries. Ours is the last house on the loch, and will be very quiet, as the road ends there. It's about 3 hours from Glasgow by a steamer that goes over the loch and 4 from Edinburgh. It all has thus far worked out as we hoped. Now, if we can do the work—.

All best love,

Joyce

MAHALI
September 8, 1956

So very dear Joyce,

Yours from London arrived in nothing short of a miraculous time! So you begin the great adventure. How I envy you. It's something so worth doing. I know what you mean about London. I miss it achingly sometimes, for its civilized way

82

of life and people, as well as for everything that life out here lacks. Even a week in Nairobi, the nearest fleshpot for thousands of miles, and not much of a one at that, wasn't enough to satisfy. I wrote you recently that I too had no friends at all, just acquaintances, and I long for your presence, to share and to *talk!* My word, I am sick of talk about babies, boys, and gardens. And how much they all miss "home," wherever that may be. I may tell you, and you alone, about not liking some aspects of life out here, but I don't blather about it all day every day, and anyway, I like most of what life here is, believe it or not. You ask, are we demanding too much? No, I don't think so. I don't think our standards are impossibly high. I think maybe most people are afraid of close friendships, that they'll give too much of themselves away (as if love and trust were expendable commodities of which everyone has only so much, like G. B. Shaw felt about his heartbeats and sperm, wasn't it?), and anyway, a good friendship is not only rare, it's immensely rewarding, which most people don't seem to see. P. is certainly my best friend, but I wish we could talk together more about real things, if you know what I mean.

I'll tell you something partly ludicrous and partly sad that happened after we got back from the Congo last month. I was feeling like a tiny dot on a huge relief map of Africa, and said to him, let's not go to the club this Saturday night, let's stay home and drink wine and read French poetry, which was stupid of me to begin with, since I don't think he likes poetry very much; he's never said so, but he never reads any. Anyhow, I fixed a super dinner and we got all dressed up and lighted candles in the sitting room instead of the ghastly Aladdin lamps, just the two of us, and drank just enough to feel comfortable. I tried to get him to read, but he wouldn't, saying my accent was better, so I was reading Lamartine ("Le Lac"), and happened to glance at Philip in between stanzas, and he had this glazed faraway expression on his face, as if he were at a really boring play and waiting for intermission. It's the first time I can remember in our three years and more together that real anger rose up in me (and for no reason! that's what's so awful) and I threw the book down and yelled, well, what the hell *do* you want? And he looked at me coldly, said, This was your idea, not mine, and walked into the dining room and started doing some paper work. It was all a total flop, and I should never have dreamed it up in the first place, let alone have got angry at nothing; after all, it *was* my idea, not his, and he really wasn't enthusiastic particularly, just wanting to be nice to me and let me do what I wanted. I'm a beast and there's no satisfying me, I guess. I just *must* stop aching for things I can't have and be satisfied with what I do have (as I am, most of the time, I hasten to say).

I'm not pregnant yet, and now don't want to be till after we come back from leave (Feb.–Mar. '58), because I don't want our lovely time spoiled by a tiny baby. We've decided to come back for one more tour because the government will pay for P. to do a diploma course in London in tropical medicine *and* give us three months further leave after that. Nine whole months in Europe! With luck maybe you three will still be there too? Christopher is such a marvelously good baby;

he still never fusses or cries or is sick, always sleeps when he's supposed to. He's very bright and loving.

Though I hesitate to sound like a patronizing Lady Bountiful doling out shillings to the poverty-stricken artists, you and I are too good friends for you to misunderstand, and I want to offer you two (three!) financial help to the best of our meager ability, if you get desperate. I really mean it. I know you would do the same for me, with love and faith, as I do it. And may I send shoes for Reinhard for the cold Scottish winter? Sweaters? Anything?

I am dying to know your living conditions. Have you hot water? Electricity? Furniture? A garden for Reinhard to play in? Tell me all, I'm insatiable for details. You are the only light in my life, I sometimes think, from the outside world. My family never writes to me (my mother is in the throes of beginning her fourth marriage) and I feel fat, faded, and fifty, even though I am skinny, tanned, and twenty-five. I was going to write you all about our immensely long and fascinating Congo safari, but I'll leave it for another time.

Do you feel like an expatriate after so long abroad, and especially after being married to a European? I do and I don't, not only on and off, but at one and the same time. *So* much about England and colonial life I cherish, the excitement of just being in Africa, the ritual and order of our lives, the slow unrolling of days exactly like one another, which sounds as if it contradicts the excitement part, but I'm sure you see what I mean. I wonder where we'll end up living, because this is only temporary. One thing for sure, it's a great place to have and raise little babies.

All my love,

Pat

(Postcard)

MAHALI
September 14, 1956

Dear friend Joyce,

On an impulse, trying to think of what I would like if I were doing what you are doing, I've subscribed to the *Times Literary Supplement* for you for a year. I hope you'll enjoy it and think of me, languishing away in the unintellectual old tropics, when you read it. I see by our Sunday *Observer* that they've a short story competition going, with a bit of prize money. Why don't you enter it? Your ever loving pal,

Lady Patricia Bountiful

September 15, 1956

Very dear, true friend (not yet fat, fifty, or faded),

Thank you. How good it is to know that there is a woman my own age somewhere who understands me and not just on theory or determination. That will solace my companionless hours in Tarbert. (Here I realize the great pity of a sexless language. You see, what I really wanted to say was companionette, or a feminine of the word, as Hans and Reinhard are, of course, good company.) But I'd so love to talk with a woman I can care about.

I'll send this off straight away, by the new method. That is, answering mail the day I receive it by boat mail, thus giving a semblance of punctuality and saving enough for our all too seldom and *ridiculously* taxed cigarettes. As you can reason from what is saved on stamps, it amounts to about two cigarettes a fortnight.

But otherwise, we're surely not going to suffer here, and the going "native" is going to be less rigorous (materially, physically) than I was all bucked up to cope with. I had visions of Hebridean exile, goats' milk, bucket-hauled water, biannual mail service, and grass soup at first, but it turned out with the BBC Third, all of our Bach, running water, a decent electric ring with little baby-sized oven underneath (to cook a single muffin for Reinhard), a doctor 5 houses down, a boat at our door for abrupt fishing needs on our immediate (and heavenly) Loch Fyne, and a bathroom with a toilet that flushes better than all the toilets I dealt with in France pulled at once.

We have four rooms—an immense kitchen with sofa, clothesline, cupboards, baby's closet, eating table and changing-diapers table (when shall I begin to train him??????????) and typewriting-sitting-and-waiting-for-the-muse table; a bathroom, hall, front room in which we sleep in one corner on a great high stiff (and unsuitable) bed and in which Hans paints (and he's already at it about 7 hours a day) in another corner; and a tiny wee (which is the only adjective the Scottish know) utterly dark room in which this little thing is supposed to sleep and does when he isn't getting another tooth, which is, lately, never. I must qualify the complaint, because he's really so awfully good. Our heating is supposed to be in open small coal fires, but we haven't any coal yet. No, we have no real garden of our own, but we have a bumpy, hollowy uphill and amorphous backyard where I can hang clothes, weather and nine hens, six cats and one dog permitting. Yes, it is so completely furnished that we allot about an hour each day for the dismantling and hiding of branching buffets, 19th century vases with orange and blue elephantiasis, and pancake-flat landscape paintings by the local Sunday painter. We brought with us a handsome big Bedouin rug, a Damascus chair and coffee table, lamps that Hans made from Chianti bottles, a black goat hair rug; and of course, our books give it the sense of us that we admit enjoying.

85

No, the Scottish, as I have thus far known them, are absolutely adorable people. I am forced by their sheer kindness to make comparisons with the French street and school scene I know, and the French become hunchbacked and wicked thereby. From what I have seen, they are *genuinely* warmhearted, open enough to avoid any strain, but restrained enough not to be either interfering or snoopy.

And how good, how excellent it is to have once more the quiet, the possibility of hearing the natural sounds through all the cacophony of population. Here, right below our window, the Loch encroaches and subsides, and beating clouds of seagulls quarrel in a trail over the amber fishing boats.

But before I rhapse waxodic over the beauties of the Scotland we have, I had better answer your question. Primarily because Reinhard is determined to tear your letter up and eat it. It's dear of you to want to send the shoes. Not long ago, I bought him a pair, his first, in Germany, which are still so big for his little thick cushion feet that they should last until March or so. So I don't really think he needs them most of all. What he really needs is something more like a little coat than a sweater.

Oh, Pat, it is so good here. I wonder if it will seem hideous going back to the States, with all its fevered momentum. Or perhaps just the opposite. What I do hope for is that together we can make enough money to spend May of this year in Paris, in the best case with an exhibit, and perhaps even without Reinhard, who could stay with his grandmother a short while. I do want to make enough money for that, before going to America. We of course have no idea what job possibilities will come our way. I don't know, to answer your question, if I'm an expatriate. I only suspect that we almost certainly will live in Europe—just Europe, not necessarily Germany or Britain—but Hans would like France. He's still most at home there. I have my stupid fears of France.

May I be honest enough to tell you that I would so very much love to have a subscription to something coming here, and we can't give the money out for it—the *Times Literary Supplement* or *Les Arts et Spectacles* or something, not to become too isolated from this contemporary world. And thank you for offering your help if we need it. It looks as if we'll be fine and all right, but I appreciate it enough that I could even ask you, if we did need something.

Write often to me. It means so very much.

My love to you three,

Joyce

Dearest Joyce,

I keep hoping to hear from you, mail train by mail train, from the depths (or heights, as you please) of outer Argyllshire, but nothing yet. I'll write all the same, since you made it clear you'd treasure mail. I'll just fill you in on a few more pieces of my life here. Of course the biggest news is this damned Suez Canal affair. Our cost of living is going to skyrocket during the next few months. All the ships are being routed round the Cape, which makes the freight twice as expensive, and it's high enough already. Thank God we don't live in Aden or Port Sudan. Poor old England. We were all absolutely terrified of war, till the States stepped in a couple of days ago with her offer to subsidize South American oil for Europe. ANYTHING to avoid another war! It's been the only topic of conversation out here for days and days now, and everyone huddles night and day round the nearest shortwave radio. We're so near and so vitally concerned.

We've been invited (along with a few thousand others) to attend a baraza in Dar es Salaam (big formal gathering) to see Princess Margaret on her state visit here in a few weeks' time, and I have to admit to being rather thrilled at the prospect. I always yearned to be part of an old-fashioned spectacle like a durbar in Victorian India in the heyday of imperialism, and this'll do in a pinch. I want to make a new garden party dress and buy a new hat and gloves, which I realize is silly, being one of the faceless multitudes and not in that fortunate group who will actually meet and shake the hallowed royal hand.

I cook more and more all the time, as the locals are pretty terrible, and I don't seem to be a particularly inspired (or would it be inspiring?) teacher. With much reluctance I began baking bread a few months ago, and I finally have got it straight now, but am not greatly enamored of the process, daily, seven days a week, ad infinitum. I also make my own sauces and jams and so on out of whatever is available (and that isn't much or often). For instance, I was given about eight dozen ripe grapefruit a couple of days ago, and I spent a whole evening looking up (in my trusty American cookbook) whatever one can do with them, except eat them for breakfast, and it's amazing what they think up. I just baked a grapefruit meringue pie; tonight for dinner we're having a sweet potato and grapefruit casserole; and tomorrow I'll devote the day to making grapefruit marmalade. So that ought to take care of a lot of them. It's rather feast or famine. For months on end I can't get any fruit except papaya, which I loathe (though Philip and Christopher like it), then suddenly I'm inundated with grapefruit, oranges, lemons, mangoes, imported apples and plums. And oh, I forgot the ubiquitous banana, tiny and green, but always there. And about 15 for a nickel! It's the same with vegetables. All through the rains, it's tins or nothing, but now my garden and the marketplace both are full of peas, carrots, turnips, cabbage and tomatoes.

One disappointing thing has happened (or rather, failed to happen). I've heard from two of the American universities I wrote to about correspondence courses, and the rest will be the same, I'm sure. They're unbelievably expensive and not only could we not afford it, we couldn't get that amount of American currency anyhow. So that's out. I've written to London University in desperation, though the systems are so very different, and my two years of credits I understand will all go for naught. We'll see what they have to offer. I do so very much want to have some sort of proper qualification to do something other than make grapefruit marmalade and bake bread the rest of my days. It's okay for a few years, but . . . I vegetate quite happily most of the time, but get all fired up about it every now and again, and worry that my mind will disintegrate entirely one of these days if I don't do *something* with it!

I think of you all the time, doing what I imagine you're doing in Tarbert (I looked it up on the map—I've never been to Scotland, but would love to go). I'm dying to hear from you.

Very much love and admiration,

Pat

(Postcard)

TARBERT
September 24, 1956

Very dear Pat,

Your three recent letters shame me that I wrote to you by boat. We're economizing in the damnedest places. But I was also sending a battered book I want you to know, and it just couldn't go by air.* Your concern is touching and helpful. I need it and shall doubtless continue to. It's gorgeous here, we're all well, radiant, in fact. But the work is devilishly hard. *Appreciate* being informed of contests, but *Observer* ones require a familiarity I can't make so briefly, I fear. I ADORE YOU for subscribing to the *Supplement* for me. As you'll see from the letter, we DO understand each other. We've got funds only to mid-January, but Hans counts on exhibits in Edinburgh soon, and he sells usually something. Prices here are encouragingly high. At this point, we're only worried for the fun of it. But it was a good idea, although as we knew, a lonely one. Reinhard is much company, but I would so love to see you! My loving thanks, Joyce

*Josephine Tey's *The Daughter of Time,* about Richard III, whose portrait had enchanted Joyce when she saw it in the National Portrait Gallery in London.

October 5, 1956

Dearest Pat,

Your several letters are so encouraging, so good that they surely serve as one badly needed spark plug at this point. It is so damn difficult! With the difficulty of course more moral than physical. I do seem to have rather little time. The housework takes a great deal, but I ask myself if I don't rather help it along that it leaves so little for what is infinitely more difficult, freedom to sit before a staring typewriter. I shall persevere to the limits of the year before I give up, and if I need to, I shall, with no yearnings or pretensions of being a bloody "writer" later. For if I can't do it now, heaven knows I never can, with more children, more social obligations, etc., etc. This year is a great big mirror, and by the end of it I shall see myself straight, which in itself is good, even if disappointing.

But it is very good that we are here. Hans is working most energetically, quite fruitfully. And you should know that he unquestionably is the one with significant talent in this family, and with a direction or a "line," as he calls it, that keeps things related, meaningful. Yesterday he worked twelve straight hours. When paintings are drying, he works on woodcuts; when he's physically tired from that, he draws. On October 22nd he'll go to Edinburgh to try to arrange an exhibit. We must make some money by the first of the coming year, or up and sail off.

My plans, which I do not articulate except to you, are to finish a book for Reinhard by his birthday (it goes well) and I hope a not too apologetic first novel near Christmas. Energetic plans? But at least the child book will get finished. I'm tormented by suspicions of my weaknesses, great ones, perhaps entirely obstructing ones. Ability to handle (because of a too weak memory) the subtleties of conversations. Poetry is the easiest for me because it demands less of memory and can be more subjective, and I cannot absent myself from the annoyingly personal. Hans is right in wanting me to abandon poetry for the year, but I don't think I can. For money-making purposes I'm working on various short stories, articles for the German-American magazine, and perhaps essays. Short prose sketches of life in Lebanon are printed this month in the *Middle East Forum,* with sketches by Hans. But as I say, and *fully* mean, it is my husband's work that demands interest. If I had known he was as gifted as he is, I might not have married him. I mean that to be understood and thought over. But I am learning from him, Pat, you cannot really imagine how much. Painting was a difficult art for me to feel—hardest of them all. He too has a glorious idea which has to be perfectly realized and if so could be not only successful, but necessary. But that too must wait to be told.

We're eating rather amazing things here, fish of all sorts, and yesterday, cormorant. Exquisite thick taste. Hans gathered mussels the other day, and they too were good, although I thought I could never greet another one after my year in Laval. We'll gather snails soon, too. I canned several bottles of plum and now blackberry jam. It grows cold, windy—wonderful silver-lit colors. Scotland is gorgeous. I must go, closing with much love and gladness too that you've begun work. *Supplement* arrived.

Joyce

TARBERT
October 12, 1956

My dear dear friend, compatriot, co-expatriate, classmate and soulmate!

Thinking of you again, imagining unrealistically you and family turning the bend of Pier Road, wheeling Christopher out to meet our Reinhard. How I do wish we could have one afternoon, one long evening that would take us into a night so late that we'd have to cook a great golluptious meal at about 4:30 A.M. We need that.

It must have seemed a long stretch of indifference before my ship-sent letter reached you. I hate doing it that way, stupid affair. So I'll send this off to let you know your letters are reaching me appreciatively, and helpfully. You're the only genuinely concerned correspondent I have any more. However, don't lose all faith; we are working.

It's just damn, damn hard. And slow. I find it rather difficult typewriting with Reinhard standing on my feet under the table, bumping his head underneath the machine with noise and discomfort. Well, what to do? My most alive thinking hours were always the morning ones, and I'm having no easy time trying to work well after he's in bed. The discipline isn't so hard. Night after night, I'm sitting here, but the spirit is not so helpful. It staggers out, and it sings off key. Realizing that we've already been in Tarbert as long as we were in Solingen, the winter seems a little space indeed, and money pressures mounting. Hans is depressed when he has to push aside the important things, trying to make a bit of profit. He says, "Better to do all sorts of tricky, easy, popular affairs than to push them [the ones that matter so much to him] down." "This is the one thing I didn't want to have to happen this year."

Well, we're doing a set of Christmas cards, too late surely, to respond to the *T. Lit. Supp.* advertisement for them. He'll do a set of landscapes in pen and watercolor of Scotland for postcards. We'll go on trying.

I'm reading only in French just now, but I'm studying daily on German, thinking that when we go to Salt Lake in May or April, I may try to pass the Ph.D. exams in both languages, for I'll probably never have them better. But who is fool enough to want a Ph.D., for heaven's sake???

All my best love,

Joyce

October 15, 1956

My very dearest friend,

I can only sympathize from afar (in more ways than geographically) about the difficulties of what you're doing there. I'm so proud just to know you two. It's wonderful that Hans is working hard and well. You've inspired me to take out old college books and old writing efforts and see if I can put my soul in order and do at least some short stories (or did I tell you this already?).

Christopher is coming along so sweetly. He's invented a new language, all growls, and when you growl at him, he growls right back. He walks all round his playpen now, holding on to the edge. Nine months is a lovely age. Every succeeding baby I like better than the one before.

And have you ever thought about coming out to Africa to a school or university teaching career, the two of you, when your Scottish funds run out? You get long leave in Europe every three years, have servants, freedom to raise your children and look after your husband and household with some degree of comfort. Especially if you're at a university, as you'd be in the capital, with a library and electricity, and rather more hint that there's a real outside world.

From the wilds I send you

My deepest love,

Pat

October 29, 1956

Very dear Pat!

You're so good to me. Not only because you're sending little unexpected gifts to the boy who is standing quite alone beside me, and because I'm very pleased you're his godmother, but because your letters always come on the right days. This shows true telepathic sympathy. I receive few letters these days.

I've been reading the Bible, at last. Tried to do it in both German and English, but I suspect I've given the German up. But it is magnificent in parts. Drama and sensuousness are probably the prime qualities of the Old Testament.

And speaking of the Old Testament, I must announce with pride that a woodcut concerning "Daniel's Dream" which Hans worked so hard upon and we printed into the "wee" hours won honorable mention and will be bought by the Victoria and Albert Museum after going on traveling exhibit throughout England. It doesn't pay enough to keep us through January, but I'm most pleased. Out of almost 400 entries, that's not so bad.

91

He leaves for Edinburgh Wednesday, the day after our second anniversary. He'll be gone about five days, trying to establish contact with professors and students in the academy there, hoping to arrange an exhibit. He's been working late into each night, trying to finish a good selection of paintings and drawings for showing purposes. It hurts me to see him put under this kind of pressure of *Having* to Exhibit, and in addition, *Having* to Sell. It's not a good atmosphere for his work. It's a great pity that we didn't receive the $200 bonus traditionally (except this lean year) given to staff.

A great rift of dissympathy separates my brother and me. It took him nine months to acknowledge our son, and in that letter he was much more excited about the pregnancy of his cats than the result of mine. He's become president of the California Cat Association—a fitting climax, I feel. Has very much the consciousness of an expatriate, but I think as much by determination as by genuine need. I mean, mentioning that New Yorkers have absolutely no connection with reality is a bit extenuated, isn't it??

How gorgeous it is here. I wish you could see it just now. Brilliantly clear, and equally cold. It's a radiant view we have. I've never lived in a lovelier one.

Reinhard is a much bigger eater than Christopher. He must weigh a good 24 pounds and he looks fat in his clothes, and perfect without them. But he is heavy to carry. His hair has not changed since the day he was born, lots, fine, and sweetly unruly.

But is it not rather bloody difficult, sticking to the ambition? The days flip by, really, and productivity always hides itself around the bend of another day. At least it moves slowly for me. If we find we have to leave in January, I'll have accomplished nothing but a few unsatisfactory beginnings. Relevance, consistency, FORM (in me first of all, and consequently in my offspring)—these are the questions.

I'm so enjoying the *Supplement.* A beautiful English is written there, isn't it? Well, you see, I'm supplanting my more demanding work by letter writing, and I'd better stop it. So, off I go. Do give Philip my best regards, and continue writing as you do.

My love as always,

Joyce

MAHALI
November 18, 1956

My ever more dearest friend,

Would you *believe* that your letter of September 15 sent by surface mail only just arrived last week? But it was good to get the description of your house and its accouterments. Your time there sounds *so* good. I hope it is productive of what you want. And I read *The Daughter of Time* immediately, and loved it. I shall go to see the picture in the National Portrait Gallery when I'm next in London —only 15 months from now, thank God. It seems sometimes as if I've been here a decade, not just a year and a half. I love it, but I get very lonely in spite of a wonderful marriage and my darling baby and all the social life in the world and more. They're nice people here, but dull in the extreme in so many ways. If only someone besides me *read* something! I've read too many Graham Greene novels, I guess, about people in the tropics worrying about the state of their souls and quoting Mauriac at each other. Never fear, they worry about the state of their booze cupboard and bank account, and quote Nevil Shute and Agatha Christie. Maybe I'm in the wrong colony? But I have a sinking feeling it's like that all over.

I'm enclosing snaps of us, house, and garden. Have you read any of this young brilliant French girl, Françoise Sagan's books? I have ordered a couple of them. Tell me what you think of her. And yet, by the sound of it, her people and context sound as silly and vacuous as I feel, in this terrible contemporary world of ours.

> Much love to you
> and Hans and Reinhard,
>
> *Pat*

TARBERT
November 26, 1956

Dear true Pat,

I should very much be working just now on Raggedy Andy, who is coming into being for Thursday's gathering, Reinhard's birthday. And wonderful packages have been coming anonymously from London with godmotherly suggestions hiding in them. Will you be disappointed to know that already he has worn the red sweater? And he found one of the Kiddicraft toys under our bed, but the other (how I love them!) remains in waiting. Your mindreading facilities are nothing short of weird. First the *T. Lit. Supp.* and then these! You're a dear and I love you truly. He'll adore the hammer, and will break everything he can find with it. Thank you so very much.

Your photos were very helpful for my imagining your life. I never expected such a wide, spacious and pleasant-looking house, for some reason. Yes, I have read both of Françoise Sagan's books, and I think they are splendid. You ordered them in French, I trust. I in no way found *Un Certain Sourire* an anticlimax, and the fact that I wept a little over it must prove something. She has a wonderful

93

economy and a brilliantly biting precision. As Mauriac said, "She's a little monster, whose literary genius shines through the first page of *Bonjour Tristesse.*" Yes, it is very good indeed—no campaigning, no championing, but a lot of truth, a lot of sadness.

Winter has come upon us here, with very short daylight hours; in fact I have the light on most of the time. I must go into town each day for food, largely because Reinhard champs so if he doesn't get the air. Today the west wind about blew us into Loch Fyne. Winter seabirds are coming too, and from about 11 P.M. on, the herons screech forebodingly along the wind. And snow was on the high hills this morning, up into the Highland mountains of Perth; I could see it. Still and all, I'm not so cold. We use layers of woolens, and a fire in the grate, and all is well.

Reinhard walks! Very sweetly. Tell me something about Philip's work there. Do you plan to go back to the States at all? Do you miss your mother very much? Will you live in England?

All my love and many thanks,

Joyce

MAHALI
December 5, 1956

My very dear friend,

It is so reassuring to keep getting your wonderful letters from that gentle land. You do know I envy you, don't you? Even the cold and the servantless existence and all. I *know* it will come to something worthwhile for both of you.

We chug along here, with the usual great preparations for Christmas, both at home for ourselves, and at the club for our little community. Plans for parties, cakes and puddings to be made, presents wrapped, decorations to be got up from something or other, all difficult here because of the lack of anything to buy, even the most basic of materials such as crepe paper! So we just have to use what is at hand and make it do. Challenging, anyhow.

You ask if I want to live back in the U.S. again—no, I don't think so. I've grown unaccustomed to much of what looms very important in American life, and Philip disliked it very much, his year interning there, though of course being poor in Los Angeles is hardly the most appropriate introduction to what is *good* about life there. We've thought off and on about perhaps going to live in Canada when we leave Tanganyika; it's close enough that I could go home once in a while, which I would very much like to do. The life, I think, is more ordered and, well, *politer* there than in the U.S.; but I don't honestly know where we'll be after

94

another tour out here, which we'll probably do, though we came out originally with the idea of doing only one tour. Philip then wanted the general experience before he specialized in whatever he later decided to do; at the moment it looks like surgery. I'll be doing the same more or less wherever we live, staying home and looking after babies and husband. But I would so very much like to go back to college and get my degree. I can't see how I can ever do it, at least before I'm 45! But if we were living in North America, I could at least afford correspondence courses, which it turns out I can't from here.

I miss my mother and my family off and on, sometimes quite painfully, but it's all in the memory, rather than being a desire to share their present life, simply because I don't know what their present life is. I feel more and more distant and estranged from those far shores of the lovely Pacific. So, unlike you, I have not that pull either. I would like Christopher to grow up knowing my side of the family though. They are nice people—open, warm-hearted, generous, eccentric. Philip disapproves of the lot, I know, though he says (and said, while we lived there) very little, because they are unambitious, uneducated, very ordinary in his eyes. But they are a hell of a lot of fun and full of love, qualities I miss exceedingly amongst the staid and dull English. When I think about it all, that is, which isn't very often.

I haven't drunk so much nor so regularly since I left college and got married. What a lot of liquor we all manage to put away at home parties and at the club! You'd disapprove thoroughly of me, I'm sure. But it's very boring to stay sober till 5 A.M. when Philip is raring to go and everyone else is falling down drunk.

This is a very uninspired letter, and doesn't look like improving, so I'll try again in a few days. Onwards to glory, O Bard of Tarbert!

Your loving disintegrating friend,
the Club Drunk,

Pat

TARBERT
December 9, 1956

Dear Pat,

Your letters are assuredly the best company I have; otherwise the unobtrusive Scottish friendliness leaves us quite alone. We spend no time at all with others; however, we are invited for Christmas dinner next door, which is all well and good since we couldn't have much of a feast here. We're not minding the utter simplicity of our lives here. Simple food doesn't bother us. But we could sometimes scream at each other or hit these leaking walls for lack of cigarettes,

95

and oh! for some cheap red wine! Those are about our only complaints. The loneliness fits like a glove these days, and we anticipate the difficulty will be adjusting to the other extreme—people, cars, telephones, stupid questions, central heating, routine, speed, etc. For coming to this calm was no jar at all. The above answers your solicitous suggestions about our coming to Africa, even though put half in jest. No, the time has come for people, the right people, conversations about his craft after four years without it, exhibitions, and the intense exchanges of other artists (which I must admit anticipating with a little fear).

You'll be ashamed of me, but I cannot but feel my own jibing inadequacies, and now that I've come to know Hans's ways, the kind of women who appeal to him and who find him irresistible, I sometimes have unworthy and shameful fears in advance. Because, oh Pat, I can help him so little—no truly European consciousness, no ability to follow along in his language, so little sensibility (I sometimes feel), about his difficult art. It's a hell of a hard, but a thrilling, effort, keeping up. For I've never dealt with anyone so compelled NOT by ambition or talent alone, but by the spiritual tenor of his endeavoring, to reach some height. And I shall not be surprised if he becomes known. And with that, I shall not be surprised if I fail to be enough. Strange, I know, but a foreboding. But, by God and all my moments of love and integrity, I'll try. I do love him, you know, and increasingly, heatedly lust for him. He's more and more attractive to me, and I sometimes am afraid.

We are thinking of sailing now on May 8th on the maiden voyage of the *Statendam*—spending Easter in Germany, a week in Berlin, and my birthday in Salt Lake. The time is speeding *so* here.

When do you plan for Christmas? Do have a merry one, and write me about it *all*.

My love always,

Joyce

MAHALI
December 19, 1956

Dearest friend Joyce,

I hope you like all the bits and pieces for Christmas, especially a last minute inspiration straight out of a nineteenth century novel.

I was rather alarmed and disturbed at what you wrote about your feelings regarding Hans. Jealousy would be a horrible consuming fire to live with, I think. It's an emotion that, oddly enough, is foreign to me. I've always felt that I am what I am, and if men don't like me for exactly what I am, then they can jolly well lump it, and that extends itself to the feeling that if they prefer someone else to me, then welcome to her. (I don't think I'm particularly arrogant about my very ordinary looks or my charms; I just feel—to hell with them, if that's what they want.)

And as regards Philip I almost sometimes wish he were more attractive to other women. I think it might spice him up a bit for me, though I hasten to assure you that all is well between us. But much of the time our feelings for each other seem more like those of good friends or of brother and sister together, rather than a romantic husband and wife. It's somehow all outside the realm of feeling adequate or inadequate for him or for any of the men I've loved. Our relationship is one thing; what more they might want out of life or other women they'll just have to cope with in their own way, as I do with wishing he could dance or that we could communicate more with each other. Do you think that all this cool assurance is a sign either that I'm insufferably vain, or that I live in a fool's paradise? Or more probably, that I perhaps have never loved anyone enough in that wild passionate way that you seem to feel for Hans? Maybe I'm destined to go through life without ever having known that. What Philip and I have is certainly very different, but then it feels safer and more secure and comfortable than what you are going through—and have gone through since just after your marriage, if memory serves me right. On sober reflection, I even would go so far as to say that I am perhaps less a whole woman than you because these feelings have never really been stirred in me beyond those of a brief infatuation.

But I have not the slightest desire to have an affair, to look for that kind of love, to disturb my pleasant life. I admire Philip in his medical work so very much. Something deep inside me does indeed thrill at the way he handles sick people and surgery and the almost magical paraphernalia of his profession. It is the best part of him, his devotion to his craft and his skill at it. I don't honestly believe Philip thinks about other women, to tell you the truth. Neither of us is at heart a particularly sensual person; and although my grandmother always told me to steer clear of men who couldn't dance, because they were invariably lousy lovers, I guess there are other things in life to balance it out. I suppose this might be an appropriate place to tell you *very secretly* that the most satisfying sensual experience I've ever had in all my life was breast-feeding Christopher, surpassing by far any sexual encounters I've known!!

I have written rather a lot of nonsense all about dull old unjealous me, instead of sending you sympathy for what must be the very real pain you go through when you contemplate this possibility of seeing Hans go to other women. *How* could he love another more than you, his wife, his supporter, the mother of his son? And you don't seem to be talking about the trivial seven year itch ahead of us all, perhaps, but about a more profound need on his part than you feel you fill. Let me ask you if he fills all yours? Of course that still doesn't solve the problem, I know. Let me know how all this transpires as time goes on.

So you leave next May. Will you have a slim volume of poems completed and ready for publication? And Hans a few crates of paintings ready for a one man show in the U.S.? I wonder where you'll settle in that strange frantic land?

I must go pour more brandy on my twenty pounds of Christmas cake ("Kilisimasi keki," in Swahili, according to my cook). I got carried away. We'll be eating it until Easter. I should have sent you some of it.

> But you have all my love
> and best Christmas wishes,
>
> *Pat*

TARBERT
December 21, 1956
And a very Merry Christmas!!

Dear Pat,

But would you like to hear the damnedest? They've kicked us out! And my love affair with things Anglo-Saxon has died a cruel death. The Home Office has sent us two letters now, stating that we must have left Britain by January 5th, so we have but two more weeks of herons and heaths and fishing boats and our lovely Loch, of things Scottish, of things British, of things European!

We've not a penny, as you know, and our half-time here has hardly given us time to make much, and we've little choice but S.L.C., where loving parents await us anxiously, having prepared space for their unwanted vagrants. We'll of course seek a teaching position, but until then we'll try to carry on at home in S.L.C. "Oh, cruel fate!" We're awfully embittered, seeing no justifiable reason for not wanting us. Times are hard here, true, but we're not stealing anything and nobody seems dying to live in Glendarroch. It's bitter, all right. We've loved it so. But—did we love it enough? We'll have to go back to Germany for farewells, rather long-term ones, and we'll probably sail from Amsterdam.

God, back into that cauldron of personalities. Oh! I'll write more later.

> All love,
>
> *Joyce*

December 27, 1956

Very, very dear friends,

I felt a little like Bob Cratchit and family receiving such an apparently anonymous turkey at just the magical time, but when that little naked African Fritz scowled out at me from the enclosed card, I knew that it had flown from the good spirits in Mahali. It came at the opportune moment when we were trying to decide between macaroni and potatopuffer, and we were delighted, down to the very broth that is left for today. Hans wants me very specifically to thank you for him, and he said he thought it was one of the most thoughtful and original gifts he'd ever received. Anyway, it was very like you, and I loved it all the more therefore.

Mother sent us a Christmas packet all full of goodies and games and stuffed animals and little trousers. Reinhard's creatures form quite a pompous list now. Acquiescing to my husband's Christmas convictions, we celebrated Christmas Eve, lit the candle-lit tree that evening, and went into our sweetly festive Christmas room. Hans is marvelous for doing everything with very little. It was a radiant, happy scene. We read the Gospel, and listened tear-eyed to many many bells, to the bells of Jerusalem where Reinhard was conceived, and where guards pace the Mount of Olives, which had been patched red with anemones when we were there. Bells from everywhere, and it made a joyous Christmas.

Reinhard too had his bell, the only gift we gave him, a brass one, and after he stopped trying to eat the clapper, and stopped muffling it, he swaggered up and down the room being our local town crier. Christmas night it snowed, deeply for this water-washed town. The mountains across the Loch are brightly white right to the water, and the impression is most arctic. A flutter kept staggering across the window that night, and we opened the snow-rimmed window to find a crippled blackbird. She joined the party, sitting on our host's Christmas tree, flying urgently around sometimes, leaving her marks.

You ask what we'll do. We don't know. We have no money, so we'll naturally hop out to S.L.C., living with parents until we have work. They'll be delighted and we'll enjoy it too, if it's not too long, and if Hans can sell enough for cigarettes. I'll write more when we know. Many thanks for the pounds too. A great help. And a happy New Year to you both, to you all three.

Our love,

Joyce

Dear Pat,

A very hasty note. We're leaving Monday for Solingen. With the help of an M.P., Sir Duncan McCallum of Argyll, we won our case, and the extension, but too late. The Hohlweins had already rented a flat for us refugees. We'll stay there till April 1st. Write to us there.

Now, if you receive anything from us, *please open carefully.* More later. A happy New Year, with all love from us. (But we hate leaving.)

Joyce

PART FOUR

JANUARY 1957–FEBRUARY 1958

*Perhaps the real challenge
is to stick at life
in all its boring routine*

January 19, 1957

Dearest friend, departed from Scotland,

Well, how very depressing, the ghastly old Home Office making it such an impossible struggle for you to stay on in your beloved Tarbert. I am so very sorry, and hereby apologize on behalf of H.M.G. for your unplanned hasty departure. Was it *very* difficult to leave the loch and the hills and the heather? I should imagine it was most painful, your love for it came through so strongly in your letters, even in your few months there.

One of your pilgrimage places will be with us here, at least—the woodcut of minarets of Beirut (tell me if I'm right) arrived, and we love its simple lines and wonderful vertical thrust. Thanks so very much from both of us. We are having it properly framed in Dar.

Christmas, New Year's, Christopher's first and my 26th birthdays have all come and gone since last I wrote you. We had an overfull social and boozy holiday season. I merely survived from one spectacular hangover to the next. Philip's mother was here, and she disapproves of women drinking at all, so I was under a cloud of disgrace most of the time. It was like college days again, milk and codeine before the party, to keep me alive the next day. I really haven't done any of this since before Philip and I were married.

Christopher is in a lovely stage now, talking all the time—the usual mama and dada, and he also sings lalala when I do. He and our Alsatian, Brando, get on very well together. Brando gets fierce and growls and pretends to gnaw on Christopher's leg, and Christopher rolls all over crowing and laughing; he says,

103

"Dortle, dortle!" for doggy, doggy, whenever Brando hoves in sight. I expect he's only half the size of your Reinhard, but though he's growing slowly, it's steadily and healthily. He's never sick, except for getting a bit weepy with teething. He's a *toto mzuri sana,* a very good child. The hot season is with us again, to my great surprise. Weather is like having a baby; you forget the ghastliness of it until it takes hold of you each time. I actually do put blotters under my wrist as I write, just like Scobie in *Heart of the Matter!*

Well, poor dear souls, I hope you are surviving and looking forward to good things, there in Solingen am Rhein. Philip sends his sympathy too.

Very much love and salaams from here,

Pat

P.S. Have you read this astounding new book by a very young man, Colin Wilson, *The Outsider?* It's quite an extraordinary synthesis of more books than I'd have believed it possible to read in a whole lifetime.

SOLINGEN
January 29, 1957

Dear friend,

Your good letter came today. Your letters are always good, always helpful and invigorating. The only sad reaction they evoke is wanting to be with you, to talk to you as I seem unable to talk to anyone else I know. Writing to you has its parallel sadness in limitation. There is so very much I should like to tell to YOU, so many pages' worth of my daily emotions, my conflicts, and difficulties, my consciousness of becoming a European, and of how this will alarm and befuddle my loving American parents, of my joys and sense of ineptness with motherhood and wifeliness, of politics and the sense of acuteness the whole Middle Eastern neurosis has created in us, of hairdos and other feminine non-sense, of cooking and cuisines, of the remembrance of things past, of Hans's work, his dedication, convictions, and his *agony* in his work, of my inability to help him, of my fears that I never will be enough for him. Of what I expect or fear about our going "home?" So much, so much.

But I should try to pick up some of what you mention. We left Tarbert tearfully, even though we won the decision and the ubiquitous "obedient servant" reversed the Home Office ultimatum. We left because by the time we knew we could stay, there had been such an intricate crisis, crossings of anticipation and depression and uncertainty and family kindnesses, that we gave up. Since in the meantime the Hohlweins had found and prepared an apartment (bombed and wretched) next to theirs, and my parents also had bought a little bed and all whatnots in the eventuality of our coming quickly.

104

So here we are back in industrial Solingen, very far from our herons and high tides and little fishing boats with the men in yellow mackintoshes, like lamps against the night. Very far indeed. But such gorgeous months as they were, we hope to carry in our bodies as well as our hearts a good time.

We eat at Mutti's table and I seem to spend most of my time carrying things (diapers, brooms, soap, potty, shirts, vacuum cleaner, hot water bottles) back and forth and back and forth, Reinhard under the other arm. This is, however, economical and we can manage here on about $25 a month. Hans is continuing to work hard, and I'm finding it goddam difficult with this little boy around.

We shall sail April 10th from Bremerhaven on the *United States.* Funny though, about our going, in a way it seems so foolish and so devious, so uncontributive to the "straight line" toward the career he seeks. Because we do not intend to live in America, and as H. says, "A success in New York or anywhere there wouldn't mean so much to me as it would were it Hamburg or Berlin or Paris." Yes, in some ways, it seems foolish.

If we are lucky—i.e., a good job, good exhibitions, perhaps a chance to save some dollars—*then* it will have proved to be good. But if we strand uselessly in some Middletown, then it will have proved worse than useless. If it weren't for the overwhelmingly *generous* patience of my most loving parents, I doubt we would go at all. I too have little longing for things American, even for people American. However, Salt Lake is in no sense unreal to me. My entire life, after all, was spent there, and I don't think one's childhood assumes this unreality you speak of, and I know so well, from other times and places. However, I have changed so (at least for Mother—I wouldn't have for you); I can well imagine Mother asking me in our first days there, "Joyce, are you happy?" "Does he love you?"—questions that are simply *unanswerable* in her terms.

The depressions I've gone through in the last two years have been the hardest but the most instructive I've ever known. But it has knocked my self-esteem down just about to nil. And living with an artist (and this I dare say, that whether great or small, Hans is at least a true one) demands an expense of spirit and patience and sacrifice and love such as makes me admire all the women who have done it well, done it so as to help and not hinder their men. This is what I want, much more now, even than writing for myself, to nourish a marriage and home such as will give him the sustenance he needs. It must be very quietly done, with much constant and searching attention to the details of daily living; practical must it be and rooted in the exigencies of *things* themselves, not remote and transcended, but physically created. With this in mind, the eight months that stretch before us homeless seem to me interminable. I have come to ache for our own place, with things no longer borrowed. We both want our proper "foyer," created and nourished by all that we can give to it.

No, I've not read *The Outsider,* nor have I even heard of it, but I shall love to read it. I've read so little of fiction lately, but have been submerging in the magnificent French of Elie Faure's *L'Esprit du Forme,* a history of art which is neither aesthetics nor pure criticism, but which opens a whole new world to me.

I'm going mad trying to iron in Mutti's kitchen all of Hans's shirts. Here you will see what a slovenly little coward I am, as I ask you for a *big* favor. Of all the grinds and feminine curses in this world, to me ironing is the bugaboo of the lot. I simply hate it! I'd scrub five floors twice before I'd iron shirts. Now, I want to ask you to help me pamper this failing. You seem to have connections with English stores that I don't. For eight months now I've wanted to buy Hans SOME TERN NON IRON POPLIN SHIRTS, but have failed at each turn in securing them. Is it possible that you would be angel enough to order three of them for me to be sent here??? Size (neck) 15½, colors: 1, white, 2, blue, 3, beige or yellow (one of each). I'll send you the money. One of the reasons I want to be able to work later is to be able to pay someone to do the ironing for me.

Best greetings to Philip!!

Your lazy, loving friend,

Joyce

MAHALI
February 20, 1957

My dearest Joyce,

I enclose some pictures of us all with very African backdrops, to cheer you up. I especially love the one of Christopher in his safari bath in the middle of the rain forest. I think I wrote to you about going up to this very hard-to-reach isolated place once before when I was pregnant. We had a glorious time and all the ladies and children I'd met there 16 or 18 months ago came to call (at least I'm supposing they were the same ones!) and had hysterics over Christopher. It was very amusing because they were fascinated with his plump little nude body, especially his genitals. Apparently some Africans believe that Europeans, pale as they are on the places that show, with clothes on, are really "normal" in their private parts and have black penises and testicles!

Your life sounds nothing short of grim there in Solingen; my heart goes out to you, and I feel guilty here in my mindless lotus-eating existence. Especially do I feel guilty over not being completely contented all of the time, as I ought to be, but no doubt it's end-of-tourishness setting in early. I wish we still had our long driving safari back to London to look forward to, but our unpopular passports would never get us through a single Arab country. Your days sound very much all work and no play. Of course I'll send the shirts for you; I've already ordered them from Harrods on our account, and they should be on their way to you now. I hope they relieve the ironing burden somewhat.

Isn't it odd what parts of housework and domesticity drive different people

106

round the bend? You say you'd rather scrub floors than iron. With me it's exactly the opposite. I've never minded ironing or washing or making beds, even dishes, but I simply loathe floors and scrubbing woodwork and doing ovens and filthy pots. It's *dirt* I can't stand. I don't mind in the least (no, that's a lie; the whole thing is a crashing bore from beginning to end—I mean, *I mind least*) things that are clean to begin with, things that don't make me feel dirty and grubby merely handling them. And there's a kind of dopey aesthetic pleasure to the damp wrinkled mess, steaming all out fresh and stiff and white and folded and tidy under one's hands. It's totally mindless and it immobilizes one too, so that I can let my mind wander and make up stories and recite poetry or learn lists of French irregular verbs or have fantasy dialogues with friends real and imaginary. Somehow on hands and knees pushing a soapy brush back and forth over a filthy floor, my mind won't work in that independent way, and I have unfond memories of gritting my teeth, with my hair falling in my eyes, just trying to get through it as quickly as possible. This is a lot of the reason that I basically still don't like the act of gardening itself, the dirt and grubbiness, though I quite like the results. That's another thing that bothers me about cleaning dirty things; I start climbing the walls if they start getting the tiniest bit mucky again, but I oddly don't mind Philip wearing his freshly ironed shirts.

I've always had a yen to live in a huge sophisticated shiny modern apartment with floor to ceiling drapes and concealed lighting and potted palms and spotlessly shining floors that one's heels click on, where one can be dressed in light filmy clothes that never get mussed or dirty, and sit down and play the grand piano. Ah me. This is a good life in its way (and I sure as hell don't have to iron or scrub floors, etc., so all my preferences are something in the way of being academic, until we leave Africa, anyway), but it isn't spotless. And yet I'm so lazy that on my own I was a pretty awful housekeeper. It would appear that one's own psyche never quite measures up to the demands of one's fantasies. What a long digression about ironing! But I sympathize heartily, thinking of the piles and piles of it all there must be.

Your depressions worry me. What do you think the reason for them can be? Could it be a long sort of postnatal depression, that I've read of women having? But you imply it's been going on almost since you married, and that it seems to have much to do with wanting so badly to make a good home for Hans. That I *can* sympathize with and more or less understand, for I too was seized with all kinds of nest-making (and beautifying) impulses—not so much the first year, though I did a lot of house (apartment, rather) painting and put posters up all over the dilapidated kitchen (travel posters are free) and made mobiles and just generally had a bash at trying to make our surroundings a little less slummy and more attractive than they were in that horrible two-room apartment in Los Angeles. But I think you mean more than just surroundings themselves, don't you? I'm referring to a sort of pleasant polished everyday ritual of meals at a certain hour and good food and wine—and here amongst the British, I'd of course add teatime—and gracious entertaining and looking as charming and attractive as one can; sewing for oneself, doing needlework for pretty things for the house —that kind of thing?

I've certainly thrown myself wholeheartedly into all of that and I love it. It lacks any kind of intellectual challenge, of course, and at my level (no murals, no self-made sculptures, etc.) even an artistic challenge isn't really there, but perhaps the real challenge is to stick at it all in all its occasionally boring routine, wouldn't you think? Of course you've scarcely had a chance as yet to test boredom in my way; you've been working, you were ill a long time, living in tiny difficult places, without a staff of servants as I've had out here. But I've vowed to myself that wherever we go to live after Africa, I'll keep up the same kinds of standards I've come to out here. I feel I owe it to Philip and Christopher and the baby that I want after we come back from leave. This business of setting high standards and keeping to them probably isn't such a sweat or new business to you as it's been to me. I had no education in living like this; we all just growed, like Topsy, in my family, every which way, higgledy piggledy, and I had to be on a sharp lookout to pick up the right signals from my surroundings, like those precious years in the convent boarding school, girl friends' (and boy friends') homes and families, even people's behavior and demeanor in the restaurants of my hash-slinging days. That's all a long way behind me now and I think I'm living up to what Philip has a right to expect of me, and I am determined to continue to do so. As you say, it's more important than writing, or anything else. I hardly ever any more wonder what it would have been like to have been an opera singer or a foreign correspondent or the first woman on an Everest expedition or (if World War II were still going on) a woman ferry pilot.

I had a few depressed months after Christopher was born, when he was three or four months old, but it was more a feeling that I was tied down to hourly schedules and couldn't do anything on an impulse any more, for the rest of my life, as far as I could see, but that went away. I don't think yours sounds at all the same. Does Hans seem to demand of you, I mean straight out, in so many words, more than you feel you are able to give? What is it that he wants? Or that you want to give? You never speak of missing the privacy of being single. Do you? I do, still, very much so, from time to time, but I'm learning to make do with what time alone I can get.

Pip, pip, old thing; you'll be off pretty soon somewhere in Europe or the U.S., and things will look up when you've your own place again and a more settled existence, I'm sure.

> Much love, my heart is with you,
> sweating over the filthy old
> ironing board,
>
> *Pat*

March 16, 1957

Dear friend,

The last weeks have been so troubled with the hecticities (coined) of visa securing that I've scarcely managed letters to anyone. After pounding the Frankfurter Embassy on the head with cables, telephone calls and letters, they finally took a personal interest in Hans's case, stopped insisting that we secure his inaccessible birth certificate in the original (from the East Zone) and altogether are being more cooperative. So it looks as if we'll make it, and be able to accept our passage on the 10th. So much the better.

The East Zone is clamping down ferociously again—letters censored like mad, touring made impossible. My two beautiful sisters-in-law were counting on going to Leipzig with their choir and very suddenly yesterday came the official Soviet refusal. It all looks rather bad.

I was so delighted with the pictures of you and Christopher and Philip. But God, it makes me want to be with you so very much. The picture of Christopher in the safari bathtub is perfect. Where our lives have brought us! We'll be in Salt Lake about the 25th of April, so from then on write us at home. Excuse this paltry letter, but all is fairly rushed just now. I thank you *so* in advance for the shirts. They've not yet arrived, but probably shall soon. Please write.

My love always,

Joyce

March 28, 1957

Dearest faraway friend,

One last letter to Solingen, to catch you before you sail away westward ho. You must be sick of packing and unpacking. Did those Harrods shirts arrive to save you a bit of work? And did Colin Wilson's *The Outsider?*

It's hard to imagine you and your wee family descending into the vortex of your girlhood, Hans for instance driving by your old high school. Will you give him a guided tour? Is he interested in that kind of thing? Philip never was, I feel, though he was always exquisitely polite as I was gushing through a Californian's version of the remembrance of things past. I'll think of you a lot in a month when you'll be back in the Rockies. It's funny, the places where people come from, one's home town, where one is a native of, and where and in what circumstances one ends up feeling "at home." You, I think, are far more bound by innumerable

109

ties to Salt Lake and the home of your parents than ever I can be to L.A. I went to thirteen schools before I ever graduated from high school! I never was a cheerleader or had any extracurricular activities, because I was always working. I didn't know a single sport except swimming; I scarcely even dated until after I graduated—no time for it. My family moved all the time, from one little pastel bungalow to another; yours stayed (unbelievably, to me) in the same house from the time you were born. And yet you and I have both ended up with the same determination to be good wives and mothers and make fine homes for our families. Beginnings *don't* seem to matter all that much then, do they? I wonder what it was that took such different material as the two of us and turned out pretty much the same product? (Do I hear a voice from the convent whispering, "God, in His infinite wisdom . . ."?) Who knows?

I wonder is Reinhard playing as nicely with his dozen beakers that nest inside each other as Christopher is now? With much impatience I restrained myself from showing him how to do it, and he's eventually found out for himself, as he was supposed to do, and sits in his playpen solemnly and carefully fitting them all in, one at a time. He's very brown, has lovely golden hair that curls over his head, dark brown, almost black, eyes, a charming mouth, small and well shaped.

Philip is studying hard for his Swahili exam, which all government officials have to take during their first two years. I've belatedly decided to get into the act and to learn it properly, irregular verbs, noun classes (eight of them!) and all. So, as civilians, or whatever we non-officials may be called, may take it at their own expense, I thought I'd study harder and more regularly with a well-defined goal in sight. I'll take my exam in September when they give them again. I couldn't be ready for this one.

I keep very busy with a variety of silly, mostly boring things; the Red Cross, being Lady House Member for the club (arranging flowers and ordering the barboy around), organizing tennis tournaments, gathering up everyone's tatty old worn-out clothes for the old-clothes auction at the Red Cross Fête in August. The Africans snatch up absolutely anything in the way of used clothes, poor ragged souls, and I'd feel like hell selling them those dregs of our wardrobes and trunks, but at least the money goes back to them again through the Red Cross. New blankets for the hospital, toys for children so unfortunate as to be there, soap for baths. Maybe even a transistor radio or two if the fête makes enough money this year. Can you imagine Philip's medical budget being too skimpy to cover these things? It's a terribly poor country; life is truly cut down to the bone and marrow of survival for the African. Half the time I feel guilty about eating different kinds of food three meals a day (four, if you count tea), about wearing different kinds of clothing for daytime, parties, tennis, all of them without rips or worn spots, about having so many books. The other half I live my own life and simply don't think about it. I think we are doing a good thing by being here though. I wonder if I'll ever get to the point where I simply cease to *see* Africa around me as so many old Africa hands seem to do?

110

Anyhow, farewell to Europe for you, bon voyage from me. Keep heart! It can't be worse than Solingen. Write from Salt Lake when you have time.

So much love,

Pat

April 26, 1957

Dearest Joyce,

I hope your long long journey was pleasant and not too wearing with Reinhard and all. I have been trying and trying to imagine your thoughts and emotions on being home again. I know, you *are* the same person, after all, but so radically altered you must be, as hardly to fit into your S.L. niche. A place, a geographical place, I mean, only has bits and pieces added and taken away, like little edges of a jigsaw puzzle, all of which can be gossiped away in a day or two, but to attempt to convey your soul's atmosphere, the fragments of everywhere that you've lived in that you carry about with you forever now—oh, does it all seem quite hopelessly impossible or has the ease of it surprised you? I'm longing to hear your first impressions of the home that you're not supposed to be able to come to again.

Philip has turned virulently anti-American, more so than ever I've known him to be before. I don't think there's a remote possibility of us ever coming back there to live, he dislikes it so much, although Canada is still number one, after we leave here. Self-government is definitely on its way, how long till, no one knows. We personally think very soon, within five to ten years, if the signs are anything to go by. But we are hooted down at the club when we say this. I just cannot imagine self government here. Ah well, it will all happen anyhow, in its own good time.

Do, do write me as long and cursive a letter as you can re: returns and remembrances. My love to your M. and F., husband and son, and any friends I may once have had,

Pat

111

(Home?)
May 6, 1957

Very dear Pat,

Many fast days have flipped memorywards since I have written. I don't like the long intervals between our letters. I write only scatteredly. Reinhard is in a most demanding stage. His span of attention is about five minutes on anything and my inventiveness is run low by the end of a day. The evenings are still given to family queries and conversations, and if I write to you at all, it must be with this stick of dynamite sizzling around me. So you'll understand any lack of cohesion or coherence.

Don't you think it's about time for us both to add to the population again? I'm not pregnant, but I'd rather like to be. It seems much the best age for Reinhard's brother to be begun and just as reasonable to be tied down with two as one. I literally cannot even read *Life* magazine until he's in bed, so I might just as well have my hands really full. Only two considerations intervene: the cost of having a baby in America without at least the Blue Cross for ten preceding months, and the fact that until this son is trained, can mount steps and feed himself, it would seem extra difficult. Anyway, this is speculation. And our reactions to America are no longer so.

We're here already, and both feeling utterly stranded. Hans says that for the first time in his life, he feels *utterly* at a loss, not knowing where he is.

Our first impressions were good. Coming into New York at the first daylight, following the shifting, almost corporeal blue shadows of the skyscrapers over ships and tugs and bay, was beautiful, unforgettable. And we had a great streak of luck in reunioning with all the people we would have cared to.

———————⇒ ⊱———————

Hurrah! Your letter just came; so good to hear! Oh, Pat, how good it *is* to hear from someone who knows—not "understands" but existentially KNOWS. Thank God for you! Yes, so far it is, aptly put, "hopelessly impossible." We feel absolutely outside the rush and the "fast chaos" we went to Scotland to avoid. Oh—oh—oh—oh—already, after six days, we want only to be alone, to avoid TV and its commercials and the people running around the set and shouting splintered tidbits about the "Ten Commandments" or a parallel waste. Fight, oh help me fight, Pat, cynicism and the sense of superiority. Distance, detachment, is inevitable and all right, superiority cannot be avoided, but oh, how all I have learned these last valuable years rejects what I meet, which equals, I'm sure, what I was. I need you. We would comprehend, at a glance.

One of the most overriding impressions is what Hans calls "a curious *lack* of self-respect." In European terms, this is assuredly valid. The American women smirk and criticize sloppy French women, but Pat, the way the quantities of wives

112

and mothers here run around in jeans and pin curls and bulges certainly gives us the right to insist on abstention. To Hans it is particularly strange to see the "demonstrativeness" of our social life here! The good silver and good china are brought out only when guests come. The women dress up with great care only when they're going to town. In the terms of our future life, this is inversion, the first thing being to establish the home spirit as the center of concern. And although this is not a peculiarly national trait, after our calmer German life, things do seem hectic here, nervous, and worst of all, *noisy*. Radio upon TV, conversation above music, one superstructure of noise upon the other. Perhaps it is just that we miss our herons of Glendarroch.

And being so badly in debt as we are does *not* help. Nor does Hans like most modern American painting, still piping on the *old* tune of "non-objectivism." We just need ourselves, solitude, long nights of love, and a few *natural* sounds. Living without water nearby will be hard. Perhaps, too, another baby. You can perhaps imagine how much I send my love, to you *all*.

Joyce

MAHALI
May 28, 1957

Dearest Returned Native,

Yesterday we were married four years. Is not life good? Four years ago today we were hitchhiking between Washington and the Pennsylvania Turnpike, getting (or trying to get) used to each other's real, as opposed to epistolary, selves. *How* a long correspondence without a previous long, stable and thorough knowledge of the other can—well, not exactly mislead one—but put garlic in the dressing perhaps, or substitute quite ridiculous (on better acquaintance) orchids for perfectly adequate and really quite stimulating daisies! Anyhow, we were just back from a horrid safari full of African itch, flu, screaming baby, drunken servant, howling bitterly cold (to us thin-blooded creatures) wind, Primus stove which wouldn't work, etc., and came back a day early to find a filthy house, last week's ashtrays not yet emptied, and of course, no boys. But flu or no, we *must* have an anniversary dinner, Philip having cleverly shot a bustard (lovely dark meat), so I whipped up (through sneezes and nose-blowings) eggs mayonnaise, roast bustard and potatoes, peas, and chocolate ice cream (from a weird tinned powder). And we had white Chianti properly chilled. All nice and cozy.

Now isn't it odd that you should bring up the subject of planned parenthood (for the betterment of humanity), just as my not really so ghastly suspicions are crystallizing? Yes—and due on Christopher's next birthday, January 5th! Of

113

course it means the end of Norway and skiing, and we must now defer leave for a month. Our latest plans are to fly from Dar to London with new six weeks old babe the end of February, find flat soonest, settle in, get (please God, let it be financially possible) part-time nanny, or go all Yank and swap baby-sitting services with opposite colonial number also on leave, if I can find one. Course Philip is taking ends on July 31st, then we shall go to St. Tropez or La Ciotat or perhaps Mallorca, rent cheapest cooking, washing, sleeping accommodation for a month, then Paris for September if we're all holding up financially and Mme. Besombes can dig up a trundle bed for Christopher in the old Hotel Normandie and doesn't mind strings of diapers across the room and me cooking on a Primus. Then we will catch the London–Cape Town mail ship back in October with our new Peugeot station wagon on board and drive back up here from Cape Town. But we have made and broken so many plans, heaven only knows.

I am enclosing a few pounds. If you very much wouldn't mind, I should so love to have a new smock or two. I've worn all my others through two pregnancies now and am sick at the sight of them. Something fairly bare and sleeveless (my smocking season will again be through the terrific heat of the pre-rains), and violently American colorful. They must be eminently washable for our half-witted dhobi, size 10. Thank you, dear Joyce. English maternity fashions are too billowy and coy and Victorian printly to be true.

Your letter filled me with love for you and a longing to be there. But how magically beautiful S.L. must be now in May. Have you taken Hans round to all your old haunts? Has he said much of his impressions of the U. and its inhabitants? He must love the mountains and the cleanliness, at any rate. Your notes on noise filled me with apprehension, we who don't even have a radio, haven't had one since we left the States. I've grown to love the creative quietness of growth in Africa. But London's noises at least are barrow boys and organ grinders and funny tin-horned cars, all meaningful somehow. Keep me posted.

> All my best Maytime love
> to you and yours,
>> *Pat*

SALT LAKE CITY
June 12, 1957

My most liebe and productive Pat,

First of all, before I forget, the Harrods shirts *did* arrive, much to my joy and satisfaction and gratitude, before we left Solingen. And now on to more important things.

An amusing irony, which nervously skirted panic, and, we feared, tragedy. Hans-Jurgen Hohlwein, scoffer of psychoanalytics, and the sort of tranquillity

114

available in capsule form, has just been pronounced by a medical jury as guilty of possessing a NEUROSIS, a legitimate one, capable of causing terrific chest cramps and the fear in all of us of something dreadful and malignant, but I think he just needs a bank account—that and a little insularity. That is why he set off Monday for the Chicago area, trying to convince deans and other responsibles that he is still better than the recommendations say. Shipping off cartloads of pleadings to anonymous department heads is worse than futile, and it would make anyone substantially neurotic, waiting for their blank answers. So I'm a straw widow for the first time, and I wonder how I'll be, manless. If it doesn't kill me, it'll be great for my character.

Your letters are such a wonderful kind of company; please keep them coming often. I almost envy you being pregnant again, but I guess logic should keep Reinhard's brother waiting. I do hope you don't have wretched sickness throughout it, and I hope you're happy about it.

Your idea of sharing a cottage in '58 is exquisite, truly. Give us a chance to try. I don't know how good we'll be on this side of the ocean for long.

I'm simply streaking through this letter to try and finally finish it before Reinhard's nap is over; it's so difficult to find concentrating time. But sometime soon, I'll develop those dialogues with you and discuss books and ideas and reactions a little. But for now, it's mainly love and a plea for patience. All regards to the three of you,

Joyce

MAHALI
August 30, 1957

Dearest Joyce,

This is but a scrappy unintelligent note to let you know I'm still around and I still love and think of you. I'm dying to know how your summer has gone, the state of all your healths, your immediate plans, your patriotic feelings. When I think of you there, I get thoroughly homesick and nostalgic for Zion. It's odd how I don't miss (or even want to see, to be cruelly honest) my family or background or friends of childhood, or any of the towns I've lived in since then —Las Vegas, Chicago, and so on—except S.L.C. I suppose it's because I wasn't killing myself with work there, and was so intensely happy at discovering adulthood and the more intellectual facets of my mind. How incredible it is to me that you are actually there, thrust back into the geographical center of your girlhood, that you are seeing the mountains begin to turn the colors of autumn, that you are playing the LP phonograph in the SW corner of your living room. Is the stain still on the carpet near the living room where I spilled a glass of red wine? Is my team still plowing? Oh well.

Send me my six-months picture of Reinhard. I will take some of Christopher and will send them on to you when developed. I am madly studying Swahili again, as I'm taking the government civil service examination in it just for fun, and it's the orals next Monday and the written next Thursday.

Write to me, dear friend. I shall write a long, decent, evening's work letter when my Swahili is over. My very best wishes to one and all, my deepest love to you.

Pat

SALT LAKE CITY
September 9, 1957

Dearest Pat,

It's been a godawful summer, through no fault of Salt Lake, or "the vortex of my girlhood," or the light on these grand mountains. It's been the most hideous four months we've had since we've been together. It's the fault of poverty, the moral inferiority to parents when you're in debt to them, the increment of medical bills by means of a nasty uterus infection on my part, and gallstones on Hans's, plus a $375 dental bill for my disintegrating teeth. I've had absolutely no spiritual (inner, put it any way you like) life for so long that I feel more like an envelope than a person. Added to this was the spring and summer-long grind of trying to "establish" ourselves in the good old biggest and greatest U.S.—i.e., job hunting. I've been waitressing every night at a local "come as you are" restaurant, where lower-class Mormons come bringing all their numerous offspring to eat greasy Kentucky Fried Chicken and deep fried shrimp. In other words, the summer has meant hash slinging, domestic discontent (and overproximity), and looking for some wee little cubbyhole we could call a "position."

So—excuse the general malaise, and the failure to write. Did you receive the smocks I sent? How do you feel? Is she a boy? Do you hope?

I've studiously neglected almost everyone here. Don't worry, it's no basic change, simply the desire to be settled rather than to be gregarious just now. And the damned political situation has me so keyed up. I set the alarm clock to wake up for the news. It's like paranoia. And ye gods! What a colossal mess! These anti-segregation problems and violences are enough to set one into moral tantrums, along with the teamsters' union corruption, the juvenile crime, the insipidity of Ike's incapacity to decide, the DAMN-ed insistence and bullying intention of the AEC to explode however many bombs they jolly well wish, despite Japanese fishermen, concerned scientists, worried public opinion. I tell you, Pat, it makes a person shudder, the capacities of human beings that come over and over again to the fore. To me, it's more and more clear, this stupid bloody handwriting on the wall.

116

If you could see these jeering, grimacing Southern housewives, throwing stones and hatred at these calm Negro parents leading their children through the crowds, you'd weep with me too, whatever Africa had taught you. The *courage* that is demanded of these Negro children! let alone their parents. And they react so often with a Faulknerian resignation: "I expected it to be like this. I just hope it will be better sometime." Good Lord above, what beasts are in us?

We have a job. Hans found it through a Chicago agency, at Drake University in Des Moines (oh, God forbid—in small print). I'm actually so relieved to have a salary, I don't give a hoot where it is. And right now, Iowa seems about as safe a place as there is. Write there, very soon.

All my love, dear Pat,

Joyce

DES MOINES
September 26, 1957

Dear Pat,

Salt Lake, Bread Loaf, Los Angeles, Canada, Laval, London, Beirut, Tarbert, Tanganyika, IOWA—when I think of addresses our many letters have known, and none of them more unlikely than Des Moines. Palma or Toledo or Maine, yes, but the Corn Belt, the Bible Belt—oh, oh, oh.

We're dreadfully busy now, cleaning up a rotten old house that has lots of space and possibilities. It's only about ten minutes from the campus, so we still find no excuse for having a car. Hans is so marvelous about making wonders of little money, by carpentering and designing everything himself. He really is so excitingly creative. It's great to live with and so pervasive as to be almost embarrassing. But the space is delicious, with a studio for Hans right in the midst. How long we'll be here heaven only knows.

It's a good job, not a great one, at a very good second-rate university—interesting colleagues—lousy landscape. It would take three years to work into an assistant professor title, which, shamefully enough, is one of the points of being here. You see, a professor title is about the only thing that would have any bearing on job-getting in that tight, tight Europe. But here are none of the advantages we've come so to love—neither woods nor water nor mountains nor cultural excitement. So three years here seem unlikely.

We seriously might have joined you next summer on your leave along the Pyrenees if it weren't that we'd have a brand-new baby to bring along, born sometime in May. I certainly didn't plan this, and I've not even told Hans yet, until some of our surface turbulence here goes under. If I made the Drake insurance program, it was nothing but a matter of hours. We surely need

117

it, and I hope I can convince them that we were under the medical deadline.

Do you, by the way, continue to study, consciously, the African world, or do you more or less withdraw into your English novels of Western problems and the European conversations you have out there? I know that as much as I adored Beirut, I slipped into a kind of unlearning stage about it all and lived it as if it were in Salt Lake or so—to my shame, of course.

I send my love and want to hear from you *soon*.

My love,

Joyce

MAHALI

October 4, 1957

My dear dear Joyce,

Apart from our friendship itself, I cannot tell you what our correspondence has meant to me these years out here. I honestly think it's been my one sane glimpse into the world over there (Europe or North America), which somehow seems to keep receding further and further away, imperceptibly, like Philip's hairline. At last, even though in (shudder) Ioway, I detected a definite upbeat in your last letter. Were you aware of it? Or in the turmoil of traveling, unpacking and settling in, was it only a delicate unspoken feeling that only manifested itself through your amanuensis?

Anyway, one year, three years, professor or bohemian starveling, mother of two or ten, I'm terribly happy for you after rather a bad year and a half. I'm happy (you sound as if, basically, you are too, though possibly a bit unnerved) about baby number 2 on his, her, its way. Nor was ours planned, though we're financially better able to cope. Now that it's actually happened, I *do* think 2–2½ years between the first two should be the absolute maximum. You *aren't* going to work this time, are you? Please take care of your health, my dear Joyce.

You looked lovely in your latest pictures, so much better than the first few after Reinhard was born. I've come to the conclusion that this is a turbulent violent period in a woman's life, and that the best thing to do is to sit and contemplate your navel and let material things go to rack and ruin around you, if necessary.

I have a book for Reinhard for his birthday which I adore and am sending it off now, so it may or may not (most likely the latter) arrive on time. Also, I'm making him some p.j.'s for Christmas, so loud, so neon-signish, you are quite at liberty to use them as dusters if you or Hans think they'll keep him awake at night. I made Christopher two pairs and he adores them. 'Nama!! he cries, when he

118

gets out of his night bath—he also says 'nama for banana and for meat, nyama in Swahili. I hope to God they fit.

I sew madly all the time these days, just to keep myself awake on these hot steaming afternoons. I feel so ghastly when I get up, I just can't get into the Memsab habit of the afternoon "liedown," as the English so euphemistically call it.

Oh! I *did* receive the smocks; they're gorgeous. They fit beautifully, and are the envy of all the other pregnant women around (that's *all* the other women around, under forty—very fertile place). I wore the blue bandanaish one for my Swahili oral exam and the striped one for my written one, and passed both, but I think I bragged about it in my last letter, though forgetting to mention my lovely good-luck smocks. Thank you so much for your trouble.

Another question, as to Christopher, he's driving me round the bend, cutting his eyeteeth. I had him completely toilet trained (or so I thought) for two whole months, and now he goes, diarrhea, morning, noon and night, and moans and groans more than he's ever done before. But he still sleeps all night, is eating well, and gradually learning boyish, as distinguished from babyish, behavior. I think I'd just as soon have another boy, but I wouldn't mind a girl.

Yes, I'm still too conscious of Africans and Asians and Europeans as such, and it drives one round the bend, to be honest. Our houseboy, for instance, whom we've had 2½ years, the whole tour, keeps defrosting the fridge every other day because the "water gets hard." This the last 4–5 weeks, after he's been taking care of fridges for twenty years. Oh well. I shall write again soon and send some pictures of Christopher. You answer *my* questions!

All my love,

Pat

DES MOINES
October 8, 1957

Dear Pat,

It's unfair! And very briefly, I'm driven to protest. I've written about four letters this summer, and I'm stumped that you failed to receive so many. Is mail characteristically unreliable there? I'm proud of you and your Swahili exam. How I agree that *that* kind of backtracking into one's testing his skills and capacities is a good, an exciting thing.

We would love to come over to see you this summer, but won't have any money, and will, also, have a one-month-old as well.

Right now, Des Moines seems a horrible outpost, but let's just hope it's all

119

from being seen through the eyes of morning sickness. There's so darn much to do to fix up this old house that I just can't write more today. I send quantities of love and good will, but rather few apologies. Will write again soon.

Joyce

October 31, 1957

My very dear friend and most cherished Reinhard's godmother,

So many goodly things, coming haphazardly one way or another from Mahali, have served to make your friendship and your very self imperatively close this week. The little undershirts, wooden fork and spoon, and Rodman poems reached me just now, after long being waylaid in Glendarroch.

You wouldn't even like me any more, I'm sure. I haven't even read *The Outsider* yet. I've scarcely read anything. Instead of dreaming in metaphors and Alexandrines, I put myself to sleep by making little lists of useless things. I'm often tired, always nauseated—morning and midnight—but luckily, not yet bored. However, I'm a misfit in America. And I don't do any of the nice things you do, such as planting geraniums, learning Swahili, or making pajamas for *my* best friend's son.

In fact, my total neglect of Christopher sickens me. I should so love to know him and to see the two boys together.

You're so decent, Pat, and such a true and generous friend, and I so seldom even have anything to offer—inarticulate reactions, antique enthusiasms, and mostly wee, paltry letters. Don't feel I am depressed. I still feel life bubbling, and expect to have a rendezvous with it again someday soon. But I certainly send you my love,

Joyce

DES MOINES
December 16, 1957

Dear friend,

It was far from my intention to wait until Christmas time to write you again. But it does go by so very rapidly. And so let me fill in many of the waiting spaces with greetings to you and to Philip and to Christopher and to the little secluded one who has no idea what it's all about. We three do hope your Christmas is a happy one with the little boy, who looks so wonderful in the pictures. I am so delighted to see them. Do let's post one another regularly by photograph; they change so wonderfully, so fast and so surprisingly. And I expect a picture of the new one as fast as possible.

I would so love to send you something for Christmas. I don't think we will ever forget our delight at the big bird that came out of Glasgow just a year ago, anonymously, and revealing upon being opened a very naked, very black little boy, who told just who was behind all that considerateness. *Do* let me know what you might like for your wee one, and I'll be so delighted to go layette-looking, as a sort of second preview of what's in store for me next May. I'm sure I could find something which you couldn't buy over there, and probably not in England. Do tell me what you would like, please.

I know that my last letters have sounded rather utterly depressed, and I'll try no longer to indulge. And it will be easier, because I dare to hope (cross-fingeredly) that the worst of my time is over, the nausea having greatly diminished, and the tiredness due to anemia being a little less overwhelming. Budgeting an American economy creates its own strains, but I suddenly seem able to cope with everything, but that a little more happily, easily.

How are you going to manage en route, and in England? Are you going to be utterly tied down, or is there someone in London who can share the burden a little? Can you nurse, and do you expect to? I'm sure that if Christopher is anything like Reinhard, traveling at this age will not be easy. Is he trained? And if he is, for God's sake, please help me out with some good strong advice. So long as the baby is hardy, he shouldn't be hard to travel with. What do you intend to do about diapers? I'm genuinely interested in these messy details, if you can ever find time to describe your plans about them. Reinhard was eight months when we were traveling all over with him, and was wonderful, still being nursed. He slept in dresser drawers, or in the suitcase, top open, you know, all the way, and thrived.

Oh, the memories and the things that make them come and go so quickly. I think about France, but it's more of an effort to *decide* to think about it as a prevention of losing it totally. It doesn't really live much in me any more. And the dear Scotland we so honestly loved sinks and falls under as I thought it never could. It persisted so achingly all summer, and I painfully ache for all it offered, all its uncluttered, unadvertised cleanliness and directness, its uncalculated naturalness, which seems so hard to find here. But this Des Moines year has moved a good third of the year away, and I realize how inaccessible Glendarrochs are in this time, this place. Only I realize it with no consolation.

Do continue to write me as often as you have, and as you can. The correspondence has been so grand. Let us keep it through many new years. I think of letters to you so often, but as you evidenced understanding, it is less easy to get around to them now than it was previously. So please never think I am neglecting you. The spaces between are larger than I will them.

121

We both send our warm and happy greetings to you at Christmas, and I send you my especially fond and concerned love as you approach the birth time of your second child.

Joyce

January 7, 1958

Beloved Pat,

God knows you're the best friend I've ever had. And God, and only He, knows how I ache to do something more for you to show what it all means. Your package came, about the happiest part of our Christmas. With perfect intuition, you know what is right. The pajamas are adorable, and I cannot imagine what you meant about their being a flop. They fit Reinhard beautifully and he looks endearingly elf-like in them. I shall take and send pictures soon. And the books! Oh, dear Pat, they are so wonderful. I've wanted to read de Beauvoir's *The Mandarins* since it first came out, and you could not have picked a book I had had my heart more set on. And the Oxford nursery book is so superlative that I cannot take the risk of giving it yet to Reinhard, who is still destructive with books, although he loves them wildly. And now it is almost your birthday and the birthday of Christopher and the birth of the new little one I would so love to hold. I want to be near you now, desperately, to help you, to care for Christopher, to visit you in the hospital, just to have the chance, a little, to share these important times. And to send you something. What could I send that would help you en route? Or anything for the infant. You must inform me in advance of all possible addresses.

We're having one HELL of a time financially. I feel like beating it from this money-grabbing country. Neither of us belongs, and yet we now fear we're trapped—never able to save, even to make ends meet. Enough of that sort of thing. Because my thoughts are so very thoroughly with you these days (except that my baby too is making itself felt, wonderfully so). I send you my love, dear friend, and I want you to feel my presence, in case you can need me.

Joyce

January 15, 1958

Dearest (and badly needed) friend, on my 27th birthday,

I am ecstatically the mother of another son, Julian, born four days ago (the 11th) at this same dreary place where I had Christopher. Julian was late too, so I've been here three weeks waiting this time. He's an adorable little mite, shorter and fatter (only by four ounces) than Christopher at birth, has great dark almond eyes, a square determined chin, long hands and feet, and is the product of a very short and easy birth (six hours from first contraction to holding him in my arms). I now have the little family I've always wanted, and am pleased beyond words that I produced yet another boy. I don't know why I haven't wanted girls. I'm not up to baseball teams, so perhaps we can form a chamber music trio in a few years.

I can't wait to get home but on the other hand sort of dread it, as I have to start packing for long leave immediately. We leave in only four weeks! I also rather dread facing life in England with my two babes, on my own most of the time, with Philip away all day doing his course, but as he says (and I take it with a somewhat bitter grain of salt), the wives out here do six-month tours (in England) and get two and a half years leave (in Africa). Ha bloody ha. I miss Christopher most dreadfully. I've never been parted from him before, and Philip tells me he has a sort of glandular fever and won't bring him over here any more. I hope he's well by the time we get home, poor love. Philip seems rather disinterested in this baby, but I guess he's too busy to take it all in, and from what I hear, that's normal with fathers until all babies after the firstborn get older. But it makes me a little sad and depressed.

Fatigue has set in, I'm off to sleep (in this ghastly heat, only stirred round sluggishly by the inept ceiling fan) before the next feeding—nursing so far goes well. I'm keeping my fingers crossed that all the upsets of the coming weeks don't dry me up. Write me in London. I hope you and baby and Hans and Reinhard go well.

Much love—I wish I could see you and have a good talk and a good cry.

Pat

January 22, 1958

Blessings on you, and on you, little man!

The good news just this minute came, and I'm enraptured with a happiness complete except for not being closer to share it with you. But despite this enormous distance, I still persist in feeling with you very immediately, so let us not complain too much. I am so grateful that the birth went well, and *easily* (you lucky one—I should not mind it being a bit swifter this time).

I'm getting along well now, feeling the infant kick, but not being able to show him enough to justify maternity clothes yet, although the sixth month now begins. I think I'm gaining weight though, which is not to be desired. Did you? Or did you lose it all, and are you as wee as ever?

I, by the way, am a very poor American wife, having a hell of a time "getting into it" here, since I see nothing much to get into. All in all, I feel as though the time were caught in some kind of vacuum, without much relatedness, and little chance of leading to anything. As soon as we can save anything, we'll be on our way back, to a culture I honestly feel more alive, more complete, more valid in. . . . At the rate of our present savings, this will take some several decades. There is only one mail service daily, and on top of this, or below it perhaps, is our annoyance at the lack of any medical benefits through the state, the puny group benefits universities aim to offer, and the overall scandalous prices the profession charges here for even five-minute consultations. Of course, the British Health Service spoiled us, but then so did the French, the German, and the Lebanese! And with no squirming glances to the subversives.

And then our foreign policy on top, and as Hans says, the shrieking dumbness of the way the high school students come, supposedly qualified, to universities. And in small letters, i don't like the landscape.

But now the little boy aches to go walking in the snow, so I shall send all love and joy, and wait for details as to your trip.

Joyce

January 25, 1958

Dearest Joyce,

The briefest of notes to enclose this funny little snap made three days after Julian's birth (for passport!). He looks rather sanguine about his prospects in this world, doesn't he? I look haggard and skinny, which I am. All is total chaos here

—packing cases and trunks everywhere, Christopher thin and gaunt from his illness, so much so that it wrenches my heart, Philip abstracted and terribly busy and short-tempered, and I full of anger at everything conspiring to ignore this darling Julian, whom I've just brought into the world. Damn it, damn it. I'd like to spend most of my time crying, but I haven't got time. No doubt I'll pick up, as I hope Christopher will, in the crisp cold and liveliness of London.

Can't write any more. Hope you progress well.

So much love, dear friend,

Pat

DES MOINES
February 3, 1958

Dearest Pat,

Julian is beautiful, and I am as great with joy for you and for him, as I am with envy, preferably more so. Because it seems I am not so great with child after all. Oh, I have been pregnant all right. My moods have shown that. But my body hasn't; my utcrus simply does not grow, and I'm as flat as can be, which for the beginning of the sixth month is odd. Not odd, however, if you suppose the little fetus to have died, which my OB does. The crisis and tears are over. I'm resigned to beginning another baby as soon as conceivable, and I suppose, if it must be, one should be grateful at Nature's taking this rather than some other course. If the rabbit test, end of February, is negative, I guess he'll help me miscarry.

Altogether, it's a lousy year. Hans can't paint. I'm up to my ears in housework; there are no interesting people here, and every little pill is a fortune. And much of America annoys me. And I *hate* ballpoint pens.

But I do love you, dear friend, and am so delighted with the lovely son. May I be a godmother, or is he spoken for? And a very very Bon Voyage!

Love,

Joyce

PART FIVE

MARCH 1958 – DECEMBER 1958

Have you read Dr. Zhivago?

March 18, 1958

Dearest Joyce,

Your sad loss grieves me, and I know how much pain you must have gone through, both mentally and physically. Let me know the details, if this doesn't sound too much like morbid curiosity. Are you in any way secretly relieved, I mean with the great burden a baby would have imposed on you in your present circumstances? And yet the only thing that gets one through this sort of time of pain is the hope for next time. I hope life is looking up in them thar flat places, the horrible old Middle West, and that you have plans for getting out of there to somewhere decent soon. I know what you are saying about America, although I haven't been home for almost four years now. I don't think I could ever live there again, and I'm sure Philip couldn't. I adore England, but life is so hard here on not much money. Though we're certainly a lot much better off than most.

We found a very pleasant flat, and had only two weeks in our grubby crowded hotel room with beds and wet diapers all over the place, not to speak of making formula and sterilizing bottles on the Primus stove, till we moved in here two weeks ago. Philip has been on his course since three days after we arrived in London, so I've seen little of him, except poring over his texts at nights and weekends. And that's how it will be until the beginning of July. I feel I might go stir crazy by that time, but chin up, I tell myself.

Julian is the best baby that ever was and a charm and delight to behold. I actually have to wake him up for his first morning feeding! Which is, you may have gathered, bottles. My fears of going dry over the harum-scarum period of going on leave were, alas, realized. I actually dried up from one feed to the next, on the airplane (30 hours from Dar to London, with an eight-hour breakdown in Khartoum—it was a nightmare—I arrived at London Airport smelling in equal parts of baby vomit and baby what-comes-out-the-other-end). Christopher is beginning to pick up finally after his lingering illness when I was away having Julian. In fact he is even a different child in a lot of ways. Sort of sad and grown up and quiet, not the blissfully unaware baby he was. Though I adore being in England, I can't say much for the life I'm leading now. I don't speak to another human being for days on end, except to say, "Two pounds of minced beef and a packet of sausages, please." And I think my brain is softening, even with *The Times* to read daily (what a delight, after three years of the pap in the *Tanganyika Standard*). At least it isn't a life sentence, and I get paroled to Mallorca in July for two months until we return to Africa. And I am getting a decent baby-sitter this week too, and can get away a bit into the civilized glories of London now and then. Why don't you join us in our rented cottage in Mallorca this summer?

My letter sounds discontented, and I guess I sort of am, but only, I trust, temporarily. The daffodils are up in Hyde Park, and no doubt my spirits will follow suit soon.

Keep a stiff upper lip,
All my deepest love,

Pat

DES MOINES
March 19, 1958

Dearest friend,

I just must get a short note off to you. The silence has been too long. In a few hours I shall enter the hospital here for a dilatation and curettage, since the baby died in uterus. A month or two ago, I ceased feeling life and went through a hell of uncertainty, but now it is resolved. The year has been bad; Hans has repeated gall colics and his gall bladder must be taken out soon. We lost our job too, last week, an honorable discharge, which nonetheless puts us out of work. They need someone who is more of a commercial artist. You see? And little Reinhard broke his right clavicle, and just escaped concussion.

So, as Hans put it, "America and I is not a very happy couple." To save the horrendous rent we've to pay here, I shall leave Des Moines May 1st for Salt Lake, Hans carrying on here with a six weeks teaching session, taking us (separately) until mid-July. We hope then to have enough to escape to Mexico, where we can get through July and August on $300; here it would last only three weeks.

If we've no job by June 1st (we have written all over, are dealing once more with these wretched agencies), I think we'll go to Europe. Things contrive to sap Hans of himself here.

How are you, dear one? I do hope all goes well. And the wee Julian. I need a word from you.

My best love,

Joyce

DES MOINES
March 24, 1958

Dear good friend,

The worst is over, and I am home from the hospital, after going through an unexpected philosophical hell, and coming out alive. The operation was calm and almost pleasant, I had thought—until I spoke with the doctor next day, who said it was the most rugged curettage he'd ever given.

To answer your question, no—I was not secretly relieved, although I understood the question. I had wanted this baby, and it took me a good month to accommodate myself to the facts. I must never have felt life at all. But today I feel a new woman, aching to begin life in a new way, and a better way. God, what a rotten year! If only we *could* join you in "civilization" this summer. I think we would if we had the dough. Your letters are my greatest stimulant. Please keep them coming.

Hello to Philip,

Joyce

LONDON
April 8, 1958

My ever dearest friend,

How I love getting your letters, even with the woes and miseries of your present life. It *must* take a turn for the better soon! You are always so sane in the midst of turbulence. I on the other hand am in the midst of absolutely nothing except a daily housekeeping and walking-the-kiddies routine that threatens to turn my already mushy mind into a vapor.

And yet, I am loving, *loving* being in London. We went last week to see Beriosova in *Swan Lake* at Covent Garden; I wept with delight. And remember my old grand passion, Ferruccio Tagliavini? I heard him sing in *The Pearl Fishers*. It took me days to get over it. He is in as good voice now as ever he was ten years

131

ago when I first began listening to the Saturday Metropolitan Opera broadcasts. I go to the movies some nights when the children are asleep and Philip studying. I can buy off the newsstands *Time* and *Paris Match* and any old thing that catches my fancy. I can buy elaborate pastries all iced and decorated by someone else. I could listen to the BBC Third (if we had a radio). I can read a morning newspaper that very same morning. I can (and do, daily) walk the tots to Hyde Park and saunter for hours through it and Kensington Gardens, and tell Christopher the story of Peter Pan. Do you know there are still uniformed nannies out in the Gardens, with their charges in prams a hundred times fancier than mine? The flowers in their calendar-appointed beds are blooming, the lawns manicured, the pale English looking as if they're enjoying spring. The Indian immigrants are being maltreated by Londoners who have looked down their long Anglo-Saxon noses at Americans for years at our treatment of the race problem, and now they have one and don't know what to do with it. If it weren't for the tragedy of the real people involved, the Asians and West Indians, I'd laugh at the idiocy of it all. And France! What in the *world* is going on there?

I am buying lots and lots of books to take back to wherever we end up next tour (please, please, somewhere with electricity and people to talk to!). I'll be my own university degree. I'd like to give some elegant dinner parties in our handsomely appointed flat while we are here. Maybe I can take time off between visits to the National Health Baby Clinic and doing diapers, and manage a curry, which I can now make rather well, thanks to a Gujarati woman in Mahali who showed me how. Someday I'll cook one for you and Hans.

We have tickets to Fonteyn in *Giselle* and to *La Bohème* for next week. It all makes up for three years in grim hot boring old Mahali.

And speaking of hot boring places, I have a very special favor to ask of you. Could you, do you think, find a plastic or rubber inflatable wading pool for me? I want one to ameliorate the heat for the children, wherever we're sent next. Let me know, and its cost and that of mailing it, and I'll reimburse you right away. I have a beatific vision of our two boys splashing happily in the cool water, sailing rubber duckies across it to one another, while I sit nearby in the ample green shade of a mango tree, reading a book and drinking endless cups of tea. But I need your help for the vision to come true, as they aren't available in cold damp old Blighty.

I send love and fond hopes that life looks up for you all.

Pat

April 15, 1958

Very dear Pat,

Your grand letters are the one bright spot lately, and your European exuber-ance is just about the only thing that purges me of the gloom which I send in wee dismal tidbits. And I fail to write you the details, the nuances of understand-ing I feel on reading your letters. It has been such a time! Reinhard was hospital-ized again for a week in the oxygen tent for a croup which was swelling his larynx to the point of suffocation. He's better—I'm better too—enjoying spring and my sex life, but not much else, excepting Reinhard, who is, I think, so beautiful. But possibly and logically I'm so fatigued under the strain of a $500 medical bill, and still more: the 22½ hour daily discussion of whether we should junk Americana and set sail for Germany in August, the goal being Freiburg, near the Franco-Suisse border.

The strain is because it would be a permanent decision. And it would mean a rather meager salary forever, *unless* he can one day prove himself a real painter and eventually make it into an art academy (also a meager salary—one that will never allow return travel to America). I find the whole subject so distressing, since it is purely catastrophic for my parents. What to do? The arguments for not staying here are not anti-American, but the rapport Hans fails to establish is a gigantic block to his work. Please send wisdom, and I will write more of the details. I can find no more to say. How I would love to come to dinner to your flat, bearing wine.

All my dearest grateful love,

Joyce

April 15, 1958

Dear Pat,

A purely practical letter. I've been inquiring about the pools. I could get you a plastic pool, inflatable, for $16, the big one and the most sturdy. But from what people have told me, they (1) need a pump to fill them, and (2) tend to puncture easily; and that once they tear, they're on the downgrade. Or there is a very large one which is heavy nylon, not inflatable. It simply sits on the ground on little legs and you fill and drain it—$27. It of course packages small. It is said to be much the more resistant, and so if you approve, I'll buy that one. Do you want it sent to Africa or to London?

Excuse my woefulness, but I already spent the remaining money on a little suit for Christopher and one playsuit for Julian. Is that all right? I'll probably be waitressing in Salt Lake all summer, so from May 1st, write there. Hans has summer teaching here in Iowa.

All love,

Joyce

DES MOINES
April 29, 1958

Dearest Pat,

One after another inanity speeds itself to you. I must remind myself to reread Madame de Staël sometime, to see how others got around to writing readable letters. I know that I've not sent you one worthy letter in the past nine months, but what's there in that? I've done little that is worthy of any kind, and I feel quite out of the best part of myself.

Hans wants me to spend the forthcoming summer retrieving myself from the dregs of this inelegant year, but the pressure to obtain (money, that is) is so great as to prohibit almost any leisure. Our bills are mammoth—the so-called insurance plan of Drake has paid nothing on three of the four hospitalizations we have had. But methinks I've wailed of this before.

I'm so pleased that you are enjoying London; I would too. Reinhard is driving me crazy just now, poking me and everything else. And I wrote mainly to confess to you in plain terms that the swimming pool was so heavy that I shall have to ask you for a pound, humiliating as it truly is. So far as finances are concerned in this, my life, I can scarcely pride myself on the generosity I can offer. Maybe someday the worst will be over, and a budget won't appear such an ominous enterprise. I only hope it won't have become too expensive a pool for you, all things told.

But I DO PROMISE A TRUE LONG letter as soon as I arrive in Salt Lake.

My fondest love,

Joyce

May 19, 1958

Dearest of all friends, Joyce,

I will try to write you a halfway decent letter today and not scraps and bits as I seem to have been doing for so long. I feel so dreadful about your financial strain and all the hospital stays—I wish I were a millionaire and could help. I enclose a couple of pounds toward sending that wretched pool which I'm so sorry to have troubled you with. Let me know if it comes to any more. I will think of you with love and gratitude every time the children use it. Send it here to London.

We have just been over to Paris to pick up our new Peugeot for our European trip and the coming tour in Africa. It was the most extraordinary time in France I've ever known. Can you imagine soldiers armed with *machine guns* standing shoulder to shoulder round the government buildings? And motorists hooting the *Al-ger-ie* FRAN-*çaise* call all the time? All these changes of government, De Gaulle standing in the wings—the latest joke there is, "Can you list all the premiers of France since World War II?" It looks a complete mess and absolutely grim for the future.

But as always, in whatever chaotic state, we loved each moment. The chestnut trees were blooming, little sprigs of lily of the valley were on café tables, great bunches of lilacs were being sold on busy street corners. We stayed in our same old arrondissement, possibly a little dirtier and smellier as the years go by, but still as cheap, friendly and atmospheric as ever. The maid in our hotel baby-sat with Christopher in the evenings—we'd left Julian in London—so that we could go sit in a sidewalk café and drink Pernod and watch the world go by.

We have been posted for next tour to a godforsaken place called Pashenzi, 400 miles from its provincial headquarters, cut off by road six months out of the year, and about a million miles from anywhere decent to go anyway. My heart sinks at the thought of three years in a place so remote and tiny (twelve government officers and no planters) and as cut off as Pashenzi is. I'm going to the British Museum a couple of times a week now to read up on its history (I mean, Pashenzi). It's *really* bush Africa.

It is presumably obvious from all this that I'm not wildly enthusiastic at the prospect of leaving Europe generally and London particularly to go to what seems from this vantage point like the far side of the moon. I live in perpetual dread that never again in my life will I have a meaningful conversation with another human being. Do you think our boys will be company and friends as the years go by and they grow into young adulthood? God knows, I could use some real human exchange. Our silences (P.'s and mine) are deafening and soul-destroying, for me. I feel desperately unloved and hence unloving. Is this just more crummy old growing up, having no friends any more and living in virtual silence with a spouse of five years? Ah well, c'est la bloody vie.

Write when you can.

Much love and affection,

Pat

SALT LAKE CITY
May 21, 1958

Dearest Pat,

Although you might have thought that by now I would have realized what a wretched correspondent I am and quit trying, I'm not through yet. How discouraging it must be, though, for you to receive nothing but these endless petulant and slightly statistical letters from me. But please don't despair of me. I have thought such endless and, alas, unwritten letters to you.

So here I am again, in S.L.C.—here, but not at home. I do not really like being uprooted from my marriage home, nor look forward to three and a half months apart. Only this heavenly mountain air, the country (it *is* lovely!) and occasional spots of understanding between self and parents along the tortuous path of diplomatic maneuvering, so as not to hurt, not to be too candid, nor to be false. There is not even the juicy delight any more in the return for learning scandals, or developments in former friends' lives. For we're aging, Pat (I am 28 Sunday), and the events that stir now happen to people we never knew, who came from afar or grew up in our absence.

I'm dying to be pregnant again, but with the pressures of this life (??), I shall have to teach next year. We discussed the possibilities into the ground of making the break and setting off for Europe now, with nary a penny in pocket. But, and I think Hans counts me for the first time a coward because of it, I could not see trying to pay back enormous debts (largely to scurrilous grasping M.D.'s, excuse me) in German marks, at the rate of exchange of 4 to 1.

So I succumbed to practicality, and my poor little beleaguered conscience is sick. And I secretly feel that Hans thinks himself trapped. The choice will, I think, take us to a tiny girls' liberal arts college, in Milwaukee, where they offer a slightly better salary, they pay the fool teachers' agency, and they move us. But Hans is not happy about it, and I'm so exhausted considering every day again and in such excruciating detail, "What is the purpose of my life?" It is similar to the force that breaks English majors—always considering the levels of reality, you know. But Hans forces it, and he is probably right.

136

There is much to say, but so much for this little one. Did you receive the clothes, the pool? How are the wee boys? How I *ache* to see you.

Do write,

Joyce

May 23, 1958

Dearest Pat,

If you were only here I'd drag you down to the Tampico and let you get me good and tight.

———————⇥ ⇤———————

Sunday: The above statement a little obsolete now, though not inapplicable. It is 1 A.M., and I just returned from waitressing at Harmon's "Kentucky Fried Chicken—Come As You Are"—and they do! God, how I loathe it. The only reason I do it is because I can't get a job teaching this summer, because we're up to our ears in medical bills, and because working from 6 P.M. till 2 A.M. (usually) leaves my days free for Reinhard. Also I miss Hans so horribly much, and it does take my mind off that. But I have (you have too) had my share of hash slinging. As a freshman at the Student Union Coffee Shop, as a grad student at Bread Loaf, and two summers here. But Hans is working so hard I only feel it's fair to help. But hell or high water, I'm going to use my fool degrees and teach from now on.

I rather look forward to Milwaukee, there being water at least, and some woods. And a mentality no longer strictly Midwestern. It is said to be a good city, an exhilarating one. The salary is only $4,500, but believe me, that is the best a young teacher in the arts can expect. How I wish we could just honeymoon in the free month before the semester begins.

Are you looking into the Brussels fair? And how does this ghoulish French crisis look from Britain? Poor dear chaotic France. What are you reading, doing, thinking? God, I miss you so, so, so. No one seems to fill your role.

All love to you all,

Joyce

June 20, 1958

Dear Joyce,

Again, I apologize. I did write you a very silly letter a couple of weeks ago all about nothing (me = 0) but burned it. I'll tell you about it when I see you next. We are chugging along happily to the end of our English time (4½ weeks) and then off on our mad continental safari with babies' beds, national dried milk, 5 dozen diapers, and heaps of naiveté.

We go (no longer to Mallorca) for 3 days to Brussels where we will do the Exposition by turns, then to Copenhagen for 5 days, then to a little mountain inn in Central Norway for 10 days (very cheap for full pension), then for a week to friends of Philip who live on Ulefossfjord in southern Norway, then for 4 days to Stuttgart to see something of Germany, where neither of us has been. Then for our last week to Paris, where we've booked two adjoining rooms in a hotel in the Rue Cujas for 1500 frs., tout compris, per day. It's probably crazy with two kids, but damn it, we won't be here for another three years. Then back to England on 5th September, sailing (via the west coast this time) to Capetown on 11th Sept., arriving 25th, then driving the 3,000 miles back to Tanganyika to arrive 17th October in Pashenzi, and that's the old leave.

I received the clothes and adore them. Christopher loves his little "diamond" and Julian looks too sweet in his little suit. The pool has arrived, a magnificent-looking apparatus, for which my thousand thanks. Was the money I sent for the freight enough?

Are you working too hard? Seeing lots of old friends? Is my godchild (to whom I *will* send a duffel coat, for the long cold Milwaukee winter) flourishing? Can I send you anything besides my love? Give your parents my warmest regards, do please.

All my love,

Pat

June 21, 1958

Dear beloved Pat,

It seems to have been an epoch since our letters caught, met, and responded, and despite the years (4 now in October, in Paris, since I saw you), I still have the immediate sense, not of thinking of you, but still acutely, sometimes, suddenly, missing you.

My address is such because of a quick turn of events. Drake University phoned me, the day before summer term began, asking me to return the next day, to teach American Lit. to teachers in rural communities who need to renew certificates. So here am I, caught again in the toils of Hester Prynne and Dimmesdale and the Magnetic Chain of Being. O memories!

The *abysmal* ignorance of these rural, but still not outlying, communities is simply terrifying. Much in America is. They have never heard of Thoreau, nor Emerson, nor Eliot, and 70% don't know whether the Civil War was early or late in the nineteenth century. And when was the nineteenth century anyway?

Have no fear, we shall have returned to civilization before very long. How are the boys? I plainly ache to see them. And I shall, soon.

All my best love,

Joyce

EMMETSBURG, IOWA

July 16, 1958

Dearest Pat,

What a great relief to know that the pool arrived, without being diverted too many times to wrong addresses, being overcharged, overpapered, overclassified, etc.! Whew! I do so hope it is what you wanted, and that it won't be too cumbersome packing it back to Tanganyika.

Typical of my recent letters, this is a mere scrawl; Reinhard and I are seated on suitcases in the station of Ottumwa (heart and grass roots of Bible Belt Iowa, and an unlikely metaphor to boot). On our way to Kingman, Kansas, where the eldest of Mother's generation, her oldest brother, is dying. I've always loved him dearly, so Reinhard and I will go there, and then on to Emmetsburg, Iowa, where I'll be teaching three weeks, then on to Milwaukee.

We termed two and a half years ago the American prospectus as a "fast chaos," I remember, and what a bitterly straight intuition that turned out to have been! Well, there are many footnotes to this private anguish of ours, and I ought to begin subjecting you to some of them soon. Enjoy your Norwegian jaunt, enjoy it a little for me, who so much would love to share part of it with you. Reinhard, by the way, too, is something of a little pest frequently. And this traveling is so damn hard on him. What did you do with Christopher in London? Can you read this? What a pen! We're coming to Europe next summer.

I send much love, between the lines of this hapless letter,

Joyce

139

July 29, 1958

Very dear Pat,

We are on the last lap now of a threefold purgatory—not really a nightmare, just a trial. And Algona is the most Midwest of them all, at least so far as my prejudices have the Midwest: flat, alien, endless. And poor Hans; he is teaching Art Education for the Elementary Schools for the tenth godawful time, to women whose art consciousness goes back no further than Grandma Moses' childhood memories, and women who eat chocolate pie twice during the coffee break. As Hans says, "My teaching only interrupts their breaks."

And all this will be over only to commence once again in Milwaukee. If only Hans had one smashing specialty—mosaic, or stained glass, for instance. In Europe, a major in Art Pedagogy is a merely logical expedient to enable painters to support selves, wives, etc., by teaching painting. Here it is sheer liability, a demerit which is as much as to say, "I couldn't make it with a fine arts major, so I got through by taking art education." Hence he teaches would-be second grade teachers, who are far more interested in Sigma Chis and will probably marry one before she (they) (always females!) applies one little nugget of aesthetic wisdom to her sprawling little eight-year-olds.

To make matters worse, Hans very much does not look forward to my teaching in Milwaukee, the school being so dastardly far away, and the whole thing involving so much darn preparation anyway. And all for $3,000, $1,500 of which is already gone (so to speak) for retroactive bills to my family. But there you have it. Whether we'll come back to Europe permanently next year, I don't know. We'll at least be there next summer. Is there any chance *at all*, at all, of seeing you? Could, perhaps, just the two of us have a rendezvous somewhere? I know it's probably out of the question, but heaven knows I miss you, and find you irreplaceable.

It is foolish to think in such terms, but it looks somewhat a mistake to have come here at all. I cannot see that we've gained *anything* at all, even the elementary family gain of understanding between parents-in-law and son-in-law. And now it is increasingly hard to return to Europe, when in Germany Hans will have to work the first two years on a salary that will scarcely support one, and where I cannot help.

After August 10th write to Milwaukee. With a wee P.S. I ask how you all are?

All my ever growing love,

Joyce

RJUKAN, NORWAY
August 3, 1958

Dearest Joyce,

I again send this to Salt Lake to be forwarded to your Middle West abode of the moment, wherever it may be, as I don't have any address with me, having packed and left London in a terrible confusion two weeks ago.

There follow twenty-five closely written pages of description of the continental trip, sent to Joyce in two installments, what Pat called "my second-rate travelogues." The high point of the trip was the week's stay with what proved to be an immensely wealthy aristocratic family in their palatial residence in the south of Norway.

MILWAUKEE, WISCONSIN
August 29, 1958

Dear Pat,

How magnificent your exhilarated letters were. It is incredible to think it almost four years now since we saw one another. I, twenty-four then, am now twenty-eight! My God! The swiftness of it all. And yet really such a brief time since we both were such primary masters of our fates, with all the foremost choices and conceptions still out of sight!

How glad I am that your leave went well. You really do have to store up for three years, don't you? Perhaps on that leave, at least, there can be a real meeting, a long one. I miss you almost uncomfortably. I have known a few men I could talk with as extensively and thoroughly as with you—but not Hans. There are many silences, not cruel or blank ones, but the feeling that this person does not like to talk about mysteries. He is after all a painter, and this is a world of difference. Who has been your closest friend lately?

Do tell me more about Paris now. Paris in early September. I feel so out of it. How incredible to think we used to daydream about visiting Europe one day! I begin teaching September 17th. It will mean great gobs of papers and preparation, and all so we can pay for my stupid dentistry, but also go to Europe next summer, perhaps buy a Volkswagen.

Enjoy it all a little bit for me, dear Pat, will you? For I feel very much with you.

Love always,

Joyce

141

September 10, 1958

Dearest Joyce,

Your last letter was the best I've received for ages from you. Things must be beginning to unravel, am I right? But *do* write me a long long letter as of yore, and fill me in on details of your daily doings, no matter how staid and dull they might sound to you.

You ask about my friends. I haven't any. Lots of acquaintances, some less superficial than others, but no simpático anywhere. Philip is rather like Hans, though less so, I think, but still a man to shy away from a spoken commitment of *personalities*. But perhaps in the end it won't burn itself out as too much exploration might. I dunno.

I at *last* got Reinhard's duffel coat. I suppose it's for his birthday. I also put in a little toy for Christmas which I fear you'll have to wrap, as Christmas wrappings aren't out here yet. The *T. Lit. Supp.* resubscription is for Christmas, m'dear, as we are *so* bloody broke after leave and our holiday and our bank overdraft (a lovely English custom, but leading us to bankruptcy) is reaching astronomical heights.

I got a book on making mobiles to while away the long hot nights ahead of us in Pashenzi. Something I've always wanted to do properly. Joyce, *five* books have been published this year by people that Philip and I know. I keep (as I have for years) telling myself I too can do it as well as they. Well, I shall be thirty when we return from Tanganyika next time, and finished for good if I don't get it out of my system now. I really and truly must, must, must. And if some of the dopes I know can actually sit still and concentrate long enough to turn out a few hundred coherent pages, there's no reason on earth except laziness and lack of will power why I (or you—all this applies to you too) shouldn't.

—————————◄ ►—————————

Here I am, at 3 A.M., we sail in six hours (or take the boat train, rather, and sail at noon), and we're still packing, but nearly finished. Tonight was glorious. We got a box for the opening night of the Marquis de Cuevas Ballet; a thrilling evening, topped off with our last European steaks and good wine in a Leicester Square restaurant and a walk back through crowded, cold and windy Trafalgar Square to the car. Oh, dear, if only it weren't for so *long!* But then we wouldn't have this long here on a decent salary. I often wish I could split in two and be aware of both personalities, one for Africa, and the other for Europe. America seems to have got lost somewhere. I must close, as we are rising at 6:30.

Much love from Europe
for the last time,

Pat

September 30, 1958

Dear, dear Pat,

September is ending, and everything is radiant. I have one hour before leaving to teach.

Really, Pat, you are so loving a friend, and I have met no one who has endeared themselves so to me. The package arrived, and since Reinhard spied it at the door before I did, I was unable to conceal its existence until late November. Thank you—oh, thanks so very very. The duffel coat is delicious, and Reinhard fits and will fit into it for a long and becoming time. And he loves it!

Also my thanks to you personally for the *Lit. Supp.* This is one of the most satisfying things I know to have coming in regularly. It is really unique in the world.

You write that I sound a little more alive. I feel it. No one would assert more emphatically than I that Des Moines was really the "Unreal City" and that I felt during most of the year precisely like a "patient etherized upon a table." Milwaukee is ever so much better. Also, I feel one hell of a lot better, which, in pure self-defense, I have to add.

However! There is so much to tell you, and since you share so much, and since I appreciate it so earnestly, almost voraciously, I want to tell you so much, and shall, if this letter runs twenty pages. Do you remember that night, a season like this, some seven years ago, when I met you on 11th East, and we walked through all the October leaves, and spoke I don't know what of? But it must have been of life and the transience of life, of men and women, and art, and it must have been intensely.

And where is it you are to be these next three years—where, exactly? What do *you* intend to do, besides live with the accumulated riches of your past leave, and besides sharing the changing worlds of wee boys? Didn't you say this is a smaller community than Mahali?

Hans amuses me with his sudden enthusiasm for the idea of a visit to Africa. He was uninterested for so long, and now is almost childishly eager to sometime visit that continent. I don't quite perceive what motivates that, perhaps a most understandable desire to slice through all the superimposed and meaningless layers of *this* kind of Western Civilization to something at least more obviously elemental. I may be way off there, but that would at least make sense to me. So much civilization here seems to revolve around prices and specialists in underarm deodorants or theorists of self-expression, that one is besieged with many a doubt of America's messianic validity.

The political, even the social, climate has changed significantly since you and I were sharing American life together. Needless to say, the McCarthy epidemic was over even before you left. The hero worship of Eisenhower has given way to a barrage of often vicious, very explicit criticism, and the sense that he is a very weak and ineffectual president is almost a common denominator of political conversation these days. Also, the Sputnik alarum brought the realities of our primitive school system to the fore; critics still speak of it, intelligently, and new adjustments for good students are already set into many a curriculum over the country.

Still, a man like Stevenson is, I feel sure, as far as ever from being able to enlist the popular sympathy. I'm sure you read about apathy and complacence and fear in whatever journals you find to read, but they are all dangerously real, and although there is more respect for the intellectual than when we were here, and a more exciting cultural life, actually, I don't believe there are any mass changes of heart at all. There are only more graduates, I fear. Anyway, the cleavage between the egghead and the regular guy is vast, enormous, and fraught with trouble.

Follow the segregation issue, and you see it. Notice even the Democrats who are winning senatorial nominations—the absolutely lowest rung of the Democratic party. There are TV programs of absolutely superlative quality steadily losing ground, being cut from half hours to fifteen minutes—lack of sponsors. These are the information programs, the articulate, dedicated and scrupulously honest CBS and NBC news analysts. One can catch them fifteen minutes a day. They have their audience. But what size of audience must demand the horrors of the other 23¾ hours? Commercials, pops, and sports. On Sundays a few bits from the Scriptures. Almost never a live concert. In fact, I haven't found one yet. When there are good dramas on TV, they are magnificent! The talent is here, the need, and the awareness of the need—all!—but the money goes elsewhere, still to back what the people want.

Have you read Milovan Djilas's new book yet, *Land Without Justice?* It must be fine. Or *Doctor Zhivago?*

As for my schedule that you assure me will not bore you: I'm teaching twelve hours a week, three a day, with Tuesdays free. I leave Reinhard with an uninteresting neighbor who is mother to a sixteen months old son, really too young to be much of a joy to Reinhard. The nice thing is that she has abundant toys, does not mind flexible hours, and impromptu services, her house is clean and just next door. So that could be worse.

Mount Mary College is one hour away by bus, which I don't really mind, since I can use the time for reading or reviewing. It's a lovely spacy place, a two-winged structure, with arcades linking the central building, and of course, the goodly sisters floating darkly here and there. They are a very genial order, the Sacred Sisters of Notre Dame, very warm and amusing. Why is it that we do not expect nuns to be quite human? They delight in our boy, spreading their gowns as they sit on the cold stone floor to play trains with him.

I enjoy all the teaching and find I have as much time as before to read, etc.

I probably accomplish more, plus having money I can dream of going to Europe with. Also, I feel a little more as if I had come of age, since I wear heels daily now—something I thought I could NEVER manage. Hans's school is old—that is, a century—and very near the lake. Small, but with excellent colleagues. As to the students, I don't yet know.

Reinhard has come into another wonderful, endearing age. He's sheer delight, and I see how easy it would be to be fatally possessive, to goad him on to perform and display all his whimsies until they are not spontaneous at all.

Write soon and often,
All love,

Joyce

Dearest friend, so much further-away-seeming than two months ago:

A scrawl, to keep you on my qui vive. We are still in a morass of unpacking and settling into a very old rambling falling to bits house, full of cockroaches and white ants' nests. We are still catching our breaths after our almost too long but glorious safari. The kids love it here already, and so do we. The house is immense and has great inside possibilities if it doesn't collapse over our heads in the next three years. The wading pool is set up on the veranda looking every inch luxurious and American. All our bits and pieces have arrived in one piece from Mahali, wonder of wonders, except a few minor bits of crockery. The people here seem a pleasant enough lot. P. loves his little (half the size of Mahali) hospital, and I'm cocking a wary eye at an enormous and derelict garden stretching for untended acres around the house.

Our car trip from South Africa to here was a giant venture, almost too much so, which left me with very mixed feelings. I *must* get this off by the plane today. We get a weekly mail plane which from December to June is our only contact with the outside world, and even now during the dry season is very exciting to have come in, bearing all our mail, a week's worth of newspapers, sausages, cheese, etc.

The climate here is a thousand times better than steamy old Mahali, and I think we're going to love it, though we'll be much poorer as the cost of living is very high due to the remoteness. It's rather like inland parts of California—many graceful eucalyptus trees lining the roads, a profusion of flowers in people's gardens (even now in the dry season), a cool breeze morning and evening.

145

I'm reading Durrell's *Justine* in snatches and loving it. We got *Doctor Zhivago* just before we left London, but are waiting till things calm down so we can devote our undivided attention to something so deserving of it.

I hope you're liking Milwaukee. *Do* write me a long letter. I'm due for one.

Much love,

Pat

MILWAUKEE
November 4, 1958

Dearest Pat,

Thank heavens! Now I know your address, and all these accusations of indifference can stop. I don't resent it, but very much regret it, that you haven't been getting my letters, particularly one truly Leviathan effort which cost me a whole evening, a batch of dirty dishes the next morning, and an angry husband who had such an uncompanionable wife. Anyway, I didn't know where you were to be, and now are, in Tanganyika, so I sent two letters on to your London bank, which I hope acts as forwarding station to you.

All goes well here, very smoothly, and so much much more happily than last year. I'm feeling just grand, except for mid-period agonies, which, after untoward expense, turn out to have the good old-fashioned German appellation of "mittelschmerz," and about which very little can be done. Perhaps a little brother for Reinhard would stop it temporarily. DO NOT get excited; unfortunately I cannot enjoy my fertility as much as I'd like. For I'm absolutely aching to have a second child, but we'll have to wait for a bit, at least long enough for me to finish out the school year.

We have great plans for the next summer. We've already put a sum down to hold reservations for passages on the new American line, Banner (we had preferred to have gone Dutch), to sail June 7th, arriving Amsterdam eight days later. Although we love Milwaukee, and I frankly deplore the idea of leaving in a few brief months, I'm sure Hans wants to get started abroad, and for that I can hardly blame him.

Still and all, I'm rather ashamed that I cannot grab the enthusiasm of living in Europe permanently, honestly, by the horns, and delight in the anticipation. I somehow or other find this difficult to do. It is not that I adore America; I am just somehow not able to identify myself with living for ten or more years in Germany.

I would probably feel the same about France or Spain or even Scotland. Strangely enough, not about Beirut, although that was still further from the

146

family. Write me about it; maybe you can understand me better than I myself.

I know this is what Hans not only wants and needs, but is determined to have, and I must go along with it, but I don't want merely to acquiesce; I'd like positively to help him, to help him rejoice in the return. But I don't—I'm a positive sop. I do realize, though, the vast difference in living abroad temporarily, for comparative purposes. France was fascinating, thrilling, because it was different, because it threw a valuable perspective on what I knew, what I was. But to shift the whole framework, so that Europe becomes the stable, and America what is compared to it, seems so unlikely to me.

I'll write again soon.

All my love,

Joyce

November 25, 1958

Dearest Pat,

I cannot but feel a little guilty, considering just the possibility that you have not heard from me. I cannot understand what happens to the mail. Perhaps by now you have all my backlog of verbiage, and the whole is clear again. But each time I put Reinhard's little duffel coat on, I think of you with all the warmth that always accompanies the idea. He looks particularly sweet in it, wears it constantly against this humid cold which cuts right through you. Together with Hans, in man-size duffel coat, also blue, they make a wonderful team.

I have been busy with this school business, but altogether enjoying it thoroughly. I'm ever so much better a teacher when I can get my hands and enthusiasm on literature, even if the girls do find all ideas so remote from them, so very tragically unreal to them.

I'm perfectly willing to grant that *I* may not be the vehicle to conduct their enthusiasm towards anything significant, but my God, nobody seems able to. All the sisters say the same. Altogether the American scene is something of an ugly and tragic spectacle, and I do mean spectacle. I'm sending you a copy of an interesting article about it in *The New Republic.* This, along with the 101st anniversary edition of *The Atlantic.* It will take a while.

There are many seeds and signs of decay, it seems to me, almost everywhere I look. Daily, with increasing insistence, myself and Hans, and others I speak with, realize that things can simply not continue as they are. "Surely the second coming is at hand"—I mean it. I should not be surprised if revolution comes within our lifetimes. I hope so. I only hope it is not that worst of holocausts. But this holding of life in abeyance cannot continue indefinitely either. Take modern art, for example. How utterly dead end, full circle it has come! There is something so nihilistic, so utterly helpless in the New York school, à la Kooning, etc.

They might go on calling it abstract expressionism, but even if it retains the term, it has to return to some calling of the human spirit, which comments more than "No. 120" or "Labyrinth" or "Haze" or "Pattern" or "Warp," etc. No. All these smeary ways out! I realize that I'm pretty much of a smear myself, but at least I try not to frame and sell it.

I look to Camus as a voice. We've never even exchanged thoughts about him, yet we have all his books, have loved and learned from most of them, and find there an unfailing source of strength. How do you feel? And then, all these trashy plays that rise and fall on Broadway. It seems that by all lots, the scarcest thing in the world is a good play.

Reinhard and Hans and I went shopping downtown—Christmas, you know, although it goes as Xmas here (the substitution of the most noncommittal of all letters). What a bodge! The gift departments overstocked with "modern" (God help us!) ceramics and lamp bases, takeoffs of Brancusi that would make him retch, wriggling beneath the base of gigantesque shades in dirt-cheap china. I swear, to be a snob, a true unconditional snob, is the only protection a poor slob has! Because as soon as the petit bourgeois get their costume-bejeweled hands on an idea, it grows pretty murky. I'm afraid I have fallen this far. Straighten me out if I'm wrong.

I do send great billowing heaps of love.

Joyce

PASHENZI
December 3, 1958

Dear Joyce,

This will not be a proper answer to your letter. I have been too tired (asthma), cross, and frustrated-feeling to write anything that sounded semi-human, but I wanted to get these snaps off by today's plane.

We are very broke, so it's just as well that Pashenzi is tiny and dull with very little social life. The general I.Q., I would say, is about twenty points higher here than in Mahali. I never in my life met a stupider lot of people than those we lived with for three years in Mahali. Here they do seem brighter and more interested in things as a whole. Which, since P. and I haven't had a conversation in about a year and a half, is greatly to be desired. I've always heard that doctors make lousy bloody husbands, and you know, I'm beginning to believe it's true. I don't

148

know, maybe everyone does after four or five years of marriage, but we just seem to have lost contact and gone on different wavelengths without quite realizing it, somewhere along the way.

We have had a constant stream of visitors for the last fortnight, all from H.Q. getting a last look before the long rains set in (they are imminent). I will write you something about my present being, which verges on the brink of nervous collapse, I believe. I really think I'm quite mad these days. Something seems to have snapped somewhere. I haven't been talking at all about your immense problem, dear friend, but I have been thinking a great deal about it, and I shall discuss it also in a day or two.

All my best love,

Pat

December 5, 1958

Dearest companion at arms,

I wrote you such a stupid letter, the last one, do ignore it. I was just feeling very depressed. I have so much to say to you, I hardly know where to begin. Not news particularly, just things simmering away.

Since our return and now that we do seem to be settled in and routinized a little, I have taken out my typewriter and dutifully peck away every afternoon. I want to revise thoroughly a few short stories I dashed off last tour in Mahali. I'm starting to keep a sort of journal, ideas, jottings and quotations book which I am beginning to think is indispensable equipment for anyone who wants to write anything, particularly if the mind is as disordered, discipline as hopeless, and memory as faulty as mine. Besides, it's good practice, like scales. If it hadn't been for our correspondence these last arid years, I should be so rusty altogether, I shouldn't even be able to write a paragraph without danger of imminent mental collapse.

But I have tried to say things intelligibly to you, with an added modicum of grace too. Thank God for you in this world, my whipping boy, my prayer cushion, my sort of Muse.

As for Philip and me—I don't know, we're just getting into a habit of marriage, I suppose. However, it has its moments, and really one can't ask too much, or you end up with nothing at all. I suppose in the last analysis I wouldn't go back to blessed singleness ever again. We've grown too much a part of each other, are terribly dependent on one another. For the first time since our mar-

149

riage, five and a half years now, I am the one who is beginning to draw back a little, to reveal less, to give a little less my soul, my personality, my ideas, my comments. And perhaps it's a good thing.

━━━━━━━━⊶ ⊷━━━━━━━

Later: You wanted to know some of the details of our life here in Pashenzi. We have a very old house, German, pre–WW I. We are cut off by road till next June by the mildest of rains, not like Mahali where it rained up to six inches in a night; no, here it patters gently down amid terrible thunder and lightning. We are on the crest of a very gentle slope leading from town up to the Boma (government offices), up to us, and then down again to the other sixteen European houses, scattered over a two mile area. Our house has two tiny and two huge bedrooms, a long narrow kitchen with wood stove, enormous dining and living rooms, and an open veranda running round three sides of the house. It's furnished with standard government furniture, plain and adequate. We have a few tables of wrought-iron legs and African mahogany tops of our own, which I designed, and, of necessity, masses of our own bookcases for the hundreds of books I forever seem to be packing and unpacking. But I'd rather part with my clothes first. We have running water, but no electricity, no telephones, no gas lines, nothing like that.

We have four servants: Saidi the headboy, who does most of the housework and serves meals and keeps the others in line; Mohamed the dhobi, who is a hopeless alcoholic and seems to have got worse since coming back here; Bahati the garden boy, who also looks after Christopher when he plays outdoors (no hedges or fences, and lots of snakes and scorpions); and Elias, our cook, the first good one I've ever had. He even offered to make our Kilisimasi keki, but I said I'd do it!

We get up at 6:30, when Saidi brings morning tea, an old English custom which has gone the sad far way of servants in England but lingers on in cheap-servant outposts of the Empire. We have breakfast (I do the children's food and feed them), and P. goes off at 8. I garden, sew, potter about, write letters, clean toilets (yes! they *don't* do that), do bills, shop in the so-called town, have morning coffee at 11:00, quite often with another Memsab or two, or them here. P. home at 12:30, kids' lunch and to bed, our own lunch at 1:00, coffee in the sitting room. P. back to hospital at 2:00, I write till 4:00 when kids get up, fiddle about with their drinks, potting, clothes, etc., till P. gets home at 5:00, we have tea in the sitting room (I got the most beautiful embroidered tea set in Madeira on this trip out), then garden or play tennis at the club (right across the road from our house) till 6:30, when I feed and bath the kids and bed them. We dine at 8:00; Saidi leaves the coffee tray in the sitting room each night for my two or three cups, and goes off.

We have our club, a rather dead affair here, except for a very high standard of tennis, and a dull booze session every Saturday night to which we've been once for appearance's sake, when we first arrived. Neither of us seems keen any more on that sort of thing, except with the right people. They are nice enough here, but not really whom one would *choose* as close friends, especially the women, who are horribly British middle-class hausfraus. I get so sick of conversation about babies and boy troubles and gardens that I could scream. But if one has to live three years with the same thirteen families, one doesn't scream.

I have started studying French three mornings a week with the Austrian wife of the police chap here. We are both loving it. There is a scheme on now to start evening adult education classes for already literate Africans who want to improve their command of English, learn history, government, etc., and I would love to teach a couple of evenings a week if it comes through and if Philip will let me.

We (I should say Philip, at least for the first few weeks) planted a large garden, veg. and flower, which is taking shape now. There are hundreds of mango trees round about, dropping their horrid squishy old mangoes all over the place and bringing mango flies by the millions, a particularly odious insect.

We get fresh meat, beef, tough as shoe leather, full of bone splinters and just hacked off the carcass; also it's water-soaked to make it weigh more, every day, a flat 3/= (42¢) a kilo. We get sausages, biweekly pork chops, and a monthly ham, all on the weekly mail plane. Also our cheese and butter come that way. We get no fresh vegetables now until Jan. or Feb. Just tins, potatoes, rice, onions and garlic. We drink dried milk, eat the tiniest eggs I've ever seen, half of which are gruesomely fertilized when you crack them open as you are baking a cake, but they only cost about 3¢ each. We get sacks of 30 kilos each of brown and white flour (from which *I* bake the everlasting bloody bread, two loaves a day, seven days a week, ad infinitum) from the enormous German R.C. mission fifteen miles away, also pork lard (5 gals. at a time), and for me, sauerkraut, and for Philip, hideous blood sausage. The only fruit just now are bananas and the odd papaya. Mangoes will be ripe in a few weeks, then avocados, then at the end of the rains, a few European fruits, and for six months oranges and lemons. We did get 30 lbs. each of imported Italian plums two weeks ago, and I made jam from the lot while P. was on safari, only to find out that he doesn't like plum jam! One of those inexplicable marital knowledge gaps. I wish I could send you some.

Because I'm more or less happy after a long period of depression, I'm getting very thin again. The happier and more hard-working I am, the less appetite I have, and if I don't stuff myself continually, I do get very thin. But as I feel fine, I couldn't care less. How is your old perennial weight problem since Reinhard came? Did the duffel coat *really* fit him? Have you read *Zhivago* as you asked me? Because I so loved it, I couldn't bear not to share it with you, and sent you a copy a fortnight ago. My God, to love like that—what must it be like?

Well, enough about me and to talk to you about you. My dear, you know my feelings on this umbilical cord business, and also where a wife's place is. I'm sorry, very sorry, that my mother has never seen Christopher and Julian. So is she. But she must come out here to see them. I could never, I think, live in the States again, and until and unless the fare to the U.S. and back for all of us wouldn't take scrimping on necessaries from Philip, I shan't go. Perhaps it's a cruel attitude, but it's crueler to bring a child up so that he or she is torn between his duties to his contemporary family and that of the next, which should be over and done with at adulthood.

One's parents have (or should have) a valid and worthy life of their own to live. The years ahead of you are long, arduous and full on their own account. The world is green and exciting and at a tremendous corner. We are in the youth of a new era, and we ourselves are young and equipped to face it. I prefer the European attitude and position, halfway between the two colossi—U.S. and U.S.S.R. I couldn't agree more with you about America, but I feel even the same about Russia. You must pick your own time and space to live out your days, uninfluenced by the pull of the cradle, and not only that, you have got a *truly* European husband as well, blessedly without the immigrant mentality (streets paved with gold, etc.), as is Philip. We still would opt, if Philip could practice in France (which he can't), to live in Paris more than anywhere else, and after this tour we just don't know where or what we'll do.

But it won't be a job or place with great remuneration or "possibilities." We just aren't interested. For me, in your situation, the greatest difficulty would be the language barrier. But you are such a gifted linguist and a European university is such a mixed bag, so cosmopolitan, that ought not to prove too tremendous a stumbling block. Am I being heartless and unseeing? Do I not understand all the ramifications of your problem? Doubtless I do not. Who does? Not even you, I venture to say, since you can't, looking into the future.

But there comes a time of a tremendous uncertain decision in everyone's life. For me, it was when I married Philip. You know how uncertain I was, when I passed through Salt Lake on our honeymoon. But the rightness of the decision has impressed itself gradually on me through the years, and the thought of a separation of any kind has never seemed a way out of anything, no matter how impossible some aspects of our life have seemed at times. What gap of loving may exist in my life I will fill with other things. What, after all, I have to keep asking myself, do I consider the most important thing in my life? And in the end, it always comes back to the good old sophomoric search of "finding oneself." All right, then how best to do that? Before you can even begin, you must realize that you have chosen someone for *life* to help you, and you to help him, in what ways you each choose to help and be helped.

A geographical and cultural situation is of prime importance in this, I believe, because no matter where you end up, you presumably have chosen this spot as the best one to solve various problems. And if financial rewards and proximity to the place where you were nurtured come first, well, so be it, and accept the disadvantages which that place gives. But as, over the past year and a half, you have been so obviously *un*satisfied, then you'd better try something and somewhere else, hadn't you? As long as you have the two people dearest to you, healthy and happy, a roof over your head, clothes to keep you warm and a full contented stomach, that ought to be the basis for the beginnings of the kind of life you're after.

I know all this is not enough, but it's the fine shadings of all else about you that can be so carefully chosen to suit the byways of your mind and own special culture. And the concrete leftovers of the past must not count in this choice! The one thing I wanted to do when we got married was to find some nice little university town to live in "for a bit," exactly like S.L.C., and if Philip had given in, we'd be there yet, rotting away in the academic ivory tower, pillars of misery, both of us. I shouldn't have given way to the desire to pour advice all over you, but I do love you so, you're my only only friend in 2½ billion people alive, and I can only see life through my own dirty little picture window, and maybe what I've said is all wrong, but you must decide for yourself and be happy (or unhappy in congenial surroundings) so that YOU CAN WRITE. I shall have to put another stamp on this if I add one more page, and I've written far too much as it is. Feel free to comment on anything I've said, as P. and I never read each other's letters.

So very much love—do write!

Pat

Most dear Pat,

Your last, alas too short, letter distressed me. Nonetheless, its distress chorded in directly with much that I'm feeling. I am anxious to know more, of course, and hopeful that the discord, although perhaps chronic, is not terminal. What do the thirties mean to you? Being near the border of them, they do not mean to me what Mother used to mean by them. "That warmest time of your life, having each other, and your children still being young." To me, even from the very early days of our marriage, I anticipated that it might mean those things, yes, but a very strong instinct told me it would mean something more, an age of infidelity. The closer I come to young middle age, the more am I certain of that unpleasant intuition. Why I hold on to the concept of faith to the marriage vow, I'm not quite sure. Is it my ancient Puritan blood rising, bigoted and determined, to the fore? Or is it because that is the better life?

I have always detested the easy faithfulness of those sound and wholesome Mormon marriages, and is it because now for the first time I become a protagonist in the issue that I seek to back away from "That dolphin-torn, that gong-tormented sea"? In such a case, I'm a mere coward, backing into the avenue of easiest retreat when adult life confronts me, who always considered herself as

153

preparing, and now seems totally unfit to confront with vigor and honesty and courage what it is all about. And yet I cannot quite believe this about myself. I was warned in my halcyon days never to marry an inexperienced man, but to choose one who had had more than surfeit in bachelor days.

Actually, from the early days in Santander, first talking with Hans, even before sleeping with him, I knew he was one who had not had enough freedom to explore and conquer, and intuited with a surety that could not be dismissed that he would have to make up for it, and would, after marriage. Every conversation we have had then and since tells me of the irresistible line pulling toward the still faceless, but not distant, women who will cooperate in that destiny.

It's more will than destiny, but the will is there, and the will makes the destiny. And so I should be prepared. But I am not. I hate it, and know that I shall detest it when it appears. I know I shall be incapable of responding in like; in other words, by taking the comfortable casual approach, not of vengeance or retaliation, but of symmetry. If, indeed, I ever come to that, then forces, circumstances and years will have changed me very much indeed. And then, whatever native honor I had about marriage vows (as *realities*, not as respectabilities) will have become merely "the insubstantial pageant faded" and I will have admitted utterly that "we are such stuff as dreams are made of."

You'll wonder what I am raving about. Hans is not in process of betraying me, only in process of being tempted, and, I should guess, sorely tempted. I only write because I feel now at that very threshold of fear, suffering, separation, and an irretrievably lost union which I have been anticipating.

Please write me, fully and frequently, and tell me of yourself. Do have a good Christmas. How I should love to see you!

Much love,

Joyce

MILWAUKEE
December 16, 1958

Dear friend,

I have your letter before me, having read and reread it several times. I don't know why I should think of domestic and personal tragedy so much in terms of fidelity and infidelity, with me on the losing end, except that I have had too much the lion's share of it the other way around, and it is perhaps poetic justice that the worst pains shoot my way, if that is the worst.

And Hans has not known that reckless intrusion into hearts that I with such nonchalance have been known to pursue. So, I don't know if it is guilt or

154

possessiveness (because I can be quite zealously, jealously, physically possessive, I find, of him). Also, I have run head-on into a sort of professional threat. I have always felt inadequate, whether rightly or wrongly, as a help (and you spoke of our being here—in this choice, I mean—partially to help) for Hans in his painting. I know so little, and understand only slightly more. I have a certain poor intuition which can sometimes help him, but no critical insights worth a damn.

My only blessing is an intensity of wanting to help, but this can easily turn sour. How easily one can try too hard! And love doesn't like that. I can model for him, sometimes do, naked, which is rather lovely, since we do enjoy each other's bodies. It can be provocative, and deliciously so (but—and isn't this the horrid bourgeois middle-aged wife coming out in me?—it might be equally provocative with other models, no?).

As an appropriate aside here, I am comfortable modeling for him, since my body, ever since, not Reinhard's birth, but my onslaught with meningitis, which took off 30 pounds, is quite new, and much nicer. He says I should tie ribbons around my breasts, and then wear nothing else but a skirt. They are not what they were; nursing took them down a few inches, but they are not ruined. Seriously, since then I have, physically, a rather new personality, and one I am grateful for. Before I knew you, at about 20, I had a nice figure too, nicer than now, for I had a small waist, which, alas, is gone. But between then and Reinhard, it was one constant battle, and in Beirut, I once went up to 150!! How miserable each day's thoughts were! It does matter. I feel more womanly, more cosmopolitan, more feminine, more gracious, more whatever you will, in this respect. But, as you can tell from my letters, the insides go on straining, shifting, adjusting, and failing to adjust.

To me the remarkable and happy thing about your letter is the writing, the spirit behind the writing which is coming out of it. I am delighted, thrilled, and eager to encourage you fearfully. You must keep up with it! I am very certain that you could; with both of us, I feel, it is discipline, and above that, will. My will is a little knock-kneed; it rubs against itself, and wears out its energy.

Would you believe it, that religion still bothers me, heckles me, pains me, troubles me, tortures me, frightens me? Shouldn't I have resolved that somehow by now? Being married to a man with beautiful religious sensitivity, being a product of a Unitarian home, being a sort of baby mystic from the beginning, and having friends who range from cynical atheists to Sister Frances, having books about the *Way of Zen*, and *The Fear and the Trembling*, and loving both Gerard Manley Hopkins and William Carlos Williams, all these do not help much either. It surely gives me a hell of a respect for the many possibilities of approach, however. Slight compensation.

Don't despair about *Doctor Zhivago*. I haven't had time, and humbly thank you in advance.

Hans does usually read your letters, because he enjoys them and you so, so much that he says he almost feels like writing you himself.

Well, America is quite ugly now, with its pink and turquoise *"Xmas"* trees and zillions of people shopping all over each other, and the hideous excess of goods. However, one can find lovely things, and Milwaukee has delightful corners here and there. We like it. It's a happy, happy contrast to Des Moines.

Thanks for all your words and thoughts and friendship. I'll write again soon.

Joyce

PART SIX

JANUARY 1959–FEBRUARY 1960

Marriages are failing all around me

January 20, 1959

Very dear dear Pat,

Your three bigger and littler birthdays have come and gone by now, without direct and punctual wishes from me. But if you know anything of how thoughts of you keep me company, you can certainly deduce from that that I was thinking of you and Christopher and of Julian and the days commemorating your and their lives' beginnings. I only don't know when Philip's birthday was, and when it repeats its acknowledgment. Happy Birthday to you all. I only wish that your year could bring us, however briefly, together, but this time literally so.

Well, there's a possibility. Europe seems more and more the destiny that approaches through the telescope's small end. And if I'm really pregnant, it will be hard to teach with a new one, and silly to stay without my teaching. It's only five days overdue, but still this is unusual for me (and I just got myself down to a delightfully vain and flirtatious size 10, darn it). You see, it's the money we're after here, for purposes of buying an abandoned farmhouse in France with orchard for $1,000. Also, I suppose a return trip would be forbidden by authorities in the eighth month? Well, all still quite hypothetical. But even if not, Hans does feel the pressure to get started over there, but heaven knows in what fashion.

I'll bet you sense a little snarl of disappointment in me growing in yourself, to think she cares so much about jobs, etc.! But we are giving up such a lovely place here, and much of Germany only alienates me . . . so there! Also, in gorgeous irony to the last, self-righteous, highly disdainful, very self-secure letter, I found myself tumulted into what borders very nearly on a love affair. Serve me damn well right! I'm fighting it daily, resisting telephoning, succumbing and telephoning, aching to be with him, delighting in his sheer proximity, under any kind of grouping, feeling very very good just talking to him. He would be, of course, a

159

colleague of Hans, an artist yet, a brilliant printmaker—woodcuts, etchings.

It's so painfully meaningful it shames me, and I'm astonished such a menial, albeit heavenly, consideration as physical attraction can be activating both of us so agonizingly. So far, no sin. Only an abysmal desire. If you want to write of it, write to Mt. Mary College.

And your woes—how are they? Yes, I do understand ever so much. You're my great friend.

All love,

Joyce

February 4, 1959

Dearest partner in almost but not quite crime,

I suppose it just happens to everyone with any hormones, doesn't it? Like that lovely short story of Colette, "Le blé en herbe"—when you're ripe you fall. And oh, dear, I've fallen. I can't remember exactly how much I've told you about all this since we arrived in Pashenzi, but I shall begin with the mundane details at the beginning.

Somehow, something in me which I thought had died has awakened now, but which certainly has been dormant for five or six years. We'd been settled down here for two to three weeks, and were playing tennis one day; I was watching my partner serve, and suddenly, in a still second, while his body was poised in that one glorious moment before the racket strikes the ball, I fell wholly and completely in love with him, and I've had hardly a thought in my head since then for three months. He's very "U" in the English sense, is eight years very much married to a dour little Irish woman, has two girls, is thirty-five, an agnostic, loves his work and the Africans, is so insulated against the impingement of personalities, so shy and wary, that I haven't a hope in the world of even a held hand in a year's time.

Why do I always fall for the impossible and unattainable? He and his wife come to the club only once every three to four weeks, and then Stephen and I usually dance the whole evening, till breakup time, never saying a word, just gloriously close and warm and real, and I wish I could die at those moments. Philip knows (I don't dissimulate well, as you may remember) and I suppose, because my feelings must appear so strong, is a bit jealous, but he is consoling himself with the wife of a game warden.

She's awful and we don't get along very well, but I'm glad for Philip's sake, because of all this. I suppose this state will drag on as long as we're all together here, then we'll gradually leave and get transferred, and everyone will forget. Poor me. I have turned the color of a ripe Mexican from playing so much tennis, as Stephen plays every sunny day (not often lately, the rains come nearly every afternoon). I have little glimmers of hope now and then when he strolls over to borrow a book or a magazine with an article in it I've told him about. He's mad on Proust, Joyce and Austen, but reads practically nothing contemporary.

God, I feel so forlorn and unloved and unneeded. I can't tell you how I ache for this wretched man. But it's such a lonely uphill battle. Batting my head against a stone wall. Oh dear, life suddenly takes on so many complications and ramifications, and it could all be so simple and clear if only we could love the right people.

It's just taken me so utterly unawares, and has my heart and soul in such an aching stranglehold, I don't care for consequences or the future or other people. Really, all I would ask would be the *feeling* to be reciprocal. That would satisfy me; I could go on my dull daily rounds feeling loved by the beloved, which is all that really matters.

Does all this sound too sordid and ridiculous? But I've only given you the bare bones of the situation, and you must fill it in with my days of longing, Philip being broody and palsy by turns, Stephen being light-hearted and friendly and warm, but never more. The barriers are too immense, the complications and consequences too tangled and noisome for anyone as essentially good and simple as Stephen to bother with. And so I fear I will go on aching uselessly away till a year from next May, when they go on leave.

And you, ma chère amie, how do your affairs march? Is all light and tremulous joy and equivalent happiness? How I envy you, if so. How difficult our lives are, after all, when we have so much good, and so many lovely things to share, and the sharing thereof is made so terribly difficult. I seem to have lost all moral sense and sensibility, and have put every thought of harm inflicted or wretched selfishness from my ego, and dwell only on this beautiful Stephen, who I wish were mine, if in our two consciousnesses only. I shall keep you posted on the progress (or non-progress, which is more likely). But I wouldn't have missed this explosion of passion in me for all the world. I thought it was long since dead and I was getting old. But I'm young, *young!!* And vital and alive and ready to be loved again, in a way that I haven't been for years. Nihil desperandum.

> All the love that is not Stephen's
> is yours, my dear,
>
> *Pat*

February 11, 1959

Dear Pat,

I am convalescing and not yet well. My letter cannot be long. I have not heard for a long time. Is all well with you? Did you receive my Christmas package and recent letters?

Since Christmas I have had a time of it. As I wrote, I thought perhaps I was pregnant. I was, but my repeated attacks of incredible pain warned me something was wrong. Last Monday I couldn't bear it. The doctor came, quickly diagnosed it as a bleeding ectopic pregnancy, and I was rushed to emergency surgery (clothesless) where they removed a ready-to-rupture left fallopian tube and a cystic left ovary. Blood transfusions, shots, and then, freedom to read (and to weep abundantly over) *Doctor Zhivago.* How I did so love it, dear Pat. Thank you! It's reassuring to know that although Zhivago is dead, Pasternak isn't.

Now I am home, still abed, but better—thinner than ever, but still clinging to the hope that what fertility I still have left will not betray me. It is painful, but I walk and feel altogether not too wretched.

Write me—soon. I need it. It will be a month before I can teach again. How is your writing going? Tell me all. I've revised some poems lately, and am happy to touch it again. Oh, that beautiful book. It moved me enormously. Life is so bewildering and so so beautiful.

Love,

Joyce

PASHENZI
February 14, 1959

Dearest Joyce,

I wonder if you would mind terribly cashing the enclosed pounds and getting five yards of a polished cotton in the sort of design or pattern you think I might like—greens (not Kelly) or reds (scarlet, not mauve)—that would be suitable for an informal dancing dress, and a 22" zipper (for straight down the back) in a color to match. It's so bloody impossible trying to get decent cottons out here, from Dar or Nairobi. They send the stupidest damn selection of samples, you know, little rosebuds in pale yellow on a pale blue background, that I've practically given up, but I'm dying to make a decent dress to wear for dancing at the club on Sat. nights.

Are you in a frightful rush from morning till night? How you've managed, all this time, working, having Reinhard to cope with, all the traveling you've done, and your illnesses too, I simply boggle at the thought in this lazy quiet backwater my life has become, full of chaotic unmeanings. Are you really pregnant again?

I'm in one of my down cycles, and it all seems inexpressibly dreary and hopeless, whether I'm loved (which I'm not) or unloved, needed or useless, creative or nonfunctioning (which latter I most definitely am). I've started writing poetry again. My poems are idiotic, but vaguely satisfying. My journal is copious and very very private. How long does one go on feeling this way before resigning oneself to ineluctable fate, before the weight of the distress of years crushes hope and joy and ecstasy out of you? God, how sordidly dreary the days ahead all seem, empty of love or understanding or empathy, just a non-entity of social politenesses and a pattern of days full of the things to be done to raise children and keep a house going.

I seem to have lost my enthusiasm for life, I suppose it boils down to. Perhaps I'm a generation too late, and it should be about 1925 now. Or am I part of this "Beat Generation" I've been reading about? Or am I ten years too old for that? (twenty-eight now, I shudder to think). Music is one saving grace, and I drown myself in our flashlight-battery-operated new phonograph every night after dinner till bedtime.

Do you remember when you and I and Liza and Benny drove down through the snow to Provo to hear Abel John's group doing the Vivaldi Gloria Mass? A sharply pointed memory for me. Oh, Joyce, tell me that life is gay and exciting and full of charm and surprises around every corner, that somewhere love waits again. I feel so gray and gloomy.

Much rapport and love from this side of the Atlantic.

Pat

PASHENZI
February 18, 1959

Dearest friend in bed,

Yes, life is indeed bewildering, but beautiful, but at the moment mostly just bewildering. Oh, Joyce, if only I could give you half of my rude health (minus the asthma) and *all* of my revolting fertility (no, I'm not pregnant again *yet,* but I keep my fingers crossed from month to month that I've again successfully avoided it). Oh, my dear, what deceptive and treacherous mediums (media?) our bodies are, but how glorious sometimes and so indispensable. My heart aches for you in your pain and sorrow of loss yet again. I do hope you were covered by an insurance scheme this time and that it doesn't greatly add to your debts. I feel so impotent to help or to say any comforting phrases here. But you know my heart and love are yours.

And now to my own problems, which I shall so selfishly and thoughtlessly, in your time of troubles, ask you to help me bear. Shall I tell you straight off, or shall I lead up to it? I think the latter. You know about my dear Stephen from my last but one letter. I have suffered from guilt pangs and conscience and revolt at my hopelessly inconstant soul, till I am down to 105 pounds, have asthma every night, am useless in the house and with the children. Stephen and I have hardly exchanged a personal word. We just dance (about once a fortnight) and moon at each other on the tennis courts or wave shyly as I trip past his office on a spurious errand to the post office. We exchange books, magazine articles, poems —with underlinings and marginal comments—but oh, so delicate and tangential, so Jane Austenish you wouldn't believe this sort of blossoming relationship could truly and sweetly exist in 1959.

I've tried not to think about the future, to tell myself that all I ever wanted from Stephen was reciprocation of affection. And yet, you know, in the midst of the turbulence of all this, I get a sudden flash of feeling that I've been cast in some ridiculous farce. Which is real?

At the same time as all this, I've been rather painfully aware of Philip's attraction to a very British and very English upper crust wife of a game warden here. Well, the long and short of it is that several times Philip and I have returned from Sat. nights at the club, each stimulated by his own particular fancy, and sat down full of confidence and Johnnie Walker to discuss extramarital relations. Were they good, bad, indifferent? Would *we* be the same? In what context should one have them? A great love outside marriage, which might be damaging to the marriage, or purely physical attraction, or just any old thing when the spirit moved you, or what? How should one comport oneself with one's marriage partner while all this is going on? And on and on and on, to no fixed agreement. I was still in agonies of guilt and adoration of Stephen, not understanding Philip's infatuation in the least, but certainly not minding it or her or her frightfully jealous husband (she's had several affairs before; she told me so). Suddenly, like a bolt from the blue, Philip goes and spends the night with her (the husband is on safari more often than he's home), and I am shattered and furious and full of venom and despair and rage and hatred.

This was ten days ago, and Philip is so bewildered at my attitude, and I too! I thought I would be modern, civilized, sane, and unjealous, and not possessive. Well, it's so bloody ambivalent, because I don't want Philip, less than ever, if anything, and I long for some sign from Stephen even more now to make me feel loved and worthy and desirable, but I don't think he is even aware of any of this, and in fact would be horrified at the whole thing.

Philip keeps saying, "But *one* of us had to be first, and you know you had the intention!" But did I? Would I have teetered on the edge of actual sex with Stephen and finally fallen into the pit? I cannot think so, but that's perhaps sour grapes morally. And now? Now I just don't know what I want except someone to make me feel unique at least momentarily. God, we are frightful messes. I've been so bloody virtuous since I got married—ME—it just isn't true.

And here I am, of all people, the still chaste but betrayed wife, and yet that's only a half truth. It was so much on the surface, and except to lie about where he was going that night, Philip has been perfectly honest all along, whereas I've kept hidden my attachment to Stephen, in sheer terror, I must add. He is so dear and so gentle, so unmodern and uncynical and trusting—and so oblivious of me! I am tired of cheap flashy witticisms from the reviews and surface (almost conditioned) responses. But here I am again, you see! Off on my schizophrenic tack of Stephen, where my bourgeois domestic self is screaming fishwife abuse at Philip for this treason to our marriage, our children, our six years of chaste companionship. How *can* I be so ambivalent?! I honestly don't give a damn about Philip's feelings for me. What I may have felt for him romantically has long since disappeared, and yet something incalculable has gone from our marriage. I really don't comprehend the beginnings of reactions, where they stem from, what gauges their intensity, why they suddenly die down only to flare up again. You know that wonderful line of Yeats: "And one man loved the pilgrim soul in you." Well, that's what gets invisible to marital vision, what domesticity kills for the partner. I'm not denying Coventry Patmore's marriage poetry, or that something perhaps bigger and better (but I rather think only different and older and tempered by experience) grows in the place of this (ahem) first fine careless *(tender)* rapture, which is lost in a marriage. But am I to be denied this for the rest of my days? Because this is only the first experience of mine since marriage nearly six years ago, and it hasn't led much of anywhere, nor will it, except to give me much inner uncommunicated rapture, does this mean it is truly unique, or only the first in a series of progressively more sordid mechanisms of escape from an increasingly dreary marriage?

But no love affair I ever had can I look back on now with anything but tender memories, some tempered with a wry smile or two. And perhaps uniqueness is conferred by the moment, if it is pure and clean, true and good in itself. What's that line? "At the still point of the turning world"—and each conjunction could be unique in time and space like this. I don't know. I just don't know. Simone de Beauvoir, I fancy, would agree with the above—and possibly rightly, who can say?

Oh, Joyce, why are we so damned mixed up and longing for recognition and love and self-awareness only to be found through *another's* awareness of oneself? Honest to God, life gets tedious, doesn't it? Stephen and I could share so much that Philip and I never had. Philip reads a little, but this deep and abiding love of literature, the written word, and sense of its supreme importance, no—but as you must realize, Stephen does. And opera, choral music, madrigals; and a sense of soul-to-soul communication that you and I have missed so in our marriages; not that much of that has ever come out between Stephen and me, as he is so flickeringly shy, but I intuitively sense that beyond a certain barrier (not sex, just articulate recognition) lies this wonderful country of analytical exploration where I haven't been in so very long except in letters to you, and in my own private world, which is growing a bit mad from too much introspection.

I still haven't told you what has disgusted me the most about Philip's sordid little affair (which continues, I believe), and that's that he's not even in love with her, though she professes (to her husband, who told P., who told me) to be in love with P., but it's all so beastly and calculated and bloody sordid, to destroy the cleanliness of a marriage. For LOVE, yes—that's understandable, but just plain old fornication, it's just beyond me.

But I keep telling myself, isn't that better from *my* viewpoint than to have him feel about her as I do about Stephen? Shouldn't it be less damaging to my pride and less humiliating? But somehow, I don't feel it is. It cheapens our whole six-year struggling relationship in some curiously undefinable manner.

Bear with me, and tell me what you think of it all (and me) from this scrappy outline. My dear, I haven't said much (so selfishly) of your pain and loss, but I think of you and love you and need you to be here and happy and well—

Pat

February 27, 1959

Dear Pat,

Your depressed letter, and money order, just arrived. The last four letters you have sent, the joy you spoke of over the writing, tumultuous uncertainty and desire about Stephen and this today—they all make me want nothing more than to be able to spend a long *long* time just being and sharing with you. A quite hopeless proposal. This note will give you no consolation at all, I fear.

Convalescence, the energies I scarcely have to give that which I must give, to keep the house and Reinhard sane and ordered enough to keep *me* in peace, the preparation I must do for my sixteenth-century course, have left me scarcely able to phrase a sentence. It's the problem of not being able to concentrate. When I'm well, I can stand Reinhard tugging at me, and still direct thoughts toward you; now, the effort ends in my near hysterics. So please understand.

We just decided on one more year here; Milwaukee is a delightful city. I'm happy to teach one more year (having already done the preps, which will largely be repeat next year). And then, Hans is beginning to sell here, and is painting well. This way we can use the summer months to investigate possibilities in southwestern Germany, but not have to cut off all security in the investigation. It may sound overly cautious, but two years is not too much to spend where one is happy.

Pat, I don't mean to inject the bitter half-theme of togetherness, but may I ask you what your relationship to and with Philip is under these pressures? It may be ugly or hard to articulate, but the issue has such real relevance to me now, in my case, that I'd appreciate it. Marriages are failing all around me, and I wonder what curbing of self is necessary, what full individuality can live when one seeks the enduring life of that strange union too. I am *perhaps* fortunate. I could in a moment let this "non-conjugal love passion" flare, fire, and take its toll. But I do wonder. We, you and I, need hours and hours and hours.

All love,

Joyce

March 2, 1959

Dear Pat,

I had better set my thoughts in order to try to approach your problems before I go back to work Friday, or I may never get to them. I try to tackle them *only* because you're my friend, certainly not because I think I can advise on the unmuddling of any of it. I sometimes wish I had more staunch convictions that could proclaim themselves, *ex cathedra*, but all I know is that approaching any problem with too rigorous a set of preconceived rules only brings ruder shocks to both the participants and the system. Conversely, to go through life letting the moment arbitrate the standard, and articulate the principles, is, I think, to ask for a different kind of trouble, the gnawing sense of inconstancy that many a pure sensualist I have known has suffered from.

They believe in the moment, yes (and rightly, I think), but they're so dissatisfied with the life that results. So far as basic principles toward sex outside marriage are concerned, I am quite positive that sex life outside marriage damages proportionately sex life within marriage, and a heartless faked-up relationship in marriage leaves only a dismal caricature of what marriage should be. It leaves but the worst kind of dutiful togetherness, a state worse than spinsterhood, I would wager.

The only place I have seen a dogmatic free love theory work was in a marriage wherein all they ever had wanted from each other was intellectual and domestic life. There was no hurt, no jealousy, no background of love to charge the treason against. But. But neither of us married in that understanding, or, let's say, that misunderstanding. You speak so little of Philip, of Philip as husband, that I don't know what you are fighting, what in your marriage you feel worth working to keep alive and healthy, what you are willing to give up in its loss. I have seen people, you have too, return to each other in new strength after torments of infidelity. I have seen others go through the worst kind of scandal and divorce over adultery for the sake of a second marriage, wherein they seemed quite happy, although both partners left human wreckage strewn all about, in many cases children to grow up fighting that.

But I don't like my tone. Still, unless I am wrong, Philip's action signaled

167

to you the beginning of a dissolution, precisely what I have written of fearing, and I understand your "fishwife" emotions to the core.

It seems so logical, unless the ones who began the motion WILL against it. I can only say, I truly think CHOICE is involved, not simply lust, or desire, or infatuation, or empathy, or even soul-to-soul communication. We have both experienced enough and paid for enough to know how and when the WILL must operate, OR to realize (at least in outline) the consequences of our choices.

Still, I am a Yeatsian, and I am not by these tokens advising security as such over risk. I still believe in "that dolphin-torn, that gong-tormented sea" with all its unpredictable agonies. But renunciation, from one side or the other, is a part of that sea—for Yeats the most cruel part. Does all this mean anything at all to you? I am neither reproaching nor advising, just articulating what I can. And by the way, I think you're dead wrong about the day-to-day drudge blinding one's insight or concern to the other's "pilgrim soul." Without love, yes, one would cease to acknowledge it. But this is the very heart-fiber that grows in our marriage, the thing I most cannot betray, the source of my confidence, a confidence perhaps tried by daily imbalances, but constantly rejuvenated and repaired by living the struggles in one another. Please continue to write me what you feel.

As for us, we are joined in the fervor of a delicious project. I've mentioned it. We intend to buy an old unused farmhouse in rural France, and we intend to find it this summer. We'll sail from here June 8th. We'll spend some time in Solingen and then go to Paris. We shall try to rent a Vespa or something and set off, we hope, with some hints to guide us. We scarcely dare hope for land, at most one or two acres, and all we ask for is a solid structure, with roof. The rest we'll work on ourselves.

I admit Stephen sounds appealing. And I do send my warmest love,

Joyce

PASHENZI
March 5, 1959

Dearest friend,

I only received your last airletter (new design, I see) yesterday, and this won't leave Pashenzi for six days, till the next mail plane, but as Philip is on safari till tomorrow, I have a plethora of peace and solitude which I will share with you. I hardly know where to begin, as nothing concrete has happened; things are just jogging along, but not very satisfactorily. Stephen has been ill, he has a very nasty tropical ulcer on his leg, which will just not heal, and he's been in bed for three weeks. He just got up again yesterday, looks very pale and wan, and my heart aches for and because of him.

Philip went on safari three days ago, and I fantasize till I can hardly distinguish reality: Stephen meeting me at midnight in the deserted Boma; Stephen coming here at 3 A.M. and tapping discreetly on my bedroom window—but as he can hardly walk at the moment, and doesn't have that sort of scheming mind anyway, it all isn't very likely. Anyhow, like all good fantasies worthy of the name, mine stop at a certain point and are blithely uninterested in complications or consequences.

And Stephen is so dear, but oh, so remote, and so I begin to weary of this one-sided plague of emotions. I'm sure it's probably much better for me that way, than getting involved in a sticky little mess like Philip's.

He is quite fascinated with her physically, and I must be fair, she has a good body, a bookish mind, and reads and ponders much. Her husband I like not at all, and I hardly blame her for the affair in a way.

Now, to try and tell you how this daily affects Philip and me, I can only do it obliquely, by a series of impressions. We are both moody and distracted at times, seldom matching times or moods. After the initial shock of the first time when I actually knew that chastity in our marriage was lost, I've settled back into my modus vivendi; that is, the children still wake up, demanding, every morning, meals are still cooked, jokes P. and I have had for years are still shared, reluctantly at first, perhaps, but we've subsided into our old ways with an ease that shocks me. Did I never really care in the first place?

It's crazy to say this, and perhaps you won't believe me after all the years and all the men you've known in my life, but dear Joyce, my body has only just begun to discover sexual arousal, since Julian was born, oh, a bit after the first baby, not half a dozen altogether, and a few after Christopher, but not the glowing surge of imminent satisfaction that one is meant to feel with one's body. It is only in myself and comes to naught, and I don't quite know what to do with it.

Do you ever hear any Noel Coward? There is a delightful little song of his called "A Bar on the Piccola Marina" about a recently widowed Mrs. Wentworth-Brewster, who goes on a world tour and Discovers Life in the P.M. I'm feeling rather Mrs. Wentworth-Brewsterish myself these days. Sex seems to emanate from the very dew on the long grass. I have to laugh (inside myself) when Philip solemnly informs me that it was practically his duty to make love to Elizabeth because she's never had an orgasm in her marriage. I dissimulate too well. And we have never been able to discuss *our* sex life.

I had a sudden visitation last night (everyone always knows who's on safari and who's home) from Derek, the District Officer, a bachelor, with whom I usually spend Sat. nights at the club dancing when Stephen isn't there, as Derek is a marvelous dancer and great fun, full of blarney and funny anecdotes, and is very flattering to me, but he came over about 9 P.M. to find me in my post-bath dressing gown, wearing glasses and reading Chaucer, on some flimsy excuse of borrowing something, so I had to offer him a drink. Suddenly he began pouring out his heart to me. My dear, I haven't had anything raise my morale at such a timely moment in years. So we sat and got nicely pickled on brandy, I drove him home, and I did something I haven't done since college days—necked in a car like any teenager, just nice long quiet kisses and words of love from him. Imagine! I really am quite mad and demoralized. This poor chap has apparently been carrying a torch for me since we arrived here. I'm yearning after Stephen, married to Philip, who lusts after Elizabeth, and yet some days are very bright indeed, and whatever lies ahead in the days and months to come, I'm sure it couldn't be so bad.

But it's rather like winning the Irish Sweepstakes when you didn't even know you had a ticket, to find out, when you're eating your heart out over A, that B has been mad about you for ages, and just couldn't contain himself any longer.

I couldn't honestly say at the moment that all this has brought Philip and me closer together; on the contrary, I find myself withholding things (sometimes of necessity) that I never would have done before, but we can't go on through the years analyzing and exploring one another as I have tried to do until now. Especially out here where all life is so constricted and circumscribed and we live on top of one another so. I'm reading a study of Chaucer which made me turn to *Troilus and Creseyde* again. One forgets how utterly charming it is, even the first stanza, "These woful vers, that wepen as I write." I know what you mean, Geoffrey, old chap. I wepen as I write too.

Anyhow, though most of my waking moments are spent dwelling on this puzzling problem of man-woman relationships, and the whys and wherefores and hows thereof, other things do happen: I garden now and then, play tennis, read, dance, cook, sew, think about the H-bomb and Chinese Communism and Little Rock, the riots in Northern Rhodesia (horrifyingly close to us), Callas singing *Norma,* the children's education, darling Stephen, so impossibly remote, Derek, the sweet District Officer who loves me, how I'd love a good rare cut-into-able steak, a fresh peach, a glass of pasteurized (not boiled) milk, a *hamburger* even —but some days, some days, life is quiet and good and funny and full of promise. As you can see, my graph has risen since the last letter. I hope yours, along with your convalescence, has.

My dear and only confidante, my love and gratitude for your understanding,

Pat

PASHENZI
March 31, 1959

Dearest Joyce,

Pardon my longish (relative to our latest letters) silence, but I've been digesting your letter and watching and waiting for developments here. Actually, though I very much admire your tone, and the obvious conviction you carry concerning our theme, I don't agree. At least for me—bluntly, though I have never really confessed this to myself, let alone anyone else, since I married, I don't love Philip and never did in that wild rapturous way. We have a good, a happy, a shared and intelligent and sensible life, we love vagabonding and get along extraordinarily well, sometimes, and I very likely might have gone on for years and years like this, except that I have begun falling in love with other people, and am suffering the agonies of the damned, twofold: first, for the impossibility of any outcome, and second, guilt, guilt, guilt, for feeling that it might be possible to give to other men that which in six years of marriage I've never been capable of giving Philip.

But, something has snapped in our relationship, so tenuous and undefinable always, with Philip, and certainly with my own married self. I've come to the conclusion that I am suddenly once again in that state you and I lived perpetually in before marriage, of waiting with a delicious expectancy for love, love around the corner of every day. I *know* my marriage is permanent, but *I* just don't feel permanent any more.

In spite of the fact that Philip is the one who has been unfaithful, I am the unfaithfulest of all, in my heart of hearts, and I suppose I must fight this and push away this longing to love and be loved as it might have been had I married someone else (who, I really couldn't say; I don't think I ever met him, to tell you the honest truth). It must show on a woman's face, somehow; I've been so absorbed with my feelings for Stephen since we arrived in this tiny place that I certainly haven't bothered with anyone else, and although with certain horror, yet, I must admit, a flattered ego, I find three men here (alas, Stephen is not one of them) much too much interested in me, and saying the sorts of things under alcoholic influence that I haven't heard for years.

It's with a sense of astonishment and certainly a bitterly ironic justice that I'm only interested in the one man who turns an utterly cold eye to me here. It's very likely just as well and will keep me from getting involved. Anyway, I think I might be getting over Stephen. His wife is so frightfully jealous and makes such awful scenes it isn't worthwhile even discussing publicly for five minutes the political situation in Nyasaland.

He certainly feels that way, and I'm beginning to follow suit. But all this present situation is beside the point, the point being that I feel I've lost control over certain aspects of my life, and that if someone should come along who *wills* events to move and I am once again overtaken by this feeling, then events will just move. Am I weak? Silly? Immoral? Bored? Colonial? Too analytical (weren't we always that?)? And then again, maybe not.

Philip is still chugging along in the midst of his affair, and is, I think, getting a little bored with her and her internecine warfare to keep him interested and things stirred up. I really couldn't care less what they do or when or how, as long as I am left in peace to grapple with this most mysterious life in my moments of aloneness when the children are in bed and all is quiet.

I'm happy to hear you're working at your poetry again. Have you submitted anything, had anything published since your return to the States? I have some ghastly African short stories I have timorously submitted to a couple of U.S. magazines, but all were rejected, and small wonder. I was always so averse to blue-penciling, *or* expansion of my elliptical style. But it's good for my soul, at any rate, to keep plugging away.

And again, for the first time in years, I've begun keeping a voluminous journal. It must sound from my letters as if I sit about and ponder men, women and love all day long, but I live quite a normal life, really, as do Philip and i together, surprisingly enough.

People can bump along together quite peacefully in the most astonishing circumstances. We are all well, Julian adorable, but very slow developing. Christopher a dear little three-and-a-quarter-year-old, very British and very well mannered, like his father. I hope you are fully convalesced and happy, dear friend, my only confidante in the world!

Much, much love,

Pat

Pat's letters written between April and September are missing, for the good reason that she begged Joyce to destroy them. These six months were for Pat a maelstrom of bewildering emotions. Philip had engaged in a second, more serious love affair with a wife in Pashenzi. This one culminated in his decision to ask Pat for a divorce so that he could marry this woman. Pat in the meantime had fled for comfort into an affair with Derek, the District Officer. He wished her to become his wife, promising to adopt her two boys and to treat them as he would his own.

Pat, with Christopher and Julian, then left Philip. He had broken down a few hours before the plane was to leave, telling her he had changed his mind and now did not want a divorce. She left anyhow and stayed in Dar es Salaam just long enough to file suit for divorce. She took the boys for a few weeks to the welcome quiet and seclusion of a small hotel on the slopes of Mount Kilimanjaro. Here she pondered the existing alternatives in all their ramifications, changing her mind from one day to the next. Finally she discontinued the divorce proceedings and returned to Pashenzi, to pick up her routine where it had been interrupted. The family life went on outwardly as before.

But the romantic yearnings, the need to love and be loved, of the past year and a half finally culminated late this year in her attachment to the man she will shortly describe to Joyce as the love of her life. She had met him earlier in the year, in the midst of all the marital and extramarital turmoil. The "woebegone letter" Joyce refers to below is the first in which Pat tells her that she and Philip are to be divorced, that Philip is to remarry immediately, that she, Pat, is very fond of the man who wishes to marry her, but is not sure she loves him. She has almost, at this point, decided nonetheless to marry him, for the sake of security, both financial and emotional, for herself and the boys.

The problem of the custody of her eldest son was central to her decision to return to Philip, who had ultimately said that if she persisted in her divorce suit (once he had changed his own mind about wanting a divorce), he would countersue for sole custody of Christopher. In a country in which she was an alien, without means of support, whose divorce laws were those of Britain, favoring the male in a divorce suit (or so her lawyer had informed her), her instinct was not to risk such a loss, but to return obediently to the marital fold.

MILWAUKEE
June 27, 1959

Dear Pat,

Your woebegone letter reached me and has made me most despondent, concurring, as it does, with other things. Dear friend, oh, Pat, I do feel so sorry. I despise messes. Isn't that a pouty attitude to take? But I've lived through enough. I can scarcely even stand to read about them. Although, of course, the uneventful life is equally distasteful. But you must be going through hell. That is, if you've any love left for Philip, it all must be sheer torture. And so ugly, too. Forgive me, but do you not now see what I meant about adultery? I mean, the act of copulating with someone else's mate. Well, physically, I can assuredly understand it. But does it not, as one act follows another, disintegrate the very fabric of which a marriage is woven?

This isn't sentimentality. It's like an organic reaction of body chemistry. The very cells of the marriage alter irreparably. I cannot help but feel this, and every infidelity I've known of testifies to it. Of course, for some the alteration is only beneficial, the genuine movement to the positive from, say, a hopeless marriage, to real fulfillment of more than physical needs. But when one just lets it happen, out of a physical itch, I don't know, it seems to me the source of marital sorrow, that is, if the marriage was sound before.

I'm just raving. I would love above all else to be with you. I ache to be with you. Are your children any comfort at all? Is any real empathy or sympathy still left between you and Philip? Do you sleep together? Anything seems possible to ask, because cruelty is so translucent everywhere. Things might as well be put bluntly; the world sort of stinks anyway. And I am yet to experience an orgasm in love-making. Isn't it all absurd! I have known men who knew how, but they were never the ones I loved, or was busy sleeping with.

173

Oh, God—and money, money, money. That's all people talk about, myself included—who makes up little lists of what and how and how NOT to spend. And creativity—that's what the rest of us talk about when we catch ourselves talking about money, myself included, and then farce away an evening being superior, and creating but NOTHING. I'm exaggerating. I do know marvelous people—you and me, etc., etc. I hate myself. The District Officer loves you. Your little boys don't know my little boy. And I'm furious as hell about something, I don't know what. Perhaps it's that I have hay fever. Otherwise, I love you very much, and wish you'd write me every day.

Joyce

SOLINGEN, GERMANY
July 10, 1959

Dear Pat,

I have no strength to write anything but the bare and cruel facts. I've had to write them already so many times, for reasons of insurance and otherwise, that I feel this is the last effort I can make.

Our summer has taken a tragic turn. Of all the struggles we've had over the past four years, this is to be the most trying and grievous. As Mother lay in the hospital in Salt Lake, having had internal surgery which the doctor feared would show cancer, Hans lay here in Solingen newly convalescing from a gall bladder removal operation. Both went well. But the next day we received back some X-rays of Reinhard's hips. We had had them taken because a neighbor here had dropped the casual remark that she thought he limped. On seeing the photo, the doctor unhesitatingly told us some very bad news. Reinhard has a disease of the hip joints peculiar to little boys, and rare. It is called Perthe's disease, and involves the wearing down of the hip joint, and if not caught soon enough, is irreparable. When caught soon enough (and this is difficult because there are no outward signs), it can be fully cured by long months of lying in a plaster cast. In Reinhard's case, both hips are affected, and the right one dangerously late. The therapy demanded is a year of lying flat in a plaster cast, and even then they cannot promise.

Oh, it's all so very, very hard. It is not a dangerous thing so far as his life and basic health are concerned, but nonetheless a very nearly tragic thing. He has been so beautiful, Pat, unusually beautiful, like a favorite of the gods. He has been one of those children who have a native natural charm that is irresistible. Everyone felt it. And to be separated from him for a year is bitter. Also, how in God's name will we finance it? American insurance programs never allow for more than sixty days. Some suggest leaving him here, in the orthopedic hospital

174

at Köln, where it is exactly four times cheaper than in America. I can't bear to think of it. You can understand why I feel that the only way I can stand the year is to be pregnant myself, with some positive sense of life growing in me. It would have to be planned, so that I could teach anyway, which, therapeutically, is only good for me.

I couldn't feel more indifferent to Europe. Please write. I'm a mess. Tell me of your life, Pat, all about it.

All love,

Joyce

SOLINGEN
July 18, 1959

Very dear poor Pat,

This letter will probably be worse than little comfort to you. I'd love to be able to say something terribly reassuring and rehabilitating to you, but I cannot, since I find the decision *so* sad. I may be a very poor realist, for I always, so nearly always, see the unhappy side of a divorce involving custody. I really cannot solace you, dear Pat, for I do love you and want to help, but, tortured and involved as I am in the grief over Reinhard, I feel that my empathy works only negatively; for I feel it would almost kill me to have to lose my oldest son. And I know it is painful for you to have to consider the possibility. Frankly, I don't see why Philip should have him. On what ground can he? And is the woman married or single? As to your future marriage plans, Pat, I can say nothing, except that, in all honesty, your letters have not sounded as if you wanted to consider this man as a husband. Repeatedly you said you didn't love him. Perhaps the relationship has changed enormously lately and you feel much surer about it.

From here, knowing what I do, I can only ask you to be careful. Everything is at stake. Oh, I wish you could come to Germany the last week in August. I *really* do. Think about it? Write me.

Love,

Joyce

175

August 10, 1959

Dear Pat,

Your bid for sympathy certainly does not go unheard, and I wish I could answer your long letter in kind. But please be patient with me. I'm up to my ears in letter writing; the arrangements that must be made through the Red Cross, the ship lines, the insurance companies, the American State Department, seem to have devoured the bulk of my European summer. When things reinstate themselves into a sensible schedule, I promise to continue our regular and already long-lived correspondence. I think about you in much more detail than I can write, and believe I understand what it is you seek, and what it is you no longer seek.

I look forward to the return journey—three weeks—just because then we can have Reinhard once more with us. He has adjusted with beautiful buoyancy. He is one of the few true blithe spirits I have met.

Yes, we'll keep him in our house. I agree with all you say about the separation of parent and child, and Hans's sister Marie will help to care for him. She's twenty-six, utterly different from us—how, I'll explain later—and I have more than a few misgivings about how it will work out. Once again, we're up to our ears in medical debts. This is a useless truncated letter, but full of love and good wishes. We'll be here till August 31st. Reinhard goes with us—on a stretcher.

Always,

Joyce

August 22, 1959

Dear, dear friend,

The world for me now, too, is somewhat hectic and I only answer in these spasmodic outbursts (instead of a decent letter) for love of you and because I want you to know my thoughts are with you all the time in your agony and your courage. Dear Pat, if only I were nearer you, how I'd love to be able to offer my shoulder to weep on. Your last letter awaited me on return from our futile trip to France, futile in the sense that we overspent ourselves looking for a house only to learn that we couldn't afford to buy.

But more important, Pat, is your new letter, with your new and anguished decision. Poor one—how incomparably hard it must all be! I find it wise to wait. Reunion may be impossible, and you may decide that life with Philip is misery, but if only you know *you* have tried and that the children will stay with you, oh, both of those things seem so important to me.

Write to me so often as you care to; be brave. I do think what you're doing sounds the most reasonable, but just because of that reasonableness, I can guess at what you are suffering.

We sail the 31st with Reinhard. How I miss him!

Always,

Joyce

PASHENZI
September 22, 1959

Dearest friend,

I did not get an opportunity in Dar es Salaam to write my promised long explanatory letter to you, so here I am, with coffee and cigarettes by me, Julian in bed with a light attack of measles, Christopher at school (9–12), and the house running reasonably smoothly after much confusion since my return four weeks ago today. It all seems incredibly dreamlike, but then so much of life does anyway. I hardly know where to draw the line between illusion, fantasy and reality. Not that it matters much, as long as one keeps traveling along the prescribed rails. The frightfulness and fear of these last months have taught me one thing anyway, to keep withdrawn and at a distance from others the things most precious to my inner harmony, not to *attempt* to share the basically unshareable, but to force myself to turn inward for communion and a sense of the justification of my own substantive values. I learned a harder lesson, which I will never tell anyone in the world but you. I found out, among other things, that no matter what is done to me, I have no redress. I found out that I own nothing except the clothes on my back, not even seafare back to the U.S., where I could support myself and Christopher and Julian, *if* I could have gotten them illegally out of East Africa. I do not even have the right to keep them with me, however good a mother I may be, if a judge or a husband says I may not have them. I guess I found that I am without legal rights or standing, and that to my astonishment I can be compelled to the will of others, by a combination of force and threats. But by God, whatever pretense I may have to keep up, in public *and* in private, my mind and soul are still my own to do with as I please.

I discovered sexual passion and fulfillment for the first time in my life, sadly with the wrong person. I never would have believed that possible. But there you are; life goes on being a continual revelation that one is perpetually wrong about everything. And now I am settled in my own home again with my two dear boys,

177

and a much needed routine and a sense of security in the future which we all desperately need, and with Philip, a good husband, despite all, to a wife who tried so hard to return his sincere love. I do my best to dissimulate now.

I did for years until this past year when I suddenly found myself emotionally astray. Philip hadn't been very understanding or sympathetic since Julian was born, and my loneliness and emptiness of heart were suddenly exposed by the shattering of this fragile shell I'd built round them. Hence the last difficult year and a half, both of us to blame, me more so than Philip, in some ways, because I married him not knowing whether I loved him or not. Not that I could begin to tell you what I think love might be. Perhaps it's only a conscious state, sparked off by God knows what, and if you're *not* conscious of being in a state of love, then you aren't *in* love. I don't know.

Anyway, because I was trying to convince myself of this emotion and that emotion, and because Philip began sleeping with this first woman here (a lot my fault; I was being beastly, but then he might have tried to help too), and I built a whole world of fantasy round that silly Stephen. And dear Derek, who was so hopelessly in love with me, right from the beginning. He was always there when I needed someone to turn to, to assuage my loneliness, to assure me of my innate value as a woman and a human being, who was such a marvelous lover and a fine human being, but, quite right you and a lot of other people were, *not* a husband for me.

Joyce, my dearest and most understanding of friends in this world, there's something vital to all this that I haven't told you. Not because I wanted to withhold anything from you, but because I haven't finally admitted it to myself until recently, it seemed so insane and illogical, and really made me feel as if I were losing touch with reality and control of myself altogether. But, well, if you're to understand this year at all (and *someone* must, as I don't believe in God; *someone* must, or I should go quite mad), I must swallow my pride in logical behavior and tell you.

Last Easter, I was just beginning to realize how silly I'd been being over Stephen, and could almost consciously say it to myself. Derek and I were the greatest of friends. I was aware of his feelings, and he of the lack of any response from me; it was all unspoken, and he'd never made any attempt to be alone with me, or to speak of his love. We had such fun together. I adored dancing with him, playing tennis with him, and his friendship and quiet adoration were having a lot to do with pulling me out of this abyss over Stephen.

Oh, dear, this is so hard; you'll think me so ungenuine and untrue to myself. I haven't even whispered this to myself, let alone anyone else, till now (upon my return home, I mean), but someone else entered the picture at this stage (Easter). Over the holidays, then, a couple named Kirkley (Ian and Alicia) came from a station in the next province, a tiny remote place, 220 miles from here, where he is District Commissioner. He's thirty-six, comes from Scotland. His wife is terribly snotty-colonial, from the Fiji Islands. Anyhow, they came to spend four days here then, and we saw a good deal of them. At the Saturday night club dance, Derek was ill and went home early, and I ended up spending hours with Ian, who to my amazement prophesied that I'd have an affair with Derek, for my own good, that Philip would get over his second woman (the affair was common knowledge by that time), a "silly little snip," and that it was all a great pity, as he (Ian) and I were meant for one another. I can't express to you how these few phrases, practically unarticulated, came out during those few hours together, dancing, in front of the assembled European populace of Pashenzi.

Well, we had just the two of them in to a Mexican dinner on their last night here. I played a record of some Scarlatti sonatas by Gieseking, and my favorite, the E major, 23, turned out to be Ian's, and something inexpressible happened between us during that music. Anyhow, they left, and I put him out of my mind as a flirt, a frightfully clever one who knew all the right things to say and moods to express to turn the head of a woman like me; and then a day or so later, I talked with the wife of the policeman here, my only reasonably close friend, and I told her jokingly of Ian's flirtation with me, and how charming and simpático I thought he was. She was aghast, as she and her husband spent the whole of last tour, three years, on the same station with the Kirkleys in the west of Tanganyika. She said he wasn't anything like that at all, but more of a misogynist, in an amusing cynical way.

I was flattered, but nothing more. I couldn't bear to think about any *more* possibilities, I was already getting so involved. At that time Philip had begun sleeping with the second woman, the one he wanted for a while to marry, and I had begun to see Derek more and more. I knew I'd end up in his arms, sooner or later, and I was tormented by this knowledge, as I *didn't* love him, I only convinced myself I did as time went by; especially after we became lovers, it wasn't so difficult.

Ian, though, cured me utterly and completely of any lingering feeling for Stephen. Everything I thought I saw in Stephen I realized was either false or only half developed, compared to the kind of man Ian is, strong and forceful, terribly, frighteningly brilliant, as musical as a professional musician, bookish, but a man. But I did dismiss him from my thoughts.

They came again in June for a weekend and I realized then the first time I saw him that second weekend how terribly attracted to him I was, hardly even physically so much as empathetically, and I felt so unfaithful to Derek and to any image of myself as a decent person, that I wouldn't even speak to or look at Ian then. We danced a bit, and he said, "Oh, no, I'm not going to say a word to you now. I'll wait until Derek is out of the picture, then we'll be back, and I want to make you understand the kind of people you and I are." I said I wouldn't be here after Derek left. Ian laughed and said, "Perhaps not, but you'll be back. You aren't in love with Derek, but only leaning on him, and Philip will come back to lean on you. You'll only be jumping out of the frying pan into the fire, exchanging bad for worse." He said, "And anyway, it's I who should hold that place in your heart, not Derek or anyone else." I left him in the middle of a dance, and went back to sit down, saying I wouldn't listen to such treacherous nonsense.

Oh, and so I left Pashenzi, and had my frightening little adventure with lawyers and being on my own with the children, and wrote a few love letters to Derek, which I truly meant, or anyway *tried* to mean, but which rang false, if I strained every nerve to listen to their phrases in all honesty. So I wrote to Philip and said how silly we both had been, shall I come back? He cabled me to return immediately; I chartered a tiny Cessna; we three flew over what seemed like half of Africa to return home; I settled into a false sense of emotional security and a true sense of bourgeois values, and then the Kirkleys descended on us for four days a fortnight ago (Philip had invited them while I was gone).

And I must tell you, it was partly the thought of Ian that brought me back. Not of seeing him again, or loving him or having an affair with him or running off to live with him, but the thought that a man like that, so true to every ideal of mine as a man and poet and dreamer and lover, exists and sees in me the same expression of his ideals of a woman. And it's too late for me, or for him, or certainly, for any conception of us. But up in my lonely hotel on Kilimanjaro, I used to walk at night in the cold mists, and think how good, basically, Philip was, and how much we shared, and our children and families and the years behind us, and if Philip was dull and had been brutally faithless with two women, and virtually forced me into another man's arms, then I had been doubly faithless all these years by not loving him and knowing I never would, and the only thing I could do, whether or no there are Ians in the world who recognize themselves in me, was to come back and be a good, if dissimulating, wife to Philip's image of me. I can now go on being that image and living a lie which can gradually become truth over the years, for all our sakes, and that is what I intend to do.

Ian said it's necessary and good to go on raising our respective families (they have two boys, just the ages of Christopher and Julian), and seeing one another at a distance now and then over the years in Tanganyika, and knowing that our illusion exists.

He's become almost an imaginary companion to me since then, over these difficult weeks, and I will *not* say to you or to myself, let alone him, that I love him or anyone; he is simply the total expression of an ideal that I'm not quite sure I'd like to see or experience as such. Please try to understand, Joyce. I'm not going to have any more affairs, to fall in love, to have secret smutty little relationships, but Ian has filled a great gaping abyss in my life, the need to love. You can't direct or force that sort of love. It just comes unannounced, and is nameless and faceless until experienced, and thank God, it has been in a brief encounter like this in impossible circumstances.

We're going to stay with them the second weekend in October, and they with us for four or five days over Christmas; then they go home on long leave, and then to the opposite end of Tanganyika on their return. But as I said earlier, I never admitted to myself my reciprocal feelings for him until they were here this last time, and then it didn't seem to matter any more. My emotions have been so battered about, I hardly know who or where I am any more in that respect. I can only go on living as a good wife, which I am doing, but in the private life of my heart and mind, this need which has yawned open wide for years has at last been filled. All the better if it's an unfulfilled illusion, an unattainable ideal. No tarnishing will come, no lessening of expectations by domesticity, just the knowledge that the other half is around somewhere, just existing and consciously *being* the other half. He's the totality of what I sought for years in bits and pieces in all the men I've known. And I intend to keep him right up there on his pedestal.

I'm so glad you're taking Reinhard back with you. You didn't make it very clear, but I presume Hans's sister is going to Milwaukee to live with you and look after R. while you're teaching. Am I right? My heart aches for you with your poor little sick child. I do so wish I could see my godchild. He's angelic-looking. Do send some snaps of you all one of these days, so I will too.

Christopher is so grown up these days, trotting off to his wee nursery school here. He jabbers incessantly in the nearly-four-year-old way, explores constantly, teases Julian, and vies for our affection with him. Julian, from such a placid fat babe, is turning into the terrible-tempered Mr. Bangs himself, beats his head on the cement floor in tantrums when he doesn't get what he wants. I've sacked half our servants and am working very hard for the good of my soul, not to speak of the good of our exchequer, as our savings and then some were wiped out by our little peccadillo—air fares, lawyers' fees, hotel bills, etc. It will take us a year to recover into the black. But it doesn't really matter. I've lots of good gramophone records and masses of books to read, my garden to till, my children to watch growing, and Philip to keep contented and at peace. That way lies sanity.

I wouldn't have bothered to tell you about Ian, had I not felt that in years to come it would help to explain a lot of this crazy year. In fact, I've read this through and it reads like the diary of a madwoman. Still and all, it's what has happened to me, not a dream. I'm very much at peace myself, and am feeling physically and spiritually better than I have since before Julian was born, nearly two years ago, so perhaps all this madness has done some good. Life seems inexplicable and meaningless to me, but I feel that it doesn't really matter, so that's peace and contentment, of a sort, I suppose.

I know you must be terribly busy getting Reinhard adjusted and yourselves back into academic routine, but I'd love a long explanatory letter about this summer and your wanderings in France. I adored your excursion into mad Gothic expenditure. You're as crazy as I am, in some ways, thank God. You're my best and dearest friend, and no one can ever take your place. You've given me so much of yourself in listening to my woes and burdens over the years. And now, yet another madness of mine I fling to you!

My love to Hans and poor wee Reinhard in his plaster.

All my fondest love,

Pat

181

Very dear Pat,

Well, it seems to take a major mishap to give me the leisure to write you, despite the constant flow of thoughts going your direction. So, for the fifth or so time, I'm home from school and on the verge of hospitalization. Nothing serious, just sad the pregnancy we were so hoping for, and which we planned perhaps too perfectly, is miscarrying. So here I am, under the influence of a hormone injection, for the moment passing no blood, but very uncertain about the future of this child. Anyway, delivery was due June 25th—perfect, we thought, for enabling me to finish teaching, for we would assuredly die without my salary. Now here I am, with very little hope about it, and knowing that so long as I have to work, parental planning will have to wait for another year.

Reinhard too has been in the hospital, but this with good news (except for the fact that it's going to cast our Christmas out of us). They took off the cast, massaged his little legs, and took X-rays. These showed such remarkable improvement for four months Perthe's that there was academic discussion as to whether his disease really was that, or something else. Anyway, it has healed thus far better than the rules prescribed. Now he's home, out of plaster, but still to be in bed for ever so long.

Otherwise, Hans is well, and working like the devil on his studies at Madison —doing nicely. Marie arrived safely, but doesn't seem to be enjoying herself too much, and is a source of sufficient worry to me, since she does so little constructively to occupy herself, and has no sense at all of how to set herself learning, etc. We are very different and I feel the arrangement might prove a little strenuous, but I shouldn't write too much about it.

Your news, Pat, struck me as good. I hope with all my heart that it may prove so. Somewhere recently I heard the statement that sometimes two people cannot learn to live together till they've been blown through the roof together. And I'm happy for Christopher's and Julian's sakes; how much, much better for them! There is so little I can say to you, individually and collectively, but that our hearts are with you, and we wish you well.

When I think of the Barrett-Browning concept of married love I carried with me at twenty, I have to either shudder or laugh. For I've not yet met one like that.

Life is often so terribly at odds with one's image of life, and I often think we live more in the irreal than the real. One's love of fiction must stem from this.

I must go back to bed. Take care of *all.* Write often, and wish me luck.

Always with love,

Joyce

November 22, 1959

Very dear Pat,

There has truly been a marked ebb in correspondence from my side of the waters. Nothing too serious; don't gulp beforehand. I find people are beginning to have a patterned response to our trials. What in heaven's name did I write you last? Do you know that I am pregnant, and that I'm having one hell of a time to avoid miscarriage? Did I write that? If not, know it now. Planned parenthood is what they call it. We aimed it so that I could make my lousy salary up till delivery time, and I think the gods have taken it out on us for trying so to tamper with their budget account. At any rate, it backfired, for the doctor insisted upon bed rest, weekly hormone injections, abstention from everything interesting, and altogether playing the part of a rather frigid woman of leisure—in no way a role to my calling. It meant that last week I had to quit my job. So down we go sli

i

   i

     i

        i ding into the financial abyss once again.

However, the sisters are, I have to admit, something like angels of mercy, and are willing to take me back full time second semester, once my pregnancy has stabilized in one direction or the other (in or out).

I'm delighted Hans is going to do a graduate degree, and he's getting a good deal from it. Also it gives him an insight into what I never could have explained about the gifts that graduate school atmosphere bestows. They are gifts that I have been searching vainly for in "real life" ever since. Also he is profiting artistically and, equally good, in terms of discipline. His paintings look better to me than they have in three years, and he's having more drive to work than since Beirut.

This has been a highly self-centered letter, and you mustn't think I'm not interested in all your many trials too. For I am often thinking of them, more often of you, and as always, wishing you great good.

Your friend always,

Joyce

183

December 19, 1959

Dear Pat,

It has been long since I've heard, and since you've such a unique place in my life of confidence and trust, it seems longer still. Yesterday I mailed two books for YOU. I decided I wanted a Christmas gift really for you alone this time, hoping to send them by air, but found they would cost over $6.00. So you'll get them for Pentecost. I'm sorry—should have done it sooner.

Our news runs like this: I had a sort of a miscarriage, or a sort of a reabsorption. Anyway, pregnancy dreams are gone, and unfortunately, so is my job. The nuns are marvelous, let me begin again at the first of second semester, but it's truly chaos until then. We are too spendthrift to subsist on Hans's $4,500. However, he was promoted, a fond old dream rooted, I'm convinced, in the German respect for a merited title, to Assistant Professor, with a $400 raise. So he's radiant. We will stay in Milwaukee another year, just to try and become solvent. Medical troubles are ENDLESS. Reinhard progresses, Hans suddenly has eye trouble, I have constant dental worries, and a nagging pain in the right side which I've got to investigate. Our money flies this direction. However, Hans sold a woodcut ($40) two days back, his first sale in three years, and I do hope it augurs well for the year ahead.

Marie drives me crazy with her midwife's superstitions (literally) and language. It makes me hate German, where I was previously loving it. All these complaints. Where is my Christmas soul? At least part of it is with you, bringing love where I cannot bring much else. Do, do, do write me. And kiss the boys for me. Reinhard delights in your birthday soldier.

Love,

Joyce

January 12, 1960

Dearest friend,

Since your first letter two months ago telling about going to bed to save your baby, you have never been far from my thoughts, muddled though they be. *How* I would like to lend you my quite revolting fertility and seemingly habitable womb and nine months of my life to have a baby for you. I would with the greatest love and good will, could I. My dear, I do so hope that one of these days the months *will* stretch out to nine, and you will produce another perfect little Fritz or

Gretchen. I feel so ashamed moaning and whining about anything when you have your health and financial problems, Reinhard, and now a miserable in-law as well to cope with.

Ian and Alicia Kirkley stayed for the five days of Christmas with us; it was so hard trying to keep from showing my happiness. Joyce, will you believe me when I tell you I've met finally the love of my life? For the first and only time I know with a certainty that we could have gone no other path but to love one another deeply and truly with a mutual understanding that shakes and frightens me. I've asked him if I may write and confide in you. He said yes, he only wishes he had someone to confide in. His marriage seems as lonely, empty and hopeless as mine, and like mine, was filled with this knowledge from the beginning, but somehow he (as I) felt inexorably bound and led into it. Ah well.

Alicia is a lovely woman, the perfect wife and mother, reasonably intelligent, frightfully sophisticated and aristocratic. She and Philip get on very well and have been carrying on a mad flirtation for months, partly defense, I suppose, and definitely not in her line, but Philip seems to be irresistible to the ladies these days. Ian and I have agreed that we would marry at once were it not for our children, but at their ages we simply cannot ignore our responsibilities.

Joyce, I've never even kissed him, although the "10% of what we feel for one another," as we call our mutual physical attraction, is so desperately strong that it's almost a real physical pain when we are together. But it's not the important thing; in fact, it would be cheap and destructive now. We have begun a hesitant, fearful correspondence, fraught with difficulties, and the necessity of trusting in other people. Very likely foolish of us. But I could not bear (though had he not suggested letters, I would have borne) the thought of losing physical contact.

When we went down to stay with them in November, he gave me a tiny book of quotations about music, a private treasure of his own; at Christmas I gave him my beloved Oscar Williams anthology, just for John Crowe Ransom's "The Equilibrists." We visited them two days ago for two nights again. On our last night there, Ian came out before dinner while P. and Alicia were still dressing, and came over to me, knelt down, and took my hand to slip a ring on my finger, telling me it was meant to be mine forever. When I looked at it, I saw it was a seal ring, set in gold. I asked him to tell me about it, but he only said he would "someday" but I presume the seal to be his family crest. It is the most treasured possession and precious gift I have ever received in my life.

I feel now as if I will never be truly lonely again as long as I live. Every lovely thing I see or piece of music I hear, I have shared with Ian this past year anyway, though only in my imagination, never those first few months dreaming he could have felt anything for me, then those awful months of trouble, the breakup, my quandary over Derek, a dear, and who saved my sanity, I think. But you see, all these extraneous things kept anything from developing between Ian and me, unhappy though I was with Philip and desperate over the children's custody and the possibility of Derek, who only wanted to look after me. I sat in my hotel on Kilimanjaro and lied to myself till I convinced myself that I could come to love Philip and knew after two days back that it was the same old story and that Ian Kirkley was uppermost in my mind. Every meeting of ours since then has only made me, in spite of being so in love with him, more determined than ever to fulfill my maternal responsibilities by being as good a wife as I can to Philip, to make a decent home for our children, and for the rest, to go on becoming a more intelligent and reasonable human being.

We have laughingly become engaged to marry in seventeen years' time, that is, when our last child finishes school, but I don't think this (at least *my*) state of affairs can go on that long. I love Africa, but I am so sick of this superficial shallow time-wasting way of life, I could die of frustration. Philip has read progressively less and less over our years out here, seems interested only in his job and our social life, which is admirable, and would be enough for most people, but I'm not going to be falsely modest and say I'm most people.

I get so tired of never having anyone with whom to share my enthusiasms and tastes, and most of all, music and books. How empty would your own marriage be if you and Hans didn't share music? I don't know if I told you before, but it was a sudden mutual discovery of music in our souls that drew Ian and me together at first; then poetry and simpático and all the rest followed, slowly and in a "nice" progression; we think and are so much alike at times, it rather frightens me. And he is so vastly more intelligent than I, I am terrified he will see my shallowness and be disgusted—my laziness, sloppiness, procrastination, mental lethargy. And as to music, I am comparatively illiterate, and it is his greatest love in the world.

In spite of what lies ahead, the long years to come, I feel so happy and justified at last, for the very first time in my life. I have at last fallen really in love and stayed that way, and watched it grow and know love for what it is meant to be. The physical recedes; I told you that the physical attraction is very hard when we are together, but we so seldom are, and only have one more time coming for God knows how long, a weekend before they go on leave. But that side of it is coming into proportion now for what it's meant to be also—lovely, attainable (given the right circumstances), but not necessary. It has come on me unbidden and unawares, and I am so grateful at having been given this priceless treasure (as I said to him), that it would be presumptuous in the extreme to demand anything more at the moment, at least till we have proven by some sort of trial (*time*, I expect) the worth and value and truth of our love.

He's a violinist and though I've never heard him play (no violin here) I don't have to, to know how good he must be. Alicia has told me so much about him that glorifies and magnifies what little he tells me. He went through boarding school on scholarships, on scholarships through Oxford, where he read history. He's bright, clear, unsullied, and too good to love me. But I dumbly accept it and pray to God he never changes his mind and heart. Seventeen years are hardly enough to prepare oneself to live with a man like that.

You must think I'm so awful, writing this when I've been married nearly seven years now, and Philip knowing none of it. But we share so little of the important things and I've ached for so long to find a worthy love. I'm sorry and I feel guilty, but I can't help this great love, and our only actual transgression is our letters, which harm no one and make us able to carry on through the lonely drudgery of everyday life.

I hardly dare think what marriage to him would be like. I've been lazy and slipshod for so long, and he's so demanding and perfectionist in his mind. How I desire it *so* passionately, instead of this sloppy acquiescence to given opinions. Neither of us has been verbally disloyal to our present partners with one another. We have too little time left, and too much to say to bother with the obvious— all the whys and wherefores of dreary marriages. It's enough that we've found and recognized one another.

They finish their tour in four weeks' time and go on long leave to Scotland for five months, then to a tiny place hundreds of miles from here, which P. and I may or may not visit on our own month's local leave next year, all depending on P. I've never suggested one of our visits to the Kirkleys. They've all come from Philip, oddly enough. Ah well, you must be bored with my rantings.

I've started really learning the recorder again, and am much enjoying it. I have lots of good music for it to get my teeth (or lips?) into. I'm doing with two fewer servants to save money and do lots of experimental cooking these days. Do you like cooking? I do, at last, though it's very tiresome on a smoky wood stove in the tropics, especially that damned bloody bread baking. I sew all my own and the children's clothes. I do quite a bit of gardening. It bores me stiff, but Philip likes to have a nice "proper" garden.

I play tennis two to three times a week, and beginning next week have to teach a kindergarten class two hours every morning, which I shall hate, but which will no doubt be good for my soul.

So you see, I don't spend quite all of my time thinking of love, although it must seem so to you at times. Can you follow with the least interest and under-standing the tangled byways of my life the last year or so, and for heaven knows how long lies ahead? I'm so overflowing with love and happiness and fulfillment I must share it, and you are my only Secret Sharer. Give my love to Hans, and a big godmotherly kiss to four-year-old Reinhard. I'm sorry I was so long in writing and won't be again.

My love and good wishes to you, dear,

Pat

Dear Joyce,

A scrappy note to fill you in and beg you to write to me when you have a moment.

My days are very full; I have tried to find more and more to do, some of it "busy" work, I'll grant you, but I'd go mad sitting around brooding. I envy you your professional center for your mind and energies. I play my recorder every day now, and take such a pleasure in it, though I do wish there were someone else here with me, one by itself being a little thin and mournful-sounding. I am doing a lot of good reading, better than I've done in years. I *try* to polish up half a dozen exceedingly bad short stories, timidly to send them off. If only I had an editor, even some addresses. Could you find me a *Writer's Market* and send it? I think I am getting a piano if we can find a cheap enough one out here for next tour. How I would love to have one again to play and to sing with. I am saving every shilling of my scanty journalism earnings for just that.

I try not to think about any future or what the years ahead may bring, but just to enjoy my daily pleasures, get along as well as possible with Philip and enjoy to the utmost the children, the basic reason for all of this.

Ian and I said a sad goodbye several weeks ago (six—is it possible?) and they have gone home on long leave. We write every week, foolishly and dangerously, perhaps, but it keeps me alive. He is a constant reminder to me of what heights the human mind can aspire to, and what standards should go on guiding me. There is not an easy or careless attitude in his entire frame of reference. He is truly a noble person. He has changed and directed so much of my life at a time when I desperately needed this change and direction. I have my ring and a few letters. The figure on the seal is a wind-hover. Is it not odd? One of my best-loved poems, which has come back again and again over the years in moments of rapture with life. And now I have my own wind-hover. Do, do write to me.

So much love to you,

Pat

PART SEVEN

APRIL 1960–APRIL 1961

Does experience ever teach us anything except that experience is painful?

April 8, 1960

Dear Pat,

Our correspondence seems to have come rather poorly across the winter. I've been working myself under, simply under, and have scarcely seen light since January. But hurrah! Vacation begins next week, for a brief ten days. My work at the university has been an awful strain, but thank God we're beginning to get a few things paid. Our April salary will be the first one this year where the wolves are not waiting at the door for it. Also it's been a cold time of it. Winter is still with us; it snowed this morning. Not a green sprout in sight. But Reinhard and I did spy sparrows building a nest this morning.

Otherwise: Hans has shifted to lithography; is going to have a one-man show here at my college next fall—not much as a gallery, but better than nichts; Marie has taken to wearing my brassieres and using my cosmetics, which infuriates the very hell out of me, because it necessitates my snooping to discover and recover them, and (p.s.) drives me crazy. It's hard for me to believe that she and Hans are kin. Reinhard is getting a little sassy, is simply ravishingly lovely; loves to read and to build (not to paint, although when we can get him to, beautiful little things result); and is not much better physically than he was three months back. I: am not yet pregnant, although I try; am glad not to be going to Europe this summer, because I want to read for a change; am tired of work and my sister-in-law, but not of Hans (although he's often exasperating too); am often tired of myself, and miss you and decent friends in general.

Politics are getting a little heady around here, particularly in Wisconsin, but I still want Stevenson, and would only vote for Kennedy if Stevenson were to be his Secretary of State. Otherwise. Well, write.

Love, much as always,

Joyce

191

June 11, 1960

Dear Pat,

It has been a long time since I've had such a full letter from you, and longer still since I've had such a relaxed and comfortable one. Yes, frankly, you do sound saner. And I'm awfully glad to hear it. Your last few years have been full of struggle, perhaps all years are, who knows? Is it not the nature of it?

This will be a poor letter, because I feel unphilosophic, and uninspired. But I wanted you to know my thoughts are with you. I was delighted to know of your many varied cultural enterprises and of your desire for the piano. I too would love to have one.

I am pregnant again. It was planned in the sense that it was hoped for; for one thing I wanted to get the most nauseous months over with before teaching, and also the miscarrying months. I'm frankly frightened that I won't manage.

It's now Saturday, July 2nd. I've had the signs of trouble. Now it is just a matter of seeing in what direction trouble will develop. Oh, oh—it is so discouraging. My élan vital is in sad shape. I could use a dose of you—but then life has tempered you a bit too.

Would you live in Britain if you had to leave Africa, do you think? Well, Pat, this is no letter at all, but merely a token from one discomfited to another discomfited. I think of you often, but I haven't written a good anything in months or years.

All love,

Joyce

One or two brief letters and postcards from Pat to Joyce covering these months are missing. Joyce's letter that follows responds to a postcard and a letter from Pat, which described a holiday she and her family had spent partly on the coast and partly on the offshore island of Zanzibar. While in Dar es Salaam, they had stayed for ten days with Ian and Alicia Kirkley, now returned from leave in Britain and stationed in the capital. Pat tells Joyce in her next letter of some of the events of this time in Dar es Salaam.

October 10, 1960

Dearest Pat,

Mail from Zanzibar! How very remote it seems. Even though our sojourn in the Middle East acquainted me with that world, how far, how very far from

Milwaukee the world at large remains. Recently we entertained people from Beirut, and the cosmopolitan air surrounding them made us heady with nostalgia.

Your trip sounds scrumptious, and I hope the time at Dar es Salaam was as delightful, with the lieder, as it sounds. Do you intend to be forever in Africa? That is bluntly put, but I wonder how long you actually will remain. Our stays are everywhere so brief, so brief as to be scarcely to the point, and I wonder at your staying powers.

It was fun to hear of your singing group, and your characteristic intensity and joy in working with it.

I of course am teaching once again, busily involved with all it implies. Furthermore, and you may have known this, we are to have a baby February 26th, which means I'm precisely halfway through with it all now. Reinhard asks, "When will it be finished?" and it is difficult to make the time seem diminishing to him. The first three months were hell, but it was good to know that I had so dramatically all the appropriate symptoms. This week I felt life for the first time.

I rather like Madeleine as a name, if a girl, assuming one could force these compulsively cozy Americans to speak a name properly, as the French do, with the accent at the end. We have here a national phobia against any name which cannot be bastardized into a -y or -ie or even -i ending, and Debbies, Kimmies, Stevies, Dickies, and Kathys are more prolific than automobiles. If they can make Reiny out of Reinhard, they can do anything.

Reinhard is running all over now, very ready for kindergarten, and just missing it because I didn't have the sense to conceive him with the eventual school year in mind. This way, it looks as if he'll be almost seven before he is in a situation where someone will teach him to read, which is a pity, because he's beautifully bright, and extraordinarily eager to expend energy in learning.

Marie is to leave in November, leaving us temporarily alone, until February, when Mother will come to help me with the baby—not that I'll need that so much, but that my school is desperate for me to offer the Renaissance course, and if I try that, I'll just have to have help.

I was in Salt Lake for three weeks in September, luckily missing an extravagantly hot summer there, and thoroughly enjoying the beauty of those mountains and that wide, wonderful valley. Saw very few people. I didn't bother with ferreting old friends out at the U. It's over, anyway, isn't it?

Hans had a one-man show, rather indifferently received, and failing to sell anything, but I still thought it strong in certain areas, and am immensely proud of the progress he has made in woodcutting and lithography. He's beginning to exhibit in national shows, good ones, and his professor at Madison considers him gifted for graphics. Altogether, apart from endless bills, and even occasional threats of collection agencies, we're holding ourselves together, praying that Nixon will be defeated, but fearing that he won't. Write often, as before.

Love always,

Joyce

193

October 20, 1960

My dear Joyce,

How very pleased I am to hear of your expected baby, and your attitude of complete assurance and expectancy of good makes me so ashamed of my present state of mind. How happy I am for you. Your medical troubles, I pray, *must* be coming to an end. We are disgustingly healthy, all of us, physically at least.

NEVER, NEVER, NEVER AGAIN. It took me eleven years to fall in love again this way. Two years of heartbreak and a rebound (and consequently broken) marriage were the results of falling in love as completely as I did at eighteen. I have not committed my emotions and heart since in that manner until now, and this is much worse, and here I sit, bitterly regretting the inward consequences. Oh, God, when will I EVER learn? But NOTHING happened, so don't worry. It is just so difficult coming back here to it all again after those ten days in Dar es Salaam, our stolen fleeting snips of private conversations, a chance phrase or look, the moments (utterly countable) dancing together; once we were left for a whole evening while the other two went to the cinema. We sang at least a dozen Schumann lieder, the whole of the Messiah, and were just beginning some Handel songs, when they returned. We hardly spoke that evening.

In fact we spoke less those ten days, and then badly, than we ever did in the forty-eight hours we used to have together when they would dash up here or we down there for a weekend. There seemed to be so little to say, after our letters, and every time I opened my mouth I said the wrong thing anyway. We have resigned ourselves to the irrefragable fact of having to get over the anguish, which simply cannot be lived with, and of seeing one another now and again (the next time will be when we go on leave, anytime from next April, when we are due, but we perhaps won't be granted leave for several months after that), as long as we are all in Africa.

I keep telling myself, everything heals in time. I read somewhere the other day, I think in Marcus Aurelius, that the healing of time is simply that of obliteration. And I am getting better and better, every day, etc. It makes it all easier, somehow, talking about it, even long-distance, to you.

I think we are going to end our correspondence after one letter each, of reassurance, I suppose. It just makes it all the more difficult to adjust to the demands of everyday life, this business of waiting in agony for the Wednesday plane. Joyce, could I ask a very great favor of you, as my oldest and dearest friend? I simply cannot destroy his letters, and I must, must not keep them any longer. The risk is too great. If I sent you a small sealed packet of them, could you just put them away somewhere and forget about them? I know I am being ridiculous, and I have brought them several times to the kitchen fire, but just could not throw them in. You are the only person I know I would dare ask such a thing of. Please? I will seal them up carefully, though the customs people might well open them on your side, but if they did, would you seal them up again, put them away somewhere in your totable-around belongings of things that you never use but cannot bear to chuck out? I'll probably write you in five years' time to burn them anyway. The great thing is to keep on doggedly repeating to myself, you are ridiculous, you will get over it, everybody gets over everything in the end, and anyway, you'll be dead in fifty years' time, and who in the hell will care then? If I have dwelt rather on the sadder aspects of this, it is because I feel primarily sad at the moment, but mostly I carry about with me a greater joy and awareness of life than I have known for years.

I wish I could convey to you the happiness and richness he has brought to my life. And a sense of duty and honor which I fear has been, not quite lacking, perhaps, but playing hide and seek with my impulses and instincts for more years than I wish to admit to. He is the most total, the realest, person I have ever known, he is not torn with self-doubts and recriminations, he quietly seeks out a path to follow, and follows it, noting down everything along the way, building up a bit here and a bit there, leaving things behind him a trifle more orderly and people with a little more self-respect and ambition than when he encountered them. He would be the most difficult person to live with that I can imagine, because he is so utterly demanding of one's (including his own) total concentration and abilities upon the task of the moment. He is terribly intolerant of laziness and hypocrisy, and demands perhaps more than people are capable of. He is a superb musician. Probably I am partially blind with love, but not deaf as well.

We have dropped all pretense that anything can ever come of our love; that was inevitable, and only came about at all from the anguish of our first parting. No, one must just stay married, raise one's children, and keep emotions out of the structure of one's days. The structure, I say, if not the interior, unseen by anyone else. And certainly the cheapness and shoddiness of affairs. That hardly needs to be said. I completely stopped smoking for several months, and only do a very little now, and joy of joys, some semblance of a voice is coming back for the first time in years. It is glorious to be able to sing an A with no effort, to breathe those long Schumann phrases without being purple of face and veiny of neck.

I've scratched about nine people up for Christmas singing, and am trying to work up a carol, solo song, and harmonium solo program, about an hour in length. I still tootle away at the recorder, most gratifyingly; I've been hammering away at it for ten months now, and can actually sight-read a few simple things with someone playing the harmonium. I expect my own piano will have to wait till we get to England, and I shall get a cheap secondhand one, and bring it back next tour, when I hope we shall be in a more accessible place than Pashenzi.

I think P. and I are going to buy a house on leave, nearish London, and spend our time and salary furnishing it. I cannot bear this rootlessness, country-lessness, any more; we *must* have a base somewhere, in some country, that the children can call home. We shall never, I think, live in America. I have become too expatriated and tropical (that's a euphemism for sluggish) to bear up under the frantic demands of life there.

I like having a big old falling to bits house, I like being able to afford household help, which one can just barely do in England now, if you make more than 2,000 pounds a year. I like being a member of an unashamed upper middle class with its attendant privileges (and obligations). And I like being left alone to be an eccentric, by the community, if I so choose. England is none of these things totally, of course, now, but it's the lesser of a lot of evils, if the tropics reject us, with all these wretched colonies coming to independence. At least Tanganyika is by far the best of the lot.

I will finish this later. I must go fix tea and get dressed for tennis and fill the lamps for tonight. Isn't it all lovely and anachronistic? You'd find me so slowed down as to be practically unrecognizable. Some of the women out here almost lose human form, mentally and physically, altogether.

October 21

I wasn't being quite honest when I said "nothing happened"; it jolly nearly did, and I believe it was only the difficulty of articulating the justification for passion that halted us. I think he drew back because he thought I didn't want a physical closeness, and I know I restrained myself because I felt he would lose the good old masculine respect for defiled womanhood, or whatever one calls it these days. So chastity still reigns; I suppose I ought to say, thank God. I don't know, it's difficult to know the right and wrong of a lot of things, but I think in the long view (that's the rest of my life, the only one I've got, staring me in the face and my children growing up with their own father and mother) that it is probably best this way, that we carry away an unsullied image of one another, and if we failed to find love or satisfaction or completeness in marriage, and feel we have found an intangible expression of it in one another, then it is best to leave it intangible, and let an image of the ideal inspire our lives, rather than wrecking a lot of other people and perhaps coming to the same thing in the end ourselves anyway.

I remember saying once to him, in the beginning, about a year ago, that I feared that domesticity would ruin and sully our kind of love, and he violently disagreed and went on about the ideal sort of marriage, Sidney and Beatrice Webb, I recall, and gradually over the past year I have sorted out emotions warped by my own and my family's experiences of marriage, and have come to believe that perhaps if we were ever granted the opportunity, we could have one of those marriages made in heaven. Now in our discussions this time, I find with wry amazement that we have switched roles. He is the one who wishes to keep domesticity and familiarity out of our relationship, while I, with confessed great effort, have come to see in him the husband whom I feel I could dedicate myself to utterly. However, as it is a purely academic question . . . Have I delineated him as perfect? He is not. He is the most terrible snob, not without reasons, but a purely British one. He, as I have said, is unreasonably and unforgivably intolerant. Ah well, any questions arising are moot and, I repeat, academic. I must take the whole lovely experience (as it really has been, even with the heartache) and weave it into the pattern of my days, hoping I have made him half as proud and happy and aware, in the end, as he has me.

You would be amazed at the physical care I take of myself these days, having always been known to you as the campus slob, or words to that effect. I make myself up carefully and religiously every morning, and am always combed, brushed, pressed, unshining-nosed. It would be most gratifying to my mother if she could only see me now. She hammered away at my insouciant messiness for years without success, and I must confess, it was only the English way of life and, finally, Ian's appreciation of femininity that eventually tamed me and turned me into a woman externally instead of a windblown college girl.

Is it not too incredible to you that we (you are, and I rapidly approach) are in our fourth decade? I simply cannot believe it. Do you remember (or do I bring this up with every approaching birthday?) walking through the snow across campus on my twenty-first birthday, you referring to it, and me bursting into tears, because I did not *want* to be twenty-one? Twenty-one. Another generation altogether must be twenty-one these days. I hardly ever think of the U. days any more. As you say, it's over anyway, isn't it?

Christopher is a darling child, terribly bright. We are not as close at the moment as Julian and I, but these stages succeed one another like the seasons. They are both very well behaved, polite little boys, with faults, naturally, but they show the results of early and steady discipline, which I have forced myself to administer. I would much rather shrug my shoulders and let them howl the place down as I did myself as a child, lacking any continuity of home or direction or mother, but mostly I have stuck to a pattern of development of sorts in manners and discipline and behavior. I would sort of like to have another, but I think I will wait a few years, two or three anyway, perhaps till Christopher goes to boarding school in 1963. I should very much like a daughter, and I will name her Joy if I ever have one.

How one does lose touch. You are the only person I write to, fully, or even half fully. I write to my mother, but never a word of what's important; she wouldn't understand, and I think it's better to go on administering bromides, long-distance. You are my diary, my mentor (of sorts: I love your badly disguised advice when you, too seldom, offer it), my confessor, the last of whom everyone needs, at least those of the flapping tongue and uncertain disposition, like myself.

So even if I ignored our friendship and what you and yours mean to me, I would still be terribly grateful for your patient and understanding ear lent to my incoherent and ill-typed outpourings all these years.

Do you write at all any more? Poetry, criticism, s.s., anything? Have you had anything published? Do you sing any more? The rediscovery of music has probably been the happiest outcome of this past year, and I can't imagine ever letting it go again. I now have lots of scores to long-owned records, sent by Ian while they were on leave, and it has been like reading a well-loved play for the first time, having seen it dozens of times, but having missed so many of the finer bits, the nuances, subtleties, brief appearances of minor characters one was hardly aware of before. Wonderful, wonderful—a whole new world.

What else do I do? I play Minibrix with Christopher, play ball with both of them; they both want to play tennis, and we do occasionally with two old broken tennis rackets of P.'s and mine, and a big rubber ball, quite insane. P. goes to the ubiquitous club, not as frequently as of yore, but he still goes; I hardly ever appear, though I have the onerous job of Lady House Member and loathe it, stubbornly refusing to have anything more to do with Red X jobs, Tanganyika Council of Women, Women's Service League, etc. My singing group meets once a week, for a couple of hours. I sew a lot, garden a lot. Shall I catalogue what is in my vegetable garden at the moment? Celery, chinese cabbage, ordinary cabbage, cauliflower, strawberries, bell peppers, parsley, lettuce, *billions* of tomatoes (I make chutney), broccoli, string beans, carrots, beets, spinach, and until recently, gem and summer squash. And every kind of flower you can think of, though the flower garden isn't much to look at, no lawn, and all the beds are every which way, with no order, just lots of flowers. I've come to love gardening, much to my amazement (and Philip's, who despaired of my ever taking an interest, let alone taking it over). We have over the years collected the odd bit of silver, which is nice in a home, a tea service, coffeepot, cruet set, that sort of thing. Old English silver is a fascinating thing to collect (if one had the money; we don't) and know about.

Our house is exactly like everyone else's out here, in furniture, at any rate, and we have muted (and inexpensive) decorations, pictures, and lots of books, and my beloved records, without which I can hardly imagine how I survived the whole of last tour in Mahali. And next tour I hope I can add: my piano.

We have a ciné camera, which has faithfully recorded the children's progress and our aging, our two houses out here, leave in England and on the Continent, the ship voyage out. Philip plays hockey every Saturday, and cricket when they can scrape a team up. The English and their sports! I had never held a tennis racket in my life till coming out here. When I realized I was a tennis and rugby widow, I took up tennis in self-defense. I thoroughly enjoy it, and am an erratic, indifferent-to-fair player. We entertain a lot (too damned much), and I do like giving a pleasant dinner party.

Last July we had to stay with us for four days our Minister of Health. He

198

is one of the best examples of what Africa can produce, but so rarely does. His degree is from Makerere (Uganda) College. He is intelligent, quick, cultivated, sensitive, and SENSIBLE. But to how many of Tanganyika's nine millions can this educational process be given? The Prime Minister, Mr. Nyerere, seems to be stalling for time; he apparently does not want self-government in the very near future; for the stability and economy of the country, he wants the status quo. But he is being besieged by the not-so-intelligent or well-informed members of Legislative Council to announce demands for self-government for next year. He stalls and stalls, but it is bound to come. What then? Who knows? One thing for sure, if anyone can make an African country work, it is Nyerere.

I only want our leave to appear on schedule next year, find reasonable boarding schools for the children to be sent to in England, if necessary, when they are of that age, no matter where in the world we might happen to be at the time; I want a house and roots of some sort that I can dwell sensuously on as MINE in the privacy of my own mind and soul. I want peace and quiet for our pleasant little family life to continue. Is that asking a great deal? After the upsets of year before last, I do not think so.

A perhaps smug, but not unjustifiable, conclusion to an unconscionably long missive. I felt I owed it to you. Now how about one as concrete and "This Is Your Life" from you? This is going to cost quids, it is so overweight! Much love to you and Hans and Reinhard. How I wish I could plan on seeing you next year. Will you, do you think, be getting to Europe?

All love as ever,

Pat

MILWAUKEE
November 8, 1960

Very dear Pat,

I speak for the whole family and some number of friends in thanking you for the splendid letter of a week or so back. Hans enjoyed it as much as I, to the point of considering it a kind of document, with parts of it quite suitable for reading to an unpredicted audience. I agree. It was the most consistently fluent letter I've had from you in some time. Not only that, it was steadier, more convincing—perhaps merely more thorough.

Tonight is a very fateful one for those of us who at all consider our fortunes (literally or figuratively) tied up with America, directly or indirectly. As I should think you might assume, I am heatedly pulling for Kennedy, though at the time of the convention I felt the Democrats could go to hell for all I cared, since they

199

would not nominate Stevenson. Now I can see, after the goopy campaign Nixon has conducted and the astonishing way its sentimentality has been swallowed, that Stevenson, being a two-time loser anyway, would not have stood a chance. As it now stands (mid-evening of election night) the race is very close. Perhaps this all seems very far from you now, but I am sure you'd be most concerned, were you here.

⊸ ⊷

Wednesday

It was a long and harrowing evening with friends, watching the tight, but nonetheless dragging, race between Nixon and Kennedy, and we left with a reasonable expectancy, but no certainty of a Kennedy victory. But I just heard —at noon the following day!—his acceptance speech, and I'm grateful (it's the only word) for his victory. I feel he's a perspicacious man with both convictions and integrity. Of course he may look better than he is, but what more have we to go on? Evidently the religious issue is passé in America. We thought his wife Jackie was a real drag, being beautiful, fashionable and chic enough to invite a good deal of antagonism. But it's nice to have a really lovely woman as first lady. Imagine! She is *exactly* my age.

As you know, I am continuing to teach full-time until the baby comes in February, half-time thereafter. Grueling but pleasurable. I wish you could send me advice at this point. You are not here, you cannot know our problems, I have told you so little. But one of my major worries, being one of Hans's, if not his greatest, source of dissatisfaction with our life, is my working. To be the proper dutiful wife, I know I should quit. Yet I'm stubborn as an ox about it, resisting Hans's every mention of it with anger, insults or tears. Why this should be so, I'm not sure, partly because it's what I always wanted to do, partly because bit by bit I'm gaining sufficient prestige to allow me the literature courses that are really stimulating, partly because I feel a twelve-hour load is not a reprehensible deviation from domesticity (although I know Hans is right in that I give many, many more hours to it), partly because we need the money. But the situation is now growing to the point that my basic delight in doing it is constantly undermined by my knowledge that a rift in the harmony of our home is the price of it all. But, I wonder, *why* need it to be? I don't want to quit, but I feel I should, as a sacrifice, or an obedience to Hans. He means it well, for the sake of more peace and serenity in my life, as well as his, but I hate to give up something I am doing so well with.

To continue, as I must, in the choppy, furtive particles of time that I steal to be my own. Hans is right—there is a great deal of expense of "paying too much for things in coin of the spirit" with my routine. I can scarcely manage anything

200

but a hodgepodge of jottings as an excuse for a letter to you. And now I have but fifteen minutes before the next class.

By the way, did *you* send me a new subscription to the *Times Lit. Supp.?* If so, a thousand gratitudes, I do enjoy it, but there was no mention of its source. A funny note: Mort Sahl, a very clever, sardonic, political comedian, said, "I hope Kennedy doesn't slip and say it was a miracle. Somebody might get the wrong idea."

Other details of our life: Hans has advanced so beautifully far with the techniques of woodcutting and lithography. It is not the technique he has the real trouble with; his difficulty is in knowing what image to create. Boils down to the same problem I have in writing: what, really, to say? His themes are essentially religious—Saint Sebastian, Veronica, some attempts at crucifixions, Jeremiah—but they give him much trouble, and he often feels he shouldn't try that. There is much pain, much anguish involved. Quite apart from the physically grueling work of running off edition after edition by hand printing. It takes hours, hours and hours.

Like you, we both are feeling and have felt for some time the desire, almost the compulsion, to buy a home. In our case, it would be on the detestable long-drawn-out time payment system, which we're trying with tooth and nail to avoid. But we have not yet found the place, and we still regret that our desires and willingness to make purchase of an old stone farm place in France fell through, coinciding as it did with Reinhard's disease.

Yes, our boy is quite thoroughly recovered. I've no idea how many, if any, photos I've sent of him, or if you've any well-defined picture of him in your mind. As I've repeated, ad nauseam, he is beautiful. He has precious, clean little features, and eyes that are sometimes appalling in their penetration, as well as the depth of their blue. He looks as he did at two weeks, quite like a little aristocrat. And by all means the most endearing thing about him, the something which I would most have wished for had I had an order to make, would have been and did turn out to be his whimsy, his charm, his Christopher Robinish nature —a quality which over the years has made so very many people comment on him, on the fact that he was unlike most American children (if such a generality is not blithering nonsense). And it was this that made his European family lay claim to his personality, whether with determined prejudice or not is hard to say. But he is very winning. He will be going to kindergarten in January.

Reinhard shows as yet no particular talent, except the phenomenally well developed one of being a skillful diplomat and a winner of friends at all levels and ages. He has resisted painting and drawing till now, and done them very badly, but suddenly now is taking real pleasure in them both.

Physically, I am a good deal changed since last you saw me. I've probably written this long since with ill-concealed satisfaction, but it has been a continuous pleasure since summer of 1955—this pleasure in my person, which I had only had at irregular junctures before. I lost all superfluous weight with the meningitis

201

while I was carrying Reinhard, and a nicer and happier person emerged thereafter. I cared more about everything, discovered I had a jolly good figure to work with and to dress, and that I could carry off just about any kind of clothing I had the courage to wear. Since then I have maintained my weight steadily at about 122, which is perfect for me. I have learned how to use makeup with some skill, which I resisted like poison until I was twenty-seven; I never am caught without heels, but always without a hat, and I have, with some abandon, recklessness, and great amusement and joy, purchased a really handsome woman's wardrobe with which I am very pleased and which I'm convinced I wear well. It took me two years of marriage before I would even abandon bobby sox, except on the occasions that absolutely demanded it, and I just now am beginning to rid myself of left-over college clothes. In other words, I'm much more likely to be seen in a violet silk blouse now than in a kelly green cardigan. It's fun, really much fun, and I have a few startlingly beautiful clothes. Hans is delightfully cooperative on this score, and cares that my lingerie is as chic as my outer garb, and often comes home with some fabulous little something, in exquisite taste. I've even gained quite a reputation around school and in social gatherings for my taste—hard to believe, isn't it? I still cannot drink. I eat with a good deal more attention than previously to what is good for me, and although I did smoke a lot for years, I've stopped with this pregnancy and perhaps won't go back to it. I never seem to get around to any sports of any kind.

Our social life is not so satisfying as we would like it to be. The people we see are either older, charmingly sophisticated and very involved in collecting amusing "art nouveau" odds and ends and doing wry or surprising things with them, and very involved in competitive entertaining (on a scale I couldn't possibly emulate) and drinking. Or they are the kind of average cross-section of less-than-the-best women's colleges, i.e., fairly stimulating, quite earnestly dedicated, and sort of pleasurable colleagues.

Will have to close here. Write much again soon. My thoughts are often with you.

Love,

Joyce

PASHENZI
November 28, 1960

Dearest Joyce,

I have felt in the mood for writing another long rambling letter to you for the last few days, but incredibly enough, in this minute isolated place, I haven't had the requisite length of time, in continuity, that is. I don't now either, but I shall write it in bits and snatches. I dwell in a depression as black and unremitting and seemingly hopeless as I have never known before, and I seek everywhere for the explanation. I have health, children, security, a reasonably forseeable future, sanity, intelligence, so I feel the reason must lie in my own inability to cope with the minor day-to-day exigencies of middle-class life; no, not the exigencies themselves, but with the insight that *this* is life, that nothing else lies ahead but this daily round, that excitement and ambition and enthusiasm and genuine gaiety lie somewhere back in my nearly over twenties.

You never even once mentioned becoming thirty this year! I find your disinterest in time, age and the somehow concrete space of years that divides things incomprehensible. You know how I have always been obsessed with this passage of time, with the importance of one's age, with pinpointing and remembering when an event took place. So perhaps my depression can be laid at the door of my approaching thirties.

I think it cannot be so easily dismissed as that, though. A great deal of it, though not all, is the agony of this love I have now put away from me. I felt I could not go on feeling that someday, somehow, somewhere . . . do you see? I couldn't live the life I must, and pay my debts to husband and children, with this spark of hope lingering on, kept alive in my heart. If I keep telling myself long enough that it is over and done with, that We Are Just Good Friends, then perhaps it will come to be so. I do not regret any of it. He has left me torn and bleeding, bereft of a kind of companionship and lifting of loneliness such as I had never known before, and the vacuum is what is so impossible to fill at the moment, but I know that time will do its appointed work, somehow, and WITH my help.

———————

I hate my fiction, it is all so damned trite and stupid, and my poems are worse. So I am going to attempt to write nonfiction articles about Africa. To judge from what I read, they'll print practically anything, providing it is reasonably well larded with Bwanas and references to the Heat and the Insect Life, etc., etc. I plan to begin a program of bombarding the few magazines I have addresses of with typical tripe. With luck I will have enough to buy my piano and a pair of silver candlesticks on leave.

God, how I wish I could see you. Can you possibly get over to the U.K. or even Europe whilst we are on leave? We have applied for April, but doubt very much if it will be granted before July, possibly (ghastly thought) they might even make us do a whole three year tour and we shan't be able to go till October. Why don't you leave that sink of iniquitous mediocrity and join us out here? I am positive you could get good jobs.

I suppose I still consider myself a reasonably good passport-carrying American; that is, I wouldn't sell H-bomb secrets to Mars, but on the whole, I think I am too expatriated after six and a half years of really enjoying myself in my

203

surroundings, and falling more and more in love with Europe (England, mostly) to ever settle down happily again in suburbia, U.S.A. Not, I trust, through snobbery, because we live a madly bourgeois life here, but with diversions of a different character.

How are you and Baby No. 18, or whatever it is now, progressing? I think of you so often, and wish again, for the umpteenth time, that I could lend you my reproductive organs. Give my love to Hans and Reinhard. How are they? We are all well, Christopher speaks Swahili and English with equal facility, Julian better Swahili than English. Both are very musical, especially Julian, who, I think, has perfect pitch. He sings "All We Like Sheep"! Not the twiddly bits that you and I always collapsed in hysterics over with the Tabernacle Choir, but the beginning measures, and he always begins dead on the pitch that the record does, whence he learned it, so that's a sign, I suppose. I'm giving Christopher a plastic recorder for Christmas, and will try to teach him a bit. I suppose I really ought to have one more baby, and we could have an instrumental or vocal quartet, à la Dolmetsch.

I really meant to end this at the above paragraph, but I now in turn have received a nice long letter from you, to make me feel in real contact again. I am so glad the pregnancy goes well. I always think of you, and indeed, you seem to think of yourselves, as temporary dwellers on the American scene, but somehow the years get into the habit of slipping by, and suddenly it is too late to make that sort of change again. I wonder, will you?

It doesn't really matter; geographical location has very little to do with it. I could settle as easily in Los Angeles or Peoria as in Dar es Salaam or the white highlands of Kenya or Chipping Camden. I suppose what one is forever searching for in all these moves (the geographical kind, the premarital boyfriend kind, the kind that takes you consciously from one age- and interest-group to another) is some sort of purpose, or, as you put it, "what to paint about" or write about or sculpt or philosophize about, not to speak of what to live about.

Ian gave me a charming little book last year, a compendium of quotations about music, and in it is quoted Sydney Smith: "If I were to begin life again, I would devote it to music. It is the only cheap and unpunished rapture upon earth." That wrenched my heart, to be sure, and made me wonder just what the content of my life might have been if I had given my second-rate talents and first-rate devotion to music. And Plato: "The man who has music in his soul will be most in love with the loveliest." So even if one's life cannot be devoted to what one loves most, or what one feels to be that of the ultimate importance to the world or even to himself, one can still have those precious hours every week, and a half hour of the day set apart for it, and create what little image, no matter how distorted, of beauty in sound, or in representation, or in *some* sort of attempt at interpretation and portrayal of the tiny segment of this instant of time we call the present, in this exceedingly small and unimportant world we live in.

All of which leads me up a crooked path to the point where I shall answer your questions about working mothers. I have always felt so sorry for you because you have missed these years with Reinhard, and the totality of homemaking all by yourself (that is to say, time, not the amount of work done), because I do think that the latter is important to the development of a woman, as such. And as for the former, although it is irksome, and the lack of money a problem (no matter *how* much one makes, it is never enough; so it is amazing how we all live on too little), the ordered simplicity (to a husband's eye), the graciousness that can only come to a home through the efforts of a wife who is nothing else first, at least in those first years when homemaking begins, and especially when the children arrive, from their birth until they are well established in school, can be begun and maintained only by a woman who does not work, or at least who perhaps might paint or make pots or do neighborhood dressmaking, but these things *inside* her own home. I feel this very strongly indeed, I fear, and I was the wrong one to ask, if you wanted a sop to your conscience, or an American-type justification for Companionship, the just-good-pals hubby and B.W. flitting out the door together every morning, cooking their television meals from the freezer together, etc. No, I'm being cruel. I know perfectly well it isn't like that at all with you, and I have great respect for your mind and your academic training and your hard work to get where you are, and believe me, no one knows better than I do what it is to live on less and force yourself to get by, but I really honestly believe you owe: 1. Hans, 2. Reinhard, 3. Yourself, K.J.H., 4. Society (corny?) your debt as a woman first to pay off before you can dwell with loving tenderness upon the niceties of Renaissance Lit. And that duty begins at home.

Damn it all, what do you think I'm doing here? I can't even stand Philip sexually; it's the most grisly pretense (this is for your eyes and heart, not Hans's or any friends; the world is a very small place), which goes on and has gone on with monotonous regularity, for years now. We get on in a civilized manner; we agree about the things that break most marriages up: money, politics, religion, raising the children, what sort of hotels to stay in on holiday, etc. But basically, we are just pleasant companions living in the same house, forced to share everything by the very fact of being married in Western society. If I didn't force myself to recapitulate, over and over and over again, the reasons why it is important that we go on this way, I would take a flyer and begin life all over again somewhere else as a ME more important to a lot more people than I am here and now. Mainly, it's raising the children. If the truth be known, I probably bore Philip every bit as much as he bores me.

And for that reason, if I am to go on here, in this life, which after all (as Ian has pointed out to me), I did choose consciously, knowing I didn't love P., then how much more must I do it properly, and be a GOOD HOUSEWIFE and MOTHER, than you who have the untold riches of a marriage with love as its foundation stone? Nevertheless, you may eventually destroy the most important thread in the fabric of a *marriage*, particularly with a Continental husband, that of respect for the Head of the Family. Nothing is so important as that. I'm afraid I *must* say what I believe to be of utmost importance in marriage, and that is for you to be there when the husband wants you, keeping a pretty, pleasant, quiet, gracious, well-ordered home without rush or absences, or working so obviously all hours to get it and keep it that way.

There are so many things I would like; I have even dropped two magazine subscriptions this year for financial reasons. I haven't bought any clothes for myself since I was married, nor for the children. My mother and aunt send nearly everything, or I sew it. Good God, I even make my own handkerchiefs out of old shirts of Philip's! I knit *all* of his wool sox for the cold season and England, all the children's knitted clothes, and even with corned beef the cheapest of tinned meat, I make our own corned beef with saltpeter.

What *am* I trying to say? It's just that you *can* get by if you really want to, but you must submerge your will. And that perhaps you are not willing to do. I feel that besides the children's ultimate well-being and security, it is unimportant, and only lying in abeyance anyhow (one's will). You once said, in a letter from Tarbert, that you knew with a perfect clarity that Hans was the one with talent in your family, and that his work was of the greatest importance. If so, then ought not his well-being and happiness, without which he presumably cannot work to his best degree, be of more importance to you than your career as eventual college professor? Can you not write at home, do research, read, search in yourself and in world literature for the reasons behind it all, if not reasons, then justifications, if not justifications, then patterns of living? That really is what it boils down to in the end for me, patterns of living.

Looking for the eleventh level of reality is merely another pattern, as is going to one's singing lessons every day, or taking time out of one's housework to play the piano for an hour every day. Oh dear, it all can be said in two or three sentences and only substantiated by dozens of examples, which, if you are determined to go on being Joyce Jerrell, girl professor, aren't going to have the slightest effect. I love you and I admire you (and I am very envious of your marriage, as you might guess). And the example of your parents, those wonderful people, must always be before you in whatever decisions you come to make about anything. I only have discoveries I made by myself: Matthew Arnold, Thomas Mann, G. M. Hopkins. And a few friends, here and there. And a forsaken lover, who more than anyone in my whole life has made me face up to realities, call them by their right names, strip them of any remaining disguises, and weave them somehow, willy-nilly, into this life I contracted so lightheartedly into. But as I get older, I find my horizons (personal ones) becoming not so vast nor so grandiose, no nearer perhaps, but better defined, and I think that at least for myself, it is better to circumscribe one's vision, put a name to it, and *then* settle down with a will and even, at times, a gay little song on one's lips, to doing the work with materials at hand, instead of vague tormented longings for that which we cannot even name, for some mystic connection with a society we cannot love nor feel really at home in.

206

Ah me, I really do seem to have prosed on for pages this time, and you must be thoroughly cross and bored with all this. But you did ask, just as I asked you, at the commencement of that disastrous last year and a half or more ago, about adultery, and you wrote me such a very good letter then, which helped a great deal (and goes on doing so).

Apropos of sex, since you once asked and I cannot remember ever having answered, my body only came alive as a woman in the last year or two, and then only with the wrong persons. It is an ever-gnawing horrible problem that I see no solution to whatever, in any future time, as people do not change in this way, and someone who is physically unattractive to me doesn't overnight or even gradually become attractive. One just pegs along, making other things count. And more than ever, we do not talk of intimate things, of feelings, of our inner selves, our yearnings.

It seems one of the saddest things of all in this forsaken love of mine, because, though we kept ourselves more or less chaste at the very end, I realized with an awful shock what sex was really all about with two people who loved one another and whose bodies were very ready indeed for one another, and then had to give it all up, over the teacups and coffee spoons. Will I ever find real love like this again at a right time and place, when there is no one left to be hurt or deprived? I cannot now, having known this kind of love for his sort of person, ever imagine responding to anyone else again except in pleasant and understanding friendship.

But still, there is always tennis for sublimation of the body, dancing, the odd whiskey, gardening, taking great and understanding satisfaction in books like Mann's *Joseph and His Brothers*, with which I am at the moment absolutely enthralled. And time heals. It does, it does. It heals everything, at least the ache thereof. And so, sex still once again escapes me, in any sort of totality. Like so many parts of life we thought to fall easily and naturally into place in the process of growing up, it seems to be made up of bits and pieces that never come together except in our minds. Fragmentary, some lost and broken, some unrecognizable, once taken out of context, some shamefaced after the event, others shining and lovely, to be remembered with love and gratitude and tenderness for the rest of one's life.

On reading this over, it appears to be frightfully smug and self-assured, which, I hasten to tell you, I think I am not! As for the rest of it, all I can say with certainty is that life appears to be very little other than a continuing battle against forces undefinable and unconquerable in the ultimate. But a battle which one must continue so as not to be submerged, and which might, with luck, be a preparation and a conditioning of strength for something which lies around the corner. Duty is such a dry and sterile-sounding word, almost disappeared from the American lexicon. I hope I have not learned it too late. I hope, *learned* it!

Yes, I am responsible for the *T.L.S.* I am glad you always enjoy it.

I have this morning sent off all my letters from Ian to you in a biscuit tin. I couldn't even bear to reread them, just popped them in, sealed it, clamped some string round, and rushed off to the P.O. before I could change my mind. Talk about documents. If I get eaten by a lion, you have my permission to read the lot.

I was glad to hear your election views. We too were pro-Kennedy, though difficult at this distance to work up the necessary partisanship for a stranger. MUST END!!

Much love, loquaciously yours,

Pat

MILWAUKEE

December 13, 1960

Dear Pat, Philip and Family,

So let our Christmas greetings come to you on the back of this messy little lithograph which Reinhard drew and colored and Hans printed off. It comes particularly as greeting to Christopher and to Julian—wishing them both and you both a happy holiday, and good year ahead.

We shall have a quiet Christmas, with Marie gone, the baby not yet here, and Mother and Daddy not coming. Please write soon, keep well, and know we think of you.

Love,

Joyce, Hans, Reinhard

PASHENZI

December 15, 1960

My dear Joyce,

Once again I bend your ear, as I am overwhelmed with pangs of loneliness, and take an interval in the midst of making a rag rug (can you imagine?). It struck me that my last letter to you was unspeakably pompous and smug, and not only in a cowardly spirit, but mendacious. I humbly beg your pardon if it created that impression. Also my whining about our poverty. Poverty is forever relative, once you get past the stage of having earned your absolute necessities. If I have canceled a subscription to a magazine or two, make my own handkerchiefs out of old shirts, make my own pickles and jams, it is because I enjoy the doing of these things and because it leaves that money to be spent on things which are

208

more meaningful. And in a tiny whisper, I admit to being envious of your working.

I only begin to realize how wrong I was ever to have entered upon this correspondence that I (we) have too recently ended, as I begin now to feel free and rid of this sick, hopeless craving which has haunted me hourly, every day, for the past year and a half. Thank God it is over. He, I think, feels the same, as I had one last (I hope) equivocal almost petulant letter a week ago, and feel relieved of a tiresome, dangerous and hopeless burden. I am still filled with gratitude for the whole thing, but terribly relieved that it is a closed book. It struck me recently how we use clichés so often which are filled with an awful truth: crazy about him (or her); insane about . . . mad about . . . lovesick, pining away after . . . etc. I think, on the whole, that the making of rag rugs and plum jam is a much more satisfying occupation than the searching of souls, one's own or anybody else's. I have the sense to realize, however, that I have probably not learned my lesson. Does anyone ever? Does experience ever teach us anything except that experience is painful?

It's like gardening in Africa: one just shoves the seeds in this unfruitful earth, forces the thought of blight, locust, drought, white ants, eelworms, failure or rains, from one's mind, and hopes for the best, and once out of a hundred times a hundred, the best happens, half of the rest is less than what you once would have thought you could possibly settle for, and the rest a dismal failure, in your eyes and everyone else's.

I also begin to see that growing up is a matter of settling for what comes, molding it to the most amenable shape, and forgetting about the rest of your impossible adolescent dreams; narrowing your horizons with good will, I suppose you could call it, but keeping in mind that it is still a horizon, and not an insurmountable wall.

January 5, 1961

Time seems rather to have whipped by, the holidays and the incessant activities of a small community like this have filled every spare moment. I have your Christmas card from my godson; I am so glad your pregnancy carries on. I can hardly believe it is next month. Do, do let me know right away.

I suppose, really, I am rather glad to be getting to be thirty (in ten days' time). It's a relief to have *young* youth over and done with. The fruitful part of one's young life ought to start hereabouts. Perhaps one's own views about dividing lines change as one gets older, but I don't really think middle age starts till mid-forties. Anyhow, what the hell difference does it make. It comes, we age, we die. So we might as well make the dutiful, fun-loving best out of it, and try to leave an orderly little spot behind, in whatever shape comes to hand.

Oh dear, I can't write anything just now. I'm all asthmatic and hot and tired and cross, and my mind won't function, so I shall adjourn till later in the week, and just miss this week's plane.

January 8, 1961

And now, I have some very exciting news. I am definitely coming home for a visit in 1961. A very short one, only four or five weeks, and without the children or Philip, as we simply can't afford it. The main thing is for me to renew my ties, friendships, relations, etc., after a very long period of seven years. We can now afford this, because government salaries are not only being raised, the raise is to be backdated, and the lump sum will about cover my air fare.

The main stumbling block is someone to look after the children. Philip's mother is the only one, of course, and she has written vaguely that because of her age she is losing her job in March, and doesn't know what to do. Well, as we have applied for leave in April, but might not get it approved till July, I want to leave here exactly two months before Philip does, so as to meet him in London when he arrives there on leave with the boys, and we begin house-hunting. So, completely dependent on whether she can and will come here to act as nanny, and when our leave is officially to begin, I might go anytime from next month to about May or June. How long could you stand me for, with a new baby and all?

How *impossible* I find it all to believe! Will I really be having a cup of coffee and cigarette with you, laced with abstract conversation, during 1961? I mustn't plan too much on it, it's bound to fall through. I haven't the foggiest notion of things American any more; I shall really be a timid immigrant. At any rate, I have kept my U.S. passport, so there won't be any difficulties there. We shall definitely come back here for another tour, if not stay on indefinitely. After all, it's a good life, one has lots of time to think and read and raise one's family, Philip is doing an exceedingly worthwhile job and loves it, and also, even better, the new terms include a shorter tour of only two years, instead of the old three. So things are working to keep on the restive European who is desperately needed here. The political atmosphere is another factor altogether, of course, and that can only be lived through and contributed to by oneself.

In any event, I am COMING. I can scarcely think of anything else, as you might well imagine, and can only pray that nothing ghastly happens to prevent it—an atomic war, drop in the value of sterling, death, illness, etc., morbid creature that I am.

End of busy talk. The bank here which you have the address of is the only safe place to write to me privately. All rather sordid, but Philip does get so cross if I don't read absolutely everything to him; all arriving mail to the medical address passes first through his hands, you see, and he knows when I've had letters from whom. Once I've read a letter to him, it's perfectly safe, as he never goes through my things. I wonder does every married couple who aren't in love any more (not that I ever was) feel as much strangers to one another as we do? We live very amicably; the only really ghastly part of our life together is this sex thing, which I have thought for years (and been told) was me, and now know isn't. We are simply incompatible that way, and that's all there is to it. I don't think it can ever be changed, and I refuse to give it any more thought or worry, or wonder about "perhaps if someone else . . ." because that's no solution either; it just makes everything go more haywire than ever, as I have found out bitterly.

I have so much else in my life—I'm moderately good-looking, I have a good figure, I have a well-developed appreciation for books and music, two lovely boys —why should I moan if this one facet of life is denied to me? It's so odd, all the same.

You just peg along, hoping for a reasonable best, and watch the years slide by, and add to your little store of knowledge and a few treasured material possessions and a very few priceless friends who cannot be replaced or substituted for or made anew. Ian wrote once, when I had written him a very unhappy letter: "When you grieve, there seems to be no meaning to our love; after all, we could have been miserable without ever knowing each other, so why waste time now? I have to remind myself that a glimpse of glory should pull me upwards, not emphasize the depth of the surrounding shadow. You have convinced me that your feet are on the upward path."

And now I am alone indeed, a more pointed and aware loneliness than I ever have known before, because of what has gone before this past year and a half, but on the other hand, I have grown in strength to be able to bear it, and find a reasonableness and joy in solitude that I have never known before, because of the mind and heart of this noble and gentle man which were so unaccountably revealed to me, who am so unworthy of his love. Whether the value of it all lies just in that, it is too early to say, but I am not unhappy; I glory that I was loved by him, and I can turn back now to what, after all, is my *real*, in a pragmatic sense, life. So sex really makes very little difference.

I slept with him a thousand times in my imagination; we ran away to Greece together every day, leaving duty, children, responsibility, broken homes, behind us. I was neither guilty nor ashamed, but rewarded in love. I grew old in the company of this love, basking to satiety in its glow, and yet here I am, the prim little bourgeois housewife, having perhaps, after all, had only a rather dangerous flirtation which five out of every six bored wives experience at some stage of marriage, all too common. My experience was unique, lovely, untouchable, a milestone in my life and a revelation of a world unknown.

It is all so odd. (This, I think, must be the most recurring sentence in my

211

letters!) I wish I could make myself sit down and write every single day, day after day, month after month. I know I could produce a book with steady effort. That is all it is, when you are given basic intelligence and a certain facility with words, which you have, which I have, to a modest extent. But it is like any other art or craft. It gets better, even if not touched with genius or extraordinary talent, with practice. I am forced to the conclusion that I must admire even Frances Parkinson Keyes and Nevil Shute more than the unwritten novels of undisciplined geniuses, because they, after all, sit down and write books. I have had my articles rejected by the *Atlantic*, as I fully expected, by the way. And now I must go and see to curry lunch, it being Sunday, and every European family in East Africa will shortly sit down to curry lunch. I am thrilled by Kennedy's cabinet. It all sounds most exciting and promising. Do let me know about Hohlwein No. 4 as soon as possible.

Much love, my dear, dear friend,

Pat

MILWAUKEE
January 21, 1961

Very dear friend,

There are hosts of things about which I want to talk to you in detail; so many, so deeply, that nothing would suffice short of a visit with you, and that such a visit is actually to be envisioned makes me more full of a happy expectation than I've been in years. You must stay with us longer than just a day or two! And feel confident that any duration will be certainly too short. And Hans is as eager to have you as I, for as I've said many times, he's grown increasingly fond of and interested in you over the correspondence. I'm delighted for you at the salary raise, and at what it will mean promptly and thereafter. I hope, though, that your mother-in-law can come now, so you could be in America in the springtime.

And then, happy thirtieth birthday! ha-ha-ha. But I don't mean it cynically at all, and I do wish it to be the inauguration of a good decade for you, as I feel it will be since my thoughts seem to coincide well with the quote you gave me about your feet being on an upward path. Altogether, your attitudes make me feel unwarrantedly immature and ill-disciplined for being *still older* than you. I think Hans is still wondering just when, if ever, I shall begin to "limit my horizons," acknowledge them, and work to some end within them. And he is so right. I'm certain he sees in me an endless and pathetic scattering of purpose and of force, and all because of some inane momentum to which I affixed myself a few years back. In terms of this alone, perhaps a visit with you could give me and us a cleansed and newer impetus.

Reinhard thanks you, by intensive play with the ferryboat you sent. He has nothing like it and is able to spin long and happy stories round about it. Baby's due date is February 26th, so it could conceivably be a March baby. The whole pregnancy has gone unusually well, with only minor skirt hitchings necessary at eight months; I still look less than that, and seem to be the type that can disguise a pregnancy months on end.

Your house-hunting in England is such an attractive pursuit. How I envy you that! Perhaps if we ever succeed in buying ours in France, we can exchange keys now and again. So, the new Administration is in. I am looking towards good things from it. There is a lot of sinew in the group.

All love and more delight
at the thought of seeing you,

Joyce

PASHENZI
January 21, 1961

My dearest (and only) friend,

I herewith enclose one last couple of letters (I think). And with them go a breaking of a link that has kept me enchained for—how long? A year and a half, at least. I dread to think of meeting him one last time in Dar es Salaam by myself, if and when I go to the States on leave ahead of Philip in three months' time. It's no good saying to myself, Be strong. I know I shall succumb, if I am wanted to. I wish I understood sex. I wish I were mistress of myself. Might as well say, I wish I were dead, which I certainly do not. Ah well. I do wish you could meet him. Of all the people who have passed in and out of my life these years, he is the one I want you to know. Who knows, perhaps you will someday, in another context. The world is so very small.

I am living in a state of suspended animation, until I can know definitely if and when I can go home for my visit. I really am very tired indeed of Pashenzi. I get very lonely at times. I have my music, the children, the house, Philip's comfortable, easy and understood company, my garden, the odd bit of entertaining, but I feel restlessness creeping up on me like the effect of hemlock. End-of-tourishness, it's called locally.

I was given lots of books for Christmas and birthday, which I have zipped through, except for two Faulkners which I have kept till last. How depressing he is! I loved Pasternak's *The Last Summer,* which led me to reread *Zhivago,* better than ever. It makes me feel less daft, allowing love so to rule my thoughts.

I haven't succeeded in my latest attempt to quit smoking, and despise myself for my weakness. This is an idiotic letter, hardly worth the name, so I had better end, and wait for a reasonable sort of inspiration to descend. I think of you so often, in your last weeks of waiting, and pray all goes well at the end. My love to you three, possibly four, when you get this.

Your aging friend,

Pat

MILWAUKEE
February 16, 1961

Beloved friend,

You shall be the first of all to whom I write and one of the very first whom I think of, on this February 16th birthday of our 6 lb. 2 oz. daughter, Andrea Dominique Hohlwein. For I love you and all the world for this wee small perfect child.

My doctor decided to induce the labor. So my water was broken at 8 A.M. and I had prompt second stage labor until noon, when I was taken into the delivery room for a most grueling hour. The baby was somehow twisted in the perineum and I still feel as if a doctor's huge fist were circulating around in my vagina. I was neither so brave nor so determined as I had been with Reinhard, and finally requested the help of gas. And it continued to seem *very* long. But now it is over and I urge you to rejoice with me. I didn't actually prefer a girl, but was full of a concern, bred by my past vagaries, that the baby be fine and healthy. She is that: long—20 inches—thin, blond, nicely wide-set eyes, small nose, perhaps like Reinhard's, his (and my) identical rosebud mouth, a head not as yet remarkable, but in no way unpleasant, and perfect small hands and feet. Hans was with me throughout labor. Mother will arrive tomorrow, full I am sure of joy over a granddaughter she can idealize. How I feel your friendship more keenly across the years!

I see very little reason to conjecture that we might make a move toward Africa. Hans is just stepping into the swing of gaining a foothold in teaching as he desires it, namely to teach printing rather than theory. We found a superlative apartment yesterday which we may take for one more year, and would perhaps be living in as you come. Please do come and plan on *as much time as possible* to be with us.

For I send my deepest affection,

Joyce

March 7, 1961

My dearest friend,

I am so very happy for you. I wept with joy when your letter arrived. Thank God it is all over, and safely this time. You must now be safely home and enjoying wee Andrea. Can I humbly beg to be (a) godmother, if this isn't being gauche? I would so love a goddaughter, if I am to have none of my own. I will send her frilly little things that she oughtn't to have so young when she is in her early teens; I will be the mysterious and world-wise and weary aunt (or godmother, if you like) that she comes to stay with when she is recovering from the pangs of her first love; she can come and study art history or tapestry weaving or ballet in London and live with us. I adore her already.

As I may have mentioned, I am sort of in the mood to have another, not desperate, mind you, but a bit "broody," as the English say, but Philip is absolutely thumbs down on it. Perhaps it's just as well; I am in a wonderful state, but rather a drifty one, and it isn't good to drift about (even mentally) with a baby. They sense it, and I am sure it unsettles them. Whether you're actually right about things or not, when your baby is tiny you should be absolutely certain of everything you are doing. If that makes sense. It's been so long since the birth trauma struck me last, and the children are growing up so, I hardly feel I ever was the mother of a tiny one, but as if I'd found them, at one and a half or two, under a cabbage. One is forever shedding old mental skins, like some demented snake.

You know, I cannot tell you what our correspondence has come to mean to me. It is like a rudder in this crazy ocean, or a lighthouse guiding me away from the dangerous shoals and rocks. What did Matthew Arnold call it? Touchstone, that's it. I know that even though you sympathize and have empathetic feelings for most of what I tell you, that you will answer truly when I ask you some things, and that you will give me an honest opinion when some half-witted project I have in mind, or idiotic state of being I find myself in, comes over too strongly. I respect you so very much, and I am so grateful to you for being my friend. The older I get and the more people I meet, the more I realize how very rare indeed is the quality of a relationship such as ours.

I am working very hard trying to learn the accompaniment to an Easter anthem my little chorus is doing. Makes me wild, as I can't sing and play at the same time. It's very good for me, though. There is nothing like accompanying to get you back in trim at double time. It's the funniest sensation, when you've never accompanied before, this feeling of being swept along in an irresistible wave of rhythm that you just *must* keep up with, and by golly, you *do;* that's what's so odd.

I have drowned my sorrows (and joys, as well) in this music this year. Philip, bless him, says I can take music lessons on leave if I wish, and we shall have a piano as well, so if we can afford it, I shall. What with buying a house and trying to furnish it cheaply and quickly, we shan't have time on our hands to travel round and be spending lots of money that way, as we did last time.

Have you written anything at all the past couple of years? Do you write poetry any more regularly, are you struck with inspiration now and again, or do wonderful lines just pop into your head, drift round for a bit, then sail off again, not having been captured on paper? I find that happening to me so much. That is the great thing about writing, to capture absolutely every worthwhile phrase on paper and file it away to be used someday, or to be developed at length and woven into something else. Do you keep a journal, a diary? I think that is very important too. I doubt I will ever have the necessary self-discipline and will power to do a long concentrated piece of work, I am coming to think.

Do write and tell me all about Andrea's first weeks, and how you are getting on.

My deepest love to you and your three,

Pat

March 9, 1961

My dearest friend,

An hysterical and hasty scrawl to affirm joyously that yes, yes!! I *am* COMING HOME! I fly to Dar es Salaam May 3rd, London May 4th, thence to New York by cheapest route available, thence to Los Angeles ditto, probably train; I stay at home till end of June, roughly six weeks, then trail slowly back to New York by bus, as I can stand twenty-four hours on a bus at a time, but not much more. Las Vegas for a couple of days (hordes of aunts and uncles and cousins), Salt Lake City one night only, to see—whom? Whomsoever is there—a quick walk round the campus, a cup of coffee at the C.I., a crocodile tear for my misspent youth —anyhow, one night—then—you!! S.L. to Milwaukee—two days? And how long can you stand me for? I must be back in London by July 15th. Philip and the boys fly there from Dar on July 19th. Would you go mad with me hanging about the place for a week? Would we talk ourselves hoarse? I'll do the dishes and walk Andrea in her pram—sorry, baby buggy—what? a week, one day for each year since we've seen one another? *Do* say if you can't manage me. I can *always* put up at a hotel near you, and for heaven's sake, say if you can't manage more than a day or two. I will certainly understand. I would come to you first, but I prefer to leave you till last, like dessert and coffee and brandy.

216

I am so, so excited, as you may well imagine. Everything else has gone out of my head with the thrill of this projected trip, now that it is definite. It sounds corny as hell, I know, but the minute I get off the plane in New York, I am going to go to a drugstore and buy the *N. Y. Times* and a hamburger and a cup of coffee, and then I am going to the top of the Empire State Bldg. (where I have never been) and then to the Cloisters (where I have been) and then to—where? I don't know—I am raving. Seven and a half weeks to go and already I can't sleep nights. Do hurry and write before I leave, and let me know.

I shall feel an utter country bumpkin, a Jamesian expatriate, I have nibbled at the alien corn for so many years now. Do you know, I haven't seen: television for six years; only one film in two and a half years; a supermarket or a six-lane highway or a diesel train for seven years? Extraordinary. The one shadow is leaving the children for such a long time, but at least they will be in good hands and in their own home. I must write lots more letters to ease the pressure before I blow up. Love to you all, my dear dear friend, whom I shall shortly hug in reunion,

Pat

MILWAUKEE
March 18, 1961

Dear, dear Pat,

Hallelujah! Only two things to clear up. First, do not apologize about asking to be Andrea's godmother. I found it not gauche at all, but terribly endearing, and the way you phrased it brought tears to my eyes for five successive readings. You know how I would love to have you.

Secondly, I cannot imagine our ever growing weary of you. One week is far too brief, but at least five days better than two measly days, and please believe me!! If you don't I'll never write you again. We have been in incredible chaos, a whirlpool of decisions and contradictions, or risks and gambles and reversals that have left me breathless. The result, in terms of your visit, is only this: I have no idea whether we'll still be in Milwaukee by early July. Certainly we shall be, and would have space for you, by the end of May, but then we'll both be teaching. And I can scarcely bear the thought of distraction from our time together. I wish we could work out something dramatic, such as meeting you in S.L.C., and driving together back east or to whatever point we'll be moving. However, at this point, only a few days after Hans's impulsive and at first perplexing resignation from his job here, we've absolutely no idea *where* we will be next year. But whatever the next year involves for us, nothing will prevent our arranging a calm and glorious time together. I can scarcely wait. I

217

shall be writing you many wee, busy letters about all sorts of busy things before you leave Africa.

Our baby is a dream; I am certain you will be proud of her. Thanks so much for the family pictures. The boys are wonderful. I yearn to see them.

All love,

Joyce

PASHENZI
March 23, 1961

My dear Joyce,

I think another six months in a place like this would absolutely finish me off. Both Philip and I are a little bit round the bend from two and a half years here, and only one vacation away, our local leave last September. Philip is terribly overworked, and is so irritable he almost matches my temper at times. We shall welcome the new-length tours. I can tell you, it's only just. For the first twelve months, you skip along a pleasant rose-lined path, enjoying and learning and beginning projects, for the next nine you are on a level plane of well-learned routine and surroundings, faces and conversations, for the next six you go gradually, ever so slightly, downhill, just a bit each week and month, but definitely downhill, and then, whoosh, deterioration, but *rapid*, sets in with a bang, and things begin to fall apart all over the ruddy place.

Not only bodily health (God, Mahali was a hellhole; I have never felt so steadily unwell in all my born days. I have *never* been so damnably unavoidably *hot* for so long, three bloody years), but in a place like Pashenzi, with a temperate climate, but so, so isolated, small and cut off, your mental health degenerates so badly the last year of a three-year tour. If someone told me I had another six months or year to do here, I honestly don't quite know what I should do.

I've been reading Robert Graves's *Goodbye to All That*. It is an incredible book. The First World War seems so remote and unnecessary, a whole way of life went down the drain with it, Edwardian England, much more than anything disappeared from life after the last war, except of course for the terrible tragedy of European Jewry. I've read very little of Graves's poetry. Do you like him?

How are you doing? How *are* you? How is Andrea? I must end, give my love to Hans and Reinhard, and do write and tell me you're not going to Alaska or the Andaman Islands the first week of July. I'm longing to hear from you. Only five and a half weeks till I leave, wheeeee.

Much love to you all,

Pat

218

April 6, 1961

Dear Pat,

Your letter came yesterday and it did me good to hear from you. Oh, I yearn and *need* to talk to you. Perhaps you can help me redirect or reaffirm a number of things. I feel no amount of time is long enough to have you near, and am trying to fantasize, at this point, some way to meet you in S.L.C. and drive together cross-country (with children probably) back to Milwaukee, or wherever. For you received my last letter, didn't you, in which I barely mentioned Hans's resignation and our search for a new position. He is quite beside himself—is such a tormented and, in many ways, ineffectual chaotic person—full of talent without discipline, desire to believe without conviction, fascination with man without the ability to reach him, compassion without a modicum of friendliness and with a shocking lack of human understanding at close range. Ah well, you'll see.

We've no idea where we'll be. Hans yearns for the Mediterranean and I only to leave the Midwest. I seek to aim at Montreal, Boston, or the Northwest, but of course would be happy to go abroad again if there is work available to challenge Hans sufficiently—some belated chance to (excuse the phrase) make a man out of him. It's rather exhausting living with so immature a man and I frankly sometimes yearn for the finished thing or the man who can control more of himself and of life, and who brings a more dynamic intellect to bear on the things of this world. There are, as you will see, rare and fine compensations, but I sometimes, right now, feel ever so ever so lonely.

Oh, Pat—I am *so* glad you are coming!

Love,

Joyce

April 15, 1961

Dear, dear Pat,

Only three weeks to go! How excited I am for you, how excited for myself, for your parents, for your godchildren and for Hans. It's all too wonderful! Why don't you call us from New York when you arrive and reverse the charges? Oh, I do so hope all goes well for you. I don't suppose I need worry about your possible disenchantment with the place, since, if anything, you probably have the expatriate's beclouded illusions rather than the immigrant's radiant ones, and perhaps you'll be pleasantly surprised. Your first hamburger and coffee in a New York drugstore might be a bit harrowing, and the shock of the American sloth in pronunciation will be a body blow, but after that perhaps you can relax and take the good with the bad, rejoice in the majesty of the geography of the land, and the variety of its humanity. You'll find much changed, much worsened, the madness of traffic hair-raising, the chic of Fifth Avenue enchanting, the intensity of all going on rather appalling. And the noise—after Pashenzi—oh, the noise! I can't wait to see you! I feel almost certain we'll be in Milwaukee that first week in July. Is there anything S * P * E * C * I * A * L you'd like to do—Chicago or otherwise—that I could plan for in advance? Shall I stock up with Chianti, zinfandel, or what? Do you have a British accent? I'll bet you do!

In any case, a thousand times welcome! You've no idea how unnerved I am and have been all winter by an incomplete love affair Hans has been having. More when you come.

All love,

Joyce

PASHENZI
April 25, 1961

Dearest friend,

It is simply too incredible that a fortnight tomorrow I shall actually be on my native heath, and in the city of the angels, and the bosom of my family— a marvelous collection of clichés to go with an experience full of banalities, no doubt. I leave here a week tomorrow, and take just a week to get there, by air, with all the various stops and waits for connections. I feel (though I haven't confessed anything but a mounting excitement to anyone else, even Philip) the beginnings of a terrifying emptiness, as if one had a tone-deaf friend who didn't know he was tone-deaf, and said to him over and over, just WAIT until you hear Beethoven's Fifth, and took him to a concert, and then . . . pouf, nothing but empty bubbles in one's head. Have I become too de-Americanized? Can one? Have I become too engrossed in middle-class values and the struggle to make myself into the image of a respectable upper-middle-class matron? To appreciate coming home again, I mean.

I have been reading William Whyte's *The Organization Man* and he most amusingly says that apropos of Thomas Wolfe, the reason why most young Americans Can't Go Home Again is that when you arrive it just isn't there, which is what I'm quite sure I shall find on arrival in Los Angeles, as it used to change so from one college term to the next. And Salt Lake, what shall I find there? I think enough to make me mildly nostalgic. Let us say, I shall very likely see the

220

empty shell of a much loved theatre where I saw some varied plays, some deeply moving, some trite, some a bit sordid, but all important to me, and all of whose runs have finished. There's no one there I want to see, except perhaps your mother and father. God, I feel ancient.

I can't put much of it down on paper, that is, I could but it would take twenty pages and several days, which I haven't got right now, to tell you about my relationship with my children, which has astoundingly (to unmaternal old me, not to everyone, I realize) turned out to be quite the most important thing in my life, and this, if nothing else, Ian did for me.

This business about my children really is fantastic, and I want at least two or three days to explore the subject with you. I am longing to make an acquaintance with my godchildren (thank you).

For goodness' sake, *do* write to me in Los Angeles the moment you know anything of your movements in June and July, as I want to make plans with my mother and I absolutely must see you. I mean, it's too silly to come all that way (and so seldom too!) and miss you, when I only am coming to see you and my mother anyway. Oh dear, I wish I could see you straight away, but my mother would have been deeply hurt if I had gone anywhere else first. If only you were where I could see you several times during my sojourn.

I must rush off and do a coffee tray. I have two silly females coming in for morning coffee, as I am having the whole station in, by twos and threes, before I go. Ugh. These two are particularly silly, and I have left them till last. Beginning tomorrow, we are going out every single night for dinner (isn't it fun, these ancien régime types of things?) and there is a farewell party at the club for me on Saturday night, all formal, men in dinner jackets and women in long dresses. Rule Britannia.

> Love, love, till we meet,
>
> *Pat*

PART EIGHT

MAY 1961–DECEMBER 1961

A long friendship without dissimulation

May 22, 1961

Dear friend,

Your little letter just came. I can well imagine from my own experience the many kinds of pressures put upon you in these Los Angeles days by family and the limits of time. In about six weeks it will seem to have been but a breath to you, half reality, half fancy. But I do intend that our time together should remain as something actual. We, all of us, are so looking forward to you, and Hans not least.

Which is one reason why I seriously doubt that I shall plan to come to S.L.C. that final June week. Hans is most eager to know you, and I do not want to have him receive the leftovers. Not that there is only so much of you and there it has an end; rather that I want him to share in the full freshness of comment and shared experience, rather than by way of any warmed-over repetition.

Furthermore, our summer funds can only go so far, and since Hans may himself be called for interview somewhere, that transportation money is actually more essential than this would be. You will enjoy Mother and Daddy and they you, but I would be jealous of time spent, to my disdainful eye, in a negligible way. I have only two more days of teaching, and I admit I'm beginning to feel radiant at the prospect of freedom from that particular pressure and commitment.

I intend to read the *Alexandria Quartet* in June, rather belatedly. Amazing how hard it is to keep up with contemporary stuff when you're teaching a few centuries back. My telephone call to you, by the way, was my thirty-first birthday present to myself. Shall we spend time bemoaning our thirties?

Write what you can, when you can,
And all love,

Joyce

June 9, 1961

Dear Pat,

Well, you seem to be experiencing an exposé par excellence. As you say, add to it the Organization Man and the Academic Man and perhaps you'll have had a fairly full glimpse. I doubt it, though. For all its horrid stereotyping, the country is infinitely various. But I am sorry you've had such a grubby session at home. The disenchantment, though, I've experienced on a lesser scale, and I know it to be something of a body blow.

I am thoroughly pooped, and I am going to try and take the cure before your arrival. This means taking naps, walks and, if necessary, tranquilizers. It means playing with my baby and reading whatever I want to, sewing on buttons and building bridges with my boy. I wish Hans could do so too. At present he is driving a cab(!).

The last weeks were an awful strain, with blue books, term papers and goodbyes. And beneath this all, our mounting concern about Hans's securing a position. So far, nothing. And only one more salary coming in. Further, we've been able to save nothing. Still, I'm sure he'll get something.

Andrea is screaming now with pain from a 4-in-1 shot she received this morning and I cannot calm her, and it breaks my heart. She is so good always and seems to be astonished at having to cry like this. She now weighs twelve pounds and is very dear.

Well, I've little to add, and my baby is so terribly unhappy. Write if and when you can.

Love,

Joyce

After seven years, the two friends were reunited for a week in Milwaukee, as Pat made her way back to New York by Greyhound bus in slow stages, and thence to London. Joyce, Hans, Reinhard (now five and a half) and baby Andrea lived in a pleasant apartment in that pretty Germanic lakeshore city. What they spoke of together during that week is now, in its details, long lost, and is referred to only vaguely in Pat's first letter from London, but it presumably encompassed much the same topics as did the letters.

Each of them now, many years later, remembers only a few specifics and some sharp impressions of the conversations. The relationship seems to have been as immediate, empathetic, warm, loving and open as in years past. They discussed love, marriage, sex, careers, books, children, parents, their probable futures. Certain impressions each received of the other they refrained from sharing at the time, so as not to hurt her dearest friend. They have since talked of these impressions and the reasons for them.

Joyce recalls her great shock at finding in Pat what seemed to her the worst sort of upper-middle-class British snob, her veneer of studied, controlled graciousness such a contrast to the impetuous, outspoken and slightly disreputable friend of a decade before. Pat in her turn was aghast to discover the dictatorial manner in which Hans ruled his little ménage, and the meek subservience of her formerly insouciant friend to what appeared to be his moody and irrational demands.

Each woman seemed to the other to have become in some ways a grotesque parody of the life she had been living and chronicling for the other: Joyce the eternal doormat to a man combining the most stereotyped excesses of artist and German paterfamilias; Pat the self-assured arbiter of an adopted set of British colonial standards and mannerisms, the compleat memsahib.

Joyce had indicated in her letters nothing about Hans's domestic tyranny, and Pat discovered to her astonishment a number of eccentric demands that Joyce appeared powerless to dispute or to refuse. For example, Hans was going through a period when he disliked artificial lighting. He had always been hypersensitive to noise, so sensitive, in fact, that Joyce remarked a few years ago that "If St. Peter ever asks me why I had to get out of that marriage, I will only answer that Hans couldn't stand even the sound of a creaking ironing board." The dislike of these two inescapable components of everyday (or rather, night) life combined to produce the following scene, repeated each evening.

The living room was chosen by Hans as the most pleasant room in which to eat the nightly meal. It was at the front of the apartment and the kitchen at the rear. The floors were of polished wood, with only their Oriental rugs here and there to deaden a few footfalls. So, by Hans's fiat, everyone went barefoot. Nightly, the table had to be set up, with Joyce traipsing back and forth along the lengthy corridor with dishes, glasses, cutlery, linen, the courses of food, drinks — barefoot and by candlelight. The five-year-old Reinhard had difficulty adjusting to the dim light and spilled something occasionally, at which there were angry words from his father, followed by tears from son and mother, and expulsion from the table of the son.

Pat protested, "Say no. This is a crazy way to live!"

Joyce tearfully answered, "I cannot. This is the way things must be to keep peace. He is an artist." Joyce remembers feeling privately that it was all very well for Pat to tell her to institute either a rebellion or a more "gracious" life style when she had a houseful of servants; true enough, but the tale remains ludicrous and pathetic in the recounting, to say nothing of the living of it.

The two also discovered during this visit that it had been at each husband's behest that they had begun dressing elegantly, stylishly, and lavishing much attention on the physical self, and not as a self-generated move in the process of becoming adult women. They both remember, however, that having once been prodded to abandon jeans, slacks and the Western American dressing styles, they enjoyed their new personae.

Each took it for granted, she now thinks, that these were temporary changes in the other. Pat thought that Joyce would rebel someday; Joyce felt that Pat would abandon her obsession with social forms and return to her old self. The unhappiness that was expressed over the years in the letters would substantiate this assumption, because what each woman was unhappy about was finding herself a square peg in a round hole, however much she may have tried to convince herself what a delightful round hole it was. In other words, each had adopted a life style and responses to fit what was being demanded of her not only by her husband but by her social setting—in Joyce's case, artistic academia combined with a German husband's attitudes about family life and woman's place; in Pat's, the anachronistic setting of colonial life combined with a British husband's attitudes about the same things.

Joyce and Pat adhered to the adopted life styles but felt uncomfortable in the false garments. Many years and many conversations passed before much of this was either articulated or accepted (and then with some reservations) by either of them.

LONDON, ENGLAND
August 14, 1961

My even more dearest friend,

Alas, alas, it is all too quickly ended, and now how many more years will it be? Not one iota different are you, except maternal, wifely, womanly instead of girlish, loving instead of flirtatious, but the sparkle, the wit, the intelligence, the charm, all there, enhanced, I think, possibly, by your trials and tribulations over these years. They have left their mark indeed, but a good one; indeed a *hall*mark, one might say. It wasn't *long* enough, that chatter-filled week! It flashed by, leaving scraps of hazy memories of this and that conversation about this and that topic, but I am *so* happy to have been with you and shared your life, even for that brief instant.

But I must do my duty now (my bread-and-butter letter, as the English say) —many thanks for your hospitality to me that week, for putting up with my sermons and alarums. I do hope something has come up for Hans and that immediate future prospects seem less dismal. Write, write, and tell me how all goes.

Joyce, I don't know what I should say about all the things we talked of. I think nothing for the moment, as it is all still too fresh, and anyway, we said all the important things and know how the other feels about ourselves and marriage and children and art. The great thing is to go on elaborating and personalizing events and people and emotions.

Here in England, Philip is terribly good about splitting our time equally with and away from the children. That is, while we're in London, he stays with them all day while I rush about shopping and gazing, and I stay home that night while he goes to a play or cinema, and the next day vice versa. We go out en masse (or rather, en messe) a couple of days a week and hire a baby-sitter two nights a week. It works very well. I love going places by myself anyway.

We had a grand reunion; the separation did us both a world of good, me especially! I think, anyway. I feel a great deal more settled and content, with P., with the children, with my lot and my chosen way of life. I have decided to give up my U.S. citizenship and to take out a British passport, but P. says wait until my U.S. one expires next year, then do it (he knows my rash ways so well). But I think I shall be unchanged then. London seems particularly lovely this summer. Is it the aching nostalgia of an aging beauty past her prime and effectiveness, her only power lying in the ability to stir men's memories of past glories and triumphs? I don't care. It is all such a slow process. I'd rather be in on the death of the Greek empire than the Roman one.

I must send you my article from the *Christian Science Monitor* of July 8th, smack dab in the middle of the editorial page, with a real live by-line! I'm frightfully proud, though probably I'll never get another published. They've even heightened it with a map of Africa, Tanganyika appropriately darkened, and a big picture of Mr. Nyerere, our Prime Minister. I have written another, on finance, and sent it off, and am working on a third, on women.

We think we have a house, for more than we had intended to pay, and a little larger—drawing room, dining room, study, kitchen, pantry, half-bath downstairs, four bedrooms and a bath up, three-quarter-acre garden (roses and fruit trees), and a couple of buildings that look as if they used to be a coach house, a garden shed, a coalbin. We have paid a 10% deposit and now just sit back and wait for our lawyer to do the rest. It will probably still be another three to four weeks before we can move in. We'll have to get a seven-year mortgage on it, and hope to God we can rent it furnished while we are in Africa, at an exorbitant rent, or we'll never be able to meet the payments. That shouldn't be too hard though, to rent it, if we can manage to scrape enough secondhand furniture together to fill the place.

Our nearest village is in a posh area, and we're surrounded by big estates, we in our little Victorian villa (villa being a condescending term in England, not at all the American idea of Mediterranean grandeur). It's a very lovely, settled, English area, rolling green wooded countryside of the Sussex downs, farms, the two nearest villages both ancient and tiny, but Hastings, from which we are about three miles inland, a not very prepossessing seaside town on the Channel. We are about an hour and a half by train from London, so we shan't be able to rent the house to commuters, which was our original plan, but it is such a good area, everyone assures us we shan't have any trouble leasing it out. It is about a hundred years old, brick, with big bay windows in front; it is set back from the road by an enormous hedge and wide lawn, and has a little road alongside the house, entered by big double gates.

We are pleased with it and hope we can move in by the 12th of September, when our five weeks in our present flat are up. We rented a two-bedroomed flat in London from a woman who went to France for five weeks, and must be out by the day she returns. It's terribly difficult to find any kind of furnished accommodation that will take children (in fact, lots of the estate agents who do rentals have signs in their windows saying, "No pets, children, or coloureds"—ugh, on all three counts). Before we moved in here last week, we stayed in a sandy little four-berth trailer on the south coast for a week!

I must say, it's tremendous fun looking at land and houses that might actually be one's own with the flick of a pen. It makes one feel rather omnipotent and regal. I think we shall be very happy with our East Sussex house, if it all goes through. The old ladies who own it now have a piano in the dining room which we have offered 10 pounds for (it's an awful old thing, but—a piano), and they've accepted, so although we owe thousands, we possess two pianos. I told you I've bought a *good* tropicalized studio piano from a friend in Tanganyika for 85 pounds and am picking it up in December when we return and pass through Dar es Salaam. The old crock here we shall just leave in the house, to be played or not by the tenants, as they wish.

I wish we could furnish it to suit ourselves, but cheapness and utility will have to be the prime considerations for absolutely everything from kitchen cupboards to beds and sofas, all secondhand from ads and sales and auction rooms —carpets too. But the great thing is that it will be ours, ours, ours. A neighbor informed Philip that the soil is so fertile, a previous owner had actually supported himself market-gardening on the ¾ acre! I feel a real land hunger suddenly.

The children are loving England and are wonderfully responsive tourists, especially Christopher, who adores the policemen on horseback, the escalators in the shops, the underground, electricity! They are very good about new baby-sitters in the evenings and being dragged all over the place by car, foot and bus. Christopher, alas, seems to have forgotten all his hard-learned letters and numbers.

We are madly looking for old battered furniture with which to fill our eight-roomed house, and have been having fair luck. We've spent about $45.00 so far, and have quite a lot of stuff—a double and a single bed, a desk, two leather armchairs ($2 each!), a kitchen table, two dining room chairs, a chest of drawers, a couple of cabinets, a big kerosene heater. England is amazingly cheap for this sort of thing, even antiques are very inexpensive.

I must end, and egg and bread the tots. My dearest Joyce, it is as if all the years had never been. You must write right away and tell me about jobs and homes.

Much, much dearest love,

Pat

My dear, dear friend,

I broke into tears upon receiving and reading this first letter of yours since your departure, this inaugurating letter of a whole new series of years, probably —certainly of experiences. And only a letter from you, I believe, or Hans, could do this to me. Increasingly I think that I should feel crushed if for one reason or another our correspondence should cease or become dilute and ineffectual.

I had been about to write you, and would probably have written you a sorrowing if not peevish letter, for I, and we both, were very eager to hear from you, to know that you crossed the Atlantic without broken eardrums, that Christopher delighted in your bright reunion, that Philip was grateful to have you back. But I had to wait to hear from you first. I hadn't your address, and now rather than send off my petulance, I must utter huzzahs and pride in your success with the *Monitor* article. You cannot guess how it pleases me—or perhaps you can, for I know you would take equal delight if ever I should have my attempts printed in such a first-rate publication. Is Philip as pleased as he should be? Good journalism is not an easy art, and a great many things can be put in that way only.

Your departure left a vacuum in my life from which I suffered as if from withdrawal symptoms. I felt great irritation in the brevity of the visit, and a certain gnawing restiveness, if not envy—which I know you marked, but which I have since come to acknowledge as unrealistic and unproductive, at least in its concentration upon detail. In any case, I have since adjusted to the fact and the truth that our respective lives naturally dictate differing possibilities, choices and chances, and it is foolish of me to yearn for things in the context of your European, your British-dominated mode.

The day after you left Milwaukee, Hans received a long-distance call from the chairman of the enormous and highly reputed Art Department of Ohio State University, announcing that Hans had been selected from twenty candidates to become appointed as an instructor at the university. We were both delighted (again, you must acknowledge the scope of our choices), for this is a real academic step forward, even though Columbus is sort of nowhere on earth, and Hans has already termed it the "green hell of Ohio"—denoting primarily the climate, but perhaps the environment as well. The salary isn't good, the loss of rank is a little discouraging, but these demerits are more than compensated for by the fact that he has been accepted by one of the big ten universities, to teach in an art department (almost unparalleled) in an American university, and to teach a specialty of his, drawing and studio applied appreciation, two courses which will beautifully concentrate and channel his gifts and natural emphases. Who knows

231

how long we will be here? Assuredly until he has proven himself in the task, probably until he receives tenure, and possibly even longer.

Furthermore (you'll consider this as mad), Hans bought us a house here on a trip to Columbus only shortly after you left. The down payment was only $500, astonishingly minimal, and the house itself, in excellent repair, only $14,000— staggering to you, but low in American terms. We are already rather firmly ensconced, and I am delighting in the privacy, the space, the garden, and the dead-end street, which frees me from, say, three-quarters of the agony I feel each time I hear screeching brakes. All our propertied friends assure us that Hans did an economically sane thing in the purchase, for in America at least, where real estate over the past decades has been the steadiest and most certain of almost all equity, anyone with a sensible eye to home improvement, and a willingness and capacity to keep a house up (are you lifting your eyebrows at this point?), can scarcely lose money, and in fact stands almost certainly to profit. Hence, if we leave Ohio after only three years, we will at least regain the rent we have paid, having had in the meantime the pleasure of living in our own sphere, and since we intend to redo the bathroom, we stand to gain perhaps $1000. If all goes well, and if I follow your good tips as I intend to (submerging my will, as you say), we shall hope to pay off the mortgage within the five years, and have the full equity to work with.

The house itself? A two-story, three-bedroomed house, with large living room, a dining room separated by French doors, a most pleasant and workable kitchen, and a quite splendid basement which Hans will use as studio. It's by no means the ordinary basement, for the previous owner had converted it into a workshop for his photography studio. Thus there are fine overhead lights quite ideal for a painter, second or third only to a skylight, and he has ample space there, besides being quite removed from the confusion of family and childhood activity. The house is white shingle, very Midwestern and architecturally not at all distinctive, but very clean and in its way attractive, with its newly painted green shutters, wide porch, and lawn front and back. We've a lovely little maple tree in front, a sprawling apple tree in back, and a back garden, albeit unkempt and weed-ridden, which slopes down to an alley through varying stages of petunias, sweet peas, lettuce, rhubarb, marigolds, carrots, hollyhocks, roses and a brick path. We both find the possibilities are sufficiently circumscribed, particularly by the tight squeeze the adjacent houses put upon ours, that it is quite impossible to conceive of this house as our ultimate one, or to conceive of it with quite the sense of futurity that you do yours. But it is rather nicely coincidental that we all became house-owners at about the same time, I feel. And please, by the way, NEVER assume that the details of your life bore me. Always assume that they interest me profoundly, as they do.

The neighborhood is not posh, as yours evidently is, but merely steady, peopled with solid, pin-curled, middle-aged, middle-class women. Goodness, how I dislike middle-class America—I feel utterly, utterly alien from it, and cannot but regard its children almost as monsters. This feeling comes and goes, but at times is quite insupportable.

I worry that Philip did not like Hans's prints. You needn't exude reassurances, but I do hope he will want them to be hanging somewhere in your new home, which is likely to be where, by the way? I do want to know where you will be at Christmas, for I have some little things to send.

This letter does go on and on—there are and I presume always will be so many endless things to comment upon, as now. The ghastly world tension, the damnable bomb shelters we are urged to build in our backyards—how seriously should a responsible person take these things? I am bursting with affection for you, with pride in our friendship.

Love,

Joyce

COLUMBUS
September 15, 1961

Dear Pat,

Congratulations to all four of you on entering your first home! It must be a grand feeling, and of a quality much more intense and thrilling than ours, simply by virtue of the fact that your intentions are more permanent, your selection was mutual, and the country of your commitment more ultimately satisfying than ours. I grieve somewhat that I cannot rejoice more in our house, and I hope it is not just a world-weariness of mine which is preventing it. But I cannot but acknowledge the fact that I will never be able to love Ohio, or any of the American Midwest, and to think of lifetime dedications must surely take the willingness to commit oneself in love? Furthermore, the house is not one I would have chosen, though I will cut my tongue out before saying so to Hans, who really tried his best. We shall have rather much to do to make it really salable (you see in what brief terms we are thinking).

The Ohio conservative bias is revolting. Local newspapers run cartoons showing Mr. Public gazing with pride at American mushroom clouds with the quip, "And we knew that our flag was still there." All editorials have the worst Goldwater touch.

Love to the boys and to Philip,
especially to you,

Joyce

233

September 19, 1961

My dearest Joyce,

WARNING: NOT A LETTER! One follows in a week or ten days, when we are a trifle more settled in. I write to share your happiness over Hans's job (I am so pleased; I was thrilled to see the Columbus postmark), to enjoy one another's feeling of first home ownership, and alas—for you to share our grief over Hammarskjöld's death, just announced this evening. My tears keep coming. He had become almost a father figure to us both, the last couple of years, as closely committed to the U.N. as we are in Tanganyika, and the life he has devoted (and now finally given) to Africa. Woe, woe, a great man goeth forth, leaving us again to chaos and darkness. He seemed to have an inner vision of strength and order and simplicity beyond the attainments of ordinary statesmen. He made the U.N. into the beginnings of a real world force. He helped to clothe it in a personality of its own, where you began to think, Oh yes, Smith (or Wong or Martinez), he's that U.N. Man. Not that American or Formosan or Ecuadorian. The proposed troika will run a shabby second to him in the race to peace, God help us. It is quite extraordinary how bitterly and unjustly bereaved we feel ourselves to be. Do others? Do you?

Damn those bloody Belgians. Should it prove to have been sabotage or the result of Belgian interference, I shall never, never forgive them. What is to become of the Congo now? Ah well.

We are trying to settle rapidly into our house and to make it a home in the three months we have left and the little money that remains. We have quite the most fantastic conglomeration of secondhand bargain basement furniture from auctions and sales rooms you ever saw. Every period, every style, even every wood (to say nothing of every condition) jostle one another for preeminence in room after room. Get a piano and join me in the joys of taking it up again. It's that *scarce* private little world we spoke of. I squash in nearly an hour a day, though the place falls in over my head and the family go hungry. I paid $28 for mine! It makes an almost tuneful noise.

Nothing more now. Oh, except to say that—selfish forgetful me—Philip loves the prints. We are having the prints of the Sappho and Islamic vases framed to match here in London, and will carefully carry them by hand on the airplane back to Tanganyika come December. The children each have their picture from Reinhard up and are most personally pleased. Christopher starts real school tomorrow—uniform, school tie, the lot! I will write a real letter answering all your questions next week.

Much much love,

Pat

October 4, 1961

Dearest Joyce,

Does this look a familiar sort of paper on which to be letter writing? It's from my notebook for school! I saw advertised a couple of weeks ago an extension course from Oxford to be held in Eastbourne, about fifteen miles from us, among the courses being one in music, "The Development of the Concerto." The class seems to be composed primarily of housewives like myself but I'm sure I'll learn something from it, and it's pleasant to enlarge upon my private little corner of my world.

We have received from London the framed prints and we are both terribly pleased with them, especially "Sappho."

How are you settling in? Are you madly painting, wallpapering, carpentering, sewing, as we are? Every moment of every day is crammed with jobs, which, I trust, once finished, shan't have to be done again for years. We bought every stick of furniture second (or eleventh, most likely) hand, and are refinishing, painting, slipcovering, or what have you, it all ourselves. All the interior work and all of the gigantic garden we are doing too, except those ghastly technical things like floorboards, chimney pots, etc., that we cannot possibly attempt. Except for a cursory reading of the *Times,* lots of radio listening (oh, thank providence for the BBC Third), I haven't stirred one brain cell since moving into the house.

———————◄ ►———————

But here it is a week since I began this poor excuse for a letter. I'm dreadfully sorry, my mind doesn't seem to be functioning very well. Really, we are killing ourselves with work trying to get the whole place done before leave ends, and time is rushing past.

You must send me some snaps, also of your house, as I do herewith of mine. Do you feel the house as an interim measure? You must do, I should think, and therefore wouldn't have quite the same feelings about it as we do ours. Anyway, you know what it's like to be part of a home. Neither P. nor I do, as I have no doubt said before. It's all very mundane and bourgeois at the moment.

———————◄ ►———————

November 16, 1961

Dearest (of all) friends,

You see from the enclosed and choppy beginning my good intentions. I can only plead that I love you more than the rest, and don't want to fob you off with a hurried airletter when I seem to have had so many of them lately. However, here I am.

We have been frantically busy and I am oh, so tired of it all—house, old friends, seeing things one must on leave. I long to get back to the P and Q of Africa. We have nearly finished the main work on the house; there are only bits and pieces of painting, sewing, etc., left. We have gone way over our financial limit. We haven't even found tenants for the house yet, but we plan to go skiing in Austria the last fortnight of our leave. We shall go to Obergurgl because it's the highest place in Austria and the most likely to have snow before Christmas. I'm longing to go, haven't either of us been since 1954, when we went for ten days to Yosemite. I shall probably have turned into a timid middle-aged matron who stays firmly on the bunny slopes, but I'll love it. The children too, I know, will adore it. So, only four weeks more of England. Quite incredible how it goes so quickly.

We've been posted to Zaliwa, the town where both the boys were born, right across the huge valley from Mahali. P. is to be District Medical Officer again. We're to have a gorgeous old German house which we've visited and will love. A decent house does make such a hell of a difference in those frightfully hot places. Which Zaliwa definitely is—hot, sticky, low, humid, full of sand and swamp, mosquitoes and flies, sisal and palms. Ugh—though I expressed excitement to Philip. He's pleased to be going back to that area, and I don't want him to know how much I hate it after those three years of sweat in Mahali. Ah well.

Anyway, I can wilt away in the heat in a static sort of colonial pre-independence grandeur; the garden even has a little summerhouse in which I can while away hot mornings. I think I'd better get a ten-inch-long cigarette holder to go with the house. At least I'll have electricity for the first time in six years. Oh, there *are* lots of amenities which we've never had before, the greatest of which will be a proper day school for Christopher and Julian.

I beg for forgiveness for not writing sooner. In here could be inserted another of my unwritten novellas: *I Married a Social Climber*—for we dash, rush, fret, stew, write notes, answer them (and the persistent telephone), follow every social lead, we entertain and are entertained by people I couldn't care less about, but who "might be useful someday" (Anon.). Well, in Africa, you see, the man's working day is at least free time for the wife, but here, my God, it's too grim trying to carry on the same sort of life with only a twice weekly cleaning woman (grandly elevated to "Mrs. Lucas, our housekeeper," but not by me). I have conscientiously taken paper and envelope on our trips to London, but unlike Rose Macaulay, I cannot write on trains. Anyhow, I will pour out everything that comes into my head, trying to atone, till I fall asleep here by the electric fire, and put this in the postbox tomorrow morning, finished or not.

I sent you off a wee Christmas parcel last week. Sorry Reinhard's is so *very* wee, but we are overspending madly doing the house up and getting bits and pieces for E.A. The book [Rose Macaulay's *Letters to a Friend*] I got two of, one for you and one for me. I love her work so. And only pray you haven't rushed out and got a copy already when you read the reviews. Is the *T. Lit. Supp.* coming to your new address? I wrote to them to change it. The crystal at last got sent off from Harrods last week when I was up in London for the day. Think of me when you have a drink at Christmas. And the gift for Andrea [an antique Victorian silver locket] is a good one.

How is your house coming on? I love the Middle Western clapboard houses, so secure and snug looking. I have turned violently anti-picture window and split level in my young middle age (you see the staid place we ended up with, after viewing dozens of ye olde thatched cottages) and our decoration has all been along very conventional, very English lines, mostly through lack of imagination and money. Is Columbus getting you down? Just think of Thurber—isn't he from there?—and how he surmounted it all. Or did he? Do you think those beastly women got him in the end, that poor little haunted suburban commuter he was always drawing? Some of his cartoon captions are so much a fixture in my imagination they pop up like a conditioned response to certain situations: "All right, have it your way, you heard a seal bark." "Touché!" "The unicorn is a mythical animal . . ." The one cartoon that haunts me is the one where he is coming home from work and his house is almost totally enveloped by the huge all-devouring figure of the wife, just waiting malignantly for him. As I confessed to you in Milwaukee, I get that feeling myself, that I'm about to be devoured again whenever I come home.

Thank God when we get back I can have a little room of my own, *lockable*, where no one can nor will disturb me for hours at a stretch, nor can it be invaded. Philip will be terribly busy, it's such a big district, the children will both be at school in the mornings. Joy, joy, selfish creature that I am. I am praying for there to be something, *anything*, musical going on in Zaliwa. At least I'll have my piano there to bang about.

Now, if you have forgiven me, you must write to me and tell me what your setup is like—if Hans likes his new work, your English classes (whatever can the students be like? are there really children called Freshmen who take beginning English?), your children, your house, your social life. Who looks after the tots while you are away? How was Mutti's visit? How are your health and finances? How's everything? I'm soooooo cold, English winters are ghastly and I long for a peek at the sun, but no doubt I'll be sick of it after half a day in Zaliwa. I'll write again very soon. Do you too, dearest friend. Much love, Season's Greetings, hands across the miles, etc.

All affection,

Pat

November 16, 1961

Dear, dear Pat!

What is it? I have developed several varying rationales to explain the long silence—the delights of householding in your own home for the first time, the attractions of civilization, long denied and now so excitingly your own, a possible effort on your part to manage some writing—and so many others. Some of them worry me.

Are Christopher and Julian well? And finally, are you all right? Is your personal life (the one I feel I know so well) going smoothly, or are there burdens and frictions, pains that have harmed or distorted the joys of the leave? It must be clear that I yearn to hear from you. In this bitterly fragmented American existence, within which I feel continuously pelted by a thousand demands and a thousand desires to help by teaching those poor products of a wretched culture to some pathetic measure of self-awareness, I need your sanity, your comprehensiveness, your idealism, and perhaps most of all—your knowledge of me. The struggle for an unflinching unity of self—albeit a unity within which myriad antitheses counter and spar. This struggle saps the life blood away. But it must be done. And of all the many trick mirrors we see before ourselves, I continue to believe that the mirror held up by a long friendship without dissimulation is the most true, the most stabilizing. The reason I want to write even bad poetry is so truly Robert Frost's reason—because it is a "momentary stay against confusion."

I fear my desires—very real ones—to send you a Christmas package will be thwarted. For I've no idea where you'll be at Christmastime.

Your loving friend,

Joyce

November 20, 1961

Dearest shoulder,

I received another plaintive airletter today, and I cannot tell you how ashamed and sorry I am. I should be in bed this very moment (it's 1:30 A.M.), as I awaken asthmatically with monotonous regularity at 6 A.M., and have guests coming for the whole day tomorrow and another lot for the whole day the next day, then two days' respite, then another lot for the weekend, and only yesterday we saw three people off on the train we'd had for the whole weekend. How I *hate* it. If I *ever* have the choice again, I hope you rush over and lock me into a straitjacket before I marry again. *Anybody!* Well, almost anybody.

Seriously, I do most heartily resent, increasingly so, the intrusion into my privacy, the lack of solitude and silence, the inability to deal with anything requiring concentration for more than five minutes at a time. I simply fail to understand this need for people round one ALL the bloody time, chitchat going on forever, meals following one another like the seasons for a lot of drabs and bores I wouldn't have thought I'd be caught dead with in previous days. Well, it's always greatly exaggerated when we are on leave; I quite clearly remember how we loathed the sight of one another by the time we returned to Tanganyika in '58. In fact it's probably what was the immediate cause of all our troubles, but that won't happen this time! All *I* want is, Garbo fashion, to be alone. I have written off over a hundred Christmas cards in the last two days, all of them (nearly) to silly stupid people, unavoidable bores, Ian used to call them, I never want to see again, but who "might come in useful someday." Faugh and ugh.

I don't know, everything is smooth enough on the surface. We adore our children, love our house, fit in well enough with one another—but really, we get terribly on one another's nerves. I suppose sex is at the bottom of most of it, but what's at the bottom of *that,* for either or both of us, I'm sure I don't know. I'm tired of worrying about it, and fending off the nagging. All I want is to be left alone, and then I am quite happy to do whatever else is required of me, with a good grace. Silly idiotic woman. I am so looking forward to the skiing.

Let's you and I run away together and set up housekeeping and only speak to one another after late breakfast on Sundays. Oh, the children . . . Ah, well, another time. I must send you Ian's letters back for safekeeping. I daren't leave them here. I'm too frightened to leave them in my bank, in case anything ever happened to me, and I absolutely cannot bring myself to destroy them, which was my whole idea in taking them back from you in the first place, in Milwaukee.

Much love,

Pat

November 28, 1961

Dearest Pat,

No, not another plaintive one—just a grateful and appreciative one. I don't really need two letters within a week, but I do need to know that all goes well

239

—or if not quite that, then roughly *how* it goes. Or to turn a phrase, how it goes roughly. Thank you for the news, busy and conflicting as it is.

I have started all kinds of letters to you—a long one (now lost) in response to your inquiry as to whether the death of Dag Hammarskjöld affected me as it did you. For it did, *immensely,* and I felt utterly alone about it here, because if Ohio is not the heart of the Fascist Belt, it at least is utterly reactionary and suspicious of anyone with any international sentiments. Ghastly.

Reinhard is six tomorrow and so pretty, so beautiful, in fact, that I almost fear for him, or fear that his beauty might dominate my sense of proportion in handling him. He made gifts for your boys. Andrea crawls, has four teeth, is very responsive, less pretty, but quick, I think, and has decidedly found her own personality, which is alert, active and funny, and easily angry.

With Mutti all has gone well, though in the end I find her simply boring. She's highly intelligent, but has allowed herself (and her capacity) to be crushed under a Prussian sense of duty. And she is busy doing things for others, *talking* about it (not self-righteously, but *technically*), and taking endless naps. She always wanted me to nap this way, and I fought it furiously, and I now know why: to need endless naps is to seek refuge—call it escape (everyone does)—and trite as it may sound, there *is* an element of the death wish in it.

My work is one prolonged agony for students and teachers and represents the folly of American Education at its worst. But I do not let it disturb me. I feel life quite fully these days. Hans is being very sweet (and if he is not a very subtle lover, he is a powerful one, and I enjoy it). Columbus is deadly dull, but the university isn't. I'm feeling well and enjoying the house enormously. It's so much easier to maintain than the apartment was. I work because we SHALL become solvent. It's terribly important to me. Towards this end we are buying no Gothic statues, eating no snails, contemplating no trip to Europe, and buying no books. And I feel optimistic.

Love,

Joyce

This untitled poem by Joyce was published in the June 1976 issue of New
Sacramento

    To my mother-in-law, who told me that afternoon naps
        were schillings in the bank of health

An afternoon nap
is a monstrous encounter
with glue, with adhesive, with suction cups.
No matter how sweet it is, how slow,
how cool on a satin pillowcase,
no matter if I conjure you, erect
and calm as a benediction.
No matter if I fall,
loose as a wet glove
into a hammock of pleasure,
nor if my small childhood calls
me to come out and play.
The backward climb is braided
with ropes of heavy molasses.
I am layered under lost secrets
whose voices are shoals of
shallow vowels, calling
Undertow. Riptide.
Come with me. Vanish.
Stay under.

COLUMBUS
December 9, 1961

Dear, dear Pat,

Oh, how can I ever, ever thank you! I shouldn't have opened the package
from Harrods, and I didn't open the package that followed from you, deserved
in so small a way, proceeding from your constant bounty of selflessness. I adore
the glasses! Each one I shall cherish and preserve as reminiscent of a brief and
luminous space of time together. And to think we scarcely fed you! They are
lovely, as all genuine and worthily fashioned things are, and Hans too, who at
present is in New York, will delight in having them, in using them. We have so
little that is genuine if even less of what is simulated. Such rare gifts as these will
long retain significance for me.

This isn't a letter. I only want to know the full address as to where to post
the children's Christmas package—and whether duty is likely to be high on it.

241

It isn't much, so duty probably wouldn't be outrageous, but if I can post it more intelligently with your advice, then I shall do so.

This is a weird city. From all I understand, one of the most reactionary in the States. Characteristically, the *only* issue which has roused the student body to action in years—and that to destructive action, violent riots and breaking down of the doors of the Faculty Club—was an issue over football. The faculty voted against letting the O.S.U. team play at the Rose Bowl, to which they were invited. The students and the *city* were up in arms and viciously prompted by a Hearst newspaper here. Very ugly. There's a broad town-gown split here (even among the faculty!). Well, well. I shall retire abroad, on a small Grecian island. I shall write a real letter soon, when Andrea's off my lap and final exams are over. You reconcile so many lesser things.

Love always,

Joyce

SUSSEX

December 12, 1961

Dearest Joyce,

Here we are, civil servants of a foreign country. Was there anything at all about Tanganyika's independence celebrations in the American papers? There's been lots here, for poor and undeveloped as Tanganyika is, politically she's a showcase for British colonial policy. We are dying to get back and see what it's all like.

I think I told you we were invited to special Thanksgiving services in Westminster Abbey on December 9th, the day of Independence, to celebrate it. Oh, Joyce, it was *so* so thrilling. What an incredible nation are the English. I was thinking of it all on the train back to Sussex, and remember something I read once about India's and Pakistan's independence back in 1947. Some English pundit remarked to the effect that in the long life of the British Raj, nothing became him so much as the manner of his leaving it. Tanganyika's new national flag of green, gold and black was flying from the north tower by the great West Door, whence we departed. Green for the land, gold for its wealth, black for its people. I was terribly impressed by the genuineness and sincerity of the service and those who attended, in fairly equal parts of black and white, with a sprinkling of brown (not many Christian Indians). We feel very proud to have been and to continue to be a part of the government of a country such as Tanganyika. Indeed, God bless her and keep her.

I have no time for more; everything is a fearful rush, only four days till we

242

fly now, then ten gorgeous days on skis, then back to dear old Africa, sunshine, servants and solitude, losing our pink cheeks to the usual sallow tropical complexions. Love and very happy holidays to you all. Give R. and A. a big hug and kiss from their godmother.

All love and happiness to you and Hans,

Pat

December 16, 1961

Dear, very dear friend,

I have time only for the shortest of notes—of thanks for the warm and wonderful letter just received, with, as I recognize it to be, the truth of damned good advice. Thank you. I am a little lean on Christmas spirit and there are things I would like to write you of in confidence. Is there any method you can advise me of that will insure a private correspondence between us?

Your letters delight me, help me, make me feel listened to—and I want the correspondence to flourish over the years ahead. Some of the quotes from your letters I like even better than those of Rose Macaulay.

All Christmas love,

Joyce

COLUMBUS
December 26, 1961
(Boxing Day, but in America just another working man's day)

Beloved Pat,

The holiday continues, and for it I rejoice increasingly, and in greater gladness of heart. I have much I wish to speak to you of, and perhaps this letter will reach you in the exciting new house. Do feel no pressure to answer just immediately—settling in anywhere is a horrendous undertaking.

I had real difficulty in achieving any sort of Advent, awareness of the Child, or even simple secular joy in approaching vacation. I was unable even to come through with the traditional varieties of Christmas cookies. And the dough still lies ignored in the refrigerator. The pain and the chaos of our age seemed to contaminate what should be the joy and the sense of blessing in the Christmas season. Perhaps it was the unrelenting signals of misery coming across the news broadcasts, perhaps the vulgarity of commercialization (and the stampede to promote it) in this country which desecrated any awareness of the holy. In any case, it was a difficult time getting going.

But then Christmas Eve itself was here. It had snowed during the night (as it had done on our Scottish Christmas), and though one knew that within a matter of hours the endless slop of splattered snow, testament to a traffic-plagued civilization, would ruin the scene, for the moment—early quiet—the delicacy of winter was inviolate.

Furthermore, *some* intelligence prevails. The university stations played magnificent recordings of Bach's *B Minor Mass,* and the *Christmas Oratorio,* and we played our own beautiful recording of *A Festival of Lessons and Carols* from King's College, Cambridge. And I realized that no matter what took place in the department and the ten-cent stores, in filling stations, homes and schools, the music of Christmas retains its power. It becomes the metaphor and all the meaning. And even though one is more likely to hear Sinatra singing "Santa Claus Is Coming to Town" or some forcedly saccharine child soprano singing "Rudolph the Red-Nosed Reindeer" than one is the *Christmas Oratorio,* nonetheless the choice remains. Because there have been and continue to be those dedicated to the spirit, and graced sufficiently to bear beautiful testimony to their dedication.

I was listening to the *Messiah* as I opened the Rose Macaulay book and read your dedication. And as with that, all things seemed of a piece this Christmas, and appeared to somehow symbolize an integrity, call it a wholeness, which I do not feel I have achieved, but which I do feel to be a possibility. I feel increasing form in our life, and I feel real gratitude for my and our dearest friends, who by the consciousness evidenced in the gifts they gave us, of the words they sent, establish a continuing rapport between the growth in their lives and the growth in ours. The book is indeed beautifully apt. I have read well into it, and am fascinated by the fineness of her spirit and sensibility. I do wonder where the years will take us both in regard to these things.

Thank you so for the beautifully old-fashioned locket. Is it *old* as well? Andrea will love it and wear it for years and (who knows?) perhaps pass it on to her daughter.

We gave Reinhard a fine electric train. He could scarcely contain himself for excitement, and he spent a full Christmas evening playing with it as reward for the long denial of waiting for darkness finally to come. Your little Scots guardsmen ride around and around too. They are delightful.

We celebrate Christmas in a fashion very different from that I knew as a child. It's very European now, I suppose, and thoroughly satisfying. We buy a huge tree on Christmas Eve—very cheap, because to Americans this is far too late. While the children sleep we set it up in the Christmas room. We *always* have only candles (I was amused and pleased last year when you wrote of doing the same), a very few plain baubles, and bits of silver icicles here and there. When all the candles on the tree and elsewhere are lit, Hans comes and calls us, and we all, in our very best finery—cocktail dresses, bow ties, whatnot—enter the room. Then Hans reads the Christmas story (sometimes in German, sometimes in English), and we open gifts. It's always very lovely, I think, and this Christmas I found the scene immensely touching.

Hans found a *gigantic* white candle, and upon hearing the heartrending description of how the West Berliners had put lighted Christmas trees on their roofs so that they might be seen from East Berlin, we decided to light the candle on a prayer for that city, as well as for Elizabethville and all the others.

Your letter about the services at Westminster Abbey for the coming of age of Tanganyika was most moving. Perhaps our correspondence will bit by bit describe the descent of one great nation and the emergence of another—if we have time.

I do hope your skiing trip was full of snow and of delight, sitz-marks but no broken bones, and much Alpine Yuletide spirit. It will be long before you have that again. The package we send with so much love and so many good wishes will be late both for Christmas and for birthdays. But sometime it will reach you.

I beg you to write me across the next tour with the honesty and candor and fullness that you have over the last two. May these years be good ones for you.

All love,
Joyce

PART NINE

JANUARY 1962 – MARCH 1963

I am a real puppet of my century

January 7, 1962

You gorgeous creature you, salutations!

How splendid to be greeted by a long letter from you here. I can't think of a nicer housewarming present. And your Christmas card and photos as well—how lovely Reinhard is; you do have pretty youngsters.

I am so glad all I sent has arrived safely. I do hope the glasses suit, and that you like the Rose Macaulay letters to the end. Yes, the locket is old, mid-Victorian, old by American standards! The chain, however, I had to get new.

I am glad you have Christmas as you do. So do we "dress" for dinner, children nodding away sleepily over their droplet of champagne and loving the flaming pudding at the end—not this year, however, but they loved their Austrian Christmas all the same.

I quite agree with you how easy and smug and pious-making it is "to be concerned at a distance" and it hardly changes the tenor of one's life at all, does it? People in large doses irritate me, and I treasure my growing bouts of solitude and self-dependence as the boys grow older. I'm a reasonable mother and adore my two, but am not really very maternal. On the other hand, I love Africa to bits, the heat, the insects, the idiocy of Africans, their often meaningless warmth, smiles and welcome. I like the romance of arriving in these crazy places with the odds so against one of making a civilized life for oneself and family and a dent in this vast amorphous Africa, but still one feels the missionary spirit and a tremendous sense of doing some sort of good just by being here, let alone Philip's work and any outside philanthropic activities of mine, like teaching English to adult Africans last tour. What I meant to say was, to each his own way. My path is not yours nor could be.

Austria was glorious—my, how I do love the mountains. I have a secret little

249

feeling tucked away deep inside that someday when I am old and gray and alone, I shall retire to a mountain town or hamlet somewhere—Rockies, Alps, Urals, who knows?

We railed down to Rome again—on arrival we'd gone straight from Fiumicino Airport to our train by dead of night and hadn't seen a thing except the Colosseum eerily lit up in orange floodlights—and arrived early in the morning at a pension on the Via Nazionale which had been recommended to us as clean, cheap and English-speaking, as our Italian, like our German, is nonexistent. We settled in and wandered round the whole day, the children enjoying it too. We were lucky in having fine December weather, and lazed away hours in sidewalk cafés, the children stuffing themselves with pastries and milkshakes.

Oh, Joyce, what a revelation Rome was! I suppose it must be one of those places that too much has been written about for too long by too many people in superlatives. I was completely enchanted and bewitched by the juxtaposition of ancient Rome, the beginnings of Christianity, the Middle Ages, the glorious Renaissance, the vulgar modern—God, such an opera house! a disgrace anywhere. The food, the language, the lilt of the place—all so familiar, yet never-before-seen-by-me. It was love at first sight, as I've only felt for one other place, Paris. I'm desperate to go back for at least a month or two next leave. P. liked it too, for reasons of his own—as a good deal of my instant love and shock of recognition was the Christian one. I got up at 6:30 our one morning there and went to mass at a little 10th century church near the hotel. Rome was an experience, not experienced, but felt and understood. I hated going, even back to Africa, which surprised me, as I was jolly glad to get out of England in the end.

On to the old BOAC Comet, zoom zoom, and there was Nairobi, perched in the floodwaters, hot, African, Swahili being babbled round one, a confused hour in the airport between planes. Then onto a little East African Airways DC-3 to Dar, bumping all over the place, chicken salad and orange juice spilling in our laps, everyone sitting in the back of the plane because of all the freight lashed onto the front seats. From Mombasa down to Dar we flew at 5000 feet and it was still hot, and when we landed at 6 P.M. it was like a Turkish bath, 85 degrees, humidity at 98. We were met by friends, went to our hotel, had an exhausting dinner and went off early the next morning to Zaliwa. It's only a three hour drive over paved roads, but a lot of the pavement has been washed away in the terrible floods recently. It was gorgeously blastingly hot driving up, grass and trees greener than I've ever seen them, Masai tribesmen nearer the coast than I've ever seen them (drought in their area till recently); we saw a nasty-looking family of baboons scuttering across the road, and a vulture picking delicately at a long-dead jackal, and a few snakes. Then the blue line of hills behind Zaliwa rose in the distance, 6–7000 feet high, though Zaliwa itself is only 1000 feet. We have a gigantic house, very old (German, pre-WWI, positively stone age for out here) and falling to bits and shabby, just like Mahali and Pashenzi, but huge rooms, high ceilings, lots of room, and three bathrooms! What luxury. There is a well-laid-out garden with lots of trees, but very overgrown and no flowers left except a few roses. I'm digging and planting madly. We've completely unpacked, and I'm making our old Pashenzi curtains do by cutting them lengthwise in half and hanging them on each side of the windows. It's so hot here we'll never draw them anyway.

I've flatly refused to join the Red Cross, Women's Service League, *any*thing, but I will be glad to do anything musical (church choir, etc.) and when Julian starts nursery school next Monday (Christopher started primary today), I shall trot along to the girls' secondary school (run by American Maryknoll Sisters) and offer my services, gratis, to teach or whatever they like, a day or two a week. I must do something to justify my existence, preferably something sensible.

We are about a mile and a half from the town, high on a hillside overlooking the valley. It's so odd to think of us six and a half years ago sitting on our Mahali veranda looking across the *same* valley! Indeed, it's odd to think of us sitting on our Mahali veranda at all, who and what we were then. Mahali is only sixty miles away as the crow flies, but rather longer by whatever of the three frightful roads you choose (pavement from Dar ends here). My piano has been on its way from Dar (120 miles) nearly a fortnight now, but not yet arrived. I think they must be wheeling it here on a footpath. Our trunks by sea have yet to arrive, as does our car. We shall settle in well here and have a happy easy tour, I think, in spite of the steamy climate. It pours with rain every day—nearly forty inches in two months, making such a din on our corrugated iron roof.

I spent the afternoon polishing very tarnished brass door fittings and furniture handles. I love polishing silver and brass, quite mad. Uhuru [independence] doesn't seem to have made much difference out of Dar es Salaam. Everything is just as hot and pokey and irritating as ever, *and* as easy and pleasant and full of the things one wants to do. Tropical villages are delightful; there's room enough for the dirt and smells and poverty to dissipate themselves, to be swallowed up in the vastness around (and Zaliwa is just a village really), but tropical towns and cities are too ghastly, physically and spiritually. Dar has perhaps the loveliest tropical harbor in the world, but that's about all, and even that is being ruined by (much needed, I'll grant you) mechanization and quayside docking facilities, instead of all the ships anchoring in the middle of the harbor and everything—people too—being off-loaded onto lighters and then the beach, as in the old days. It's all happened only in the last couple of years. Even I, inured to Los Angeles, find this overnight change in a people, a town, a nation, quite incredible to watch from within.

I've had half an hour's break, getting the children to bed, and I seem to have dried up rather. Oh yes, one little quiet veranda room I have semi-furnished and turned into a sort of morning room cum study, just for me, inviolably so! Something I have always wanted and never had. I think that if and when I ever get another choice, I'd stay single almost no matter *who* was around. I miss solitude

251

and peace and quiet more with every passing year. Don't you? But then you get rather too much of it in large doses, and I never seem to. My trip to the U.S. did have that one drawback, that I enjoyed the sanctity of privacy so much during those ten weeks, I longed for it dreadfully for months afterwards. However, count one's blessings, etc., with which I am more than liberally endowed.

My, what a long letter! You'd better go lie down with a pad soaked in witch hazel over your eyes.

All love and blessings,

Pat

COLUMBUS
February 8, 1962

Very dear Pat,

Last evening I attended a French film about a family of four British children from Sussex spending a summer in the Champagne country of France (from Rumer Godden's *Greengage Summer*). I don't really need much prompting to think of you, but their continuous backdrop of emotion was "home," and their frame of reference made me almost nostalgic for an area I've never seen, and am not likely soon to.

I am reading the Simone Weil recommended by Rose Macaulay. It, too, is a series of letters, entitled *Waiting for God*. She was a most amazing woman, perhaps indeed, as Leslie Fiedler says, a "saint for our time." Do you know her? She has a force and an urgency in her statements which seem to me due almost entirely to an unbelievable candor, a candor which leaves me feeling quite denuded and erring. Anyway, she has a stern and compromiseless attitude towards the search for faith. She doesn't believe in it. She feels one must simply wait and let God choose. My first contacts with Catholicism were of the absurdly hypocritical sophomoric variety. Did I not ever write to you of my conversations with my one and only significant French friend, M. Tricaud, Prof. of Philosophy at Rennes, who, on the strength of those conversations, arranged meetings with Gabriel Marcel for me? Not that I pursued them, as a person with greater drive toward conviction might have, but they (the conversations) and it (the impetus toward faith) have never, never, never left me. You had a touchstone of understanding in your childhood convent days—I gained what I have, which is assuredly less than yours, through reading, and a few people. But really, the way doesn't matter. Is it St. John of the Cross who wrote that "Each way is good / And each way is the same"?

But of course, I have enormous reservations, and the reservations, being

252

intellectual rather than emotional, of course derive from my rationalistic upbringing. Further, I cannot yet understand the concept of complete obedience. For she says, "If it were conceivable that by being disobedient I should gain salvation, whereas by obeying God I should be doomed to eternal Hell, I should have to choose obedience." Now, I admire this, but I cannot help it, there is something in me which admires Prometheus too, when he tells the messenger of Zeus, "I care nothing for Zeus. Let him do with me as he pleases."

In other words, I cannot quite choose Job's answer in preference to that of Prometheus. But perhaps gradually I shall learn that such alternatives are absurd and beside the point.

I am very sad about the packet—very sad that you failed to instruct me as to how I should list contents in relationship to your customs duties there. Look, Pat—I included a print made by Art Thrall that is a likeness of me. You may not like it at all. He's an excellent craftsman, but the image may not please you, and you might not want me hanging around. I'd originally got it for my parents, who didn't like it: "It wasn't my sweet Joyce. . . ."

> Love to you, to Philip, to Christopher, and to Julian,
>
> *Joyce*

DAR ES SALAAM, TANGANYIKA
Mid-February 1962

Dearest Joyce,

As you see, we have been moved, just as I finished digging, mulching, manuring and planting my garden, got a final coat of much-needed polish onto all the furniture and floors, and made curtains to fit the windows. Not to speak of the poor children getting settled in new schools, making friends, Philip getting to know his job. Still, this is the first time this has happened out here to us; some people get transferred three and four times per tour. Anyhow, it's for a specialized new public health job.

Maybe this will lead to something in the World Health Organization for us, which is more or less what we want eventually anyway. Philip is sorry in a way to be leaving clinical medicine; he'll miss the patients, especially surgery and obstetrics, but general practice is a dead end, and most specialities are so very cut-and-dried and specialized.

As to living in Dar, that's the ghastly part of the whole thing. The climate is beastly, the slightest effort to do anything brings on total lassitude and an outpouring of sweat. You wake up drenched in the mornings, you go to sleep drenched at night, the whole house smells of mildew and mold, even swimming in the sea is no palliative, at least to me, because the water temperature is lukewarm and it's full of seaweed, which I find off-putting, to say the least. Well, at least the cost of living (food mainly) is so low compared to upcountry that we can afford to eat steak once in a while and to get the odd packet of prepared food, and God, I CAN STOP BAKING BREAD. *How* I hate cooking in this climate. I fear we'll eat out of tins and frozen packets till the end of the hot season in April or so.

I asked a friend what he thought my chances were of getting a job with the new American Embassy as a spy at 100 pounds a week, and he said, don't take a penny less than 150 pounds. Embassy, schembassy, it's so bloody silly here, Russians, Chinese, Israelis, Germans, Yanks, all over the place, acting as if it (and as a consequence, they) were really of any importance. It's just like (and getting more so every day) one of Evelyn Waugh's early novels; have you ever read *Scoop* or *Black Mischief?* You ought to, they are among the ten funniest novels in English of the twentieth century, especially *Black Mischief,* where the army eats its first consignment of boots because they hadn't been told what they were for.

Last month when things started going awry and getting crazier and crazier here in Tanganyika, and the Prime Minister quit his job to "reorganize the Party," I took out all the old Evelyn Waugh novels and read the lot, to convince myself that nothing here was really to be taken seriously. It's the same with the Congo. The thing that sticks in my mind about the Congo happened to me in England. I was listening to the BBC news one evening, and the announcer in his perfectly modulated BBC voice was reeling off the news about The Bomb, strikes, etc., and then something to the effect that some United Nations personnel had been captured in the north of Katanga by Baluba tribesmen, and, in a strangled voice full of disbelief, said, "and they . . . they . . . *et* them . . ." and trailed off into a momentary silence. Philip and I looked at one another for a moment, and roared with laughter. We simply couldn't stop. I mean, it's the only way you can take Africa these days. It's that, or weep. Anyway, Dar is a very good place to be for the next couple of years, and the job that P. is doing now is a very good one to be doing.

I liked your comments on the thirties, which we both are now well into. I didn't mind thirty-one at all; it was thirty that really stuck in my throat, and hurt for months. Now I couldn't care less. I'm going to turn into a fascinating woman of uncertain age for a few decades before *I* give up the ghost. I had a few bad moments when we first arrived here in Dar, remembering last year and Ian, but I've pushed it all behind my conscious level; the letters have stopped completely, and it's all finished.

When we get well organized here in our house (we haven't moved into one yet, and have been camping out in a two-room service flat next to the cemetery on one side and the Hindu burning ghat on the back!), I shall join the Dar Music Society, and that will be the extent of my social life. To hell with charitable organizations. I've had my fill of them all out here. We've been allocated a nasty two-bedroomed house in the middle of town, no garden, as hot as blue hell, and old and falling to bits, and very tiny. I can't imagine where we'll cram all our bits and pieces. It hasn't any but the bare minimum of furniture.

I'm down to one cretinous servant; I'm doing the cooking in this damnable heat, trying to save money, and we are limiting our social life to one movie a week. Ah well, who in the hell cares? Enough moaning. Before our move, I was thoroughly enjoying my piano, and as soon as we get into the house here and can unpack, I shall enjoy it here too.

I've dried up. This has been a stupid letter, and I meant to say so much. I am longing for your odd parcel to arrive, also a long letter. I hope all is well with you. You are a dear thing. In this best of all possible worlds, you are the best of all possible friends.

> Much much love—*do* write,
> soon and lengthily,
>
> *Pat*

March 5, 1962

Dear Pat,

How very good to receive the details, and to know all is well, if somewhat confused. À la Rose Macaulay, I must account for letters—for I wonder if you've received the three I sent since the one greeting you upon return? I really marvel at your resilience and affirmation. I know I should be very full of complaints if I had had to move after all that work to a worse climate and a smaller house.

If you are pleased with Philip's change, I assuredly am. The World Health Organization would indeed be a goal which could involve all one's concern and knowledge, and open up fresh prospects in a myriad of ways for you. I hope for all details you can manage in the heat, about Dar, the boys, the politics—all.

Our baby has since turned one, and she walks. She is so diminutive altogether, and never went through a fat stage comparable to Reinhard's. Her face increasingly takes on the proportions of his as a baby, but she remains an awful towhead.

I'm troubled, strangely, about something which has been with me for years and which never seemed anything but natural, and our intimate conversations of last summer made me realize you were probably the only, and certainly the most logical, person in the world to discuss sex with in any detail. Besides, I think we seem to have similar problems, and while, as you said, "One could be a hell of a lot worse off," I increasingly realize that I am missing something very

255

important. Furthermore, I suddenly feel myself labeled—as "frigid," something I considered myself most unlikely ever to be called. But if failure to achieve orgasm indicates frigidity, then the conclusion is inescapable.

What's it all about, Pat? I have always satisfactorily blamed the artlessness of the men I've known; was it, in fact, myself? If this is the curse of the well-educated American woman, is there no hope? All very juvenile, but I read (and I am snooping in this overly available literature, like a teenager fearful of worlds unopened as yet to him) that any man can tell whether a woman is frigid or not by the actual involuntary internal muscular spasms, which she has, and he feels, or rather by the lack of them.

I can imagine there's nothing in the world you feel *less* like thinking about, in the heat of Dar es Salaam, than my failure to achieve orgasm. But write me frankly, if and when you've the inclination, for I suddenly feel sort of obsessed and sad about it. Otherwise: all well enough, Reinhard reads beautifully, prints (as you will see) ABOMINABLY. Hans gradually finds acceptance with good national shows.

Love,

Joyce

Joke: Dmitri: What would you do, Alexei, if the bomb fell?
       Alexei: Get into a shroud, and walk slowly towards the cemetery.
      Dmitri: Why slowly?
      Alexei: To avoid panic.

DAR ES SALAAM
March 14, 1962

My dearest (and only) friend,

Alas, my lost one, how can I, being compass-less (and so encompassed) guide you to anything save confusion, despondency and sordidness? It's all so squalid and pointless and respect-robbing, I'm beginning to think perhaps St. Paul was the one who was right. I HATE SEX. At least married sex. My body is totally attuned; I shake with aroused passion when physically in contact with the odd person or two. But whether it would come to fruition, who knows? The one opportunity, there wasn't time; for the rest, there's no opportunity, nor do I really want one. Unless a *really* undetectable one arrived with a *right* person (know any?), and I'd slide soooo easily into adultery. I hate myself, I hate Philip sexually. I hate sex. It's just a great big crashing bore. It's all so futile with us—and with an American lifetime's buildup, not to speak of all the books one's read, the real product is like using excrement for lipstick. Do I shock you? The simile came to me at a particularly bad moment the other night, and when it was over, I got up and read Hopkins' "A Nun Takes the Veil."

> I have desired to go
> Where springs not fail,
> To fields where flies no sharp and sided hail,
> And a few lilies blow.

> And I have asked to be
> Where no storms come,
> Where the green swell is in the heavens dumb,
> And out of the swing of the sea.

There is good, there is beauty; they *must* be concerned somehow with what we name truth, but I honestly wonder if they really are concerned with sex? That is, copulation, orgasm, relief, disgust—the four horsemen of the modern Apocalypse. Or is this sour grapes? You know, I think we are both losing our sense of humor, that magic of youth that made us resilient to every sorrow, reeds that bent in the strongest winds, and immediately raised their indomitable heads again. We *wonder* so little nowadays. So seldom do I feel either of us take a recent hour, or a new scene, in both hands, and gaze spellbound at its freshness and loveliness and clarity. But (and I will tell you how I came to see this a little further on) I feel that our ability (may I quote you?) to "listen to the birds" decreases with each new financial burden, material possession, bits of one taken away by one's children (this I *know* is why the really great women writers were *not* mothers), hourly, daily, expanding into yearly and decade-by-decade commitments. It's all these bloody commitments. One feels in the end like a filing cabinet full of all the right responses and solutions, but still, a filing cabinet, to be sure.

About the only conscious pleasures I can think of (non-material, I mean, excluding the travels, children, etc.) are the bitter ones of rereading books I read at eighteen and understanding the meaning of futility for the first time. Has growing up for me been a fifteen-year battle to understand the meaning of that one eight-letter word?

Oh, Joyce, what hope is there for us? I still cling to a forlorn hope of creativeness of some sort, self-expression. But very forlorn, and not much hope. I am a lousy wife, at least with Philip, and I'm fairly sure I would be with anyone else too. Oh, I do all the necessaries reasonably well and fully, to compensate for the lack of any real emotional basis on my side. I feel (but this I *cannot* fully admit to—it's a sometimes thing) a moderate (could it be?) failure as a mother. And for heaven's sake, what *else* have I been doing the last eight years? You at least have been teaching and have been a real success at that. I have nothing to claim. In taking stock, I can see only two things I do well—knitting and cooking. Some achievement! The only time I am happy with the children is when I am alone with them for any length of time. They fight so abominably and continually when

Philip and I are together, I can't bear them. Nor can P., and he is lately talking of sending Christopher to boarding school next January, which I *could not* bear. Joyce, he'll be barely seven, *so* tiny, so unprepared to cope with boarding school life. But Philip and his brother went at that age, and "it will be good for him, toughen him up!" God, but I feel a really desperate failure. How can I make it all up to him in the less than a year that may be all that's left to me? I really cannot bear it, and will never forgive Philip if he really insists on it. I am so sick of it all, I wish I could be somewhere quiet with a tiny house and garden, just the children and myself, out of this mad chaos of marriage and two dissident personalities and the endless pressure of sex which I hate and this phony stupid social climbing life of Dar. Oh hell, enough moaning.

I shall talk of your last letter—sex last. I loved your joke. (P. never laughs at jokes, he thinks they are stupid, and it's an idiotic thing to come between us, but it makes me unreasonably cross. There used to be—and still is, with other people—so much humor in life.) I long to get your—what? likeness. Also to see Reinhard's printing. Give Andrea a tardy birthday kiss from me. I am over halfway through a size two sweater set begun about eight months ago! I shall, as you see, send this to your English Department, and I request you write to me a long answer, c/o Poste Restante, Dar es Salaam, as Philip gets so cross when I don't read my letters to him, as I did not read your last, and he was quietly upset about it. You know, everything goes to his office first, so he knows exactly what mail I receive.

When there is no love, *so* much subterfuge must be employed. I miss the *privacy* so much! Sorry, I forgot I wasn't to moan any more. Dar is really okay, except for the climate, and I'm getting sweatily accustomed to it.

We are already, alas, caught up in a network of old acquaintances and the diary fills up daily, weekly, with morning coffees, dinner parties, picnic Sundays on the beach, teas, receptions, all of which must be returned. Sickening. Also the children started piano lessons last Monday and seemed to be quite happy with the teacher, an enormous, ancient, slightly dotty Frenchwoman who's an African character out of Evelyn Waugh.

You speak of my resilience, but, dear friend, it's nonexistent. I get headaches, asthma, dizzy spells, suddenly remember a hem to put up, or that I haven't read last week's *Observer,* or decide to make scones for tea, or just flop and read —*any*thing to put off the evil hour of coming to terms with myself and my will. I read a funny epigram by Maurice Chevalier the other day: "Old age isn't so bad when you consider the alternative." Uh huh. Maybe. I'll tell you when I get there.

As I said, we've settled into the house, the piano's been tuned, the fridge (still on kerosene) is sort of working, and all in all, I'm fairly pleased with the move. I mean, it's here, at least *I* am, so I might as well like it. Remember that old saw, "If rape is inevitable, enjoy it"? Well . . .

I *am* fairly good at settling down and liking a place soon, well and consistently, except along towards the end when I know I'm off soon, and I get fed up with the whole shebang. But I'm pretty awful about people, especially poor old P. He must loathe me, I'm so cold and unresponsive, and I *care* so little. I mostly try to hide it, but even a person who lives as little on his emotions as P. does could hardly fail to sense my indifference. Not just sexual, but general. Well, here we are at sex again.

What can I tell you? You are quite right that a man who knows anything at all of women and/or biology knows whether she has had an orgasm. You cannot pretend to the real thing, they say, but I've gotten away with it for years, just to get the whole thing over and done with. Maybe I'm frigid too—at least, I can be aroused, tremendously so, but the only way I've ever been satisfied, I might as well be doing it myself, as I told you in Milwaukee. However, I know I can be aroused by ordinary love-making, for the last couple of years anyway, so, like you, I cling to a sad little hope that it's the artlessness of the lover, not the inability of me.

As to my heart getting involved, that is over for a very long time, if not forever. I still feel that I've only been in love once in my life, and hope to God I never shall be again. But this is all dull old me.

As for you, I cannot imagine you *not* responding. I would hardly advise you to go and have an affair, which is what advice-givers in brightly contemporary novels and plays always do. Anyhow, you don't just go out and *have* an affair. Does *no* one attract you? Does Hans? Do you—well, I can only repeat myself rather lamely—come alive with passion, ever? Feel your flesh quiver, your stomach and soles of feet burn, and you crave to hop behind the nearest bush or into the nearest bed with anyone? Someone? Hans? I mean, if *that's* there, then maybe you're a late starter. Heaven knows I was—twenty-eight or thirty—and still nothing—I mean, not *the* thing—has happened to me. But I don't give a damn just now. And I wish I could pretend to respond to P., think about platonic dialogues or gardening or imagine myself in a brothel, but I absolutely cannot bear his touch or methods and it's a teeth-grinding ordeal, less and less frequently gone through, I might add, and what the end of it all will be, I refuse to think about. I hope to heaven you aren't like me. It's the most ghastly ordeal. For me it's as if I'm being raped every time. And never, *never* will he allow any of it to be discussed or brought into the open. It's all so depressingly dishonest. I'd never have said all this and won't dwell on it again, but it's all I know about sex. I'm not even tempted by solitary pleasure any more. It seems too sad and futile and ludicrous somehow.

An obscene thought: I wonder how they managed that bit in the film of *Tender Is the Night?!!* Well, m'dear, it's very late. I've rambled on purposelessly for pages; I don't suppose this will do anything except to depress you more deeply. But perhaps the great thing is not to feel alone. I recently often think it would be a great pleasure to live out the last years of my life in a pleasant little villa with you when we are old and gray and past all this, and be visited frequently by our sons and their families, and lots of interesting people we've met from all over, but mostly to live a quiet bookish life, tinkling at the piano, two garrulous old ladies reminiscing over the Italian meals cooked and served by the one little maid, writing memoirs and exquisite short stories and lots of letters. I think in the end you will be the only one who ever understood or cared.

Good night, dear Joyce, God bless and keep you and yours. Heaven knows what's ahead for either of us, body and soul, but I expect we'll bear up.

Great love,

Pat

Or as the woman in labor said in the delivery room, "Bear down? I can hardly bear UP!"

COLUMBUS
March 21, 1962
(the first day of spring?)

Dear Pat,

Your "hello" letter received yesterday inadvertently prompts me to write to you from all the torment I am feeling, since your complaints and general disquietude unleashed my own, and simultaneously the certainty that you, as I am, are willing to hear the querulousness of the heart. I had the impression in the summer that you rather permanently trounced me for complaining, quite rightly and with the best wisdom there is, to change or to accept. But, as I witness in your letter (*not* that I noted with any glee any gloom on your horizon, for I do so hope for, as you wrote, a "good tour" for you all), and as I know from both our temperaments, life does have its invidious little ways, its chameleon unpredictabilities, of reserving new demands for our ability to accept, or more difficultly, to change. If not a lover, then an illness, or insolvency, or friction with a growing turbulent child's spirit, or fear of the great abyss of non-being, or the sense of irrecoverable distance from you—my only friend—or the appallingly minuscule sense one is with of himself after realizing how we (the earth, its mess, and ourselves with our grandiose sufferings) are but a dust-sized fringe at the outer edge of one galaxy among hundreds of thousands of such galaxies . . . and the ultimate worry, anxiety or hope that Christ really did suffer for our petty and miserable sins. Always the new neurosis, the new source of self-examination—the effort at new self-approximation. In this context, it was rewarding to see even Rose Macaulay considering herself to be but a bundle of poses, recognizing the "self" in the fact that one cannot assume poses really TOO alien to what one ultimately is.

By the time you read this, perhaps the worst of your hot season will have

260

spent itself, and you will feel a happier interaction between you and the rest, and thus can establish the counterpoint to my sadness today, and cheer me. But oh, oh, how preferable it would be to have you near. Having you this summer made me realize that in fact conversation is better than correspondence. But despite that, this correspondence is the best communication I have, since Hans and I ignore or do not know or cannot know so much in each other.

He just left for Chicago, to make a trial run of the galleries there, carrying with him his folio of new prints, drawings and rubbings—a not unexciting collection. I thus have time (it is spring quarter vacation) and liberty (he will not read this) to write you as I will, full of all bitchiness and self-solicitude. How vulgar it all is, and how incumbent upon the would-be artist in this cutthroat and highly organized exhibition and gallery world, to repeatedly expose and advertise oneself, with or without humility. There is such bitterness in this profession; the fear of passing the line from the "young promising" to the tenured and "spent" professor is a harassing one; and the colleagues one observes here do all sorts of gymnastics and pirouettes to escape the label of being a merely locally known artist. There is much that is sad in it; there is the inescapable feeling that modern art (as I believe you inferred) is not what the world needs; and when one is honest, there is the horror of confronting one's own void, which must double for the source of fertility, creativity and love. What results is a spiral of delusion and anxiety, networked with enough talent and satisfaction in *technique* that one continues, always hopeful of vision, of compassion, of inspiration. Despite my tone, I believe in this; I believe that trying to cope with oneself, even the most bumbling self, in form, may be one aid to self-recovery. As St. John Perse said, "I live better when I write poetry." But I lie, since I don't write now, and I've lost that joy which I did know—of living better.

What is it I am getting at? No, there is no one most painful climax. I am bombarded on every side by varying pains, and it will be a long letter indeed if I hope to cope with them all. Columbus is hideous; there is no natural beauty, not even that contrived of the will to fabricate one, by parks or self-respecting upkeep of gardens—and the first glimpse of a landscape not peppered with gas stations and used car lots is too far. One can only SEE here by a process of exclusion, rigorous exclusion, by elimination of all civic, architectural grotesquer-ies, by staring raptly at what one believes, in his highly idiosyncratic way, to be beautiful—a Gothic statue, a child's face, some anonymous hands. But to relate to the city and its life is an impossibility. One lives within the confines of the university (itself a series of buildings which look as though they should house insurance or dental offices, rather than the fine arts) and the confines of a not too harmonious household.

How I yearn for some loving interchange and intercourse between myself and the environment. America is such a God-damned place! Why the rape of the landscape, the assault on one's most precious capacities? Outside, the chil-dren: "I'm gonna shoot the guts out of your stupid head, buddy!" "Bang! Bang!"

Next door: Woman in bedclothes at noon shoos a poor cocker spaniel outside on his three-foot perennial chain to howl in misery for a little freedom; she returns to two sets of TV, and at two o'clock, in a sudden explosion of false elegance, goes to a department store lunch with the girls or whatever. At school, the six-year-olds are already thoroughly indoctrinated in "rugged American individualism," and competition is established as the way "to get things done" from the very beginning. On Sundays, of course, "the meek inherit the earth." "In God We Trust; all others pay cash." How can two such hopelessly irreconcilable aims —loving one's neighbor as oneself, and getting to the top in the fastest and most ruthless way—ever result in a people not mortally sick?

Kennedy is having no luck in Congress. Probably his bills for everything important will go by the board: aid to colleges (the pressure is becoming staggering); cooperation with the Common Market; bill to help finance the U.N. with bonds—there is such resistance. Oh, Pat!

I couldn't help being stirred by the John Glenn flight, by the sense of man's refusal to be contained, by the sheer glory of a masterful job well done, of the amount of mind that has gone into such a thing—not, what most Americans felt, the recapture of prestige and the sense that we can show 'em! But will all this not be put to military use! It seems to me a certainty. And the misery of Algiers, the sorrows of Berlin, the starving in China. God help us.

Well, I began with conscious intent to disparage Hans, and my malaise has widened to include all the discomfits, which is perhaps a fairer locating of cause. I think of religion a great deal too, but (perhaps, as usual) to little effect. I feel I am fighting a background even more resistant than yours; the need to examine critically was nurtured in me as a child; the technique of satisfactory examination less so. Thus, I never became one truly scientifically oriented, but skeptically oriented, yes. And each little venture towards belief, each study of theological implication, even each coping with my ignorance of Christian terminology, has been a break from my background. For I have to admit that the freedom from orthodoxy of my parents was an ignorant freedom and hence no real one; they did not KNOW the Christian tradition that they broke from; they merely, in a typically American Bible Belt way, associated Christianity with the negative Calvinistic strictures which ruled their lives. Hence, I never did learn the Bible, or the grand superstructure of theology Christianity implies. Mother doesn't to this day know what the word Incarnation means. I was twenty-five before I heard of Pentecost. So before I could even apply my trained talents in skepticism, I had to forage clumsily for that peremptorily disregarded doctrine. And now, with some imprecise knowledge of it, a mixture of Unitarian onslaught, of Mormon memory, of deep and natural longing for meaning, of literary awareness of what's been done with Christian symbology, of admiration for French intellectual Catholicism, of awareness of Romanesque and Gothic spirit through study with Hans of their art and architecture, of monastical life as I've known it through fairly close observation of the School Sisters of Notre Dame, of increasing distaste for Protestant secularization ("Is Jesus Christ on *your* Christmas card list?"), and of an overpowering sense of marvel at the beauty of the liturgical life—these are all I have to bring. Perhaps the fear of death does not count, but I know so well what John Updike means: "Young as I am, sometimes in the middle of the night, I feel my death rushing towards me like a freight train."

And then, when I want to believe, I am nonetheless fully conscious that my right hand is doing what my left cannot see, for it will be years, if ever, that I can drop the feeling that reason just won't allow for these things, and that reason is important. For all the evidences of the forfeiting of reason are *terrifying*. I saw a documentary on Nazi Germany recently; the mindlessness of it all was devastating—the power of unreason; the willingness on the part of the untutored or lazy to be impassioned with the unworthy, with evil. Yet, as I said before, the reason behind rocketry is probably equally wicked.

Result: I am a real puppet of my century.

As a parent in the religious training of Reinhard, I am an abysmal failure. I do not know what to do. I can read him the Bible, but as literature rather than as truth, as partial but not total history. I can answer his questions by telling him he is tired and must sleep now, but I cannot tell him he will live on and on. I can send him to Sunday school in order to acquaint him with a tradition he should know; but I cannot vitalize it into reality for him at home, and he can easily escape any sense of urgency related to it. Hans leaves it up to me, with the feeling that it is the mother's job to pray with a child at night, that it is she who should decide how and what is to be said before meals, etc., and he is disappointed in my paralysis on the subject. But I suppose my children will grow up as so many of my generation did—questioning, and tormented.

All metaphysical, spiritual, philosophical problems are accentuated in proportion to the harmony or disharmony of the life most immediate to me: the maternal, domestic and wifely life of Mrs. Hans Hohlwein. When this theoretically closest of all unions is out of focus, most else jars blurred for me too. Does this indicate an overdependence on Hans? In any case, it is no dramaturgy to cast him as a most difficult and erratic character. When I married him I married disquiet and utter unpredictability. And often I am near despair about it, Pat. You say, leave him or live with him. I do live with him; I do choose this, as does he (for I know he thinks over these alternatives too), but I think it is increasingly for both of us a life of quiet desperation. We talk less and less, about less and less. He tells me where he is showing, and who else is being shown, etc. We never discuss the children; I cannot even get the subject of schooling into any momentum.

I count on your sympathizing with my NOT wanting to separate, despite the resultant turmoils and beefing, because of what YOU realized when the problem came to breaking up a home. How wretched a thing to do! But I feel so sterile with Hans. It came as a shock to me the other day when a very bright student and very eccentric, but real, told me that "You seem to be so naturally what so many other people try to be and are not." The compliment upset me terribly, because it pointed out how very much more I do come alive outside, a fact Hans has always noted with company and at parties.

Apart from nostalgia or regrets, I in all honesty have been trying to make a good marriage. This you know. I have worked where I shouldn't have, managed ill where I should have managed better, but I have been unswervingly faithful and devoted to all Hans's efforts, to my role as wife, to all the clumsy sacrifices entailed in being married to an artist of these sensibilities and these neuroses. I think I'm a decent mother, but our family life is a gloomy thing. Once again, Hans and Reinhard are at complete odds. I feel convinced Hans has not even much love for him. He loathes having him around, never does anything with him, will not listen to the boy's simplest comments about school or anything.

"Vati . . . ?" begins a conversation.

"No!" terminates it.

These things crush me, fragment me, divide me one against the other. I overcompensate by being more mother than wife, by preferring to read or walk with Reinhard than to be in bed with Hans. These are serious turns, Pat, for once become habitual, we are destroyed. But this lovely boy, so curious, so resilient that he will always come back smiling, so quick, is being slowly trampled, trampled, trampled down, and tears are in my eyes right now when I think of any quenching of intelligent spirit. You can't help me, I know, but what can I do? Hans adores the baby, but she's tiny, soft and dependent, and I notice that he is only really good with her when she's amusing and quiet. I have seen him throw things on the floor and scream at even her for crying.

And for all of it, through all of it, I am blamed. "The baby doesn't cry like this with me." "Of course, Reinhard is right; of course, I'm wrong." But isn't he wrong when he screams at Reinhard for something so innocent as trying to help Andrea walk, or for showing her how a ball bounces? I am lost, lost, lost, Pat, and very lonely. I know very well that the least person who had intelligence and the attitude of my student could lead me willingly astray, and if he loved the kids, could lead the three of us astray.

Hans too is, and always has been, eagerly waiting for his chance to be unfaithful. I've spoken of this quite enough, but he's always asking me what do I think they (the university) would do if an instructor had an affair with a student, or telling me that he's eager to meet an elegant Oriental woman, and so on. Of course, I am convinced that what he really wants and probably needs in a woman is a sexually aggressive mistress who otherwise indulges in a seven-day-week, twenty-four-hour-day assuaging and caressing of his ego, whose goal in life is to be lusciously available to him at all times, rather than a semi-intellectual who is far more at home with ideas and people than with things (or with him).

The baby is an adorable little thing, full of charm and very diminutive appeal, looking ever so much like her brother aged one. She walks now, but sideways, like a very blond and unlikely crab. Sooner or later she'll have to confront the issues squarely. Reinhard reads very well, and though the youngest in his class, is of the top three. How I wish he could know and grow up with Christopher. One of those things that would be nice.

What sort of house have you now? Is Philip satisfied with his work? Please write me as fully as you can.

All love,

Joyce

COLUMBUS
March 25, 1962

Dearest Pat,

Today was the first day of spring quarter, and upon arriving at the university, I was greeted with your wonderful, kind, good good letter. Yes, the great thing —the important thing—is to know I am not alone and so long as you write and keep link with me, I am not. This is so good to know, for I can (and shall) tell you anything, absolutely anything, a relationship unique to you.

The crisis of last week, which prompted the long verbose letter you will receive perhaps concurrently with this, is over. A family feud it was, perhaps similar to the kind of atmosphere you described when Philip is fed up with the children. Hans left for Chicago on a very negative note, but called me that evening to compensate. Nonetheless, he most curiously informed me, he telephoned to Milwaukee to the woman who troubled my last year so and whom I miraculously failed to inform you fully about when we were together. They had a fairly subterranean affair during most of my pregnancy, yet it caused me ever so much discomfort, as she is a remarkably impressive woman of twenty-nine, sultry and dark-eyed, very informed and acutely involved in art—handsome, sharp of mind and tongue, adulterous of inclination, and alone five days a week, when her equally impressive husband—an anarchist whose political savvy about Europe makes him fascinating to Hans and VERY well informed on art, music, literature, etc.—is away. Anyway, he phoned her, and she came down to spend some time in Chicago with him. Of what nature the episode was, he didn't bother to tell. Anyway, these things always do and probably will continue to crop up with Hans, and they're disconcerting to say the least.

As for me, I believe I still have the power to attract men, but I don't have the time. I mean that. I am barely down at the university long enough to sort out those to whom I respond (answer: Yes, of course, I *respond*, if that includes

265

all reactions of excitement, rapport, enthusiasm, interest, sexual and otherwise, short of orgasm), before I must return back to the fold which has me thoroughly circumscribed. Not that this frustrates me; I am not looking for an affair, though in all honesty, I recognize my susceptibility to such as being far more heightened than ever before. Why, it is hard to say. Perhaps Hans's nonchalance about his own sense of limit and restriction has eased mine. I wonder if I shall ever, in practice, counter that well-meant advice I wrote once to you about adultery.

In any case, Pat, I do not have a wretched sex life. Hans, as I am certain to have told you, is potent and strong and I do know that powerful rhythmic pulsing you spoke of as the very nature of my sexual experience. I have never disliked this, but as I grow older, I grow increasingly worried about my failure to consummate it all. And surely Hans can't remain so ignorant forever. I am being awfully blunt, but I can be. Does Philip, knowing all he must, as a doctor, consider you frigid? Or is this only ultimate incapacity very common? Especially among American English majors, perhaps? Does it infuriate men? Do they watch for it? Would you be self-conscious about it with any casual (or otherwise) lover? Oh, I don't know, I'm sure, it's all such a crazy uncontrollable thing, and I shan't be pestering you about it ad nauseam, I promise. It's probably a passing obsession.

There is so much else to answer to. At all costs, we must retain joy in life, and a conviction that at least life, if not art, is worth practicing. The reverse of this, which you suggested I and perhaps the two of us are falling into, a loss of the wonder and glory and joy of the moment, is painfully evident in the lives of others (as well as my own). A very dear and intelligent friend of mine from Milwaukee says that she simply can no longer respond so vitally to music, that the genuine aesthetic experience, seized and cherished, is practically impossible for her to achieve. She is marvelously sensitive and intelligent, but no longer spontaneous. She is a Shakespearean scholar, and says that even poetry no longer reaches her whole being. It is intellectually exciting; it no longer makes her feel as E. Dickinson wrote, that upon reading real poetry, she felt "as though the top of her head had been blown off." I KNOW, alas, what she means. I remember, in Salt Lake, lying on the floor of home, submerged in a total ecstasy of delight in hearing the late Beethoven quartets. I can't do this any longer. I can't. Your delight in music excites me, helps me, prompts me—and I do love it, increasingly more than any other art.

What I write is merely symptomatic. I really did think life was a process of accumulating new abilities and capacities of understanding and awareness, not a bit-by-bit lopping off of the gifts one had to bring to life. I will not yet give in to that. It just must be possible to maintain and perpetuate one's own joy in the awareness of living, not to be increasingly plagued by one's bitterness or sorrow in the awareness of living. Because there are glorious old people, and they must remain as mentors. But you're so so right about the obligations to respond and to perform desiccating one on the limb, dehydrating the very sap of one's best nature out of him. Everything I'm saying is perhaps just a rather long-winded version of a little joke that "Life is a trap and you can't get out of it alive." Or

> Forgive, O Lord, my little jokes on Thee,
> And I'll forgive thy great big one on me.
> —Frost

> You mean so much to me,
>
> *Joyce*

April 29, 1962

Dear Pat,

It seems ages since I heard from you, and in a persistent and often, I suppose, subconscious fashion, my relationship to living seems subtly altered when I don't know how you are. There is a nagging little sense of loss or discomfort, as when one slip strap is broken.

It is spring here, and even grim, ill-proportioned unseemly Columbus is beautified. Every year spring is more meaningful, more devastating. Perhaps it is merely the horrid prolongation of all unaesthetic properties of life and character here in Midwest U.S.A. that makes me almost grieve with joy at the resurgence of beauty unfettered and unclaimed. I cannot stay inside. I must abandon all pressures of housekeeping, paper-doing, and compulsion—living to be outside, to watch as yet unopened apple leaves darken, then brighten and almost whiten against a falling evening sky. It won't last long. Soon it will be humid and hot, too many fat women in shorts, too many teenagers dragneting their bopped-up weapons, too many children with popsicled fingers, and I complaining.

But right now it's glorious. I feel absolutely resexed. I feel as though I could take on any seventy-odd men as lovers. Isn't it fantastic? I've not had such frivolous bodily thoughts for almost a decade. Quite a contrast to my past letters, but it's the season, and it will soon pass. Is your hot season over, and are you feeling better? And how is little Christopher doing?

This is a perfectly dreadful letter, I know, but it stands merely as a voice of love and concern, of desire to share and to communicate. With the leisure I now have approaching, I shall be able to write more fully again.

> All love,
>
> *Joyce*

267

May 18, 1962

Dearest Joyce,

I am just going to sit down and write this and to hell with everything. I absolutely loved your package which at last arrived day before yesterday—quite incredible, how bad the posts are getting here. Your very Joycean woodcut I am thrilled with, to say the least of it. It is very like you, some kind of scrubbed inner bones of Joyce-you, "the horror of it all" but still wide-eyed about it, and not a Dorian Gray. I am very taken with it indeed, and it is now away being framed. I neglected to tell you that all of Hans's prints are framed and hanging around our house; very proud possessors we are too, and I especially love Sappho. But none more than the new Joyce. My feeble thanks for a gift which goes beyond gift-giving.

I had practically finished one each of the Pooh and Alice painting books myself, with the children nagging away at me to let *them* do it, before I could tear myself away. They are delightful, and I have never seen a painting book like them. The blouse is a perfect fit, and I am wearing it at this moment. *The Wapshot Chronicle* I shall read with enjoyment, I know. All in all, a *very* well received and recipient-happy-and-grateful-package.

I had the oddest letter from you the other day, all about your incipient sex life, and the reason it is so odd is that I have had a difficult time even sitting still in one place these days. I feel like slinking round felinely, or showing my bare bosom at the window to likely passers-by. As you say, all sorts of weird and wonderful thoughts, none of them, alas, having any effect upon my marital sex life. Perhaps it is the season, spring here being the end of the hot season, bringing a great resurgence of energy and ability to cope. I feel very pagan about it all, I must say. But it is such a dull, domesticated world, and everybody else, like me, sits around and waits for someone else to make the first move. It must have taken a great effort on Ian's part for him to make a declaration when he hadn't the foggiest notion how it would be received. I think the latter is the biggest barrier to love as one gets older and more sensitive and cautious and out of practice, so to speak, the idea of rebuff being uppermost. However.

I am so damned busy I have hardly time to take a breath. I won't bore you with details, but I have found several jobs to do in my spare time, at home mostly, typing, etc., to make the odd pound now and again, and they are adding up to most of my waking hours, suddenly. One of them is doing guided tours round Dar, for passengers off the ships that call here, and now the wretched tour agency has been thrown in my lap because the owner is off to Europe for three months, so Joe Soap me is stuck with it till the end of June, and I haven't any idea what it is all about, all the organizational side, I mean. But the tours themselves are crazy and fun to do, palming off all sorts of ill-digested misinformation on unsuspecting tourists. I am being paid to organize the European Parents' Association (now wisely name-changed to the Tanganyika Parents' Assn.!) into a viable unit. We only have sixty-two members in Dar, and we are trying to get up to about four hundred, nearly all of whom must be interviewed personally in the next month, with the eventual end in view of building some sort of new school for the non-Tanganyikan population of Dar. And a couple of other things. The Parents' Association job has been fun though, because it's been an entrée to the embassies and biggest firms, right to the ambassadorial or managerial level, and I've loved meeting all the diplomats and execs.

May 25, 1962

Ah la! I really am hopeless. I can only beg your indulgence, with overwork as an excuse, but even that's not good enough. However, I really will finish this today. Philip has been away for three days seeing to a famine and flood combined. I must say, it's a terrible admission, but I do so enjoy being on my own. The children are angelic; I'm in a good temper from the moment I get up till I go to bed; my time is mine and the children's; I get time in the evenings after they are abed to contemplate my navel (alas, not novel), etc. The peace is almost tangible. However.

The children are my love and joy these days, and fill my heart with happiness. I am gradually coming round (after about a year of being broody, as the English say) to the idea that I would not just like, but would adore, another baby, a girl preferably, but Philip doesn't want one. We shall see. I must have it out here, it is so much easier with servants. Mind you, I have only one servant left now, and do all the cooking myself, and never have him back in the evenings, and cook and serve the dinner, and I usually wash the dishes. Not like the old days, with cook and houseboy hovering about, every single night, and three-course dinners! It all started as an economy drive, but I think I will continue with it even after we are caught up. Life is so much simpler and less complicated without all of them.

I cannot write a decent letter, this is just to let you know I am still alive, and love you dearly as the best friend a girl ever had. Bags of love and best wishes on your twenty-ninth birthday (ha)—may all the rest be pleasant and non-aging.

Much love,

Pat

269

June 7, 1962

Dearest Patience,

I sent you off a silly little birthday card a couple of days ago. Only about a fortnight late! I think of you much these days. It is so very lovely here at the moment—perhaps too warm still for your northern blood, but perfect for Tess of the Turbulent Tropics here. I am frantically busy, which is why you are not getting any real letters, but the jobs will all have ended except one by the end of this month, and that's a nice steady calming type, not frenzied and nerve-wracking like these wretched guided tours. However, it does help to pay our bills.

Things are not actually unpleasant here, but it's becoming a rather frightening sort of place and one must tread very carefully indeed to avoid offending a black man. We hardly ever see any of our African friends any more. They're too frightened of being called "black Europeans" or "neo-colonialists" by their own people. All very sad, and we no longer feel an integral part of Tanganyika's day-to-day life.

Other than that, no great excitement. Philip and I not getting on very well (that's news?)—nothing serious, just fed up with being too much together, and I very much look forward to a *whole* month on my own while he's away on a conference in July and August. I have refused to go except for the last week of it at the end of August. Other than that, I play my piano when I have a minute, see the odd flick (*Hiroshima, Mon Amour* was a shattering experience—marvelously well done). I read a teensy bit—no time! And I see rather too much of Stephen—remember my crush in Pashenzi at the beginning of last tour? He's now stationed in Dar and works two doors from our house and is always popping in and out on this and that pretext. Also he sings in the Music Society, as I do, and neither P. nor S.'s wife do—so as the attraction and mutual fondness were always there, you can imagine what is happening. As for me, I couldn't care less. I adore Stephen, but I'm not in love, nor ever could be, with him. I'm very much attracted physically, but not to the point of thinking about it when we're not together. So I'm just drifting, letting things take their course.

Much much love,
a gorgeous summer to you,

Pat

August 5, 1962

Dearest Pat,

A recurrence of rhythmic communication from you always gives me a resurgence of confidence in the reality of the heart. I am sorry for the long silence. I see ominous hints on the horizon of the Day of the Locust, and this is why I've not written. I cannot be specific really, except insofar as the baby comes at an inopportune and unbudgeted time, that Hans's mounting disgust (shall I call it "hatred"?) for the formlessness and ugliness of American life and mores augurs some sort of rebellion, and that he has profound disquiet at the role of art in today's world—a disquiet underscored by the marked concentrations and egomania of all his fellow workers, whose aim, above all, is "TO MAKE IT." I cannot quite ignore a comment you made in Milwaukee—"Is art really needed today, Joyce?" We wonder—seriously—and Hans fights this within himself. I feel an almost admiring envy of you, of Philip and his work, and of the sense of relatedness, call it purpose, which most certainly would accompany a good job in WHO, certainly has been in the work he has been doing, and would be inseparable from the work in the U.N.

Yes, in many fundamental ways I envy you. I envy the formality you have access to, a formality which, if one insists upon it here, is sheer anomaly and discomfort for the children. I envy you the closeness, the inextricable thread of political awareness that must constitute part of the texture of each day in Africa. I envy the intimate, the "known," knowledge which proceeds from this. I rather envy the fact that you have already had (perhaps) "the" crisis in your marriage, that it is over. And, altogether, your life is more seemly.

Of course, I know you far too well to relegate all crises to the past. Surely, you will find yourself drawn to other men; there will probably be religious crises if the pattern of the year unfolds like the "multifoliate rose." I know you're not immune, but you *have* weathered a serious personal jarring.

Reinhard, alas, and confusingly, seems practically tone-deaf. There is *no* tune he can sing correctly. Is there *any* chance it will come later? He is fascinated with fossils and prehistoric times, and it is my constant battle to preserve him from the worst aspects of the boys' world around (the love of violence, the horrid language, the hatred of Negroes, the suspicion of fantasy). Andrea is tiny, delicate, and blond as a dandelion. She's very clever and audacious physically and scares me out of my wits. I'll write soon again.

Love,

Joyce

August 8, 1962

Dear friend and counselor,

I shall write small to give me space to convey as many of the perplexities I feel as I can. You wrote me in such detail at the time of your agonies and separation; perhaps just writing does help. At what price does one save a marriage, Pat? Here I am, carrying a third child (due in February again), and Hans and I have *never* been so far apart, so remote, indeed. At times there is a tangible, or audible, at least an almost *sensible,* momentum towards mutual hatred. I must write the truth and I know this is so. But I remember the same word from your letters, and has it passed? Can you enjoy life together now? Ah, Pat, Hans has taught me something I thought no one could, how to dislike life. He has, at so, so many points, mimed out a weltschmerz of such colossal proportions that a whole half-hour could be swallowed up in the grim undertones.

I used to delight so; now I anticipate almost more than anything else the time when I can sleep—close out, exclude, deny, forget—do I dare say *destroy?* What is masochism? The willingness to be annihilated? At times I scarcely know myself this summer, so dour and tight-lipped I have become. I am still greatly at ease with my children *when I am alone with them,* but I can't make the right move when we are all together. People still find me pleasant, gay, quick, but I am another person with Hans, and I wonder at my ability to shift.

I gave a rather dazzling dinner party the other night, but since, Hans and I have screamed, slammed doors and avoided each other like the veritable pestilence. I am always so ill in early pregnancy and so sleepy, I think I am growing dim-witted and all this annoys Hans so. He has no sympathy whatsoever for it. But the division is more serious, and I wonder whether it is sheer cowardice which prevents me from allowing the word "divorce" or at least "separation" to come into our brief and intermittent high-pitched flurries of conversation. Oh, I could use a long talk with you, my dear friend.

Shall I enumerate a few petty things which reveal a serious division? Hans never gives anything to Reinhard. I know this sounds like a caricature seen in outline as only an hysterical woman can see things, but it is utterly utterly true. He will not put him to bed, read him a story, listen to what he says, or ask him anything. He will command him; he will complain to me about him. He wonders at the lack of communication and says the boy *cannot* be gotten to. I love Reinhard; we fight and we have fun; we read—all sorts; and we play football. We rearrange the furniture and we make up stories. And he said, quite without prompting, "Vati forces me. And I won't take forcing! I'm sorry, that's just the kind of person I am." This, at *six.* So far as I can see, Hans has only one *genuine* interest in Reinhard—his table manners. So, no matter *what* else the boy may try to say at dinner, the *only* response he receives is a correction of table manners. All this, you will understand, grieves me.

He adores Andrea, who is a little doll, and very flattering to the male ego, no doubt, BUT if she cries, as babies do, he whops her off to bed, to languish there and to completely upset the rather nice schedule I'd succeeded in establishing. He won't have her around at dinner, so I have to devise some unlikely spot for her.

If he should come home when I've a record going, he will grab it off, saying, "This blasted chamber music all the time," quite willfully scratching a beloved record of mine. This drives me practically to spitting at him.

And I am pregnant! And much as I often want to leave him, I cannot now long support myself. This is agony. Do you feel such crises are over with you— are in the past—and that, having been experienced, future recurrences will be manageable? I may go to a psychiatrist in the fall. Everyone says Hans is the one who should go, but he never would, and lacking that, perhaps it would give me more strength to cope.

Yes, he's doing well at Ohio State, got a good raise, but characteristically, makes no friends. He's the bugaboo of the neighborhood, and all the children hate him. I remember the laughing, crowded, joyous games in my parents' backyard—a world away.

My love,

Joyce

BARIDI, TANGANYIKA
August 18, 1962

Dearest Joyce,

As you see by the postmark, I had to accompany Philip to his conference, like it or not.

This will be a rambling effort which I will write off and on for the next few days. Your sad sad letters only arrived a couple of hours before I flew off up here. I am deeply sad to learn of your new pregnancy. I think it is a burden you simply can't be asked to bear. *Why* do you play "Vatican roulette" as you call it? Oh, Joyce, Joyce, I wish I were there to hold your hand! However, if it must be, so be it, and I send you all my love and prayers and best wishes for a sound and easy pregnancy and delivery and first months.

Joyce, my dearest friend, what can I say to you that could possibly hold a ring of truth *and* hope? Your situation isn't at all like mine of three and a half years ago. You've done nothing overt to bring it about, as I had. Hans has not done any series of specific actions very uncharacteristic of himself, as Philip had. Your daily life isn't basically changed from a year before. It's only *more* so, in its less attractive aspects, if you see what I mean. I know it sounds beastly and

273

most uncomforting at this time, but I can only repeat what I said to you in Milwaukee last year: *People don't change.* They can modify or disguise their responses and outer personality trappings to fit the society or milieu or group in which they find themselves, if it is different from the one for which they were trained and in which they grew up, or like an Oscar Wilde or a Gauguin, who find themselves incompatible by nature for their own milieux, can search out and escape to another, better suited to them; or, the hardest thing of all, for one who is trapped in "impossible" circumstances, like a prisoner in a concentration camp, or a castaway on an island, or (is it "The Lost Girl"?) one of Lawrence's heroines who find themselves in a marriage which is intolerable, but which must be tolerated, make every adjustment to fit the circumstances, every alteration of one's own self, give way to every pressure and have one's own escape valve tucked away in some completely unobvious place.

Do you still love Hans? Is marriage as such sacred to you, in the sense that there is *no* alternative to it, only alternatives for your own state of mind? Do you feel you would rather Reinhard grow up with (a) his own father, harsh, unyielding, but, indubitably, his own; (b) no father; or (c) another father whom you would very likely marry in a few years' time, if you divorced now and gave yourself time to heal the wounds, which, believe me, are really terrible, even in the shortest of separations (ours was five weeks only!). As for the psychiatrist bit, DON'T!! You need a psychiatrist like another head. No, I'm dead against this psychiatrist thing. A lot of morbid wound-probers we Americans have become. The psychiatrists are great for the helpless, but you're not that, by a long shot.

As for Hans's attitude to Reinhard, my dear, this is the typical German upbringing, cold comfort though I know that might be. The father is *very* harsh, the total disciplinarian, unemotional, unyielding, unwavering and ungiving. Vati is *always* right, and when *you* (or he) become Vati, *you* are always right. It's not a matter of lack of consciousness or tenderness or father feeling in Hans. He is perhaps an extreme of Teutonic discipline, but he is only living out the mores of the society in which he was raised. I *know* Thomas Mann was raised in the same society too, but he was hounded into exile, wasn't he, by that same society?

All of the foregoing is so harsh and hopeless, it makes me quite ill to think of poor pregnant you sitting there in the Columbus August heat, reading it, looking for a glimmer of silver lining. Have you ever bearded the lion in his den, asked him if he realizes the ultimate consequences of his forcing you completely to *his* way of life? Have you threatened him with separation, loss of his children, etc.? Have you asked him if he would genuinely prefer to be free of it all, than to go on living so unpleasantly together? Have you thought of going to one of those marriage counselors? My poor poor Joyce, it must be so joyless and thankless an existence. The children are the only things that must make it worthwhile.

You ask about Philip and me. Yes, I truly do think we have put the time of great crisis behind us. Frankly, ours is no great romantic love; we (at least I) never even started out with that, but I honestly wonder if any marriage is that, on both sides anyway, after a few years and the odd major crisis together. I accept Philip as he is, coldness, aloofness, incapacity to communicate, and all. I determined that we should be and now we are friends, and have built a very intimate private structure of our life together, which is sound, intelligent, ambitious, forward-looking and family-minded, almost what an "arranged" marriage turns out to be. In fact, on my side, it almost *was* an arranged marriage, as I instinctively knew P. could give me a great deal in life (*not* material things) I could never get on my own—the security of mind, the purpose, and frankly, the entrée to an international world which I wanted so much more than suburbia or even academe, that what I might have "given up" for it is worth it. And I don't even know that I might ever have found the other anyhow. And I do think both of us feel that after what we went through and the good things we now have, and THE CHILDREN, that we are determined—no, not even determined, to be married to one another for good—more a fact, like death and taxes. I still make abortive attempts at a closeness which isn't possible because P. isn't capable of it, and P. is still too ambitious in a way that almost frightens me, and is, I think, bitterly disappointed that *I* have not lived up to my earlier intellectual promise and ambitions.

But you know, on reflection, he is a more suitable husband for me than Ian might have been, for whom I would have rapidly become the complete hausfrau. My extrovert independence belies a really fearful inner insecurity which in times of rock-bottom depressions has led me too to dwell lightly on the possibilities of permanent, quick and easy escape—Marilyn Monroe's death shook me terribly. We still have rows, but who on earth doesn't? No, I would say on the whole we *have* passed our biggest crisis and it is well behind us, and I look forward with immensely heightened anticipation to the next decade in our life together.

I simply don't know what to tell you. I know if it were me, having seen as I did what the domestic Hans is like, that I couldn't have stuck it half so long as you. But I'm not you. If you *did* leave him, what would you do? Back to Salt Lake and live with your parents and teach at the U? Overseas where jobs have rent-free housing and servants are plentiful and cheap? Anyway, write out your heart to me, and I will answer honestly and to the best of my ability. I long to hear from you again and frequently, just jottings on airletters, if you've no time for rambling epistles. All my best love and hope and good wishes to you.

Dearest friend in all the world,

Pat

Dear Pat,

Have weeks or months gone by since I wrote? I received the long, honest and rather hurting letter. Time, as you know, heals, preparing me for future wounds. I'm over the nausea, and the baby moved last night for the first time. I look well, and being on thyroid as a result of low indications on a basal metabolism test I had, am feeling quite perky and buoyant. My ups and downs with Hans do unnerve me, and they do seem to be chronic, but there are ups.

He decided, before autumn quarter began, that we should go to New York as a respite from the Midwest and from domesticity. And we did go—on a shoestring. He bought me a really handsome maternity dress beforehand; I had my hair all chopped off, and we deposited the children at our very fine baby-sitter's and took off. I never fail to find exhilaration at the city itself, though the surroundings reveal a squalor of spirit that is devastating. New Jersey and Brooklyn seemed to me an endless traffic jam, bordered by endless junk, on either side. The ugliness, Pat, oh, oh, oh, the UGLINESS!

But Manhattan excites me. I love the flair of it, the elegance of it seen from the ferry, the alertness of the responses, even if chilly. Such a contrast to the lassitude inescapable in Columbus, etc., etc., etc. We went to *too* many art galleries, saw too much abominable experimentations for mere novelty's sake, and the Guggenheim Museum made me absolutely fold up with nausea—first from the architecture, second from the "show" itself.

We've solved one hair-raising problem, one whose acquaintance you made —how to bear the tensions of having an artist TRY to work at home. He doesn't any longer, and I am immensely grateful. The university has given him a fine and capacious studio, and I on his thirty-third birthday gave him an excellent FM transistor radio, so he will have both peace and good music, and I can vacuum when I need to. This has been a source of so much much woe, and it is better this way.

The children are proving my enormous delight, as with you. Reinhard was, to our great joy, and even greater expense, accepted into the University School here. He is very happy there, and the move successfully uprooted him from the grisly neighborhood play and companionship. Andrea is very funny somehow, as I've undoubtedly said, for reasons difficult to describe. She jabbers incessantly, and forcefully, but she still is "talking scribble," abundantly so, which is an unexpected charm.

We still have a small kernel of hope left that we may leave for Europe in June. Financially this would be a real tour de force if we could swing it at all. But Hans is desperately nostalgic for Europe and such visits seem far more important to him than "getting ahead" financially. Well, we'll see.

So many questions you asked I cannot truthfully answer, because I cannot find the truth. Do I hold marriage so sacred a bond as to be unbreakable? No; many marriages are far better broken off, but I do so *hate* to divide a *family*—father from children—and why should I share them? I do believe I am better with them, but not that I necessarily therefore love or want to have them more. My marriage isn't easy, God knows, but there are some compensations, and I painted Hans blacker than I ought in that unhappy letter.

Our cultural lives are very truncated; the great source of delight remains the movies, which give us tremendous pleasure. We've an excellent foreign film studio nearby, and when I've the courage to face the local murderers (there are many), I go alone to some magnificently moving films. *Good* films are a great help and escape to the larger world.

I send, forever, so much love,

Joyce

COLUMBUS
October 20, 1962

My dear and only friend,

Many warm and significant things tell me of you, only in my chronic dissatisfaction, I yearn for yet more of you. It seems very long since a letter, and I do wonder, continuously, how you are.

Oh, Pat, the adorable sweater set—precisely so right—arrived two days ago. You always succeed in reaching me in some very private way, and I love you for the work and care you put into them, and for the charm of the result. I bought a navy blue pleated skirt for her, and the ensemble is utterly winning.

Winter is nearly upon us. A radiant fall, such as must be unknown in the tropics, is just diminishing into gray and ash, and we're all bundled up in sweaters. The last rose is brilliant against all the shadowy doors, and the smell of burning leaves is everywhere. Inside, a record of Elizabethan lute music. I wish I could share more life with you.

All in all, things go well. Hans receives increasingly demanding assignments, and increasing respect. Reinhard is reading beautifully now, all sorts. And Andrea is an absolute crackerjack, full of lust, and very clever. I'm teaching a bunch of cretins, all with ambitions to be doctors, in English 400 (remedial). Quote: "I think a great deal and am very intelligent—in fact, some people consider me quite imaginary." Or: "The United States is a good example of capital punishment." What does one do, feed them vegetable food?

Write me—please. No one replaces you.

Love,

Joyce

277

My dear friend,

Our positions are reversed. I must ask you why, oh why, do I not hear from you? It does seem so endlessly long since I've heard of *you*, or yourself, of the patterns that make up your inner life. And without these, I feel desolate.

Despite the really egregious agonies promoted by the Cuban mess, and an all-too-real consciousness of the potential futility of all self-examination, I cannot help but be absorbed, often most miserably, by those personal problems that hound us all. Teaching thus remains a very real shock-absorber. I cannot call myself a scholar, but I am able to *get across*—as person to persons—in the classroom. It so often seems all I have. I feel like a dried fruit in my marriage, Pat. And indeed, this is about how my body behaves sexually. The only sense I have of being in a warm, fleshly, woman's body is the sweet awakening the baby's movements create inside, truly inside me.

But this whole frigidity syndrome, or whatever the head-shrinkers would call it, is obsessive and sad. I'm reminded of all the tortured boys—some disgusting, some brave but futilely unhappy—who, in one way or another, during university days, released, often in drunken conversation, their fears and refusals to accept their full or partial impotence. I have thought of myself as at least potentially whole, potentially an entire person, whether through art, or marriage, or faith. But just this simple inability to achieve a stupid f—— climax, ever, deprives me of that hopeful wholeness. Ah, well, perhaps it can be lived with. Perhaps it is, at the end of one's life, no sadder to have missed that than to realize, say, that one has missed music or literature. And yet the loss of these could seem so tragic.

I adore the children, both of them. I never resent time spent with them, as some friends I have do. But this is surely only because I have at least one genuinely adult outlet. They are interesting children, but they, too, become thorns in the flesh because of the way the family doesn't work. Oh, I've said all this before, but why—why—why is Hans so contemptuous of the boy? It seems to be far less a problem of Teutonic authoritarianism than of Hans's own personal dislike of this lovely youngster. I am baffled. Is there, after all, a truth in Freudian sexual jealousy? Can it be because Reinhard is growing up *too* much an American? It is on the relationship between these two, I feel, that my resistance or refusal to continue in the marriage will hinge. *You* saw it. You put your finger squarely on his unkindness to the boy while fawning over Andrea. Or do all marriages splinter themselves thus, Pat?

I read and read. I look well and keep the house up nicely—I do. But I'm an awful wife, I guess. We sit in stupid silence or I ask the anticipated questions about *his* work in a gesture of self-abnegation. Please write. You're so dear to me.

Joyce

November 4, 1962

Dearest dearest friend indeed,

Your letters are not dropped into a bottomless pit. I digest every word, I re-re-read them, I think sadly and at length about your problems, and I haven't got the foggiest notion what to tell you to give you even cold comfort, except a pocketful of aphorisms. Those sorts of things are just the same as ever with me, only I never have time to worry about it any more. I have just taken on a *new* job beginning in a fortnight, again a job I do in my own time and in my own home, stuffed with filing cabinets, etc.

I have dropped all my daytime social life, sports, French classes, sewing, just no time. And we are out so often in the evening, it's ghastly. I never read anything except the *Observer* and *Encounter*—no time. This week we went to a reception at the Russian Embassy (as they said on the invitation, "to celebrate the 45th anniversary of the Great October Socialist Revolution," rather nicely put!). Then the day after, we went to the American Embassy for a farewell party to a couple who are going on transfer to Liberia, poor things. The Russian do had about seven hundred guests, it seemed as many waiters, lashings of vodka and Ukrainian champagne, lots of food (real Beluga caviar), and more than half the guests were African. You wouldn't believe it, but the American party had not one single solitary African there. Incredibly dense of them.

Philip flies off tomorrow to Kampala for a week's conference, and I have refused all invitations for the week. I shall stay home and get something done, like Christmas cards and writing to you. Again, I am very worried about Christopher, who is quite good at the piano, but just plain slow at school, after all my hopeful ambitions for him. He *refuses* to learn. He's very sweet and a dear at home, everybody loves him, but he's nearly at the same point now in school that he was two years ago. It's a dreadful worry. Maybe he's a late bloomer and will suddenly be into abstruse mathematics in his teens, à la Einstein, or a political genius at twenty-five, like Churchill. God, I hope so.

Must close and mail this and go to work on today's pile of bumph. I will write a long letter next week. All my love, my sympathy, and, I hope, my understanding.

Ever yours,

Pat

December 21, 1962

Dear Pat,

I just send these recent photos of the children as a sort of late Christmas greeting from this side of the waters. Hans continues to plan—I merely to speculate—on March 28th sailing date plans. It's folly, I feel, not because of the baby, but because of the shortness of funds. Hans is adamant. If so, we'll probably be in Barcelona from April through October; at least, is there the remotest chance of seeing you?

It is not continuation of the past that I cherish and value so in you. It is contact, the hand across the great breach of time and circumstance. Were you able to live the Advent Season? Is there glory in it, truly? And a Happy Birthday to you, dear Pat, to Christopher, and to Julian. I've no idea how long surface mail takes. Write—please—more this year than in the last.

Love,

Joyce

DAR ES SALAAM
December 25, 1962
Christmas night

Dearest ever friend,

I adored Reinhard's Christmas card. How very clever he is! I hope your Christmas has been joyous and *good,* family, children, turkey, carols, the coming of the Infant into the New Year (which for me, always begins at Christmas). Here there is no commercialism to speak of, but also no Christmas, except within your own heart and home. We try very hard to make it so, for the children.

Christopher wrote his letter to Father Christmas (I wrote Julian's and he signed it), and they were duly and solemnly stamped and posted, I think they fervently believe.

My mother-in-law bought a tiny battered little black Ford Anglia for me to go to my job at the Soviet Embassy in. And we got lots of lovely stuff from one another. I feel very rich and very lucky and very happy—except for her having moved in with us, about which I have serious reservations, which I must not express to Philip obviously. But perhaps she is a good influence (unawares), as we can't bicker and be beastly in front of her, and it's good for the soul to repress a bit (our souls, anyway). The children love her to bits and don't seem to be getting on her nerves in the old way yet.

280

As to my job at the Soviet Embassy, I am to begin to teach English conversation and idiom (the village idiom) to their staff next week and I haven't the remotest idea how to set about doing it. Still, I suppose some kind of inspiration or other will appear. As usual, I lied my way into the job, practically told them I'd been a Berlitz teacher for years. I had a curious experience over the job. I was visited by a delegation of ladies from the *American* Embassy and told I mustn't for patriotic reasons take the job! I told them politely it was none of their business and that I was a Tanganyika civil servant, not an American one, and that my patriotism was my own business. Isn't it all sad, this whole Cold War business?

I will write a proper letter when the holiday simmers down in a day or two. I trust you are keeping fit with the wee-est one.

All love and warmest greetings to you all,

Pat

COLUMBUS
January 8, 1963

My good dear friend,

I was so pleased to have such a happy letter from you. You seemed in such far better spirits than at the time of the last letter. Your Christmas sounds warm and good, and perhaps the presence of a real grandmother will be good for all. I am sorry that my wishes were not present in the form of the book which has perhaps arrived for the boys by now. The gifts from Africa via England arrived beautifully, late Christmas Eve afternoon. As we open gifts that evening, the timing was perfection. How I do adore that little Scottish beret and mittens! It is such that both children can wear it, though Reinhard, growing as he is like a weed, will soon be too large, and I shall with love pass it on as a cherished set from child to child. Reinhard is a tall boy, nearly to my shoulders now. On Christmas day he lost his front tooth. Have the boys, Christopher, I mean, lost any? Reinhard so far is one of those children of the Graces, who manage the worst stages easily. He *is* fun, a great reader now, trying all sorts of hard things. Both you and I seem more absorbed in our first than our second child. I feel I know Christopher ever so much better than Julian. Do tell me about him, sending pictures, if you can.

I'm envious of your Russian Embassy job. It should be ideal for you and vice versa, despite any lies perpetrated in getting it. I want full and embossed details. I also have no sense what is happening to you and music. Do you practice much? Sing lieder? Who are your good friends, women, I mean? Be more precise about

281

your 1964 plans. Will you be in Sussex long? It now seems unlikely that we will be able to profit by Hans's quarter off. We're too poor to go to Europe, though Hans feels desperately in exile. Columbus is an ugly, ugly place.

Well, let this be a tiny Birthday greeting to you. You seem to be started upon a good year, and I hope so. I wish I could say the same for myself, but perhaps some manna will drop from heaven, after all. I wish and shall always wish you the best of the good things in life. Oh, and my loving thanks for the badly needed lift to my femininity. I love such things as the sachet and have had very few of them.

Love,

Joyce

Dearest Pat,

Your letters come infrequently enough of late that I make a real celebration upon receiving one, with cigarettes, coffee, rereadings, and allowing myself time for ruminations and contemplation. I do wish I had you nearer to talk with, or equally happy, simply to be with. Your reference to your mother-in-law reminded me that there are magnificent old people. I've known some I would pay to have live with me, so reassuring they were. But you make that little trick of "keeping one's responses alive" sound so easy. It is just because it isn't that deterioration sets in. Habit assaults the freshness and delight until most people fail to remember what they thought they were looking for. I'm not at all convinced I can maintain enough awe and joy to achieve this beauty and grace in old age.

Ah, yes—the death of Robert Frost. I wept and wept. His poetry had not meant so much to me before knowing him. But three Bread Loaf summers of watching that man live, of knowing the marvel of his conversation, made his poetry painfully beautiful to me, and I'm convinced that if American letters has not lost its greatest poet, it certainly has lost its greatest and wisest conversationalist. I still know no definition of poetry that more accurately sums up the reasons I need and delight in it—as "A momentary stay against confusion."

The baby is due momentarily. Mother will arrive here on the 10th, and I'm much looking forward to her, though Hans is *not*. I feel like I'm going to explode, and wish it were all over with. Hans, by the way, now (still tentatively) thinks he'll go to Europe alone this spring. I'll go to Salt Lake City. The expense for all is just TOO much. More details of the Russian lessons, please. It's great fun to hear.

Love,

Joyce

February 20, 1963
Riverside Hospital

My only real friend,

The pregnancy seemed interminable. The delight now dispels the memories of all that. Monday, February 18th, 2:45 P.M., after an induced and easy labor, a second little daughter was born to us. She is perfect, and the relief on this score seems a far greater release than ever before. Seven pounds, four ounces, twenty inches long. She is the biggest of the three, but resembles Reinhard closely as an infant. We're not yet determined upon the name, either Anna Elizabeth or Laura Elizabeth. I prefer the latter. Never having had a godmother of my own, and coming from a family which doesn't buy such terms, I don't know the proper protocol. I only know that I wish for you, of all friends, family and acquaintances in this world, to be spiritual overseer for this little girl. I don't want to oblige you to gifts and a sense of commitment on that score, but will you, across whatever distance, give me the moral backing for her sake that you alone so well do? If that makes you her godmother, will you be so? You're the only woman I feel I really know, the only one I know I can trust.

Mother is here and gets on well with the children, plays Monopoly by the hour with Reinhard, delights in Andrea.

Hans will leave alone for Europe in about three or four weeks, and I shall probably go to Salt Lake with Mother and kiddies. From June on, the future remains open. I feel very alive, and grateful, more optimistic than in months. Do, do, do write.

Love,

Joyce

March 15, 1963

Dearest Joyce,

Excuse this ghastly Christmas air letter form, but I must use them up! I can't apologize enough for yet another non-letter, but time presses so horribly. We have been out every night except Sunday for the past fortnight, and have yet another week of the same boring rounds ahead. Life is anything but dull, as long as I can stand the pace. Philip has just had confirmation that he is to attend two conferences, one in Italy next month, the other in Edinburgh in August, lucky devil. I am going to disconnect the telephone, and except for going to my Russkis in the mornings, not stir out of the house.

The latter are getting on splendidly as friends, but so-so as students. They don't really work very hard at it. I don't have much time for the men, who are very political-minded and full of all their Marxist nonsense, all terribly illogical and stubborn and naive. I can't be bothered to argue with them, I just correct their grammar and accent. The teaching itself, aside from some of the students, I enjoy very much too, all most challenging and rewarding; in depth, I should imagine, even more so, not superficially, as I am examining it. I find to my astonishment that they are more racially prejudiced (when they're safely alone with me in a lesson) than the wicked old colonials!

The lovely de la Mare book for the kidlets arrived; they will shortly write to say "thank you." We loved Reinhard's letter. It was Christopher's idea, as he is absolutely mad on stamp collecting. How are you in your new motherhood? How are baby Laura (lovely name), Andrea, Reinhard, Hans and your Mum? Are you really to be in Salt Lake for the summer? I *promise* to write at length. This is just to send my love.

And all of it,

Pat

March 24, 1963

Dearest Joyce, Mother of three,

Clever you. I can hardly credit it that you now possess fifty percent more children than I. I would adore to see my goddaughter-to-be. I am delighted to be it again, too, most gratifying to one's sense of responsibility and the continuity of events. And all that jazz.

Life goes on at the same dizzy pace here. I can hardly keep up with things.

I've got myself far too involved with all sorts of daft enterprises, and never have any spare time to tell the boys a story or to play the piano or make a new dress. It won't do, and I must begin withdrawal. Of course, I recognize it for what it is, simply a shameless orgy of *doing* after seven years in the bush. However, it still won't do.

Philip and I have had an endless procession of official visitors, mostly United Nations people, technical experts and advisers. Nearly every night for the past six weeks has been busy, and now to cap it, Philip's mother (who had left us only five weeks ago and gone back home after three harrowing months here) has now *re*-changed her mind, and is coming back. I feel very bitter and uncharitable about it. For me she casts an aura of dourness and depression about her, almost tangible, and seems hypercritical of absolutely everything I do, in a monotonous boring way. I told Philip bluntly that I couldn't take it again for very long, and he promised to get her a flat near us, which will of course cost us a fortune. Ah me.

How are you? How are all your summer plans maturing? I am still pegging away at my Russians, but am getting very tired of their endless politics and jingoistic bragging just like a bunch of Texans, they are! What a perfectly horrid letter—forgive me! I have just finished Solzhenitsyn's *One Day in the Life of Ivan Denisovitch*—do you know him? Superb, and so moving.

I send all my love,

Pat

PART TEN

MARCH 1963– JUNE 1964

I am a person in process, as we all are

(Haunt of collegiate memories)
March 28, 1963

Dear Pat,

Do you think you write often? You don't. In fact, our correspondence has dwindled to a quarterly affair, and I'm sad about this. Shall I, or shall you, embroil ourself in some emotional turbulence so as to need and solicit consultation and exchange? Quite seriously, I do need more word from you. So much seems stale and profitless, so much mere vanity. Our correspondence seems neither.

Hans is in mid-Atlantic now, on the *Queen Elizabeth,* and I am here in Salt Lake with my three. By all logic, I should be jealous, but I am more glad to be in the West after all those grim flat lands than I would be to be heading for industrial Germany. Imagine! I drove up Big Cottonwood to Brighton, where Reinhard and I had the time of our lives watching the National Collegiate Ski-Jumping finals. Glorious. He was overwhelmed with excitement. There are difficulties here, of course. There always are, I suppose, when generations try to meet somewhere in between. It seems incumbent upon me to unearth some old and ill-fitting habits, since the stabilization of Mother's ego is necessary if all is to go smoothly here. Daddy seems to accept more easily that I am a person in process, as we all are, and less tortured at the demise of gay, singing, seventeen-year-old me. In any case, they are dear people, and I'm glad they can be with the children for a while.

Hans will return in June, and perhaps we'll go to Mexico for the rest of the year. We shall see. How are the boys? Your Russian students? You? Baby Laura is a dream, both lovely and easy. And I'm feeling fine, though somewhat inelastic mentally. I must discipline myself to some sort of arduous study. Do, DO write.

All love,

Joyce

289

April 5, 1963

Dearest Joyce,

Salt Lake! I had thought you were not going there until June, for some reason or other, and was most surprised to see the postmark. That world is all so very buried in the past, so irretrievable and lost for me and to me, that somehow it seems magical for you to be there in the flesh. It's as if the *people* all ought to be dead and gone too, with my youth (*that* youth anyhow; I'm in the midst of a renascence), and there you be, communing with them. How very odd it is.

Joyce, forgive me for the long silences. You know without my saying what this correspondence, finishing its tenth year, means to my life and ability to think at all clearly. I've been a complete fool here in Dar and got involved in too much. I am stopping half my activities this month, and what a relief it will be. I love my Russians and find them endlessly fascinating. I teach English nine hours a week, and also one hour of absolute beginner's French, which I didn't really feel I ought to take on, but I was begged, and in spite of better judgment am having a bash at it. Consequently, to get back a semblance of conversational French myself, I am having two one-hour lessons a week. Perhaps I'll have a stab at Russian too, as the First Secretary's wife goes on leave to Moscow this month and is bringing me back at the end of June the Russian Linguaphone set, just out on the Russian market.

They are great present givers, and the other day, March 8th, a solemn little deputation of my two men students filed into the room in the embassy where I teach, and looking rather embarrassed, made a ponderous but short speech and presented me with a gaudy little black and gold cardboard box in which were a bottle of cologne and one of perfume, "Moscow Nights," really wild stuff—I smell like a petunia in heat. Apparently March 8th is Eenternaseeonale Voomanz Day, I suppose like our Mother's Day. I was *so* touched, really! Then a very dear girl, a frail ethereal wisp of a thing, pale reddish-gold hair, a fine fine alabaster skin, the most delicate bone structure and carriage—Lara (Larissa) Kuznetsova by name—went off to Moscow a couple of weeks ago. She'd been very good at her lessons and done well. I liked her enormously and thought I'd give her a wee souvenir of Africa, an etching of a head of a Gogo chief done by a friend, very nice and simple. I brought it to class on her very last day before flying off to London en route to the Soviet Union. She had brought me a set of Gorki's *Autobiography* (in English) and a little folio of picture postcards of Gorki's life, friends, habitat, etc., and we each shed a tear and patted each other awkwardly on the shoulder.

They really are very nice simple people, very much more genuine than *any* other of the diplomats I've come to know, and I'm sure are dedicated to the downfall of us all. Although I personally am far too erratic and idle to be even a good socialist, let alone communist, I'm not so sure that it isn't at least an equally good, if not a better, system than the one which shapes our half of the world. They are a very *clean* people. Their mentalities have sharp definable clear clean lines and distinctions. They are madly emotional and very leaden-footed in their humor(s). Politically the men are fanatics, and I try to steer clear of logistics and categorical imperatives. The women dismiss "all that nonsense" with a Slavic shrug.

One and all they hate and fear the resurgence of Germany and the erratic approach to "peace" of the U.S.A. I am trying very hard to see all this as a Martian might. My God, how they suffered during Stalin's day and during the war. Again, one and all, they say over and over how Russia is at last "herself" (mother Russia, not father) again, how this terrible burden has been lifted. Perhaps it's only by comparison with Stalin, but they revere Khrushchev. Young Vadim Kuznetsov (dear Larissa's husband—I teach him French) said to me: "Our Khrushchev is one of us; he is our father, but he is Russia's son too. The land bore him. He is a peasant's son, and is still a peasant. We love him as the best leader, but *of*, as a *part of*, us. How can you say this or feel this of your Kennedy with his private schools and million dollars at twenty-one and private mansions? He is your Czar." What could I say to him?

Alas, I feel *so* un-American. But I could never never live *away* from the Anglo-Saxon English-speaking traditions. I wouldn't want to. Compared to the rest of the diplomatic corps here, the Russians come out very well. The English are unquestionably the worst: snobs, arrogant, conceited upper-class monomaniacs (loss of empire and the uppishness of the wog these days). The French and Americans tie for second place for beastliness and sheer thick skins. The Israelis are dear—again a pure simple dedicated people with a goal (though I know I'm exaggerating).

I don't know whether you'll shudder with shame or die laughing at this. But I went last night to see *El Cid*, which has only now reached East Africa. And I was very deeply moved. All through the film Chaucer's line "parfit gentil knight" was running through my head. Then of course at the end, the Moor (or whoever it was; I couldn't see through my tears!) kneels down and asks God to welcome the soul of "This best and purest and noblest knight of them all," as the beautiful white charger gallops away into the hills with Rodrigo's still upright body on it. Isn't the legend that he never was found and that he still rides, awaiting a call to come back in the hour of Spain's greatest need? However, I was very deeply moved, 70 mm. staggerama, or whatever it was, and all, by this austere vision of a great simple noble man's dedication to a moral value and a goal in life. What has happened to us? Where are these people of steadfast glowing courage and immense moral fiber today? *Does* the East have a priority in them? Actually, I have known a few, but for the greater part, *older*, much older men. Perhaps from another time than ours?

And the Peace Corps—you might think it a vision of just the sort of person I yearn for in this world. I had the honor of a few moments' conversation with Dr. Nyerere the other night at another interminable reception. I asked him what he thought the Peace Corps might effect in our Tanganyika. He smiled, looked at the night sky for a bit, and said, "I see them spending a year unpacking, mentally, that is, and then the second year repacking. It was better when you of the Colonial Service did your three-year tours and knew you were coming back here for another and yet another." And I suppose he's right. I imagine the youngsters think their two years away from the U.S. an endless penance. But I was only twenty-four when we arrived in Mahali for a three-year tour! Ah well.

I sometimes wonder how I can ever unmesh myself from my tangled messy life. There are so many rubbishy bits and pieces that I'm sick of. I love music, great and good books, a few people, my children immensely; and a very clouded vision of something I can't even articulate. I think you are the only person alive who understands me. I'm very contented with my own little private life (inside me, I mean) these days, and the need to probe the bottomless depths is leaving me as I get well into my thirties. I think I might be growing up a little.

My dear, dear friend, I think of you so often. I am sorry if I have been neglectful. I especially wonder how you fare in Salt Lake, that beautiful raw place, the mountains I love so, the footstool of the desert at your feet. My love to all three little ones, but most to you.

Have a happy April,

Pat

SALT LAKE CITY
April 8, 1963
Palm Sunday

My dear friend,

It is hard for me, too, to get around to writing a letter with any degree of coherence, not because I am so busy as you just now, but I am troubled in some ways, quite occupied with maternal cares and *very* eager to have what time is left after both motherly and daughterly duties to try to come to myself, to read, to re-establish abilities I feel in danger of losing, the ability to learn a system, or a logic such as a language and to hold it together, for example, so forgive my roundly chastising you (or oblongly, perhaps). It's just that I do hope our letters can be exchanges instead of synopses. I'm sending to you a print of Reinhard's for the boys' room. I hope you might like it. He's sold two, and the money goes toward his cherished hope of a bicycle.

After arrival here, I felt only introverted. I called no one, and deliberately avoided some few I might have called at a recent lecture. I can easily get to the point where I just refuse to answer phones. If the phone behaves tactlessly and interrupts the privacy of my reading, I scorn it.

Tell me of your experiences with the Russians. I hope they do not become a jaded part of your day. Yes, I knew you would love teaching, because it would come so easily to you. God bless you, my dearest, dearest friend, may your Easter be joyous—

Joyce

DAR ES SALAAM
May 7, 1963

My dearest Joyce,

We have just arrived back from the most wonderful safari, nine whole days in a little rest house, no electricity, eating out of tins (off plates, I mean, but the food out of tins). I read, read, read, and did my tapestry and played with and read to the children. Philip spent the days working, but we had two Sundays and May 1st (national holiday) to go on picnics in the gorgeous surrounding country and rock-climb for hours in the crisply hot sun. Very dry and invigorating air, at an altitude of about 5,000 feet, such a difference from this lazy enervating climate. It made me wistful for the California desert of my childhood. Really, the upcountry East Africa is very similar!

I read Robert Graves's *King Jesus,* a work of great scholarship, I'm sure, but somehow very sterile and unsatisfying, considering its subject. It left me with a faint distaste. I also read a most electrically entertaining work of African exploration, Alan Moorehead's *The White Nile,* very good indeed. What men (and some women) they were indeed in those days! It is about the exploration of the headwaters and source of the Nile, 1830–1900. Africa is still such an exciting and new place. All the deaths, the misery, sickness, fever, sense of aloneness, are only very recently done away with. Frustration and puzzlement with Africans, although it stems from a different source, is ever-present still. It really is a very good book, so alive, as so few histories are. I read right through the week, all sorts of things, till my eyes nearly fell out of my head. I had an absolute feast after famine, which I must, in all fairness, admit has been self-imposed.

Also my tapestry. Have I told you of my recent passion for our long-awaited tapestry? Alas, I'm not clever enough to do my own designs, choose wools, amounts, etc., and must pick them out of catalogues. So, no unicorns, medieval ladies strumming lutes, or oddly perspective castle grounds. I finished one smallish one and had made out of it a piano stool, by one of the very good local

Hindu carpenters. It is very nice, if I do say so myself. Tapestry is enormously satisfying and soothing, and it's so simple, so mindless, that you cannot make a mistake or forget what it was you were doing, if you happen to mislay it or the time in which to do it for six months or so. You ought to take it up. So very undemanding and quiet.

My Russians are coming on very well. I find them endlessly fascinating. I teach eight to ten hours a week, quite enough, and I have resigned all my other three jobs. I really was getting impossible to live with, tired, fat, neglectful of the children and the house, the mending, et bloody cetera. So I feel very footloose and fancy free at the moment, and very nice it is too.

Christopher is coming along nicely on the piano, but his schoolwork is still impossible, as he is so lazy and seems to lack all powers of concentration. It drives me frantic, but I can't see what there is to do about it. Julian is somewhat better for his age, but would appear to be falling into the same trough. I wish they could understand the wonderful world that awaits them in books once reading comes easily. I am convinced that Christopher will turn into a bookworm once he just understands that it is not word by grinding word, but phrase by phrase. However, it doesn't do to worry.

I loved the pictures you sent! What absolutely gorgeous children you seem to have. I think I told you I am deferring a christening present for Laura until we get to the U.K. on leave in February, as the selection here is very limited and expensive. She'll get something from the old godmother, though. Never fear.

I must end this now and rush off to help get the collection boxes ready for Red Cross Flag Day. How one gets involved in all this sort of thing, I don't know, but I have become a real Helen Hokinson type—on the surface, I trust.

Love to all,

Pat

SALT LAKE CITY
June 4, 1963

My dearest friend,

All this time and leisure have made me delinquent and lazy, and I'm sure it's ages since I've written you. We've had an endless stream of illness here, chicken pox and colds, separately for each child, and the flu for me (twice). A colossal nuisance! And now this episode terminates as Hans is on the return trip and I prepare and pack for the next curious interim before we return to regulated duties once more.

I have seen few old friends here. I'm quite accustomed to being without any very close friends any more, excepting only you. I do not pride myself on that position, however.

Reinhard and I had a delightful, arduous, nine hours' hike up Big Cottonwood. My awe was renewed at this glorious country. How I do love the bare protrusions of rugged cliff. One sees the structure as well as the covering, the forest, and both are grand.

Oh, God, how I wish we might enjoy each other at closer range. The death of Pope John has touched me most, most deeply.

Love,

Joyce

July 22, 1963

My dear friend,

I do so especially not want to lose the sense of your days and doings. Don't wait for the long safari letter, nor even for the musings of a briefer letter. Now and again just send off the facts, though of course I'm always grateful for interpretations. What is your summer like? Is the Russian teaching finished and is it to be resumed, or not? Are you hot, sluggish, ebullient, despondent, pious, or in love?

I am as bad as you. I've not written a very real letter to you in a long while, and I've not even the excuse of being busy. For this has been the most prolonged vacation I've had in years—no teaching since mid-December, then three months' freedom from being even a wife. Just nursing a fat and jolly baby under the blossoming hawthorn here, listening to the chatter of cedar waxwings, watching the winter's snow day by day vanishing from the Wasatch Mountains. It was very pleasant, really, though in no significant way very constructive, except insofar as respite from pressure is gainful. And Laura has been sheer joy. Perhaps by now you've received her photos. She is so much like Reinhard, pretty in just his way, gay, and so immeasurably *good*. But the spring was rife with sickness (had I told you?). All minor matters, but collectively quite a siege.

Well, Hans returned brown, too plump, virile and enchanted with Florence, where he'd spent an exhilarating two weeks. He ran head-on into Mother's mistrust and dislike, which took all the joy from him. But it's coming back now, with the beauty and leisure of our time here in the Pacific Northwest. This country is glorious, and the situation relaxing. One day at the spectacular shoreline, another in a true logger's wilderness. We came to Eugene in particular because of a very dear, gifted poet friend of ours who's poet in residence here at Oregon University. We're exploring, camping out, fishing, playing tennis and being nicely physical. It's marvelous *not* to be pregnant and to feel so well. Apart from caring for my three, there's small reason to be compulsive about domestic cleaning, etc. So I read. We both quit smoking, and I'm about to decide (again) to try my hand at writing poetry. My poet friend urges it, and I know myself that it's my most successful way of unearthing and encountering my best self, such as there is of it.

I continue always to miss you, and to consider what pleasure it would be to have long hours together.

Much love,

Joyce

DAR ES SALAAM
August 6, 1963

Dearest Joyce,

Again, again, it scarcely seems credible that I have been so beastly a correspondent. Partly busyness, partly withdrawal from the world, partly living in a complete daze. The International School has taken up so much of my time and energies, both physical and mental, that I haven't even been able to be a decent wife or mother for months. But that is no excuse.

We are so very proud of our efforts on behalf of the school. Have I talked about it much over the past year? It all stemmed from Philip's and my becoming chairman and secretary of the Tanganyika Parents' Association (guess who is which!). There was a great and pressing need for an English-language medium primary school here, to take the place of the (still) government-run ones, which were then, and are now (at an accelerated pace), running rapidly down in efficiency and standards. I remembered having read of the excellence of the International School in Geneva, and on a chance wrote to the headmaster there asking him if they could give us any advice on how to go about beginning one, we being interested parents. They (he) could and did. We started out with a few brochures and odd little mimeographed "histories" from all sorts of schools all over the world who started out in much the same circumstances as ours, though none with so large a potential student body.

It has taken us nearly a year and a half, but here is how we stand. We have now a board of governors, of which Philip is chairman, very august indeed, including bank managers, ambassadors, the head of AID here, a Member of Parliament, the general manager of the East African Division of Anglo-American Tobacco, the general manager of Tanganyika Shell, etc. We have received

296

$67,000 from the American Government, apparently the first time in history that the U.S. Government has aided an overseas school which is not, and will not be, American; $6,000 from Her Majesty's (British) Government, and an assorted $10,000 in donation from industries and parents, in money and in kind. A few loans have trickled in, but it's almost 100 percent straight grants. We have a headmistress (English), who was given to us by the Geneva International School —she has been head of their Junior Division for several years—we have four overseas staff on contract terms, and about five locally recruited teachers.

The funniest things have dropped into our laps. We spent months looking all over Dar es Salaam and environs for suitable buildings, only to have the Minister of Education call in Philip one day last March and tell him confidentially that if we could raise £20,000 capital, the Tanganyika Government would sell us at flat cost price a brand-new fourteen-classroom primary school which would be (and was) completed in April. The reason that the Government wanted to sell us their school was because someone discovered in an awful moment of truth that it had been built in the wrong place—wrong for them, but just right for us. Scarcely credible, but to our great benefit. Philip talked it over with the board, and with representatives of the people who were going to give us money, they all took a hard gulp, and signed on the dotted line—*without* any money. That only came *after* we'd bought the buildings, an awful risk! So we have this beautiful pristine school, built for the purpose, lots of playground space, etc. We have two hundred and twenty-five children enrolled to begin on September 16th, our grand opening, equipment swimming over—we trust in time—from the States and England, and eighteen nationalities waiting for the day. We also have a waiting list of around fifty! It's all too wonderful. A small but I trust not insignificant triumph I can call all mine was to do with the Russians. I talked two of my students at the embassy into coming to some of the organization meetings for parents of prospective students. They very warily did so. I got tons of literature about the U.N. school in New York to prove to them that Soviet citizens could indeed send their children to approved schools, and they went ahead and applied for approval for *our* school, and got it! So now the little Russians will be a part of it too. Not only that, they even shelled out some teaching materials as their contribution to the scheme.

It's at last reached the stage where it doesn't matter if Philip or I drop dead. It will go on of its own volition now, an enormous relief. It really is the most gratifying feeling of accomplishment, to have created from absolutely nothing something of this magnitude, which one hopes will go on and create its own tradition and mystique. Wouldn't it be glorious to visit it in twenty or thirty years' time (now that it looks as if we will all still be around, barring lung cancer, since the Test Ban Treaty has been signed), and see it all still functioning smoothly and internationally? Philip really has the most stunning organizational mind. He sees every possible contingency, and deals with it all in advance. He would have made a brilliant general, or criminal. Actually, he's making a brilliant tropical specialist. He just flew off this afternoon, to an International Congress in Edinburgh.

I am still teaching the Russians; no summer vacations there. I feel at the moment as if I am doing it just for the money, as I am rather bored with the lot I have now.

We have all taken up shell collecting to make our Sundays on the beach seem more purposeful. It's enormous fun and gorgeously tan-making, as the best low tides all come in the sunny late mornings. We are sort of specializing in cowries, big and little, as there are so many lovely ones on this stretch of coast. The children love it, and it is something they can join completely in with us to do, and have the thrill of their own odd discoveries, and the fun of helping to catalogue them afterwards.

I too was moved by the death of Pope John. I was so terribly impressed by his sanctity and achievements. If ever a man flew straight up, unencumbered by sins, it was he. But I am doing nothing about my own sins. I'm in a morass of stupidities, all entangled in obligations, meetings, things to type, Philip's papers to edit, people to telephone, parties obliged to attend (we refused eight invitations for the one week that we managed to get away from here in July!), and people I'm obliged to have back.

We have finally and irrevocably handed in our resignation from the Tanganyika Government, and haven't the foggiest notion where we'll be (geographically and financially) when our leave ends in April.

Well, I'm going to pop this in an envelope and mail it tomorrow and do the same thing again in a couple of days, as this was only filling you in on details, not what I'm thinking about and all that jazz. I hope your holiday was perfect, and that you are all flourishing and Hans full of beans from his European jaunt. Give him my best regards, and Reinhard a hug, and Andrea and Laura a chuck under the chin(s). Would a little opal ring be too outré for Laura as my christening present? Do say.

All love,

Pat

September 23, 1963

Dearest Joyce,

Just a short note to accompany the enclosed clippings from the *Tanganyika Standard* on the opening of our International School. As I told you, this is what has been keeping us so busy the past months. We are *so* proud of it all. Not only

298

do we have, as the editorial says, Arabs and Israelis side by side, but five Russian children (my embassy staff students' children), two Bulgarians, lots of Americans, and probably, in this time and place, funniest of all, about half a dozen Afrikaans children (Dutch Boer South African, I mean) and the three children of the King (Mwambutsi) of Burundi. It is all very exciting. We got all but about £8,000 of the money we needed, and we opened with a great flourish a week ago.

Now we are just leaving it to itself. I refuse to have another thing to do with it. The last gesture was that we gave on last Saturday night a reception for sixty-five people, including staff and husbands or wives, all the board of directors and wives, and all those who had been instrumental in getting the school large sums of money or given moral support when most needed. I shall not even make so much as a cup of tea for a visitor for months and months. I spent two days making trays and trays and trays of canapés. However, all very invigorating once it's over with. I'm sure my friends here are sick to death of being pressed into service licking envelopes, mimeographing endless God-knows-whats, and so on. What are you now doing? I have not heard from you since you left Oregon. Didn't you get my long letter when you arrived back in Columbus? I shall be very cross if it was lost, since it represents about five months.

I have, of all things, begun a correspondence course with a commercial education outfit in Oxford with the view to getting myself accepted as an external (correspondence) student at London University. The first thing is to pass what constitutes entrance exams to an English university, and I am doing Latin, English history, French, and English literature. The Latin is the ghastliest, the rest are fun but an enormous amount of work. I absolutely must have some kind of genuine credentials and be able to get some kind of *real* professional work wherever we end up next, not this tentative easy-come-easy-go sort of thing.

But I still teach my Russians, a new lot, as they seem to be forever coming and going. I consider it a great victory having got them (and the Bulgarians followed in their wake) into our International School. I really do like them immensely. I've been reading a lot of contemporary Russian short stories, and one or two novels, terribly naive style, or maybe it's just the pedestrian translations, full of enthusiasm and idealism, impetuous and emotional, but really rather dull in subject matter, except when they touch on the war (WWII). I don't think any of us realizes how much the war really affected Russia, nor how deep the scars are. They are a funny lot, and I wouldn't have missed this experience for anything. I am impressed in particular with one novelist–short story writer named Solzhenitsyn. Have I mentioned him to you before? Do you know him? And a novelist named Dudintsev. Bureaucracy and the unbelievable sufferings of the Soviet masses under Stalin seem to be their themes.

Well, as to our own future plans, they are still very hazy. The furthest we have looked ahead is that we sail on January 22nd, and will spend at least two or three months at our house in Sussex, hoping to get in a skiing trip and/or a couple of weeks in Paris. I am back at the good old Alliance Française, brushing up my French for the correspondence course. I am trying to read a novel by Mallet-Joris (in French) but can't make head or tails of it. Maybe I couldn't in English either?

Must close and get off to my English lessons. *Do* write and say you've forgiven my bad lapses the past few months. I haven't been very well either, lots of stomach trouble, but I hope to be looking up. No love affairs (how dull), no religious perturbations, no nothing, except busy work, frenetic social life, the correspondence course. I can see I'm not cut out for the social life, in particular. God, it is the very worst sort of life imaginable, to be a diplomat's wife. I cannot see how these people stick it. Out every night of the week, same old faces, same dull conversation, same vapid bright smiles.

You didn't answer about Laura. How is the family, how is everything? Are you back teaching? Give me all the latest gen.

Much, much love, dear friend,

Pat

COLUMBUS
September 28, 1963

Dear good friend,

I've been remiss in answering your letter, and I have no worthy excuse. I had pots of time all summer and glorious leisure, to the point that I was quite inebriated with beauty, the scope, the scale of Oregon grandeur. So I wrote no one. I nursed my baby in the wilds, made love on the beach, rolled down sand dunes with my kids. And I read a host of books, a couple of which I hope to send you to arrive—this time in time—for Christmas. But before all that . . .
I AM SO PROUD OF YOU!!

The photo of little Julian giving the flowers to the wife of the Minister of Education was so dear and touching—the occasion likewise represented so worthy. Oh, Pat, how good a thing! It may even seem in a decade that of all the little abortive efforts one makes across his youth to realize some lingering idealism, this one fruitful and determined crusade of yours was the most rewarding. Just to know of its future continuance, of its diversity of student, of its certain *need*—how good to have promoted any working symbol of internationalism. Bully for you! And for Philip! I shouldn't wonder if this proved more cohesive a force in your marriage than any number of midnight congresses. I don't want to denigrate sex, but how vitalizing it must be to have this sort of accomplishment between you. Is it so?

300

How long will you be in Sussex? You can't answer that, of course, but give me an approximation. How I'd love to visit you!

The children are all in great form—only Andrea is at a ghastly stage, two and a half, and very hard. She is so extreme a child, a veritable Sarah Bernhardt, and while this may bespeak intelligence and certainly does vitality, it's an enervating quality. I really thought Reinhard's beauty would go, but on the contrary, he grows more so. But Laura is much like him—and she should turn out well (physically, that is—the least important part, really). Yes, dear one, I do love the idea of the opal ring.

There is so much more to write—later this week, I'll hope.

All love,

Joyce

DAR ES SALAAM
October 12, 1963

Dear Pillar,

I'm so happy you had a pleasant summer. You deserved it after the last few years. I hope you are settled down to Midwest mores again. I send a photo or two of our opening ceremonies and one or two more clippings from the paper. I was so thrilled by what you said. We really *are* terribly proud of it all, and don't mind saying so! One unexpected bonus of our investigations into this kind of education has been that Philip has just about changed his mind about sending the children away to boarding school, if there is *any* kind of a school like ours in the various places we might end up in.

It now appears that we might be in England about a year. Have you ever given any thought to something I mentioned to you when I was with you, that is, sending Reinhard over to us for all or part of the summer holidays? It would be perfect this year and I would so love it; he and Christopher I *so* want to meet, and Reinhard is old enough now to get something out of it. There are various cheap charter fares for children you could investigate, if you feel you could part with him! We should all love to have him. As his godmother, I'll see that he goes to Sunday school regularly, and practices his harp, etc.

No time for more just now.

Much, much love,

Pat

November 10, 1963

My dear long neglected Pat,

Would that I had an excuse as valid for myself and for our times as you did with the International School! For weeks and months go by, and though I almost certainly think of you daily, my letters are becoming fewer. Bear with me, and we can perhaps reestablish our former rhythm.

Apart from teaching, wifing, mothering, and working on the miserable local political lethargy, a good hunk of my time recently has been going into trying to prevent a friend of mine, wife of a lawyer, Catholic mother of six little ones, from taking her life. She has had two severe crises, hospitalization, and electric shock therapy following both, and this week another relapse. She spent hours and days at my house while I cared for nine wee ones and she went through ebbs and flows of terrifying physical manifestations of the agony of our times. Her hands and face would *freeze,* both in rigidity and in temperature. And the reverse would be a hot band of red flush on her throat (not hot flashes, however—she's thirty-five). She's a beautiful girl, suffering from what increasingly is apparent to me as the most egregious illness of our congested times—isolation. She's just a mass of floating anxieties, terrified of beginning the day, of being *alone* in her suburban home.

I read the most persuasive article by Agnes de Mille commenting on the "Twist" as (and I'm convinced all art forms are) symptomatic of the times. She mentioned how dance has always been some form of expression of *community,* of cooperative movement, that the "Twist" is isolated, introverted, sexual preoccupation. She'd taken her son, a great "Twister" (as is Reinhard) to a square dance, where he was appalled (but converted) by the demands of so cooperative and communal a dance form. It seemed to me that just as the minuet was the 18th-century social manifestation of seduction by the rules, so to speak, that perhaps the twist is really just ostentatious, externalized masturbation. This is also what "action painting" seems to be. It's purely for the glory of a self-induced state. There really is *no* intent, not even an impulse to communication.

Which of course brings me to—what is it? My annual lamentation about the difficulty of sex. This only proves, of course, how much one is a part of his time, how inescapable, that one's children perforce shall be too. But—oh! Pat —when I observe and think upon the pathetic and myriad forms of isolation in American society, I could weep. I do. The minority groups, the outcast aged, the straitjacketed housewife, all the miserable high school dropouts, bored, scared and violent, the paranoiac rightists, the masturbating artists. God! I saw Ingmar Bergman's *Through a Glass Darkly,* which did nothing so much as to put human isolation onto a film strip. I wonder, is it so bad in the underdeveloped countries?

I am well, the children are fine. Reinhard reads like a fury, placed in the

99th percentile on an academic achievement test, in reading and language skills; 96th in math—place him at the equivalent of a sixteen-year-old. It doesn't matter, Pat. I don't take it seriously. Increasingly, precociousness seems to me of minimal importance. What I am *much* more concerned about, and interested in, is that a child learn *kindness* and the ability to *respond* (hence to communicate), to see, to be aware. Lord, the hypnotic trance most people (and American children!) are in! The baby is heavenly, though far too fat. When do you leave? I did, for a change, get off your Christmas package in time, I hope. Yes, I do consider flying Reinhard to you—God bless you!—though I am not yet certain. Do take care.

Love, much love,

Joyce

DAR ES SALAAM
November 26, 1963

Dearest Joyce,

What is there to say? I cannot remember ever having grieved so continuously, so deeply, and having felt so bereft and afraid of the future at the loss of anyone as I do now, four days after this appalling and still unbelievable crime against America, against humanity, against us all.

The memorial High Requiem Mass in the cathedral here yesterday afternoon was a shattering experience. I had only begun to hold my shaking sobs and tears inside my weak body, and the Mass, which I know so well, completely unnerved me. President Nyerere was sobbing unashamedly, every woman was in tears, the cathedral was packed with every American, every diplomat, the entire cabinet, and well- (or ill- ?) wishers. His loss is inestimable. I cannot see how it could happen at all. If we could do this terrible black thing, and follow it up with the violence of the next day, where is it all to lead?

Where will Johnson, either in strength or in weakness, as time will show, lead us? I have awful and grave fears for my country. You cannot imagine the impact this terrible sad thing has had on the English. We (you know how I am schizophrenic about my alliances) are deeply afraid about the future, not because, as I said, of the loss of Kennedy itself, but because of the forces of evil which caused that loss, and which may be unleashed in its train.

This beautiful intelligent brave young man, struck down in the middle of the most brilliant of careers life can offer, his lovely and devoted wife, young children—I cannot bear to think of her, though I constantly do so, in her moment of grief-stricken revelation that he was dead. There is one picture of her in the

303

paper which arrived today clutching Bobby Kennedy by the hand, her face wiped clear of every expression but that of frozen horror, watching the coffin being taken out of that Dallas hospital where that life, which could have been the making of so much good for us all, slipped so quickly away. The blood which spatters her skirt is the blood of the dead body of all our highest hopes. I feel shame, grief, even guilt. I hate Texas, and Texans, I loathe myself even, for having at times given way in minor matters to just that sort of impulsiveness and violence which is so characteristic of America, mindless, physical, inarticulate, hating this careful, aristocratic, philosophic, patient approach to problems, but hatred is what killed him (and who knows what else?), and if anything, his death must be kept before us of his generation as the symbol of the steadfastness and courage before whatever fate may next deal us.

I went to the Soviet Embassy as usual to teach. The entire staff of the embassy was waiting for me by the reception desk. I stopped as I came in the door, wondering for a second why they were all there. Then the Ambassador, dull little Mr. Timoshenko, came forward to hug me, I burst anew into tears, the whole lot of them crowded round in one hugging mass, all of us weeping and patting each other in impotent sorrow.

I am too shocked and sad to go on. You know the rest. There is no news. We sail in eight weeks. You should have Laura's ring by now, which was taken to the States by a friend and he was to have mailed it from there last week.

Love, and love—
we must stand together,

Pat

DAR ES SALAAM
December 3, 1963

Dearest Joyce,

Why do you not write to me and share with me what I know must be your grief, mingle your tears with mine? I am as stunned, even now, as I was ten days ago. I simply cannot bring myself to believe the facts. I feel as if some of me had died at that moment in that bleak city. I say with Lord Hume, "His death diminishes us all," and with our dear Adlai Stevenson, "Every one of us who knew him will mourn his death until the day of our own."

What a world. What creatures we are. I want suddenly terribly, *terribly*, badly to come back home. I belong in my country. It needs me, and I need it at this hour. It is as if this act had been some sort of declaration of war and I feel as if I must come home and enlist my small services in the cause.

Do write to me. I feel so lost and depressed and homesick.

Love,

Pat

December 8, 1963

Dear Pat,

Beloved friend in history and space! How I would love to embrace you in sorrow. Oh, Pat, your letters have articulated so passionately my grief as well as yours, and the grief of millions. You expressed my experience exactly in saying, "I have never grieved so deeply and for so long." In addition to grief, I have known a corollary depression so intense as to inhibit my proper functioning. I could write no one, and only now, to you, do I begin to articulate, to cease weeping and waking in the predawn stillness, to horror or anguish. What will become of us? The only amazing and heartwarming, though in no degree reconciling, aspect of this has been the deep genuineness of the mourning across America (oh, Amerika!) and around the world.

The students, generally so apathetic and callous from sheer ignorance, have been deeply touched. Never have I seen more massive and uninhibited sorrow. One boy student broke down and wept on my shoulders. The Negro janitor, tears in his eyes, stared at me shaking his head for a full two or three minutes. Infuriating students who'd been brainwashed to think Kennedy was Satan and Goldwater God saw clearly, in proportion, but in grief. The old professors, the good ones, whose lives have been directed against madness and meaninglessness, were stooped and shaken. And of course, Jackie Kennedy was as regal as Antigone. I've never, I mean *never*, seen any human gestures so eloquent as those of this beautiful woman in bereavement. Her control, her pain, her sense of history and of this nation, of her motherhood to those two small wounded children, and of her wifehood to a husband and a man of great eminence—all pulled together into the elegance and pure dignity of all she did. It was truly remarkable.

But oh! that interminable weekend. The sound of the drums, the rocking of the caisson, the riderless horse. My God! We've all been ripped from our daily trivia and placed firmly in the scroll of recorded history, and having been brought so close to the abyss, I cannot but look on this sometimes as from a place in eternity, acknowledging it as one of the momentous tragedies of time past. I love you, my dear friend, and I embrace you across water, lands and many peoples.

Joyce

DAR ES SALAAM
December 10, 1963

Dearest Joyce,

If someone doesn't write to me from home, I shall begin to think I've gone mad or am shortly about to go. I've not had a single letter from anyone, relative or friend, since before the assassination. For God's sake, *write.* I am, I suppose, getting over the first terrible shock of it now. I guess everyone must be. But I can think of no other event in my own life, outside my *personal* mainstream, which has affected me so much, nor made me so determined to do something personally about the forces which caused it. I feel more American and more homesick and more personally involved and responsible than I would have believed possible.

We of course are in the throes of beginning to think of our departure and what the future holds for us (and *where*), and Philip has had a couple of nibbles from the States. I am desperately keen to get home at least for a year or two, and he knows this and is trying very hard to follow up these vague leads, but it's very unlikely he can get an appointment, not being American and not wanting to become a citizen. However, we'll see what happens. I must *never* let myself get into this smug Jamesian self-imposed state of exile again.

I think we could all of us, with profit to ourselves, examine our consciences with respect to J.F.K.'s demand for personal excellence to the degree of our ability to give. We die if we stagnate. We set the stage for death for our children if we slow down and become complacent. The barbarians are hammering on the gates of Rome. Are we going to shore up the defenses, make them Romans, alert the Empire? All of these and more.

It's obvious to you that I am very moved, to the roots of my being. As much, I think, by Jackie's incomparable performance, like something out of Greek tragedy—noble, inexorable, ineluctable in her bearing of the unbearable. She stands with Antigone or Zenobia.

I must get back to my Latin declensions, the bloody old Faerie Queene, Anglo-Saxon Britain, and Candide. I have great doubts about ever passing this foul exam, but I'll sure try. Maybe when I do qualify to register, I won't do English after all. But I don't know what I want to be when I grow up! Not anything scientific. My mind doesn't work that way (work, period).

WRITE.

Love,

Pat

December 15, 1963

Dearest Joyce,

Your letter of the 9th arrived this morning and shed a ray of light. How thankful I am to have you to share this with. Things are coming into focus at last, slowly, but it is all too painful to be able to dwell on for very long, in depth. I came across a notebook of three or four years ago in which I had jotted down something you might well have cut out and sent (or written) to me. Adlai Stevenson, in introducing the candidate John Kennedy to a political rally, and trying to illustrate the difference between himself and J.F.K., said, "Do you remember, in classical times, that when Cicero finished speaking, the people said to one another, 'How well he spoke!' But when Demosthenes finished speaking, the people said, 'Let us march.' "

This is exactly how I feel. I want to march. The train of thought this event has started off has stirred the quiescent blossoms of my patriotism and political fervor in a manner I can only remember (and then it was intellectual, I feel, not both emotional *and* intellectual) during that sad frantic autumn of Stevenson in '52. I said to myself over and over again, in tears, those first two or so weeks after the assassination, I want to go home, I *must* go home, I WILL go home. And so, my dearest friend, to my wholly unexpected and, somehow, fantastically coincidental news, positively Zhivagoish in its connective proclivities: Philip has been offered a two-year fellowship in Boston, beginning in May of next year! I am elated and bowled over by getting this sort of prayer answered. My children will at last see their heritage. I can really and truly see New England—I've never been north of New York City. And perhaps, *perhaps,* I can finish my B.A. I can campaign for Teddy, enjoy the intellectual splendors of Boston. This of course is an immense honor for him, and he is thrilled to pieces.

It's all so sudden and marvelous and unexpected, it has quite driven all other thoughts out of my mind (i.e., goodbye Tanganyika, hello England, civilization again, a rosy future with U.N.O.). All I want to do is to get home, plant my nomadic roots in America again, drink deeply of her waters (at the fount of liberty, if you'll pardon the cliché), and not think of any more tomorrows for a bit. Isn't it odd, how this news came only a few days after I wrote you of my homesickness and my need for my country? I should warn you (and myself) that it's not absolutely certain for a couple of months yet. It will break my heart and spirit if this falls through.

Love,

Pat

December 20, 1963

Dear Pat and Philip,

This letter must be to you both, as I'm so delighted for both of you, so *proud* of you, Philip. What a magnificent turn of fortune for you, and incidentally for us. I am thrilled over the possibility of real proximity once again, and more thrilled yet about the ascendancy and merit of your career, Philip. It's a veritable Christmas present just to receive the news.

And to think of your being here, possibly, so soon. We'd thought Reinhard might visit you in Sussex, but perhaps we can all hike the Long Trail together or canoe into Maine, or speak French in Montreal, or mournfully visit Cape Cod together. The fact that you've been made homesick by our tragedy, Pat, has moved me deeply, that you want to return to your erratic, dreaming, chaotic country, that you love it—all this has touched me, and made me wish for some way you might return. I'm *very* happy.

All love and Merry Christmas,

Joyce

(UNICEF card, with picture of many schoolchildren)

COLUMBUS
Christmas, 1963
[*mailed in October*]

Dear Pat, Philip, Christopher and Julian,

Here are lots and lots of Godchildren for you! May your final Christmas there in Africa be lit with great family happiness amid all the surrounding gloom and despair. You'll be remembered in Dar for your wonderful work. Thank you so for the packages which have been arriving so abundantly, and for the beautiful, beautiful ring for Laura! How glad, how very glad I am to have you as their godmother. It means so much to me. To all of you—I hope the new year and its many changes for you will all be good.

Joyce, Hans, Reinhard, Andrea, Laura

January 14, 1964
Amerika! Amerika!

My dear dear friend,

Where will a birthday letter find you! Is this to be the last letter I shall write to you in Africa, your home now for so so long? I never did have the exact date of your departure, even less so the exact form of your projected itinerary, but perhaps you have already left, sailing out from the beautiful harbor of Dar es Salaam, carrying with you the mementos of nine years' time in that new and striving nation. How much you must weep!—"For what is past, and passing, and to come."

On your birthday I am thinking of you. I hope the year will bring you here, to your own soil and source, if only for a while. I hope the passion that you felt for our wounded country can be lived with, and towards the dedication you want to give. And I hope for the children, this change, this abandoning of their African childhood, will be full of happy surprises, of good things. Besides all this—I want to see you—and will.

All the dear and lovely Christmas things were beneath our tree on Christmas Eve. Thank you, dear Pat; the continuity is worth all to me. The inclusion in my package of the Lincoln assassination notice was a timely irony, wasn't it? I do hope the package reached you.

Don't be seasick, do know I'll drink twenty-nine toasts to you, and more than that, know that I can, with some fullness of understanding you, I think, suspect how you feel at leaving.

A twentieth-century epigram: "I'm convinced life is meaningless, but I don't have the courage of my convictions."

Love,

Joyce

January 24, 1964

Dearest and best of understanding friends,

Your letter reached me this afternoon. We sail tomorrow! I must answer all of your questions, but first (even before our "revolution" tales), thank you, thank you, for such a gorgeous Christmas parcel! Thank you for *every*thing; you are dear and careful and thoughtful.

I gave up trying to cope with my really wild correspondence course (now

309

deep in the intricacies of Latin verb conjugations) last week, ten days ago, to go into hospital to have my bunions chopped off (or, more grandly, "an orthopaedic operation for the removal of an exostosis of the bone"), and three days after I am out of hospital—still immobile and feet like pumpkins swathed in yards of bandages—bloody old revolution. Very bitter I was too, first at the thought of being left behind, hobbling along as the mobs swept all before them, and secondly at the unfairness of not being able to get out and see anything of the excitement, when it became obvious it was "only a veddy *little* revolution," as a lady recently arrived from South America remarked acidly.

I won't go into the whys or wherefores here; they're not really comprehensible without the prior background, which I'll tell you all about when we meet. Back to the revolt: funny stories, horrid stories, unbelievable stories (Philip spent the three hours of the first morning, the most critical time, locked in our house with the Minister of Finance, who was too terrified to stay alone at his own house). No one knew where the President was for thirty-six hours (and still don't —he isn't telling). The whole thing was ostensibly a pay and promotion revolt, also wanting to remove all British officers (seconded here from the British Army at the request of the Tanganyika Government!), so the prim and starchy British officers were rounded up in the middle of the night, bundled onto an airplane in their pajamas to get the mutiny on its way. Their families followed the next day, and off they all went from Nairobi to London. Anyway, these events this week have almost made us feel as if we were in a foreign country. But I suppose that was bound to happen in the end. I mean, it *is* a foreign country, isn't it? Under colonialism, it never felt like it. It's too unbelievable for words.

But as for last week's "people's revolution" in Zanzibar, that was another story altogether. Refugees here tell us it really was ghastly, an absolute massacre of Arabs by Africans, heaps of unidentified bodies chucked in pits. Goans on their way to Mass on Sunday morning shot down for no reason and without warning; whole families (Arab, mostly) knifed and hacked to death in the most hideous fashion. Our ship hovered around the outside of Dar es Salaam harbor for the few days entry was barred, then came in, but contrary to custom, will not be calling at Zanzibar, as the port and airport are sealed for another three weeks, we hear. The stories we hear are so awful. They say the harbor at Zanzibar ran red with blood for days.

Thank you for the twenty-ninth birthday sentiments. Must take my aching feet to their last African sleep. Perhaps I'll be back someday. Africa has been very good to me. I leave my youth here. I leave the place where my children were born, my first real home, the love of my life, much sorrow, much happiness, much puzzlement. But I do want to get home to America.

Much love and warmest thoughts,

Pat

March 4, 1964

Dearest friend, whose understanding and love I always need, but now more than ever,

You must gird your loins (or whatever it is females have instead of loins) and prepare for another stormy few months from me after such a long period of calm. Yes, dear friend, the long-ago-made appointment with Ian was kept. Our ship arrived in the Thames in the middle of a snowstorm and after the usual tedious formalities, made even more tedious with our car on board, we disembarked and drove down here through the lovely snow-covered countryside. It was wonderful going straight into the house, made all clean and warm and ready for us, even with tea ready to be poured, by our faithful cleaning lady.

One hour after entering the house, I answered the telephone, to hear that beloved voice. Three years it's been, and do you know I was as petrified as any high school girl? I must have been very abrupt and uncommunicative, with Philip breathing down my neck—thank God the English don't go in for extension phones. We invited him to come and stay the following weekend, ten days ahead, and he accepted, and hesitated a moment. Then he said, well, he'd kept *his* side of our resolve; he still loved me, and—well, just that, really. He's working in London, while his wife and children are in Yorkshire until he's posted abroad by his firm.

So, delightful as it's been being home, seeing old friends, etc., I was in a progressively deteriorating state before he arrived last Friday. By the time we met him at the station, my knees had turned to jelly, my brains to sawdust. Three years, Joyce, since we saw one another, over two since our last letter, and I had just forced myself to stop thinking of him as future, but as *past*. I knew I still loved him, and no doubt always would. I even flirted with the idea of another (as yet unmet!) lover to help push him out of my heart. I was convinced long ago that he had not felt so deeply for me as I had him, and that whatever he had felt four or five years ago had certainly by now disappeared.

One look was all I needed, and apparently all he needed too. We spent a heavenly forty-eight hours, just being with one another again. We even snatched a couple of hours alone, Philip suggesting one morning that I take Ian to see some of the local sights while he got on with some writing.

Oh, Joyce—all you need to do is find some of my old letters to see how I feel about him and what sort of person he is. I just cannot fathom why he loves me. To me he is godlike, perfect in every respect. So here I am, throwing myself for the first time in eleven years of married life into a full-fledged affair, assignations, the lot. I'm very frightened of it all, but I just cannot help myself, nor do I want to. I trust him implicitly and love him so truly and so deeply that I know he will see us through somehow. Today was the first time we were able to be alone. Philip and I went up to London to see a play, and Ian told me that if I could get up in the early afternoon alone, he might be able to snatch a couple of hours from the office. So I did and we had two pure crystalline utterly private hours alone, the *very* first time we've ever done so, been *able* to do so.

God, I just don't know what I should do. No, it's silly to say that, as I know perfectly well I am incapable of following any other course. I have never known anyone who locked his personal life and inmost thoughts and feelings inside himself as he does, and yet he's told me over and over that I know more about him than any living being. I started to say that I haven't any idea what his life with his wife has been the past couple of years, but pretty grim, I would imagine (judging by my own married life). He asked me once if I'd ever lost faith in him over these various jobs he'd started and dropped since leaving Africa and the Colonial Service, and I said no, never. He said, well, you're the only one. The last thing he said to me today was that he felt wrong done only towards four people. I asked, whom? And he said, our children. And then we parted.

This weekend and today, we jokingly referred to our long Victorian engagement, of the seventeen years of which five have already passed. Only twelve more to go—I'd be forty-five and he fifty. Some joke. What frightens me is not the affair itself: if people are very careful, they don't get "caught" (ugly word with ugly connotations); nor the thought of love dying—che sarà sarà—but that he himself is changing his mind over whether the price we would have to pay for an earlier marriage would be too high. I just know at the moment that I'd go without so much as a toothbrush, if he beckoned, like the lady with the raggle-taggle gypsies O! I just cannot make myself think of a future bereft of my children, nor his own without a father, left to their mother's sole care. And, God help us, what it would do to her and to Philip.

God, what a shambles my neat tidy little planned-out life has suddenly become. I remember once, in the same circumstances, you telling me you hate messes—and here I am, embroiling myself in yet another one. Or rather, the same one. I need love! I want love! And I am in the middle of my very difficult correspondence course, to enter London University as a correspondence student —but perhaps scarcely necessary now, since it's definite we're coming to the States. Then my mother is arriving for nearly four months next week and she's a full-time job. I hate myself for it, but even before Ian suggested it, I know I will be using her as a "cover," to get up to London for the odd day every week or two and snatch a few precious hours now and again. I don't think I dare tell her. She disapproves very strongly of adultery. She keeps saying she made all hers legal—all four—and she adores Philip. I'm in a terrible quandary.

Listen, when you find yourself giving courses on the Russian novel, and your students object to the part coincidence plays, to the vast sweep and passage of time and places, just read them a few passages from my letters. Ian took me in his arms and kissed me in Hastings, that truly hideous resort town where we went on our two-hour outing, and burst out laughing, saying he'd never have believed it if anyone had told him five years ago he'd be making love to me on a back street in Hastings (a stock joke kind of place, like Peoria). Well, there you are. I'm doing a Scarlett O'Hara and refusing even to think about it until some tomorrow. Talk about *The Wilder Shores of Love.*

I feel such a complete sewer rat, mucking about with dynamite in people's lives like this, but I just can't help myself. I never knew such love was possible. I doubt any future is possible for us. I am not British. I despise the international life abroad which he is about to go into. Maybe he'll end up a knight? And I honestly cannot imagine myself as Lady anybody. In spite of the training in that life Dar gave me the past couple of years, I really don't know if I could keep up the pace and the strain and the artificiality of it forever. I'd be terrified of letting him down; any mistake I made I'd never be forgiven.

I am so beatifically happy, joyous, above and beyond myself, again, as I felt five years ago. I never thought it possible life could offer anything like this. Somehow this time I feel it won't fade or be snatched away as I did before. Well, early days yet. I shan't make any rash statements until another five years have passed by.

What must you think of me, I who preach so sanctimoniously when I am forced to lead a blameless life, and then throw myself back into the arms of this man whom I positively worship, but who belongs to at least four other people (including his mother) and another life, I who belong to three other people and who am not free to do as I please? Do not judge me harshly, Joyce, if my world comes crashing down about my ears. He is springtime and eternal youth, gaiety and love and deepest seriousness about the right things. He is honor, courage, steadfastness, brilliance—i.e., as near perfection as I'm likely to get in this life. Would you, could you, ignore this or turn away from it if it were offered to you? And there still nags in a tiny corner of my illogical mind—he's wrong. I couldn't possibly be what he thinks I am. His image of me must eventually tarnish, and then what? A pit too black, an abyss too deep to contemplate. Ah well, no more.

Here, it is terribly cold, little gusts of snow which melt immediately; the countryside is beautifully green, snowdrops and yellow and purple crocuses blooming, and the daffodils just beginning to come up.

Do write to me (at American Express) and give me your opinion, sound or unsound, pro or con. I know I'm crazy. I have been going along on this nice even keel for three years now—no troubles, no mixups, lots of hard work, and now, just wildness and beauty and love, and God knows what lies ahead. Must close, it's 3 A.M. We've just come back from seeing Uta Hagen and Arthur Hill in Albee's *Who's Afraid of Virginia Woolf?*—absolutely terrifying and hilarious and brilliant. I rather wistfully envy those kinds of hysterical knock-down-drag-out fights in an unhappy marriage, instead of long cold silences, and total suppression of what one really wants to say. You must at least read the play, if you can't get to see it.

Much much love, dearest Joyce,

Pat

313

March 20, 1964

Dearest Joyce,

Well, I popped into American Express day before yesterday, when I was in London, but no letter from you. God, how how *how* I wish you were here. I'm bursting with emotion, confusion, wildness, joy—I've never known anything like it (in spite of the fact that I sit hours and hours every day typing Philip's manuscript—this happens to be the reason why I've been allowed a day now and then to go up to London on my own, as payment for my labors). No, worry not, dear friend, nothing will come of it, except maybe that I'll lose my mind along the way somewhere, but what the hell. No, it's for a very short time; it's not what you'd call transient, but in the nature of things to be experienced and absorbed and remembered for a lifetime.

In the first heat, as ever, thoughts of home and children and sanity simply flit away, but soberer reflection brings back stern duty. In spite of that, I am the weaker one, which is a good thing.

And now I can tell you that the U.S. is definite. We come to Boston for two years, Philip in mid-May, I at the beginning of July, to give the children an extra five weeks of the school term, and the hope that Philip can find us a place to live. I am determined to get back to some kind of college in Boston and get my B.A. in our two years there. We'll have both children with us (no boarding school yet) and intend to live la vie Bohème for the two years, as we are paying our own passages and can't afford to ship anything other than a few books and our Persian carpets. What more does anyone need anyhow? I imagine we'll have barely enough to scrape by on, but I do not intend to do anything other than go back to college, try of a sort to keep house, and put my heart in cold storage.

What a mess. But whatever happens, I regret absolutely nothing, not a single minute, nor can I imagine myself ever wishing things had been any different. It'll be hell when I leave England, for a few months, but at least I shall be going to a new exciting life and city and back to college, which all help a lot. Can you, will you, come and stay with us this summer? Can Reinhard? That was one of the first things Christopher asked when I told him we were really going to America!

Of all the times I've needed you, this is the most. I'm torn a thousand ways. I'm a nervous wreck. I only live inside one interlude, and am in suspended animation from one to the next. Well, well, it's all very odd and difficult. For God's sake, burn these letters and do *not* comment on them, except to me at American Express, and don't talk about it to Hans.

Much much love, dying to see you,

Pat

March 23, 1964

My dearest and beleaguered friend,

Appropriately enough, I am listening to the Kreuzer Sonata on this balmy spring day, and thinking intensely of you, along with Russian coincidental effects —and yours. Since your last letter, I have been thinking of you with more intensity, concern and love than ever. You will perhaps be dismayed at my reaction, perhaps pleased, or, alternately, both.

Even in my remote, my easy distance, I cannot somehow counsel restraint, and my major reaction is that of jealousy, not censure. I sometimes am so hopelessly *bored* with my undynamic husband and life, and with the curious admixture of marketplace mentality and cultural snobbery which afflicts the academic artist. I am so conscious of sharing and conversing only a small portion of my experiences, of my capacity, that I truly feel I could not personally resist a love and a life which could involve, could want me totally.

But I am no less caught domestically and maternally than you, perhaps even more. I could not, I believe, ever ever give up my children to someone else's custody, and the question of whether I could ever deprive Hans of them remains one I can scarcely confront. And larger questions intrude. I am not *certain* one really has a "right" to happiness, as such a right is so often interpreted here. The right to be careless of other's lives, I mean, in what turns out to be a ruthless pursuit.

Dear Pat—I do not know—I only know that a part of me is awaiting the inception of just such a dilemma for myself, and I cannot speak for what I would do, for what you should. I only wish you NOT to suffer inordinately, whether through guilt or through your great renunciation. Et voilà—the tragic dilemma. May your Easter be somehow blessed and somehow joyous.

I am very much with you.
Write.

Joyce

April 26, 1964 (!)

Dear Pat,

How lovely to be in Shakespeare's England this year, this time of year. It is his only centennial which we will ever know, and I rather envy you your being there. The Shakespeare stamps arrived today, duly and gladly noted by Reinhard.

If your dates and plans have not changed, Philip should be beginning, however tentatively, to think of departure. Apart from your arrivals, we shall and certainly must have times together. There are all kinds of possibilities. Reinhard counts on having some time with the boys, and we must arrange it.

Did your mother come, Pat? And how do the boys feel about America? As for us, we are thrilled you are coming.

And we send much love,

Joyce

SUSSEX

May 9, 1964

Dearest Joyce,

How gorgeous to think of ourselves and our children actually being together this summer! You must of course come to stay with us in Boston for as long as possible. But we, I fear, shan't be able to think of a holiday this summer, financially, as the move is costing us so much. Philip won't hear of me going off on my own, after having been apart for a month and a half. He hates separations. But if you and the children can come and stay, I know we can have lovely days exploring the countryside, etc., if you don't mind whatever unpalatial pad P. manages to find for us.

My mother, the children, and I sail on the old Cunarder *Sylvania,* and arrive in N.Y.C. July 7th. How I should love to see you standing on the dock! I am in great trepidation about settling down in America for even two years. I've been away ten, nearly the whole of my adult life, and honestly, Joyce, I found it so noisy and brash and horrid three years ago. I'm a bit frightened for the children too. They're terribly naive and innocent and *protected,* I guess you'd call it, from TV, supermarkets, ads, noise, gadgets, you know. I'm just a cowardy custard, I suppose, a grizzled old colonial or something. Imagine getting cold feet at this stage.

Aside from all this, my affair of the heart is driving me into mild insanity. This side of it (does he love me?) is one I've never explored before, but I find that utter physical capitulation and enslavement (literally) have driven me into an uncharted land I'd never imagined the like of before. Bleak, horrid, lonely, silent, and so frightening. I can only suffer in silence and comfort myself with the thought that five years could hardly be considered a brief encounter or a casual dalliance, but God, it's hard, hard, hard.

And he helps me not at all. The verbal reassurances I need are simply not forthcoming. *Why* can men not share their souls and hearts, only their bodies? The suffering is so intense that it will be with a great lightening of the heart that

316

I shall see the slums of the Liverpool dock area (how inappropriate a setting for my lonely farewell) fade into England's mists. I don't ever remember knowing such abysses of unreasoning or lonely unaccountable misery, to follow such perfect joy and physical bliss. If this is truly love, may I be spared it ever again. I'm really sorry if I have ever caused anyone this in my life. I am not saying he doesn't love me; I just don't know if he will go on doing so. Ah well, it palls.

Mother and I join Philip in Paris day after tomorrow for five days, where he has been on business. I haven't been over since '58. Everyone says de Gaulle has ruined everything, but I can't believe that. I shall visit the Rue Dupuytrens and think of you. Such a long time ago it all was. Haven't we suffered through a lot together, you and I, via the international postal services? Four continents, innumerable countries and crises, new unnamed and now mostly forgotten friends, births, deaths, illnesses, joys, despair, depression, books, music—what a lot our lives have held. And soon they will physically touch again! How glad I am for the fact of you in my life!

My mother is so touchingly sad and amusing at one and the same time, with her Norman Vincent Peale philosophy and the ability to gloss over past deficiencies with half-truths and deft (though easily unconscious) changes of tone, shadings and substance. I realize more than ever how alone we stand on that rocky shore, the aware Prometheus. How Olympian I sound!

I have awful shuddering premonitions that perhaps, in twenty to thirty years, my own children might stand on these heights of youth and look down on me, wallowing in a dirty little pool of clichés, lies, unfulfilled promises, broken hopes, forlorn dreams, glossing over the lot with tired jokes and conditioned responses, and they, shaking their heads sadly and hopelessly, look on towards *their* future —*so* different will it be—and so on, ad infinitum. Is it always thus? I have been for so long at such a remove from my family, I can't ever remember crystallizing this as strongly as I know you feel it. And yet one is tied by these silken cords, those sinister velvety bonds, which may in the end strangle one.

How ghastly it all is; better to make one's children hate you and beat it forever, than to pity you and feel *responsible* for maintaining your safe little unreal world. Ugh.

I am terribly thin, smoking like a chimney, and can't sleep nights. But I'll no doubt stop all this and fatten up when I break off this disastrous relationship again. I pray, *temporarily;* otherwise I think I might die inside, really. Well, it's 1:00 A.M., the only time I am ever alone; God, for a monastic cell. I sometimes think the nonentities of daily conversation are slowly driving me batty, along with everything else. I cannot WAIT to see you, to be with you.

All my deepest love,

Pat

May 15, 1964

Oh, my good dear friend,

Your troubles, my troubles. Here I am very nearly thirty-four, which means I've been around for thirty-five, and while not deep in the miseries you write so poignantly, so painfully of, I am teetering on the edge of the selfsame abyss. And as usual, there's not one individual soul in the world to whom I can tell my woes, my real hopes, my real frustrations, my sexual dilemmas, my all, but you. How good that we can really truly see each other, despite (ah, yes! I do understand) the hideous realities of everyday America, despite your inevitable sense of loss and dislocation at the time I shall see you.

What will you have to tell me, what will I have to tell you? I'm suddenly so caught up, so nervous, I haven't been able to eat anything for two days. On Tuesday, I received a phone call at about 3 P.M. It was Jim Wild, whom I've never mentioned, knowing him only so slightly as I did. He was in a bar, desperately needed me to come, would pay the taxi, baby-sitter, anything. So I went, and found him waiting, ready within ten minutes to tell me that he loved me—that he had loved me for two years! I thought he might have wanted to tell me of professional woes, of dissertation miseries, of the hell of being divorced, or even that he found me irresistible and wanted to sleep with me. But this I did not expect. But I believed it, drunk though he was. So, who is he?

He is simply a thirty-five-year-old classicist, as I said a divorced man, a hell-raising, irrepressible, somewhat bombastic, incredibly fluent, by no means "perfect man," but by all means a man I could love, and a man I could passionately desire. All the girls in his classes are mad about him, and the Department considers him brilliant. I too, for two years, nearly three, have wondered about him, have hoped to see him in the halls, have translated some things into French for him. He seemed remote, above, charming but superior, and altogether both unavailable and unattainable.

I think that he really is a wretch, devastatingly incisive when drunk, sensitive and penetrating when sober. He drinks too much. And I never, I mean really truly NEVER even dreamed he found me anything unusual or interesting.

So this afternoon happened. He meant that—that he loved me—that he "would marry me tomorrow," that he "felt complete joy in the thought of me," that he "was aching with the need to go to bed with me," and that he found me "incredibly beautiful," a "fantastic woman." All enough to flatter any aging adolescent heart straight into sin!

So ye gods, Pat! Is life the process by which one assiduously and circumspectly avoids frustration, or is it not? I cannot tell you, though you surely know, what my body is doing to me now. I can scarcely walk, through sheer physical lust!

Furthermore, he is a father, of three small children. He is leaving to teach in Texas in August, and he wants me not for a night—for he wants me. So when I sanctimoniously preach about adultery, consider your friend's heart and mind: that given the chance, I am that very moment either undressing in a very-nearly-missed man's bedroom, or that I am longing to be so. And, as you can at least tell yourself, it took you five years, with and without proximity. If I am *strong*, this will take me two weeks. Do you know, Pat, despite your warnings and your sorrow, I think this will happen to me. Curiously, three years back, Hans once mentioned that he feared this man. Oh, God! Oh, Life!

I have an honor. Apart from the above one, I mean. I have been appointed to the Comparative Literature Department. I have a new rank as a real full-blooded member of the Faculty. I got a real plum and was competing with a host of men to get it. It involves a $600 raise (very good in academic circles) and it will mean only nine hours of lectures. No papers (after a decade of them!). No student conferences! No stupid mimeographing of quizzes and student essays. And hosts of prestige! And most importantly, the chance to read, to teach, indeed to lecture about, great literature. It took more courage than I thought I possessed to confront the Chairman and ask for what I felt were my rights, through years of menial service and through sheer capability.

Oh, Pat—I've kept our secrets, and your letters. Will you, might you, would you, take care of the kids for two days while I race off on a sinful weekend with my paramour? How silly? But I mean it. New England is my trap, and I utterly adore it because of that! So you'll see what a poor consolation I shall be.

Always,

Joyce

If you answer this, do so c/o English Department, O.S.U.

COLUMBUS
May 21, 1964

My dear, my really beloved friend,

La femme adultère, les femmes adultères. Ah! Pat! I was even closer to the truth than I knew in that last hasty letter. So that if you did in fact envision me at about the time I suggested as committing myself to a passion heretofore denied as possible, you were right. So at the present moment, I am high on muscatel, trying sensuously to remember the beauty of this man making love to me, trying otherwise to get through an ordinary evening's activities of feeding and bathing three children, and of facing up to the intellectual, or semi-intellectual, disci-

319

plines involved in my work. My heart feels stripped, and I'm living not with any feeling of guilt, only of fear that I cannot have long enough to sin, not long enough to let this really grow. The wee beginnings of terror, the feminine anticipation of what comes next? I am thinking of you too, if possible with an even heightened closeness and compassion. I yearn to see you, my dear true honest friend. Ah, what will become of us both? Mine is so much less founded, so much less known, so much more indeed the casual dalliance you speak of, yet, ironically, I'm not at all certain this could not develop into love, mutually, nor perhaps even into marriage. Yet I know him so little. You know Ian so well. But he makes love to me like a god. For ten days I've eaten nothing but an orange for breakfast, and have reverted to cigarettes myself. I don't even seem to need coffee. I have lost eight pounds in this incredibly short span.

Contrary to you, I'm not even sure this is a good man, or even a gifted one. Brilliant, yes, but that is different. And otherwise, he seems to be the sort of person whose relationships end up tragically, and who hates himself in some basic ways.

Still, you might like him. I feel at such a total loss with Hans. He is so paralyzed a person and so goddamned passive! Worse yet, he really is so hopeless a father, particularly to his son, that quite without rationalization, I could believe that Reinhard would be happier and better off without him. Harsh words, true words.

I feel the whole misery of infatuation returning to cloak me in yearnings, and the agony of waiting to know when next I may be with him, naked and alone, is almost too much.

Well, I can tell you anything, and no doubt shall. My heart is very much with you, Pat, and I can imagine how painful it all is for you. It is but a few days now till Philip flies. How free will you be in the ensuing month? How often do you get to be with Ian?

What a birthday present, turning thirty-four to be newly loved and physically wanted. Do write, c/o the English Department.

My love,

Joyce

SUSSEX
June 9, 1964

Dearest dearest only Joyce,

I only yesterday had for the first time in a month the opportunity of being alone in London, and nipped straight over to American Express to find your *two* letters awaiting me. Dear God, what strange parallels our lives have! Or are all women's lives so, and they just don't talk about it? All I can say is, my heart and soul are with you. I only hope that you escape with less of the agony and turmoil than I've known the past five years, especially these last months. Still, I do not turn away from love. This is the one definitive moment of my life—series of moments, collection of still lifes.

I am so happy myself I am moving in a kind of golden dream, and he is so marvelous, and for the first time in these five years so giving of himself without restraint and so joyous and sharing, that I have gone even past shame or guilt or even the feeling that I will burst in a delirium of happiness. I am simply floating in a nether world. It all ends in July—I to America, Ian to India and his first post abroad.

Philip on the other hand appears to be pining away in Boston, is terribly lonely and comes all unstuck without me. Our outward life together has finally gotten very close the past couple of years, with all the projects we have worked on together drawing us together as a team. He relies on me more and more, and we are happy and friendly together and share jokes, friends, private busy-ness. You know the sort of thing. Physically, we are just about at a standstill, as of old (as of always, I should say).

And great news—Boston University has accepted me! So I am about to embark on my career as America's oldest coed! And I can drop this beastly correspondence course, thank God.

Whatever life may hold for me, whatever lies ahead, nothing can dim or mar the image of this man for me, nor will I ever be less than grateful to life until the moment of death for this transfiguration—quite literally—I am a different person than five years ago, even from three years or six months ago. He remains a beacon and a goal and a touchstone in my life and will do so if I never see him again

I finally had to tell Mother I'd a reason for going into London (without details), and she's being an absolute brick, which astonishes me no end, as she adores Philip. We've had so little! Only half a dozen evenings together since our arrival here in mid-February—not very much! But enough. And only one or two more. But, Joyce, I think, so sadly in a way, but with a kind of desperate relief in another, that there will be no divorces. I just cannot imagine setting the machinery in motion to wreck Philip's or Ian's wife's lives, not to speak of the four children involved, and all the peripheral nuisances. So all in all, I have gradually had to push the idea of a permanence ahead out of heart and mind, and live with (and be grateful for) what is. So be it.

And as for you, I am SO PROUD OF YOUR ACADEMIC SUCCESS! How brave of you to march into your Chairman's office and *demand* a proper full-time appointment with a real salary and future prospects, after all these years of grueling part-time work with such paltry financial and professional returns. Bully for you, courageous soul. And you deserve it. We both seem to be off on new paths at this point, don't we? I mean, I have some kind of professional goals in mind. You are now there. We both are full-fledged adulteresses, whatever that might mean.

But how I wish you were at Boston University and not Ohio State, so you could ease me through to my B.A. You know, I have awful moments of fright that I won't make it. Oh, how I look forward to and long to see you, soon! Play it cool. You have my love and understanding and every gram of sympathy I possess.

Love to you, ever dearest friend,

Pat

COLUMBUS
June 11, 1964

My dear and most true friend,

I am thinking of you at some time in each day and with a combination of an empathy only you can understand and gratitude for you. These last few English days must be unbearably painful for you. It is only two weeks until you sail, and what a tangled and turbulent profusion of emotions you must be struggling through I can well, very well, imagine. Your letters reached me on my last day in the English Department, the last day on which I would be able to meet him professionally in the halls, professionally with, no doubt, a readily recognized gleam of lust, joy and private understanding. Oh, Pat—dear Pat—at least through our sorrows and renunciations we do maintain ease in communicating our lives to one another—a meager substitute, I know, for that fulfillment each one of us might feel, might inhabit, if, as you say, we could "set the machinery in motion to wreck all these others' lives. . . ." How seriously have you two been considering this? Have you given up even talking of it? Well, what with distance, time, study at BU (don't be silly, you'll do beautifully) and your rebellion at the Goldwater platform, perhaps the worst of it can be worked out of your abdomen. Still, so much pain will remain, the agony of a diminished, a skeletal, sex life being but one part of it.

My maneuverings are extremely hazardous. Each stolen moment, each fugitive delight, represents a real tour de force of arrangement. It is a Tantalus-like situation. I almost convince myself that it is a mark of the quality of the feeling that it can withstand and override what we have to perpetrate to acknowledge it. As you say, it is both difficult and beautiful. Perhaps it is the vacillation that creates the intensity, though of course I like to think the beauty might flourish yet more luxuriantly in the peace of marriage and resolution. He denies this, assuring me he is a beast, that he does not last, that he ends up hurting those

322

he loves. And he does go drinking night after night after night. I've been going with him, happily, whenever possible, and drinking more than you've ever known me to. Still, do not worry about the framework too much for my sake. All hair-splitting aside, I really have lived enough to recognize a scoundrel when I meet one, and to find repellent a sordid nature. But defrocked priests (and he very nearly was one) perforce must carry some ambivalences around with them.

There is a beauty in this man that I find infinitely precious, a beauty he seems innocent of knowing, and very needful of. Evidently people react to him with a combination of alarm, anger, obsequiousness and lust (his female students are mad for him), but not with the intelligent respect and delight which he would like, and which I feel in the mind and in the viscera.

If I could, I would meet you at the boat and, aging demoiselles, we would weep upon the other's shoulder. This total confidence, this clarity of complete understanding, Pat, is one of the very few certitudes of my life.

Dear friend—write soon—let me know.

Joyce

SUSSEX
June 14, 1964

Dearest Joyce,

Alas, your happiness unfolds at the time of the greatest sorrow of my life. I have made an end to it, once and for all. Am I mad, have I gone completely insane? Yes, yes, yes. But I could not bear the dichotomy in my life any longer, the thought of the hurt that lay ahead for so many people, the terrible wrong I was doing Philip. And even more, the thought that our physical rapture together this spring might lead one or both of us to bringing matters to a head Five years I have had of this agony-ecstasy, and I could not bear another five of it. If I were free, yes, but not at the cost of this deception to Philip.

We have in the last two or three years really begun to build a marriage, à convenance, to be sure, without great love, without a sex life, but with children, with a future to be considered, and with faith and trust in one another. I just could not go on breaking that faith and trust. It's so odd how much more strongly I felt it once Philip had gone.

We met once again—then I wrote. And that is the end. I can scarcely bear it. But at least I have done it, and hope I have the strength to stick to my convictions. No, I need not worry about that. The sort of person he is, I shall never hear from him again. He will withdraw utterly from my life, and that will be that. Physically and spiritually I am wrecked and cast ashore on some unknown nameless desert island. However, as Helen Waddell had Abelard say, after his

323

castration, "But what is the desire of the flesh beside the desire of the mind?"

My one gratitude is to the thought of the next two years of Bostonian grind that lie ahead of me. I sail a fortnight from next Tuesday. I cannot bear to write more just now. Do write here before I go. I hope your *tendre* is formulating itself, but not, I pray, to the disintegration I suffer. I am only half a person now.

Lots of half-love,

Half-Pat (half-wit, too, I know)

COLUMBUS
June 25, 1964

My dear Pat,

All my love, all my understanding, and a great longing to have you near, to talk once again all through the night. All my tears and frustrations are as nothing compared with yours, and do not believe I am comparing our two loves. I suspect Jim is nothing of the man Ian is. There has been no test of time, none at all. Mine is an affair; yours is a true, reciprocal love, and for that your renunciation seems heroic beyond belief. Mine will be over soon, as he leaves for Texas to teach. And he is a man who would cause me pains, not only the viable precious ones of loss, but assertive, unnecessary ones.

True, he offers me eloquence and brilliance, but a caustic tongue, violence and some ugliness (and desirability). Hans is simply neutral in these areas, but he loves me. We have a dear family; he just got tenure and promotion to Associate Professor. And I'll probably never leave him.

I cherish you,

Joyce

AFTERWORD

But Joyce did leave him. She had written, years before, "Marriages are failing all around me." Now came our turn. Nearly a decade later, both unions came to the end of their long tortuous roads. During these years we wrote to each other as before, but as our lives were changing so drastically, so did the letters, so indeed did the friendship itself.

We each began to make our own decisions, however tentatively, to take our life into our own hands as we had not done previously, although we didn't realize it at the time. The events of our lives made such decisions necessary. A bare chronology of the ensuing years lists crumbling marriages finally ending in divorce; children growing up; parents dying; struggles with our professions; efforts to build fresh lives, each in our own way, in a profoundly changing society and in new settings, Joyce in the West, Pat in the Northeast.

There were several short visits in the year that followed Pat and Philip's move to Boston. Joyce and Hans came with their children only a week after they had settled into their small Boston apartment; this was the first time Joyce had seen Pat's boys, the first time the children had met, the first time since that brief visit in Paris ten years earlier that the men had seen one another.

In Ohio the following year came another short reunion, and a final one the next summer, when Joyce (alone) visited Pat's house in the English countryside. Then Hans moved his family to California (where Joyce still lives), and Pat, after continuing her studies in Boston, except for summers, moved with her family to New York. All this time we went on writing faithfully, but the candor and reaching out diminished as our daily lives became more and more difficult and the problems remained as insoluble as ever.

Therapists, marriage counselors, books, experiments of one kind or another —nothing solved the sexual problems within each marriage. Again, Pat bluntly called Joyce a doormat to Hans's demands. Joyce was hurt and called her unfeeling. She wrote that each cared for the other, but naturally saw things from her own perspective. She asked Pat for an answering sympathy for the almost suicidal depression into which she was sinking in Columbus. Pat could only say, from within her own experience, that *doing* something, anything, was the solution. Neither seemed able fully to understand the other's situation.

Our short reunions had hinted to us that our sensibilities, our perceptions of how a life could or should be lived, were moving further apart than the three thousand miles about to separate us. Our choices reinforced this. Pat buried herself in work and the camaraderie of people with whom she worked in both the antiwar movement and the new women's movement. Joyce too began moving outside her marriage, although in ways other than her friend's. She began a relationship with a man other than Hans and at last found the kind of physical satisfaction so long denied her in her marriage. As Pat was returning to formal studies toward her Ph.D., Joyce was studying Homer, writing poetry again, and exploring the contemplative life.

But we kept trying to stay close because each of us felt great pain over the developing strains on the bond between us. So our letters shared views on politics, the ongoing tragedy of Vietnam, children, our sense of aging, the agonies of the time. Pat wrote, in 1967, "Ten thousand Reinhards and Christophers have gone to their deaths in that Godforsaken land. Even the children argue endlessly about it out in the garden under the ginkgo tree, where I can hear them. From seven years of age and up, the debate is endless and sterile." Joyce wrote, on the verge of her fortieth birthday, "I ignore the classic suburbia we live in. But of course the children cannot. And when I think of all the dizzying contrariety of values they are and will be exposed to, I fear. How does one help children? I think of you and your boys, of the many children of different friends, and see so much painful groping. I hope they all make it, the whole dear restless troubled lot."

During the process of divorcing, within one year of one another, we shared our agonies over what this meant in terms of losing traditional family life and the sense of failure that haunts most divorced women and men. Both of us were also frightened at not being able to foresee the consequences of so irrevocable a decision.

Joyce, visiting Salt Lake City with the children to fête her ailing parents' golden wedding anniversary, reflected, "It is most odd celebrating family and marriage when I am losing one. My interlocutory decree will take place in three weeks. That will mean one life truly ended, and without being foolishly nostalgic, it is probably the only family I'll ever know—pregnancies, little kids, and all that." Pat replied later on the telephone that one's youth got consumed anyway, and *that* kind of family life was lost even if one stayed married until one was a hundred.

We took to phoning each other in moments of crisis through the period of breakup, separation and fresh divorce. Grotesqueries emerged amid the tears and traumas. One night shortly after Joyce's separation, Pat sleepily answered the phone at 3 A.M. to hear her sobbing incoherently. Joyce finally managed to stammer that Hans had broken into the house while the family was out, and had sawed what had been their marital bed in half. Dumbfounded, Pat could only think to ask, "Horizontally or vertically?" "Diagonally!" said Joyce, and broke into louder sobs.

And Pat, hysterical late one night in New York, dragged Joyce out of bed to weep noisily into the phone, "Do you know how *hard* it is to break one of these damned plastic records? I nearly broke my kneecap trying to break up *Jesus Christ Superstar!*" (a record Philip had purchased in warm memory of a date he had taken to see that show when out of town shortly before).

So we sustained the bond, however shakily at times and despite sporadic misunderstandings and hurt feelings. We had always been very different women, more different that we had had occasion to realize before the ending of the marriages set each of us on a course the other could not accord with.

Pat fiercely savored her privacy and independence. She wrote, in language and from an emotional stance inconceivable a decade earlier, "Such a lot of repetitive experiences and articulation of them it took for the two of us dummies ever to get off our asses, learn how to fuck (such ladylike language and equivocation in our letters, tippytoeing around the edges of everything!), throw out those two shitty marriages of ours, and shout defiantly to all the bastards this world is made up of, I COME FIRST! And then, my dear, to make damned sure we *do* come first, both in fucking and in life, ho, ho. I feel so good most of the time these days that I'd jolly well fly away if I were not firmly anchored to the ground by finishing the Ph.D. and getting a job."

Pat's commitment to the political issues raised by the women's movement had touched Joyce only slightly, concerned as she was with the interior life. The issues raised not only by our different choices but also by our sharply opposing positions on feminism divided us again and again—in letters, telephone conversations and visits through the 1970s—and became a barrier between us. Joyce felt that most women would still seek to define themselves as mothers and presumably therefore as wives. She asked, "And do you think that the *ideal* of a harmonious male/female union, as the union of opposites, is faulted at the root? Whatever the answer, it still seems to me the most happy and satisfying means of making your life *feel* meaningful."

She was living her own philosophy, though the relationship she was deeply involved in had its difficulties as well as its rewards. "The most excellent thing in my life has been the intellectual, spiritual and sexual closeness I have had with Daniel over the past two years. We have become perhaps morbidly intimate. The very things I missed so terribly with Hans, mainly a friendship that put me completely at ease, have existed at the price of all but total isolation from the rest of the world. I envy you the support and closeness of your women friends, and I know I haven't had them partly because I've not been active in the movement, partly because I've had a husband who heartily resented my closeness with women friends. But for two years my only confidant has been Daniel. The values of such intimacy are very real. I will not know how to do without them."

Pat felt otherwise. "This 'one true love' thing is the downfall of us all," she wrote. "I had a student in a women's studies course who said that all of us women from about eight years old onward, each time we meet a male of *any* age over fourteen for the first time, have a two-inch-high adolescent girl who runs to the front of our brain, clasps her hands together, goes all starry-eyed, and breathes, 'Is He The One?' There are just too many men who exploit the relationship with women, extract all kinds of conditions, play games, double-talk, and make us feel like idiots. I'd greatly prefer the sorts of friends I've made over the years (who turn out to be mostly women). Just *look* at the procession of ex-lovers, ex-fiancés, ex-husbands, crushes, strewn behind us! How many of them mean a nickel to us today? What can we recover from the wasteland of spent emotion, tears, moments of ecstasy, but some precious *self*-knowledge? And I'm sure there's a better way of going about learning who and what one is than through the romantic shtick of My Own True Love(s). And you, my oldest, dearest friend—what is there between us that Philip or Hans has contributed one iota to?"

This exchange was repeated over the years, but we were not hearing each other very clearly. Joyce appeared to agree with the substance of what Pat was saying, but not its importance. She kept answering, Yes, the price is very high. I do suffer from my relationships with men, but the suffering is worth it, compared to the loneliness you must feel. And Pat kept responding, No, you are wrong. There is something drastically wrong with relationships that make us suffer like this. And I am not lonely; I choose to live alone, which is not the same thing.

Each of us was brave in a different way, each fearful over different challenges. Each had difficulty appreciating the other's courage, for it lay in areas in which she was not interested or was hesitant to enter. Pat's occasionally sharp feminist anger appalled Joyce; Joyce's willing subservience to the traditional male/female standards infuriated Pat.

But with time, circumstances restored empathy and brought back knowledge of what we had shared over half a lifetime. Middle age was upon us, and we both watched our mothers die slow, painful deaths, Joyce's from a series of brutally dehumanizing strokes, Pat's from the helpless agony of breast cancer. After Joyce's mother died, her father lived only a few months, and she went to Salt Lake City to be with him when he died. She wrote sadly, "He is withdrawing. He didn't recognize me at first, but finally did. Oh my God, I dread what you are having to go through with your mother. Cancer is slow and ugly. I have spent almost twelve hours today and yesterday sitting by his bedside. I'm glad he knows I came, but there is almost nothing beyond that that I can do. I've cried and cried, but one can only cry so much. One can only touch beloved and familiar objects so much, stare in amazement at beloved handwriting so much. I thought I would feel frightened alone in this house, but I don't. It's home, comfortable, though emptied of those who created it."

Knowing each other's parents well, we wept together, phoned after the funerals, tried to comprehend what it meant to be orphaned in one's forties, to have no barrier left between oneself and death. After Joyce's mother died, Pat wrote of growth and aging and death. She quoted Gerard Manley Hopkins's poem "Spring and Fall," and the necessity simply to accept death and loss as "the blight man was born for." And she lamented to Joyce, "Is this *really* so? Is it a blight at all? Why must we be blessed with the knowledge of our growing, changed selves and necessarily cursed with the knowledge of our own mortality? Is there a lesson to be learned in such sadness, such ineluctable grief? I must lose my children, or they me. I must lose you, or you me. There will come a time when the familiar handwriting of our quarter of a century from one of us can never be expected in the mail again. Must we only count our blessings and not rail against this terrible knowledge of what must inevitably come? You and I have won our wars of husbands and abysmal marriages, jobs, health, and halfway decently raising our children—but still, do we not mourn what is past?"

Memories of our quarter-century of sharing resurged when Pat came across an old trunk as she moved from New York to her first full-time job. In it she discovered "an enormous box of knitting yarns, patterns and equipment. I have it all sorted out in piles on the living room rug since hours ago and I can't decide what to do with it. It begins (you will understand the need for a chronological history) with one ounce of the gray wool from which (under your tutelage) I knitted the sweater for Philip when we were engaged. It ends with a few skeins representing socks and a couple of professorial sleeveless sweaters I knitted, again for Philip. And in between, baby yarn, and patterns, patterns, patterns—your children and mine. My God, it's so painful, Joyce. If I were not post-Christmas broke, I'd phone you and cry. You spent so much of that decade working and being ill and having babies and moving about in perpetual poverty. I spent it knitting and having babies and organizing Red Cross fêtes and studiously practicing airs and graces for people who bored me to distraction and whom I despised anyhow. What on earth was going on in my *head?* I feel like a medieval astrologer confronted with the irrefutable truth that Galileo was right."

Joyce responded to these memories at once, but less in bewilderment at the past and more in sadness for a present in which she now found herself living alone, having broken with Daniel. She longed for "community," but not so much a social community as the traditional family life, now gone forever, with children growing up, without a marriage partner. Pat had ended her letter, "We are our old selves and our new selves, the voyage, and indeed the ship itself, encrusted with the barnacles of old love affairs, books read, places gone to, drunken and glorious and awful parties, bad times with families, childbirth and its endless consequences. Isn't it odd to think that we are other people's shoals and barnacles too?"

Joyce wrote back, "You asked on the phone how it will be for me when my children are gone, and reading your letter, I am caught up in thinking of that —since in effect, yours already are. You must adjust to familylessness now; I have

329

some years more, although I feel I'm already into it since Hans is long since gone. I am a fairly brave person, but I don't relish the thought. The suddenness with which they will go seems almost terrifying, yet it doesn't seem to torment you, and I must become like that. Oh, Pat—all those years and fates behind us. You put it well when you asked if it wasn't rather amazing to think that we are others' shoals and barnacles."

As our children grew into young men and women, staying friends with one another and with their parents and avoiding the worst pitfalls for the young in the 1970s, the two of us have come to know that what we longed for was constancy, and that for all the differences that had seemed to separate us, we have remained constant. We have learned to be honest and to accept the consequences of each other's honesty. Slowly and sometimes painfully, we have come to understand that we will probably never agree on that which divided us for a time. We have agreed that it doesn't matter very much. Faithful and loving friends are too few to quibble over the rightness of each one's differing solutions to the endless difficulties of being alive.

Pat was greatly stirred when she reread all the early letters for the first time. "What moves me so deeply, in the light of middle age, lots of affairs, the end of innocence, too many Ingmar Bergman movies, cheap exploitation awareness, or whatever, is the enormously deep well of love and affection for one another, the trust, the reaching out for answering love. I'll wager that very few relationships of such depth and knowledge and intensity have survived from youth to middle age. Perhaps it is just *because* of the nature of the changes that it survived? Both of us were so dreadfully lonely, even in the midst of children and lots of social life, all those dreary years. Each of us, at various times, would cry out from the void, Write! Write!"